Maths for Intermediate GNVQ Application of number

and other courses

Ewart Smith M.Sc

MACMILLAN

First published 1995 by
MACMILLAN PRESS LTD
Houndmills, Basingstoke, Hampshire RG21 6XS
and London
Companies and representatives
throughout the world

ISBN 0–333–62779–2

A catalogue record for this book is available
from the British Library.

10	9	8	7	6	5	4	3	2	1
04	03	02	01	00	99	98	97	96	95

Typeset by Wearset, Boldon, Tyne and Wear

Printed in Great Britain by Unwin Brothers Ltd,
The Gresham Press, Old Woking, Surrey.
A member of Martins Printing Group

Contents

Acknowledgements

The author and publishers wish to thank the following for permission to reproduce copyright material.

London Electricity for the sample bill on p. 103.

Mercedes-Benz (United Kingdom) Ltd, for the equipment specification on p. 41.

The Post Office and Parcelforce, for details of letter and parcel rates in Unit 5.

British Rail Intercity Great Western, for details of train timetables in Unit 7.

Thomson Holidays, for travel brochure information in Unit 7.

Going Places, for the photograph on p. 244.

J. Allen Cash Ltd for the photograph on p. 72.

Format Photographs Ltd for the photograph on p. 300.

GR Photography for the photograph on p. 161.

Every effort has been made to trace all the copyright-holders, but if any have been inadvertently overlooked the publishers will be pleased to make the necessary arrangement at the first opportunity.

How to use this book

We hope you find this book interesting and useful for it is rather different from many of the maths books you have used before. Whether you are a student or a lecturer/teacher you will find lots of things to do and discuss that will be helpful whichever course you are following. Apart from the vocational applications of mathematics there are discussion topics and numerous 'easy reference' sections which you can go back to as often as necessary should you need another try.

If you need maths in your vocational area, you should find it here.

A note to users

If you are a student studying for one of the new General National Vocational Qualifications you will study three core skills, one of the most important of which is mathematics. This book aims to help you with this part of your studies whichever GNVQ course you are following. It provides you with the skills and techniques you need to solve problems in your particular vocational area. The book consists of 12 Units and covers all the Performance Criteria and Techniques up to Application of Number, level 2, which link directly to the corresponding National Curriculum Attainment Targets.

Each unit begins with a summary of the topics studied, covers a wide range of applications under one main heading, and includes numerous Worked Examples and Exercises. See the GNVQ matrix on pp. vii–viii for a guide to which units cover each technique you need to master.

Towards the end of each unit is a Multiple Choice exercise made up of questions of three different types. This is followed by a Self Assessment exercise, the purpose of which is two-fold. It can be used by you to test whether or not you need to study the unit, or it can be used for consolidation or later revision after you have completed the necessary study.

Revision Papers are placed after every third unit to give practice in the work covered in those three units. General Revision Papers, which are near the end of the book on p. 304, contain questions that revise all the relevant topics.

Possibly, you may have problems with some of the basic skills. Should you need help, the concluding section of the book (pp. 323–56) gives a clear explanation of, plus practice in, all the basic skills thought necessary up to level 2. The first time a new skill is involved, whether it is in the text or for an exercise, you will be referred to the Guidance Notes: Basic Skills section.

Most exercises begin with a worked example. Study this carefully before trying the examples that follow. A new worked example in the middle of an exercise indicates that the examples that follow are slightly different. They may ask the question in a different way, be a little harder, or tackle a new type of problem. Some exercises begin without an example. This is because the work has been fully explained in the text or because the work is already familiar to you. To get the most out of each exercise study the worked examples carefully. In this way you should make a lot of progress even if you have to do most of the work without outside help.

After you have used a section a few times you will have a fairly clear idea of what it contains. You can then refer to it whenever you feel it is necessary. If you are in doubt about anything, look it up in the index – you should get help there.

Calculators are an essential weapon in the battle to solve problems with the minimum of effort. You are encouraged to do calculations in your head and to use pencil and paper methods, but if such advice is obviously slowing down your progress you should use your calculator quite freely. In case you are not as familiar with your calculator as you would like to be, Section **G** of the Guidance Notes: Basic Skills (p. 350) should help you.

If you need extra help you will have to look at your calculator instructions.

EWART SMITH
1995

GNVQ Matrix

This matrix gives the principal Unit (or Units) in which each Technique is studied. Additional work on most Techniques will be found in some of the other Units.

UNIT(S)

ELEMENT 1.1

Gather and process data at Core Skill Level 1

☐ Make estimates based on familiar units of measurement, checking results. 1,2

☐ Conduct a survey on an issue of the individual's choice. 8

☐ Convert between different units of measurement using tables, graphs amd scales. 5

ELEMENT 1.2

Represent and tackle problems at Core Skill Level 1

☐ Solve whole-number problems involving addition and subtraction. 1

☐ Solve problems involving multiplication and division. 1

☐ Use fractions, decimals and percentages to describe situations. 2,4

☐ Use simple formulae expressed in words. 6,9

☐ Find perimeters, areas and volumes. 3

ELEMENT 1.3

Interpret and present mathematical data at Core Skill Level 1

☐ Use mathematical terms to describe common 2D shapes and 3D objects. 6

☐ Construct and interpret statistical diagrams. 8

☐ Use the mean and range of a set of data. 8

☐ Use symbols and diagrams. most

UNIT(S)

ELEMENT 2.1

Gather and process data at Core Skill Level 2

- ☐ Make estimates based on familiar units of measurement, checking results.   1,2
- ☐ Conduct a survey on an issue of the individual's choice.   8
- ☐ Convert between different units of measurement using tables, graphs and scales.   5
- ☐ Design and use an observation sheet to collect data.   8
- ☐ Design and use a questionnaire to survey opinion.   8

ELEMENT 2.2

Represent and tackle problems at Core Skill Level 2

- ☐ Solve whole-number problems involving addition and subtraction.   1
- ☐ Solve problems involving multiplication and division.   1
- ☐ Use fractions, decimals and percentages to describe situations   2
- ☐ Use simple formulae expressed in words.   9
- ☐ Find perimeters, areas and volumes.   3
- ☐ Use networks to solve problems.   11
- ☐ Find areas of plane shapes and volumes of simple solids. 3
- ☐ Calculate with fractions, decimals, percentages and ratios. 2,4,10
- ☐ Solve simple equations.   9
- ☐ Know and use the formulae for finding the area and circumference of circles.   6

ELEMENT 2.3

Interpret and present mathematical data at Core Skill Level 2

- ☐ Use mathematical terms to describe common 2D shapes and 3D objects.   6
- ☐ Construct and interpret statistical diagrams.   8
- ☐ Use the mean and range of a set of data.   8
- ☐ Use symbols and diagrams.   most
- ☐ Use 2D representations of 3D objects.   6
- ☐ Identify the outcomes of combining two independent events.   12

UNIT 1 Whole Numbers

After studying this unit you will be able to
- [ ] understand the different symbols used in the media
- [ ] solve problems involving addition and subtraction
- [ ] solve problems involving multiplication and division
- [ ] round off whole numbers
- [ ] round numbers to the nearest 10, 100, . . .
- [ ] use rounded numbers to check calculations.

For further help on 'Whole Numbers' see Guidance Notes: Basic Skills, Section A, p. 323.

How numbers are used

Whole numbers are often used as a shorthand way of referring to a group of words that describes something. For example, instead of saying 'I want the bus that goes from Kensal Rise to Hackney Wick' I would be more likely to say 'I want a No. 6 bus'.

Similarly, at a sporting event it is often easier to draw a friend's attention to a particular player by referring to the number on his/her back rather than by using the player's name.

Think of cases in your own experience that describe things by using numbers, for example:

The rooms in your college/school
A seat at a concert
A business invoice
A cheque from a bank – what do the different numbers on a cheque mean? Is every unused cheque different?

Live in

HOTEL MANAGER

£18K

This is part of a newspaper advertisement for a job as a hotel manager. The letter K after the number stands for the number of thousands.

This advertisement is offering the job for a salary of £18 000.

If the word 'circa' or the letter 'c' appears in front of the figure, it means that the salary is in the region of the figure given. For instance circa £14 K means 'about fourteen thousand pounds – it may be a little more or it may be a little less'.

Property advertisements sometimes use the letter 'm' after a number.

FACTORY UNIT

Factory Unit £5m

In this advertisement the price being asked is £5 million, i.e. £5 000 000.

National finance is concerned with much larger numbers: 'The government expect a deficit next year in the region of £54 bn': 'bn' here is an abbreviation for billion. In the media a billion is a thousand million so £54 bn is a short way of writing £54 000 000 000.

Exercise 1a

Now let's try some examples before we look at a worked example and then give you some more practice.

For further help on 'place value' see Guidance Notes: Basic Skills, Section **A1**, p. 323.

1 Write, in figures, the number referred to in each sentence:
   (a) This coach will seat forty-four passengers.
   (b) Kingston Hospital has five hundred and twenty-seven beds.
   (c) Last year, British Airtours carried twenty-seven thousand, three hundred and seventeen passengers.
   (d) The number of new cars sold in the first three months of this year was two hundred and forty-eight thousand, five hundred and fifty-four.

Question	Write in figures (a) £70 K (b) £3 m (c) £2 bn.
Answer	(a) £70 K = £70 thousand (1 thousand is written as 1 with 3 zeros
	= £70 000 so 70 thousand is 70 with 3 zeros after it)
	(b) £3 m = £3 million (1 million is written as 1 with 6 zeros after it
	= £3 000 000 so 3 million is 3 with 6 zeros after it)
	(c) £2 bn = £2 billion (1 billion is written as 1 with 9 zeros after it
	= £2 000 000 000 so 2 billion is 2 with 9 zeros after it)

2

SALES ENGINEERS	Circa £18K

Technically orientated, possessing high levels of commercial acumen.

BUYERS   Circa £16K
Exposure to volume manufacture preferred.

PRODUCTION SUPERVISORS   Circa £15K
Ideally with experience of high volume manufacturing facilities.

PRODUCTION MANAGERS   Circa £20K
Electronics consumer product manufacturing background preferred.

DESIGN DEVELOPMENT ENGINEERS   Circa £23K
Mechanical and Electronically biased candidates required – a number of positions available to include, as an example Telecommunication product design.

PRODUCTION ENGINEERS   Circa £18K
A background to include Electronics manufacture advantageous.

MOULDING SPECIALISTS   Circa £18K
Positions available for technically orientated Blow and Injection Moulding specialists.

Use this newspaper cutting to write in figures the pay offered for each of the following jobs:
(a) Production Managers   (b) Buyers
(c) Production Engineers   (d) Moulding Specialists.

3 The budget for Kingly School next year has been set at £12 m. Write this number in figures.

4 Smith Beeston has just announced plans for a £12.5 m expansion at their Aylesford plant. Write this number in figures.

5 Exports for the last quarter amounted to £956 bn. Write this number in figures.

6 (a) Write the year 1995 in words
   (b) Write the number 1995 in words.

Addition and subtraction

Exercise 1b

First we shall see how to work out one of the examples, then you can try your hand at a few yourself. Each time you come across another worked example it will teach you something new and make the examples that follow a little easier for you to do.

See Guidance Notes: Basic Skills, Sections A3 to A6, pp. 324–25 if you need help with the 'mechanics' of + and –.

Question At a conference, one of the speakers was more boring than usual. Of the 224 delegates, 39 fell asleep, 82 retired to the bar and 68 read their newspapers instead. How many delegates were still listening to the speech?

Answer Number not listening to the speech   = number asleep + number in the bar + number reading their newspapers.

= 39 + 82 + 68
= 189

Number still listening   = number of delegates − number not listening
= 224 − 189
= 35

∴ the number still listening to the speech was 35.

1 Ross wants 75 bread rolls for a party. He goes to buy them at the local bakery. They can only supply him with 57. How many short is he?

2 At the beginning of a week a garage has a stock of 28 new cars and 56 second hand cars.

   (a) How many cars do they have altogether?
   (b) During the week they sell 5 new cars and 8 second hand cars. They take in 3 cars in part exchange, but do not take delivery of any new cars. How many cars do they have at the end of the week?

3 Zelda was born in 1977. Which birthday will she celebrate
   (a) in the year 1998   (b) in the year 2042?

4 In a local election Mrs Aldridge received 1364 votes, Mr Bean 983, Mrs Court 63 and Mr Denham 475 votes. How many people voted?

5 In a parliamentary election the votes cast were as follows: Joyce Edwards 8493, Lyn Shelley 24 537, Tim Grocutt 16 943 and Jim Johnson 4357. In addition there were 164 spoilt voting papers and 6584 registered voters failed to vote. What is the size of the electorate?

6 During the first six months of the year the following numbers of visitors paid for admission to Bentley Zoo: 1536, 2543, 4627, 13 073, 25 476 and 38 576. Find the total number of paying visitors during the six months.

7 Motorway exits along a section of the M4 are numbered from 6 to 28. How many exits are there, assuming that there are no complications in the numbering?

8 Last year the number of vehicles each month failing to get an MOT certificate at Gary's Garage were: 14, 24, 9, 21, 15, 25, 17, 14, 19, 15, 23 and 12. How many failures were there altogether?

Question   The crowd at Old Trafford for a Premier Division game on a particular Saturday last season was 42 867. On the following Saturday there were 4876 fewer spectators. What was the attendance for the second game?

Answer   Number in attendance on the second Saturday is the difference between 42 867 and 4876 i.e. $42\,867 - 4876 = 37\,991$.

---

9 On consecutive Saturdays the attendance at Highbury was 37 564 and 35 246. Find the decrease in attendance.

10 Lytton's Financial Services have 137 fewer staff now than this time last year. It is expected that there will be a further reduction of 83 staff by this time next year. If there are 1536 employees now, find the number of staff
(a) employed by Lytton's this time last year
(b) expected to be employed this time next year.

Question   In the local dancing club there are 13 more women than men. If there are 55 members altogether how many of each sex are there?

Answer   There are 55 members and 13 of them are definitely women. This leaves $55 - 13 = 42$ members unaccounted for. These 42 members must be equally divided between men and women i.e. there must be 21 of each. The membership is therefore made up of 21 men and $21 + 13$ i.e. 34 women.

---

11 In a Department store with 897 staff there are 189 more women than men. How many men are there?

12 In a factory the workforce is made up of 314 men, 645 women and 107 young people, 796 of these employees are paid a weekly wage whereas the remainder are paid an annual salary. How many employees are paid a salary?

Multiplication and division

For further help see Guidance Notes: Basic Skills, Sections A7–A12, pp. 325–27.

Exercise 1c

Look carefully at each worked example before you attempt the questions that follow. A worked example indicates a slightly different challenge.

Question	A circular running track is 400 m long. (a) Georgio runs in a race that is fifteen times round the track. How long is the race? (b) How many laps of the track must be covered to run 10 000 m?
Answer	(a) Length of race = distance covered in one lap × number of laps = 400 m × 15 = 6 000 m (b) Number of laps = $\dfrac{\text{length of race}}{\text{distance covered in one lap}}$ = $\dfrac{10\ 000\ \text{m}}{400\ \text{m}}$ = 25 i.e. a 10 000 m race requires 25 laps of the track.

1 A box of chocolates contains 14 chocolates in the top layer and 15 in the bottom layer. These boxes are packed in cartons, thirty-six to a carton.
How many chocolates are there
(a) in a box   (b) in a carton?

2 A farmer packs eggs on trays. Each tray has 6 rows and there are 8 eggs to a row. The trays are packed in boxes. Each box contains 6 trays.
How many eggs are there
(a) on one tray   (b) in one box   (c) on a lorry carrying 56 boxes?

3 A bus company operates 26 fifty-seater coaches, 15 forty-five-seater coaches and 6 twenty-four-seater coaches. How many seats does the coach company have available at any one time?

4 At a concert 236 seats were sold at £15, 527 at £10 and 425 at £7. What are the total receipts?

5 Robbie Dence plays soccer and estimates that he runs about 8 miles during a match. If he plays twice a week for a thirty-five-week season, about how far, in total, does he run during all the season's matches?

6 A farmer bought 30 tons of fertiliser at £40 per ton. The government paid him a subsidy of £12 per ton. How much did the fertiliser actually cost him?

You need the information given in the following table to do Questions 7–10. The table shows the populations, in millions, of India, China and the United States of America in recent times

Year	India	China	USA
1971	551	852	208
1981	675	1008	230
1991	844	1116	253

7 Write, in figures, the population of
   (a) India in 1981   (b) China in 1991.

8 In 1971, how many more people lived in China than
   (a) in India   (b) in the USA?

9 Which country shows, and by how much,
   (a) the greatest
   (b) the smallest, increase in population from 1971 to 1991?

10 Which of the following statements are true?
   (a) The population of India is more than the population of China.
   (b) From 1971 to 1991 the population of China increased by more than the population of the USA in 1991.
   (c) The population of India increased more between 1971 and 1991 than the population of China increased between 1981 and 1991.
   (d) The population of China is more than four times the population of the USA.
   (e) In 1981 the population of the USA was less than half that of India.

The worked example and Questions 11–13 refer to the following information. The minimum number of staff required to run a hospital kitchen where long-stay patients are fed is:

Hospital size (beds)	Minimum number of kitchen staff (staff per persons fed)
under 100	1 per 15
100–300	1 per 25
300–700	1 per 35
700–1000	1 per 40
over 1000	1 per 45

(if any number of staff works out as a fraction that fraction must be increased to the next whole number.)

Question Grangely Hospital has 1120 long-stay beds and has 768 staff. They employ 39 kitchen staff.
(a) Do they meet the minimum requirements?
(b) If not, how many more kitchen staff do they need to employ?

Answer (a) Number of persons to be fed = number of patients + number of staff

$$= 1120 + 768$$
$$= 1888$$

Since the number of beds is over 1000 the minimum number of kitchen staff is 1 per 45 persons fed.

i.e. $\dfrac{1888}{45}$ = 41.95 ...

= 42 to the next whole number.

The hospital employs 39 kitchen staff but should employ 42 i.e. they do not meet the minimum requirements.
(b) Number of extra staff required to meet the minimum requirements = 42 − 39 = 3 i.e. three extra staff are required.

11 Cornfield Hospital has 163 long-stay patients and 112 staff:
(a) How many persons are there to feed?
(b) What is the minimum number of kitchen staff required?

12 St Bride's Hospital has 534 long-stay patients and employs 318 staff. How many kitchen staff must they employ?

13 Buxford Hospital employs 435 staff to look after 623 long-stay patients. They advertise for 3 additional kitchen staff to the 19 they already have. Do they satisfy the minimum regulations:
(a) before they make the 3 new appointments
(b) after they have made the 3 appointments?

Questions 14–17 require the following information:

A Public Health Act requires restaurant owners to provide Water Closets and Wash Basins as follows.

Water closets (WCs)
Male 1 per 100 up to 400 persons plus 1 extra WC for every 250 persons over 400
Female 2 per 100 up to 200 persons plus 1 extra WC for every 100 persons over 200

Wash basins
1 for up to 15 persons, 2 for 16–35 persons, 3 for 36–65 persons, 4 for 66–100 persons. Add 1 wash basin for every 100 persons over 100

(Calculations that give fractions of a water closet or wash basin are increased to the next whole number.)

14 A restaurant caters for up to 300 persons at any one time.
(a) How many WCs must it have for males?
(b) How many WCs must it have for females?

(c) How many wash basins must it have altogether?

15 How many WCs are required for
   (a) males   (b) females,
      by a restaurant with tables to seat 500 persons?
   (c) How many wash basins must it have altogether?

16 Montecellini's Restaurant can seat 368 diners.
   (a) How many WCs are needed altogether?
   (b) How many wash basins are needed altogether?

17 Spangero's, which can cater for 145 persons, has 2 WCs for men and 3 WCs for women.
   (a) Are the regulations concerning WCs satisfied?
   (b) How many wash basins should they have?

18 The table shows the present known world oil reserves by region:

Area	Reserves thousand million barrels
North America	40
Latin America	120
Europe	10
Africa	60
Middle East	660
Former Soviet Union	60
Asia and Australasia	50

   (a) Which area has (i) the greatest (ii) the smallest,
      amount of the world's reserves of oil?
   (b) Are the reserves in the Middle East more than the rest of the world
      put together?
   (c) How many barrels of oil reserves are there estimated to be in
      Europe? Write your answers in figures.
   (d) What do the total known world oil reserves amount to?

19 When a cruise ship arrives in Naples passengers can either opt to go on
an organised tour or make their own arrangements. When bookings
close the numbers for tours are: Tour A 187, Tour B 324, Tour C 97 and
Tour D 152. The coaches for all tours are 47-seaters.
   (a) How many coaches do they need altogether?
   (b) How many additional passengers could they have taken on each
      tour without increasing the number of coaches?
   (c) The fares for the tours are: Tour A – £12, Tour B – £15, Tour C – £25
      and Tour D – £35.
      Find the total receipts for the passengers booked on these tours.
   (d) By how much would the receipts have been increased if all the
      available seats had been taken on all the coaches?

20 Fifty-three-seater coaches are available to carry tourists from an airport to the city centre.
   (a) How many coaches are needed to transport 1278 tourists?
   (b) How many spare seats will there be on the last coach assuming that all the others are full?

Using addition, subtraction, multiplication and division

Exercise 1d

If you need help with these examples, refer back to the worked examples in the previous three exercises.

1 A hotel has 12 double rooms and 7 single rooms. How many guests can it accept?

2 A residential home has 23 single rooms and 6 double rooms. How many residents can be accommodated?

3 There are 31 young people in a group and there are three more girls than boys.
   (a) How many boys are there?   (b) How many girls are there?

4 There are twelve No. 8 screws in a packet.
   (a) How many screws are there in 6 packets?
   (b) Ted needs 60 screws. How many packets should he buy?

5 At a party there are 7 more girls than boys. If there are 35 boys and girls altogether, how many boys are there?

6 In a darts match Simon threw: treble 8, double 12 and 3. What was Simon's total score?

7 In my street the houses are numbered from 1 to 31.
   (a) How many houses have odd numbers?
   (b) How many houses have even numbers?

8 Nine coaches are hired to transport supporters to an away match. Each coach holds forty-five passengers. All the coaches are full. How many supporters are there altogether?

9 Christopher Columbus is said to have discovered America in the 15th century.
   (a) What are the first two figures of the year in which America was discovered?
   (b) The sum of the four figures in the year is 16, and when the units figure is subtracted from the tens figure the answer is 7. In which year did Columbus discover America?

10 How would you read
   (a) the number 1887   (b) the year 1887?

11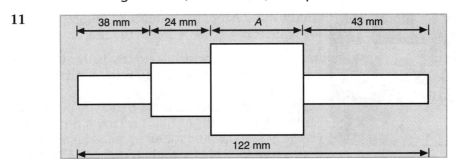

The diagram shows a shaft from an engine. Find the dimension marked A.

12 A typist can type 70 words a minute. She has to type a manuscript of 56 000 words. How many minutes should it take?

13

Mon	Tues	Wed	Thurs	Fri	Total for week
542	607	597			2847

The table shows the number of radios produced in a factory one week earlier in the year.
(a) How many radios were produced in total on Thursday and Friday?
(b) If 145 more radios were produced on Thursday than on Friday, how many were produced on Friday?
(c) Can you give a reason for the lower production figure on Friday than on any other day of the week?

14 A bookseller buys 56 packets of a new book, each packet containing 24 books. He stores them on shelves, at the rate of 42 books to a shelf. How many shelves does he use?

15 A lorry operator owns fourteen 20 tonne lorries, six 15 tonne lorries and thirty-eight 10 tonne lorries. How many journeys will have to be made to remove 28 500 tonnes of hardcore, assuming that all the lorries make the same number of journeys?

16 Dorien has some CDs and some plastic bags to put them in. If 9 CDs are put into each bag, one CD is left over. If 11 CDs are put into each bag, one bag is empty.
How many CDs and how many bags does Dorien have?
(Try to be logical. What if there's one bag? What if there are two bags? And so on.)

Rounding numbers Frequently it is useful to round numbers. For example, a newspaper headline giving the number of spectators attending a sporting occasion has more impact if it is given to the nearest thousand rather than as an exact figure.

Consider the number 568. To the nearest 10, this is 570.
We write this: 568 = 570 to the nearest 10

BIG FIGHT SELL-OUT

30,000 tickets sold

On the other hand, the number 563 is 560 to the nearest 10.
We write this: 563 = 560 to the nearest 10.

In the case of 565, which is exactly halfway between 560 and 570, the rule to give it to the nearest 10 is to round up, that is 565 = 570 to the nearest 10.

Suppose a newspaper reported that 5000 people had died in an earthquake. This means that the largest number they believe had died was 5499 (5500 would round up to 6000) and the smallest number of deaths was 4500 (4499 would round down to 4000).

Exercise 1e

Study the worked example, then attempt the examples that follow.

Question   Round the numbers given in each of the following sentences to the nearest 100.
(a) Newbridge Youth Club has 279 members.
(b) Topclass Autos have 824 second-hand cars.
(c) There are 550 seats in Brockley Town Hall.
(d) At Frinton's last home game there were 5328 spectators.
(e) The population of Kidborough is 6752.

Answer   (a) 279 rounds to 300
(b) 824 rounds to 800
(c) 550 rounds to 600
(550 is halfway between 500 and 600. It is the custom to round halfway figures up.)
(d) 5328 rounds to 5300
(e) 6752 rounds to 6800.

1 The area of the main hall at college is 27 698 square feet.
(a) What is the place value of   (i) the 7   (ii) the 6?
(b) Give the area of the hall correct to   (i) the nearest hundred square feet   (ii) the nearest thousand square feet.

2 This year the number of registered students at Purseley College is 5835. Give this number correct to
(a) the nearest 10   (b) the nearest 100.

3 In an air disaster 357 died.
(a) The first news item on the radio after the crash gave this figure correct to the nearest 100. What figure did they give?
(b) In a later news bulletin the figure was given correct to the nearest 10. What figure was given in the later bulletin?

4 Last year Honro Automotive produced 1 576 439 cars worldwide. Give this figure correct to the nearest
(a) thousand   (b) hundred thousand.

Greatest and least values

Suppose the personnel manager reported that 300 people had applied for jobs at his factory. If this figure is correct to the nearest 100, what is the greatest number of applicants possible? What is the least number?

If 350 people applied then this would have been rounded up to 400, whereas if 349 applied this would have been rounded down to 300.

Similarly, 250 would be rounded up to 300 but 249 would be rounded down to 200. Hence the largest possible number of applicants was 349 and the smallest possible number was 250.

Exercise 1f

Question Correct to the nearest 100, there were 2300 students in college yesterday. What is
(a) the largest number
(b) the smallest number, that could have been present?

Answer (a) the largest number that, correct to the nearest 100 is 2300, is 2349.
(b) the smallest number that, correct to the nearest 100 is 2300, is 2250.

1 What is the smallest whole number which, when rounded up to the nearest 100, will give
(a) 500   (b) 1600
(c) 1800   (d) 27 600?

2 What is the largest whole number which, when rounded down to the nearest 100, will give
(a) 800   (b) 1300
(c) 7600   (d) 18 400?

3 What is the smallest whole number which
(a) when rounded up to the nearest 10, gives 190
(b) when rounded up to the nearest 100, gives 1400
(c) when rounded up to the nearest 100, gives 27 000
(d) when rounded up to the nearest 1000, gives 59 000?

4 What is the largest whole number which
(a) when rounded down to the nearest 100, gives 700
(b) when rounded down to the nearest 10, gives 1850
(c) when rounded down to the nearest 100, gives 52 000
(d) when rounded down to the nearest 1000, gives 38 000?

5 Correct to the nearest thousand, 45 000 attended a concert.
   (a) What is the largest number that could have been present?
   (b) What is the smallest number that could have been present?

6 The population of Romania is given as 23 000 000 correct to the nearest million.
   (a) What is the largest possible population?
   (b) What is the smallest possible population?

7 The area of Poland is 310 000 sq km correct to the nearest 10 000 sq km.
   (a) What is the largest possible area?
   (b) What is the smallest possible area?

8 A college reported that it had had 4000 applications for the 180 places on its foundation course. If the number of applications was correct to the nearest 1000 and the number of places was correct to the nearest 10 find
   (a) the greatest and least number of applicants
   (b) the greatest and least number of places.

9 An aircraft engine needs a full service after 10 000 hours flying time. If this figure is correct to the nearest thousand hours what is
   (a) the shortest time
   (b) the longest time
   that the engine should be used before servicing?

10 At a demonstration the organisers claimed that 100 000 people attended, while the police stated that the figure was nearer 55 499. Both claims were correct – it all depends on how the rounding is done. Explain the apparent contradiction.

Checking calculations

If you need help, see Guidance Notes: Basic Skills, Section G, p. 350.

Often we use rounded numbers to check calculations.

Suppose Una wishes to find the weight of 769 packets of bolts, each of which weighs 347 grams.

Using a calculator Una finds that 769×347 is 266 843. Is this answer reasonable?

To the nearest 100,   769 is 800
and   347 is 300
Without using a calculator $800 \times 300 = 240\,000$.

This is a six-figure number that is reasonably close to the six-figure number 266 843 and so confirms that her answer is about right.
If she had got a number that was close to 2400 or 2 400 000 she would know that she had made a mistake and would need to start again.

1 Given below are the calculations needed to find the areas, in square feet, of four rectangular buildings
(a) 86 ft × 48 ft (b) 67 ft × 24 ft
(c) 77 ft × 48 ft (d) 977 ft × 87 ft
By giving each number correct to the nearest ten, estimate the ground area of each building in square feet.

2 (a) Use a calculator to find the exact answers for the calculations given in Question 1.
  (b) Do the answers you got in Question 1 help to confirm the answers you got in part (a)?

3 By giving each number correct to the nearest 100, estimate the area of four rectangular plots of land whose dimensions are given as
(a) 798 m by 547 m (b) 374 m by 285 m
(c) 1287 m by 646 m (d) 8975 m by 633 m
(Area of rectangle = length × breadth).

4 Check your answers to Question 3 by using a calculator to find the exact answers.

5 By giving each number correct to the nearest 100 estimate the value of

(a) $\dfrac{723 \times 977}{693}$ (b) $\dfrac{446 \times 864}{376}$

(c) $\dfrac{1187 \times 654}{837}$ (d) $\dfrac{5447 \times 8519}{4475}$

Use a calculator to check your estimates.

6 By giving each number correct to the nearest 1000 estimate the value of

(a) $\dfrac{1944 \times 3073}{5814}$ (b) $\dfrac{2842 \times 4329}{6253}$

(c) $\dfrac{7774 \times 5288}{10\,429}$ (d) $\dfrac{39452 \times 8299}{12\,784}$

Use a calculator to check your answers.

Negative numbers

We are all familiar with temperatures on our weather charts. In the summer temperatures are always positive but sometimes in the winter they are negative.

Apart from temperatures, negative numbers can be used to describe other situations. For example, if I say I have −£20 in the bank it means that I have a £20 overdraft, that is, I am £20 in debt.

Positive and negative numbers together are called *directed numbers*.

Exercise 1h

Question

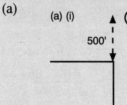

The diagram shows a hot air balloon as it is about to take off for a trip over the Grand Canyon in Arizona.
(a) Draw a sketch to show the position of the balloon when
   (i) it rises 500 ft above the lift-off point   (ii) it drops into the canyon a distance of 450 ft below the lift-off point.
(b) If we describe 500 ft above the lift-off point as +500, how can we describe a position of 450 ft below the lift-off point?

Answer   (a)

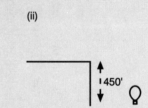

(b) If 500 ft above the lift-off point is described as +500, we can describe the position of 450 ft below the lift-off point as –450.

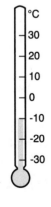

1 Wilf is standing halfway up a hillside. If +10 means 'walk 10 paces up the hill' what is the meaning of
   (a) −10   (b) +50   (c) −100?

2 If +3 means that I am 3 metres above the surface of the water in a swimming pool, what does −1 mean?

3 If +50 means that I have a credit of £50 with my father, what does −30 mean?

4 (a) What temperature is shown on the thermometer opposite?
   (b) What would be the reading on this thermometer if the temperature rose by   (i) 5°C (ii) 12°C (iii) 20°C?
   (c) What would be the reading if the temperature fell by   (i) 6°C   (ii) 13°C?

5 Which is colder and by how much
   (a) 5°C or −5°C   (b) −18°C or −12°C   (c) −6°C or 3°C?

6 The temperature of a cold store must be kept at 4°C. Temperatures above 4°C are recorded as positive temperatures and temperatures below 4°C are recorded as negative temperatures. For example a recorded temperature of –3 means that the temperature is 3°C below the desired level i.e. the temperature is 1°C. A temperature of 6°C is recorded as +2.
   (a) Find the recorded temperature if the actual temperature is   (i) 8°C   (ii) 0°C   (iii) –5°C   (iv) 10°C.
   (b) Find the actual temperature if the recorded temperature is   (i) +3   (ii) −2   (iii) 0   (iv) −8.

7 In a quiz 3 points are awarded for a correct answer and 2 points are deducted for an incorrect answer. Sally attempts ten questions. She gives correct answers to all of them except questions 2, 3, 6 and 7. What is her score
   (a) after 3 questions   (b) after 7 questions
   (c) after attempting all the questions?

8 Kerry stood on a bridge overlooking the M1 and facing towards London. She estimated the speeds, in m.p.h., of six cars in the order in which they passed her as +70, − 75, −65, +80, −70 and +75.
   (a) Which cars were travelling towards London and which were travelling away from London?
   (b) Assuming that all the speeds remained roughly the same which cars overtook one or more of the others?

The number line

$$-8 \quad -7 \quad -6 \quad -5 \quad -4 \quad -3 \quad -2 \quad -1 \quad 0 \quad 1 \quad 2 \quad 3 \cdot 4 \quad 5 \quad 6 \quad 7 \quad 8 \quad 9 \quad 10 \quad 11$$

We can mark positive and negative numbers on a *number line*. Positive numbers are marked to the right of zero and negative numbers to the left of zero.
On the number line 6 is to the right of –1. We say that 6 is greater than –1 and use the symbol > to mean 'is greater than', that is 6 > 1.

Similarly –2 > –5 since –2 is to the right of –5 on the number line and 4 > –6.

On the other hand –2 is to the left of –1 on the number line so –2 is less than –1. Using the symbol < to mean 'is less than' we have –2 < –1.

Exercise 1i

In questions 1–12 write either > or < between the two numbers.

1	−6	3		2	−7	−4		3	−4	−3		4	0	−8
5	5	−2		6	−3	−7		7	−12	−4		8	2	−3
9	−3	0		10	−4	−8		11	−5	4		12	−3	−2

Adding and subtracting directed numbers

$$-8\ -7\ -6\ -5\ -4\ -3\ -2\ -1\ \ 0\ \ 1\ \ 2\ \ 3\ \ 4\ \ 5\ \ 6\ \ 7\ \ 8$$

To find $3 - 10$ we start at zero, move 3 steps to the right followed by 10 steps to the left. We are now at -7, so $3 - 10 = -7$.

Adding a negative number is the same as taking away a positive number, for example $+(-6) = -(+6) = -6$, and taking away a negative number is the same as adding a positive number, for example $-(-8) = +8$.

Exercise 1j

$$-13\ -12-\ -11\ -10\ -9\ -8\ -7\ -6\ -5\ -4\ -3\ -2\ -1\ 0\ 1\ 2\ 3\ 4\ 5\ 6\ 7\ 8\ 9\ 10\ 11\ 12\ 13$$

Question   Find
(a) $4 - 7$ (b) $5 + (-3)$
(c) $-6 - (-9)$

Answer   (a) $4 - 7 = -3$ (b) $5 + (-3) = 5 - 3 = 2$
(c) $-6 - (-9) = -6 + 9 = 3$

Find, using the number line if it helps
1 $5 - 10$ **2** $7 - 12$
3 $13 - 15$ **4** $12 - 23$
5 $12 - 20 + 3$ **6** $-4 - 8 + 11$
7 $-3 - 8 + 5$ **8** $-7 + 10 - 5$

Question   Find $4 + (-5) - (-2)$

Answer $4 + (-5) - (-2)\ =\ 4 - 5 + 2$
                         $=\ 1$

Find
9 $4 + (-3) + (-1)$ **10** $(-3) + (-3) + (-3)$
11 $4 - (-3) + (-2)$ **12** $-8 - (-4) + (-2)$
13 $7 - (-6) + (-2)$ **14** $10 - (-4) - (-7)$

Question   Find $3 - (10 - 3)$

Answer $3 - (10 - 3)\ =\ 3 - 7$
                     $=\ -4$

Find

15 $7 - (4 - 3)$

16 $6 - (8 - 3)$

17 $-5 - (5 - 3)$

18 $4 + (12 - 15)$

19 $(2 - 9) - 8$

20 $(5 - 10) - (5 - 3)$

For further work on Directed Numbers see Sections A25 and A26 of Basic Skills (p. 331) and Using a Calculator (p. 350).

Multiple choice questions

In Questions 1–5 several alternative answers are given. Write down the letter that corresponds to the correct answer

1 A salary of £28 K a year is

A £2800

B £28 000

C £280 000

D £28 000 000

2 The lamp standards in my street are placed at 50 metre intervals along one side and are numbered consecutively from 127 at one end of the street to 159 at the other end. The length of my street from one end to the other is

A 1500 m

B 1650 m

C 1550 m

D 1600 m

3 Teri lives 1 mile from work and goes home for lunch every day. From 1 September to the end of the year she worked 5 days a week for 17 weeks, without missing a day. The total distance she cycled back and forth to work was

A 34 miles

B 68 miles

C 156 miles

D 340 miles.

4 On his first turn in a darts match Len scored 19, double 6 and treble 14. His total score was

A 39   B 73   C 45   D 67.

5 By giving each number correct to the nearest 100 the estimated value

of $\dfrac{9349 \times 793}{627}$ is found to be

A 12 000   B 1200   C 9000   D 10 000.

6 The attendance at an England–Scotland international was 76 928.

Which of the following statements are true and which are false?

A Correct to the nearest 100 the attendance was 76 900

B Correct to the nearest 100 the attendance was 77 000

C Correct to the nearest 10 the attendance was 76 930

D Correct to the nearest 1000 the attendance was 76 000.

7 The largest number of components ever produced in a day at Microcorp Electronics is 86 000, correct to the nearest 100.

Which of the following statements are true and which are false?

A The largest number that could have been produced in a day was 86 499

B The smallest number that could have been produced in a day was 85 500

C The largest number that could have been produced in a day was 86 049

D The smallest number that could have been produced in a day was 85 950.

8 The following statements have been made:

Statement 1 Victor earns £18 700 a year which is less than his sister, Vicki, who earns about £21 K a year.

Statement 2 Capital expenditure of £2 bn is less than Research and Development costs of £200 m.

How are the two statements best described?

A True, True

B True, False

C False, True

D False, False.

9 The Barrett family set out on a 2500 mile trip from home to Moscow via Vienna and Bucharest. The most they wanted to travel in a day was 320 miles. On the first day they drove 287 miles, on the second day 315 miles, on the third day 292 miles and on the fourth day 189 miles. The following two statements have been made:

Statement 1 They still had at least 6 days driving left.

Statement 2 There was more than 1500 miles driving still to do.

How are these two statements best described?

A True, True

B True, False

C False, True

D False, False.

Self assessment 1

1   Write as a number (a) £65 K   (b) £5 bn.

2   The table shows the number of washing machines a factory warehouse took into stock each day on a particular week together with the number of machines dispatched to distributors:

	Mon	Tues	Wed	Thurs	Fri
Number produced and added to stock	372	392	405	386	307
Number dispatched to distributors	406	418	397	482	114

(a)   How many washing machines were
(i) produced and added to stock on Wednesday?   (ii) dispatched to distributors on Thursday?
(b)   At the start of the week there were 294 machines in stock. How many machines were there in stock when the factory closed for the weekend?

3   In a knock-out competition there are 8 teams, with 15 players plus 2 substitutes for each team. How many players are involved in the competition?

4   For the rugby league cup final at Wembley there were 72 854 spectators. Write this number correct to the nearest
(a)   100
(b)   1000
(c)   10.

5   Correct to the nearest thousand pounds, Ken's annual pay is £16,000. Find
(a)   the largest amount,
(b)   the smallest amount,
       that he could be earning.

6   A pallet of building blocks consists of six layers with 27 blocks in each layer. How many pallets of blocks must be ordered for a building that is estimated to require 120 000 blocks?

7   In a school with 846 pupils the estimate is that each pupil will use 16 exercise books during the course of the year. At the beginning of the year there are 2873 exercise books in stock, and during the year they receive two deliveries, one of 6500 books and the other for 6000 books. How many books do they estimate will be in stock at the end of the year? Give your answer correct to the nearest 100.

8   A train pulls into a station carrying 1453 passengers.
(a)   What is the least number of carriages on the train if each carriage has 64 seats and every passenger has a seat?
(b)   If 347 passengers get off and 138 get on how many passengers are there on the train as it pulls away from the station?
(c)   As the train pulls out, how many spare seats are there?

9   Screws from a machine fall into a hopper at the rate of 58 a minute. They are packed in boxes, 288 to a box. The number of empty boxes required to pack one month's production of screws from this machine is

$$\frac{3480 \times 744}{288}.$$

(a)   By giving each number correct to the nearest hundred estimate the number of boxes required.
(b)   Use a calculator to find the exact number.
(c)   The empty boxes can be bought only in packs of 250. How many packs should be purchased to cover one month's production?

10   Nick Redman has thought long and hard about increasing production at his factory. If he can sell more he can reduce the price per unit. At present he sells 30 000 units a week at £2.40 each, receiving £72 000 from these sales. His total costs amount to £73 000. This is obviously unsatisfactory. His estimates for different numbers of units sold weekly at different prices and with different costs are given in the table.

Number of units sold (000)	30	40	50	60	70
Selling price per unit	£2.40	£2.30	£2.20	£2.10	£2.00
Value of sales (£000)	72				
Total costs including overheads and raw materials	73	88	120	140	130
Profit (or loss) (£000)					

The entries in the first column show the present figures.
(a) What income does Nick expect to have if he can increase the number of units sold to
  (i) 40 000 (i) 70 000?
(b) Copy and complete the table to show the total value of sales if the stated number of units are sold at the given price.
(c) Can the business afford to carry on at existing production and price levels?
(d) Does the profit always increase as the value of sales increases?
(e) On the basis of the information given above how many units should Nick aim to produce to maximise his profit?

11 Sid Barnes has an agreed overdraft of £500. How much is in his account after each of the following transactions?
(a) His account is £230 overdrawn and he pays in £175.
(b) He is overdrawn by £156 and writes a cheque for £144.
(c) He has £125 in his account and writes a cheque for £196.
(d) His account is £120 overdrawn and he pays in £210 in cash.

UNIT 2 Fractions and Decimals

> After studying this unit you will be able to
> ☐ compare the sizes of fractions
> ☐ add, subtract, multiply and divide fractions
> ☐ express one quantity as a fraction of another
> ☐ find fractions of a quantity
> ☐ solve different types of problems involving fractions
> ☐ understand place value
> ☐ add, subtract, multiply and divide decimals
> ☐ give decimals to a given number of decimal places and/or significant figures
> ☐ use rounding to estimate calculations.

For extra help in understanding fractions see Guidance Notes: Basic Skills, Section **B**, p. 331.

The meaning of fractions

If $\frac{5}{12}$ of the spectators at a sporting event are girls we mean that five out of every twelve are girls:

The bottom number in a fraction is called the *denominator*.
The denominator gives the fraction its name. It tells us of the number of equal-sized parts into which the whole has been divided.

The top number in a fraction is called the *numerator*.
The numerator states how many of the equal parts are being considered.

For example $\frac{5}{12}$ of a bar of chocolate means that the bar has been divided into 12 equal-sized parts and 5 of these are being considered

$\frac{5}{12}$ of this bar is shaded.

Exercise 2a

Question The shading shows the part of a circular pizza that has been eaten. What fraction is this?

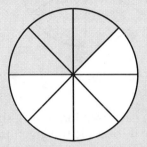

Answer (The circle is divided into 8 equal parts and 3 are shaded.)
$\frac{3}{8}$ of this circle is shaded, so $\frac{3}{8}$ of the pizza has been eaten.

In Questions 1–6, write down the fraction of the whole shape that is shaded.

1

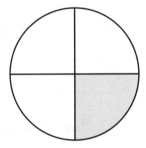

The shading shows the red tulips in a circular bed.

2

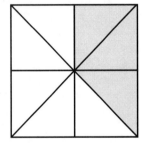

The shading shows the part of the lower tier of a wedding cake that was used at the reception.

3

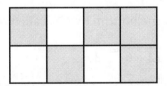

Part of a bar of chocolate is shaded.

4

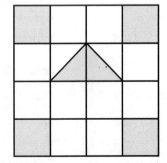

A floor design using tiles.

5

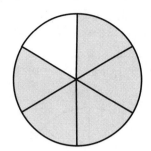

6

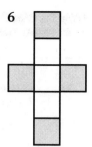

A fruit cake.

A design with paving stones in a garden.

7 For each fraction draw a shape like one of those in Questions 1–6 and use it to shade the given fraction of the whole.

(a) $\frac{3}{4}$ of a rectangular field
(b) $\frac{7}{8}$ of a circular flower bed
(c) $\frac{7}{12}$ of bar of chocolate with twelve pieces
(d) $\frac{9}{16}$ of a square title.

Equivalent fractions

Suppose a rectangular area is divided up in three different ways:

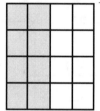 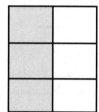 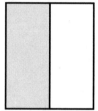

From the diagrams it is clear that there is the same amount of shading in all three diagrams.

so $\dfrac{6}{12} = \dfrac{3}{6} = \dfrac{1}{2}$

$\dfrac{6}{12} = \dfrac{1 \times 6}{2 \times 6} = \dfrac{1}{2}$

Writing $\dfrac{6}{12}$ as $\dfrac{1}{2}$ is called reducing a fraction to its lowest terms

or *simplifying* the fraction.

Dividing the top and the bottom by 6 is called *cancelling*

i.e. $\dfrac{6}{12} = \dfrac{6 \div 6}{12 \div 6} = \dfrac{1}{2}$

Similarly $\dfrac{14}{49} = \dfrac{14 \div 7}{49 \div 7} = \dfrac{2}{7}$ i.e. we have divided the top and the bottom by 7.

When a fraction has been simplified to give the smallest possible numerator (top) and denominator (bottom), the fraction is expressed in its lowest terms.

Equivalent fractions are found by multiplying (or dividing) the top and the bottom of the fraction by the same number.

e.g. $\dfrac{12}{20} = \dfrac{12 \div 4}{20 \div 4} = \dfrac{3}{5} = \dfrac{3 \times 5}{5 \times 5} = \dfrac{15}{25}$

Exercise 2b

Question

Show, by glazing a rectangular window in three different ways, that $\frac{4}{8} = \frac{2}{4} = \frac{1}{2}$.

Answer

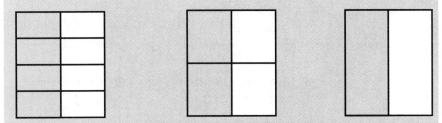

In the first diagram the window is divided into 8 identical rectangles. Four of them (shown shaded), cover half of the window.

In the second diagram the window is divided into 4 identical rectangles. Two of them (shown shaded) cover half of the window.

In the third diagram the window is divided vertically into two identical pieces (one of which is shown shaded).

In all three cases the shading covers half of the window, i.e. $\frac{4}{8} = \frac{2}{4} = \frac{1}{2}$

1 (a) Draw diagrams like the one in the worked example to represent $\frac{9}{12}$ of the area of a rectangular table top and $\frac{3}{4}$ of the area of the same table top.

   (b) Is it true that $\frac{9}{12} = \frac{3}{4}$?

   (c) Write another fraction which simplifies to $\frac{3}{4}$

Question Give three fractions that are equivalent to $\frac{2}{5}$

Answer $\frac{2}{5} = \frac{2 \times 2}{5 \times 2} = \frac{4}{10}$

$\frac{2}{5} = \frac{2 \times 3}{5 \times 3} = \frac{6}{15}$

$\frac{2}{5} = \frac{2 \times 4}{5 \times 4} = \frac{8}{20}$

2 Copy and complete

(a) $\frac{3}{5} = \frac{3 \times 5}{5 \times 5} =$ (b) $\frac{3}{7} = \frac{3 \times 4}{7 \times 4} =$

(c) $\frac{7}{9} = \frac{7 \times 3}{9 \times 3} =$ (d) $\frac{5}{11} = \frac{5 \times 6}{11 \times 6} =$

3 Give a fraction that is equivalent to
(a) $\frac{1}{3}$ (b) $\frac{2}{7}$ (c) $\frac{4}{7}$.

4 Complete the following statements

(a) $\frac{3}{5} = \frac{}{10} = \frac{}{15}$ (b) $\frac{3}{4} = \frac{15}{} = \frac{}{24}$

(c) $\frac{1}{2} = \frac{}{14} = \frac{21}{}$ (d) $\frac{5}{6} = \frac{}{24} = \frac{25}{}$

5 Give three fractions that are equivalent to
(a) $\frac{1}{5}$ (b) $\frac{5}{7}$
(c) $\frac{7}{8}$ (d) $\frac{4}{9}$

6 Give
(a) $\frac{1}{2}$ in sixteenths   (b) $\frac{3}{4}$ in twentieths
(c) $\frac{3}{5}$ in tenths   (d) $\frac{1}{4}$ in hundredths.

7 Change into twentieths $\frac{1}{4}, \frac{3}{10}, \frac{1}{2}, \frac{3}{5}, \frac{4}{5}$

Comparing the sizes of fractions

The area of Joan's garden is $\frac{3}{5}$ hectare and the area of Hilary's garden is $\frac{3}{4}$ hectare. Which one has the larger garden?

To compare the two fractions we need to express them as equivalent fractions with the same denominator

$$\frac{3}{5} = \frac{12}{20} \quad \text{and} \quad \frac{3}{4} = \frac{15}{20}$$

Since $\frac{15}{20}$ is bigger than $\frac{12}{20}$, $\frac{3}{4}$ hectare is bigger than $\frac{3}{5}$ hectare i.e. Hilary's garden is larger than Joan's.

To keep the numbers involved as small as possible it is sensible to find the least common multiple (LCM) of the denominators

$$\text{so} \quad \frac{5}{6} = \frac{15}{18} \quad \text{and} \quad \frac{8}{9} = \frac{16}{18}$$

i.e. $\frac{8}{9}$ is bigger than $\frac{5}{6}$.

(see Guidance Notes: Basic Skills, Section **B3**, p. 332)

Whole numbers, mixed numbers and improper fractions

Whole numbers can be expressed as fractions

e.g. $5 = \frac{5}{1} = \frac{5 \times 3}{1 \times 3} = \frac{15}{3}$.

In reverse $\frac{24}{6} = \frac{24 \div 6}{6 \div 6} = \frac{4}{1} = 4$.

Fractions that are less than 1 are called *proper fractions*

e.g. $\frac{1}{2}, \frac{7}{8}, \frac{3}{16}$.

$1\frac{3}{4}, 2\frac{1}{2}, 10\frac{3}{5}$ are examples of *mixed numbers*

$1\frac{3}{4} = 1 + \frac{3}{4} = \frac{4}{4} + \frac{3}{4} = \frac{7}{4}$.

Fractions where the top (numerator) is larger than the bottom (denominator) are called *improper fractions*.

Adding and subtracting fractions

If we add 3 cars to 2 cars we have 5 cars.
Similarly, if we add three sixths to two sixths we have five sixths

i.e. $\quad \frac{3}{6} + \frac{2}{6} = \frac{5}{6}$

If we have 5 plates and remove 1 plate we have 4 plates left.

Similarly, if we have five eighths of a cake and take away one eighth of the cake we have four eighths of the cake left

i.e. $\quad \frac{5}{8} - \frac{1}{8} = \frac{4}{8}$.

In each case the bottom number (denominator) is nothing more than the name of the item we are considering.

Exercise 2c

Question	Which is the larger, $\frac{5}{6}$ of the trees in a wood or $\frac{4}{5}$ of the trees in the wood?

Answer

$$\frac{5}{6} = \frac{5 \times 5}{6 \times 5} = \frac{25}{30} \quad \text{and} \quad \frac{4}{5} = \frac{4 \times 6}{5 \times 6} = \frac{24}{30}$$

Since $\frac{25}{30}$ is bigger than $\frac{24}{30}$ of the trees in the wood, $\frac{5}{6}$ is larger than $\frac{4}{5}$ of them.

1 Which is the larger
   (a) $\frac{1}{2}$ of a loaf of bread or $\frac{5}{12}$ of a loaf of bread
   (b) $\frac{7}{12}$ of a kilogram or $\frac{5}{8}$ of a kilogram?

2 Which is the smaller
   (a) $\frac{3}{8}$ of a mile or $\frac{5}{12}$ of a mile
   (b) $\frac{5}{7}$ of the passengers in an aircraft or $\frac{8}{9}$ of the passengers in the aircraft?

3 Some students each choose a potato from a bag and weigh it. The weights of the potatoes are $\frac{11}{16}$ lb, $\frac{9}{16}$ lb, $\frac{7}{16}$ lb and $\frac{13}{16}$ lb. Arrange these weights in order of size.

4 Another group of students do the same thing. The weights of their potatoes are $\frac{5}{8}$ lb, $\frac{9}{16}$ lb, $\frac{1}{2}$ lb, $\frac{3}{4}$ lb and $\frac{13}{16}$ lb. Arrange these weights in order of size with the largest first (Express each fraction in sixteenths).

5 The members of a committee are asked to read a report. After half an hour the fraction that each person has read is: Joe $\frac{4}{5}$, Vera $\frac{7}{10}$, Mandy $\frac{17}{20}$ and Nick $\frac{3}{4}$.
   (a) Express each fraction in twentieths.
   Who has read
   (b) the greatest fraction of the report
   (c) the smallest fraction of the report?

6 The lengths of four nails are $\frac{5}{7}''$, $\frac{1}{2}''$, $\frac{3}{4}''$ and $\frac{5}{14}''$. Arrange them in order of size with the smallest first.

Question	In a class of students, $\frac{1}{2}$ of the students come by bus, $\frac{2}{5}$ come by car and the remainder walk.
	(a) What fraction of the students walk to college?
	(b) What fraction do not come by car?

Answer (a) Fraction of students that do not walk to college
       = fraction that come by bus + fraction that come by car
       $= \frac{1}{2} + \frac{2}{5}$

$$= \tfrac{5}{10} + \tfrac{4}{10} \text{ (expressing each fraction in tenths)}$$
$$= \tfrac{9}{10}$$

Fraction that walk = 1 − fraction that do not walk
$$= 1 - \tfrac{9}{10}$$
$$= \tfrac{10}{10} - \tfrac{9}{10}$$
$$= \tfrac{1}{10}$$

i.e. $\tfrac{1}{10}$ of the students walk to college.

(b) Fraction that come by car $\qquad = \tfrac{2}{5}$

∴ fraction that do not come by car $\quad = 1 - \tfrac{2}{5}$
$$= \tfrac{5}{5} - \tfrac{2}{5}$$
$$= \tfrac{3}{5}$$

i.e. $\tfrac{3}{5}$ of the students do not come by car.

---

7 At a pop festival, $\tfrac{2}{3}$ of the groups were all male, $\tfrac{1}{5}$ of the groups had one female and the rest had more than one female. What fraction of the groups
(a) were not all male (b) had more than one female?

8 An airline allows each passenger to take 66 pounds of luggage. Maxine has one case weighing $26\tfrac{5}{8}$ lb and another weighing $13\tfrac{1}{4}$ lb. How many pounds is she under the limit?

9 On a GNVQ course $\tfrac{1}{8}$ of the time is spent on each of the four mandatory units, $\tfrac{1}{6}$ of the time on each of the two optional units and the remaining time is divided equally between the three core skills. How much time is devoted to
(a) the three core skills (b) one core skill?

10 A reel of rope is $41\tfrac{1}{2}$ yards long. Lengths of rope $5\tfrac{1}{4}$ yd, $7\tfrac{3}{8}$ yd and $13\tfrac{7}{8}$ yd are cut from it. How much rope is left on the reel?

Expressing one quantity as a fraction of another

Suppose we go out in the evening three days a week. There are seven days in a week so the fraction of the evenings in a week that we go out is $\tfrac{3}{7}$.

Similarly, if we have 75p in change, the fraction of a £1 we have in change is $\tfrac{75}{100} = \tfrac{3}{4}$

so   75p is £$\tfrac{3}{4}$

To express one quantity as a fraction of another, first express both quantities in the same unit and then put the first quantity over the second quantity.

Exercise 2d

Question	Write 5 pairs of jeans as a fraction of 20 pairs of jeans.
Answer	$\dfrac{5}{20} = \dfrac{1}{4}$
	so 5 pairs of jeans is $\frac{1}{4}$ of 20 pairs of jeans.

1 What fraction of £1 is
   (a) 50p   (b) 25p
   (c) 60p   (d) 85p?

2 What fraction of one hour is
   (a) 40 minutes   (b) 10 minutes
   (c) 45 minutes   (d) 6 minutes?

3 Last September it rained on 12 days. On what fraction of the total days in September
   (a) did it rain   (b) did it not rain?

4 A youth club has 112 members, 70 of whom are girls. What fraction are girls?

5 Krimpfil plc advertised for machine operators. They had 504 applications and took on 63 operators. What fraction of those that applied succeeded?

6 A doctor prescribed a course of 105 tablets, to be given at the rate of 3 per day. What fraction of the total tablets was to be taken
   (a) each day   (b) each week?

7 Bina saves £3.50 a week towards buying a radio costing £42. What fraction has she saved after 8 weeks?

8 Jen has £130. She spends £65 on clothes and £52 on food. What fraction does she
   (a) spend on food   (b) have left?

9 Tim painted 12 m^2 of the walls of the lounge. The total area of the walls is 30 m^2. What fraction of the walls
   (a) did he paint   (b) remains to be painted?

10 In a Town Band $\frac{3}{20}$ of the players are men, $\frac{1}{5}$ women, $\frac{7}{20}$ girls and the rest boys. What fraction of the band are
   (a) boys   (b) not girls?

Fractions of quantities

To find a fraction of a quantity, multiply that quantity by the numerator and divide by the denominator.

e.g. $\frac{2}{3}$ of $36 = 36 \times 2 \div 3 = 24$ ('of' means 'multiply')

or $\frac{2}{3}$ of $36 = 36 \times \frac{2}{3} = 24$

Multiplying fractions

Suppose the records show that $\frac{3}{5}$ of Derek Johnson's land is put down to cereals and $\frac{7}{8}$ of his cereal crop is maize. To find the fraction of his land used to grow maize we must multiply $\frac{7}{8}$ by $\frac{3}{5}$.

Two fractions are multiplied together by multiplying their numerators (tops) and multiplying their denominators (bottoms)

e.g. $\dfrac{7}{8} \times \dfrac{3}{5} = \dfrac{21}{40}$

Hence $\frac{21}{40}$ of his land is used to grow maize.

When a mixed number is multiplied by a fraction it must first be changed into an improper fraction.

e.g. $\frac{3}{4} \times 2\frac{2}{3} = \overset{1}{\cancel{\frac{3}{4}}} \times \overset{2}{\cancel{\frac{8}{3}}} = 2$

and $5\frac{1}{3} \times 2\frac{3}{4} = \overset{4}{\cancel{\frac{16}{3}}} \times \frac{11}{\cancel{4}_1} = \frac{44}{3} = 14\frac{2}{3}$

Notice that if possible, it is sensible to simplify the expression before doing the multiplication (see Guidance Notes: Basic Skills, Section **B7**, p. 334).

Reciprocals

If, when two numbers are multiplied together the answer is 1, then each number is called the *reciprocal* of the other.

e.g. $3 \times \frac{1}{3} = 1$ so the reciprocal of 3 is $\frac{1}{3}$ and the reciprocal of $\frac{1}{3}$ is 3.

Similarly, since $\frac{4}{5} \times \frac{5}{4} = 1$ the reciprocal of $\frac{4}{5}$ is $\frac{5}{4}$.
The reciprocal of a number is given when 1 is divided by that number.
The result is the same as turning the original number upside down, e.g. the reciprocal of $\frac{6}{7}$ is $\frac{7}{6}$ and the reciprocal of $\frac{3}{13}$ is $\frac{13}{3}$ i.e. $4\frac{1}{3}$.

Dividing by a fraction

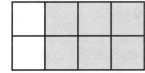

Jonathan has a pile of $\frac{1}{8}$" washers and wants to know how many he needs to raise a gate by $\frac{3}{4}$".

This means that he needs to know 'how many $\frac{1}{8}$s are there in $\frac{3}{4}$'.

The rectangle has been divided into 8 equal squares so each square represents $\frac{1}{8}$ of the whole.

$\frac{3}{4}$ of the rectangle has been shaded.
There are six eighths in $\frac{3}{4}$
i.e. $\frac{3}{4} \div \frac{1}{8} = 6$
hence $\frac{3}{4} \div \frac{1}{8} = \frac{3}{4} \times \frac{8}{1} = 6$.
Jonathan therefore needs 6 washers to fill the gap.

To divide by a fraction multiply by its reciprocal

e.g. $\frac{2}{3} \div \frac{1}{4} = \frac{2}{3} \times \frac{4}{1} = \frac{8}{3} = 2\frac{2}{3}$

and $6\frac{4}{9} \div 1\frac{1}{3} = \frac{58}{9} \div \frac{4}{3} = \frac{58}{9} \times \frac{3}{4} = \frac{29}{6} = 4\frac{5}{6}$

Exercise 2e

Question

Three-quarters of the boys in my class can swim. There are 32 boys in my class. How many of these
(a) can swim   (b) cannot swim?

Answer

(a) Number of boys that can swim $= \frac{3}{4} \times 32$
$= \frac{3}{4} \times \frac{32}{1}$
$= 24$

(b) Number of boys that cannot swim $= 32 - 24$
$= 8$

---

1 Ross had £60 and spent $\frac{5}{12}$ of it.
   (a) How much did he spend?
   (b) How much did he have left?

2 Joy bought a 1 kg bag of sugar. She lost $\frac{1}{10}$ of it through a hole in the side.
   (a) How many grams did she lose?
   (b) How many grams did she have left?
       (1 kg = 1000 grams.)

3 Shavi bought an 8 litre can of engine oil. He poured $\frac{3}{8}$ of it into his engine.
   (a) How many litres of oil did Shavi put into his engine?
   (b) How many litres remained?

4 During the month of June Hank spent $\frac{2}{3}$ of the days at his workplace, $\frac{2}{15}$ of them working on the house and the remainder going away for day-trips.
   (a) How many days are there in June?
   (b) How many days did he work on the house?
   (c) How many day-trips did he make?

5 A man left $\frac{3}{8}$ of his money to his wife and half of the remainder to his brother. If he left £160 000, how much did his brother get?

Question

On a shopping spree Jan spent $\frac{2}{3}$ of her money on clothes and $\frac{1}{6}$ on compact discs.
She had £24 left.
(a) How much did she start with?
(b) How much did she spend on clothes?
(c) How much did the CDs cost?

Answer

(a) Fraction of Jan's money that she spent $= \frac{2}{3} + \frac{1}{6}$
$= \frac{4}{6} + \frac{1}{6}$
$= \frac{5}{6}$

> Fraction she had left $\qquad = 1 - \frac{5}{6}$
> $\qquad\qquad\qquad\qquad\qquad\qquad\qquad = \frac{6}{6} - \frac{5}{6}$
> $\qquad\qquad\qquad\qquad\qquad\qquad\qquad = \frac{1}{6}$
>
> Since she had £24 left
> $\frac{1}{6}$ of the amount she started with $\quad = £24$
> i.e. the whole of the amount she started with is $£24 \div \frac{1}{6}$
> $\qquad\qquad\qquad\qquad\qquad\qquad\qquad = £24 \times \frac{6}{1}$
> $\qquad\qquad\qquad\qquad\qquad\qquad\qquad = £144$
>
> (b) Amount spent on clothes is $\frac{2}{3} \times £144$
> $\qquad\qquad\qquad\qquad\qquad\qquad\qquad = £\frac{2}{\cancel{3}_1} \times \frac{\overset{48}{\cancel{144}}}{1}$
> $\qquad\qquad\qquad\qquad\qquad\qquad\qquad = £96$
>
> (c) Cost of CDs is $\frac{1}{6} \times £144$
> $\qquad\qquad\qquad\qquad\qquad\qquad\qquad = £\frac{1}{6} \times \frac{144}{1}$
> $\qquad\qquad\qquad\qquad\qquad\qquad\qquad = £24$

6 My school is divided into lower school, middle school and upper school. $\frac{1}{5}$ of the pupils are in upper school, $\frac{1}{4}$ in middle school and 396 in lower school. How many pupils are there in the school?

7 In a college election there were two candidates. Allan got $\frac{5}{12}$ of the votes and Beryl got $\frac{1}{3}$. A total of 300 students did not vote.
   (a) What fraction of the students (i) voted (ii) did not vote?
   (b) How many students are there in the college?
   (c) How many votes did Beryl get?

8 In a business the total receipts for the year were used as follows:
   $\frac{2}{5}$ was spent on materials, $\frac{7}{20}$ on wages, $\frac{1}{10}$ on fixed overheads, $\frac{1}{20}$ on dividends and the remainder was put into the reserve fund.
   (a) What fraction of the income was placed in the reserve fund?
   (b) If $£\frac{1}{2}$ million was placed in the reserve fund how much was spent on materials?

Question   How many bottles of wine, each holding $\frac{7}{10}$ litre, can Sheila fill from a cask holding $10\frac{1}{2}$ litres?

Answer   (We need to know how many times $\frac{7}{10}$ will divide into $10\frac{1}{2}$.)
   Number of bottles $\quad = 10\frac{1}{2} \div \frac{7}{10}$
   $\qquad\qquad\qquad\qquad = \frac{21}{2} \div \frac{7}{10}$
   $\qquad\qquad\qquad\qquad = \frac{21}{2} \times \frac{10}{7}$
   $\qquad\qquad\qquad\qquad = 15$
   i.e. 15 bottles, each holding $\frac{7}{10}$ litre, can be filled from a cask holding $10\frac{1}{2}$ litres.

9 How many jars of marmalade, each of which holds $\frac{1}{2}$ kg, can be filled from a tin of marmalade holding 21 kg?

10 How many $4\frac{1}{2}$ cm lengths of wire can be cut from a coil a wire that is 180 cm long?

11 It takes $3\frac{3}{4}$ minutes to read 50 lines of a novel. How long does it take to read
   (a) one line   (b) 350 lines?

12 A doctor estimates that it takes him $3\frac{1}{2}$ minutes to see a patient in his surgery.
   (a) How many patients does he expect to see in his morning surgery which lasts $1\frac{3}{4}$ hours?
   (b) Evening surgery is time-tabled to last $1\frac{1}{4}$ hours. Twenty patients attend to see him. Should he be able to see all of them in $1\frac{1}{4}$ hours?

13 A motorcyclist travels $351\frac{1}{2}$ metres in $9\frac{1}{4}$ seconds. How far does he travel in one second?

14 A retailer marks all the beds he sells at one half more than they cost him. Find:
   (a) the sale price of a bed that cost him £200
   (b) the cost price of a bed that he sells for £270.

15 Bakehouse Publications publish local history books. For any given publication they estimate that the fixed costs are £2500 and in addition the cost of each book produced is £3.50. These books they sell to the retailer at £8 a copy.
   (a) They decide to print 1500 copies and are surprised to sell $\frac{2}{3}$ of them in the first month. Have they got their money back?
   (b) After one year all the books have been sold. How much profit have they made?
   (c) The book retails at £12.50 and one local outlet takes $\frac{7}{10}$ of the books sold. What profit does this retailer make? Does he make more profit than the publisher?

Decimal notation   For extra help on decimals see Guidance Notes: Basic Skills, Section C, p. 335.

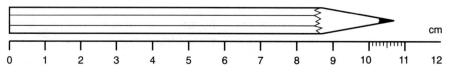

I measure my pencil on a ruler graduated in centimetres and tenths of a centimetre. The length of the pencil is 10 centimetres plus seven tenths i.e. $\frac{7}{10}$ of a centimetre.

In decimal notation we write this as 10.7 cm.

When the part near the tip of the pencil is magnified ten times we can measure the length of the pencil more accurately.

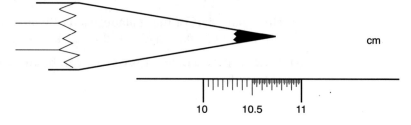

Each small division on the ruler is one hundredth of a centimetre.

We can see that the length of the pencil is 10.7 centimetres plus three hundredths i.e. $\frac{3}{100}$ of a centimetre.

In decimal notation we write this as 10.73 cm.

The dot is called the *decimal point*. We read this length as ten point seven three centimetres.

Place value

The first number after the decimal point means tenths and its position is called the first decimal place.

The second number after the decimal point means hundredths and its position is called the second decimal place, and so on for the third and subsequent decimal places.

We can set out the number 10.73 under headings

tens	units		tenths	hundredths
1	0	.	7	3

Exercise 2f

Question   The width of a paper clip is being measured on a ruler marked in centimetres and tenths of a centimetre. Write its length in decimal notation

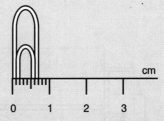

Answer   The width is seven tenths i.e. $\frac{7}{10}$ of a centimetre.
In decimal notation we write this as 0.7 cm.
(We put zero in front of the decimal point to show that there are no whole centimetres.)

In this exercise write the dimension (i.e. length or width or diameter) of each object as a decimal.

1

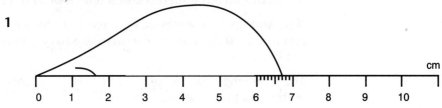

2

3

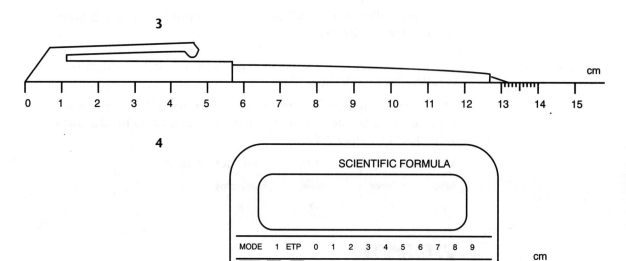

4

Adding decimals

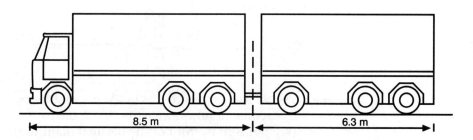

This lorry is 8.5 metres long and the trailer is 6.3 metres long.

8.5 metres means 8 metres and 5 tenths of a metre.
6.3 metres means 6 metres and 3 tenths of a metre.

If we add the whole metres we have 8 metres + 6 metres i.e. 14 metres and if we add the tenths of a metre we have 5 tenths + 3 tenths, i.e. 8 tenths.

The total length of the lorry and the trailer is therefore 14 metres and 8 tenths of a metre i.e. 14.8 metres.

This is easier to see if we set it out in columns:

tens	units	.	tenths
	8	.	5
	6	.	3
1	4	.	8

Exercise 2g

Question The handle of a knife is 6.7 cm long and the length of its blade is 8.4 cm. How long is the knife?

Answer

tens	units	.	tenths
	6	.	7
	8	.	4
1	5	.	1

The length of the knife is 15.1 cm.

1

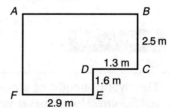

The sketch shows a fish slice. Find its total length including the handle.

2

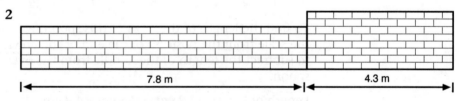

Find the total length of this wall.

3

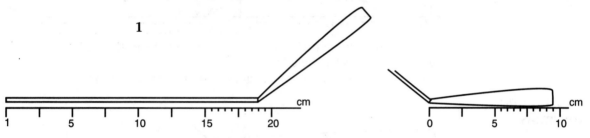

This is a plan of Jo's house. All the corners are right angles.
(a) How long is the wall *AB*?
(b) How long is the wall *AF*?

4

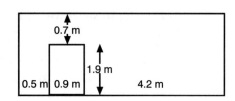

(a) How long is this wall?
(b) How high is this wall?

5

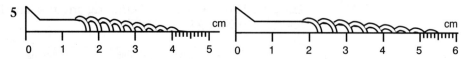

What is the total length of these two screws if they are laid end to end?

6

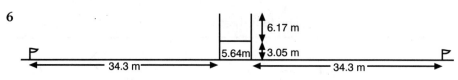

The sketch shows a rugby field viewed from behind the posts.
(a) How wide is the field?
(b) How high is the top of the goal post above the ground?

Subtracting decimals

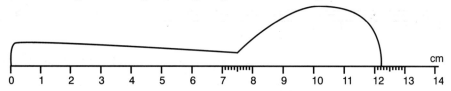

To find the length of the bowl of this spoon, we could count back on the scale from the position of the end of the bowl. However, it is easier to subtract the length of the handle from the overall length of the spoon.

Length of bowl = 12.2 cm − 7.5 cm = 4.7 cm.

Exercise 2h

Question   The overall height of a new car is 127.25 cm and the ground clearance is 18.7 cm. How far is it vertically from the lowest point of the car (excluding the wheels!) to the highest point of the roof?

Answer
We need to find the difference between 127.25 and 18.7

   127.25
    18.70   (We write 18.7 as 18.70.)
   ――――
   108.55

The vertical distance from the lowest point of the car to the top of the roof is 108.55 cm.

1

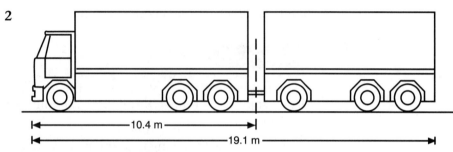

  (a) How long is the threaded part of the screw?
  (b) What is the greatest distance this screw could rest in a hole with the head above the hole?

2

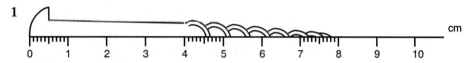

How long is the trailer?

3

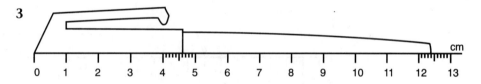

How much of this ballpoint pen is visible below the top?

4

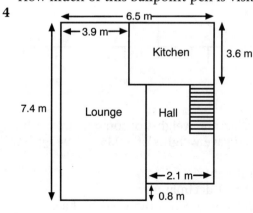

  (a) How wide is the kitchen?
  (b) How wide is the lounge at its widest part?
  (c) How long is the hall?

Rounding off

If we find $\frac{3}{7}$ as a decimal using a calculator, the figures fill the display.

i.e. $\frac{3}{7} = 3 \div 7 = 0.428571428...$

We do not always need all these figures so we often give a number correct to the nearest tenth of a unit or to the nearest hundredth of a unit.

Suppose we wish to give 7.3578 correct to the nearest tenth.
We have 7 units and 3 tenths.
Mark a dotted line after the tenths   7.3 ¦ 578.

If the next figure after the dotted line is 5 or more, we add 1 to the number of tenths.
so   7.3 ¦ 578 = 7.4 correct to the nearest tenth.

However, if the figure after the dotted line is less than 5 we leave the number of tenths as it is.

e.g.   3.4 ¦ 287 = 3.4 correct to the nearest tenth.

Similarly 28.927 is 28.93 correct to the nearest hundredth.

Exercise 2i

If you understand the explanation in the text you should be able to do the examples that follow. If not, look carefully at the text again.

The diagrams show a magnification of a ruler graduated in centimetres.
Give each of the following measurements correct to
(a)   2 decimal places   (b) 1 decimal place.

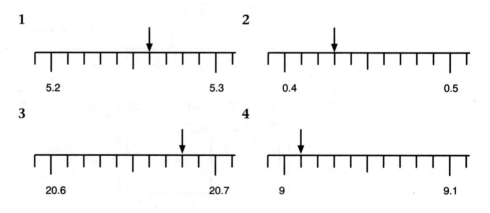

1 ... 5.2 ... 5.3   2 ... 0.4 ... 0.5
3 ... 20.6 ... 20.7   4 ... 9 ... 9.1

5 Selina checked the weights of some metal washers. The first five she weighed gave weights of 5.935 g, 5.947 g, 6.006 g, 5.983 g and 6.018 g.
Give each weight
(a) correct to 1 decimal place
(b) correct to the nearest hundredth of a gram.

6 A new car is 4.724 metres long, 1.751 metres wide and 1.422 metres high. Give each dimension correct to

(a) the nearest tenth of a metre

(b) two decimal places.

7

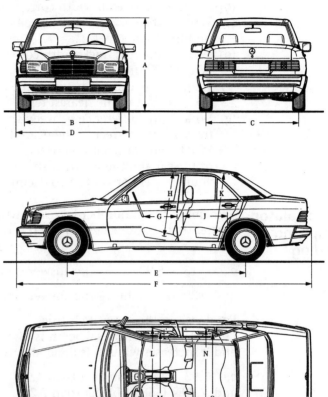

		190 D to 190E 2.6			190 D to 190 E 2.6
A	Overall height	1.375 m	K	Seat height, rear	0.934 m
B	Track width, front	1.441 m	L	Width at hip level, front	1.296 m
C	Track width, rear	1.421 m			
D	Overall width	1.690 m	M	Width at shoulder level, front	1.360 m
E	Wheelbase	2.665 m			
F	Overall length	4.448 m	N	Width at hip level, rear	1.298 m
G	Steering wheel-driver's seatback[1]	0.490 m			
			O	Width at shoulder level, rear	1.352 m
H	Seat height, front[2]	0.965 m			
J	Driver's seatback – rear seatback[1]	0.665 m		Boot space (VDA)	ca. 410 l

1) Measurements vary according to seat position.

2) Measurements for driver's seat vary according to seat position.

Source: Mercedes-Benz (United Kingdom) Ltd.

The table shows the lengths, in metres, for the various dimensions of a motorcar that are marked on the accompanying sketches by letters.

(a) What is the overall length correct to the nearest metre?
(b) What is the overall width correct to the nearest tenth of a metre?
(c) What is the length of the wheelbase correct to the nearest hundredth of a metre?
(d) What is the rear track width correct to 1 decimal place?
(e) What is the front track width correct to 2 decimal places?
(f) What is the distance between the driver's seat back and the rear seat back, correct to the nearest tenth of a metre?
(g) What is the difference between the front track width and the rear track width, correct to the nearest hundredth of a metre?
(h) What is the difference between the width at shoulder level in the front seat and the width at shoulder level in the rear seat? Give your answer correct to two decimal places.

Using a calculator for multiplying and dividing

Remember that a number increases when it is multiplied by a number greater than 1 and decreases when it is multiplied by a number smaller than 1

e.g. 15×5.92 – the answer is bigger than 15

and 29.47×0.93 – the answer is smaller than 29.47.

For division, the opposite is true
i.e. a number decreases when it is divided by a number greater than 1 and it increases when it is divided by a number smaller than 1

e.g. $1.93 \div 2.47$ is smaller than 1.93
and $7.29 \div 0.58$ is bigger than 7.29.

Exercise 2j

Question	Find $57.82 \div 0.7$
Answer	$57.82 \div 0.7 = 82.6$ (5 7 . 8 2 $\div$ 0 . 7 $=$:) (The answer is reasonable. It is expected to be bigger than 57.82.)

Use a calculator to find

1 43.2×12

2 12.2×1.8

3 43.1×0.8

4 45.2×5.5

5 $6.3 \div 0.7$

6 $26.6 \div 14$

7 $42.5 \div 0.34$

8 $260 \div 5200$.

Question	A packet contains 25 screws, each of which is 3.25 centimetres long. How far will they stretch if they are laid end to end?
Answer	Distance the screws will stretch = number of screws × the length of one screw

$$= 25 \times 3.25 \text{ cm}$$
$$= 81.25 \text{ cm}$$

i.e. the screws in the packet, when laid end to end in a line, will stretch a distance of 81.25 cm.

9 There are 100 buttons in a box. Each button weighs 5.7 grams. What is the total weight of all the buttons in the box?

10 Wall tiles are 0.4 centimetres thick. How high is a pile of 24 of these tiles?

11 Sally worked $37\frac{1}{4}$ hours at an hourly rate of £5.84.
(a) Express $37\frac{1}{4}$ as a decimal
(b) Find Sally's gross pay.

12 An operator takes 0.78 minutes to solder a joint. How many minutes should this operator take to solder 350 such joints?

13 A bag contains 36 nails. The bag weighs 15.8 grams and each nail weighs 3.6 grams. Find:
(a) the weight of the nails
(b) the weight of the bag together with the nails.

14 A lorry weighs 2.54 tonnes. It is loaded with 30 boxes, each weighing 0.046 tonnes. Find:
(a) the total weight of the boxes
(b) the total weight of the loaded lorry.

Question	The total weight of 56 identical steel washers is 137.76 grams. Find: (a) the weight of one washer (b) the weight of 148 similar washers.
Answer	(a) if the weight of 56 washers is 137.76 g

the weight of 1 washer is $\dfrac{137.76}{56}$ g = 2.46 g

(b) Weight of 148 similar washers   = 148 × weight of one washer
$$= 148 \times 2.46 \text{ g}$$
$$= 364.08 \text{ g}$$

15 Karen's car travels 94.5 kilometres on 7.5 litres of petrol. How many kilometres per litre is this?

16 The instructions on a bag of fertiliser state that it should be used at the rate of 0.04 kilograms to the square metre. How many square metres should the contents of a 2 kilogram bag cover?

17 A bottle holds 0.7 litres of wine. How many glasses can be filled from this bottle if each glass holds 0.0875 litres?

18 From a 500 centimetre length of tape, Rebecca cuts off pieces 30.25 centimetres long.
(a) What is the greatest number of pieces she can get?
(b) How much is left over?

19 A jug holds 1.5 litres of milk. The capacity of a glass is 0.125 litres. How many times will the milk from the jug fill the glass?

20 Last week Ernie earned £278.25 after working for 37.5 hours. How much was this per hour?

21 A builders' merchant marks prices without including VAT. The price to be paid is found by multiplying the marked price by 1.175.
(a) What will I have to pay for a saw marked £14?
(b) I pay £14.10 for a pair of glass pliers. What is their marked price?

Significant figures

The length of a car could be given as 4.53 metres or as 453 centimetres or as 4530 millimetres. Each of these measurements has the same degree of accuracy, i.e. each is given to the nearest centimetre. In each number the figure 4 has a different place value. It is, however, the first figure in each number. It is called the first significant figure (s.f.). Similarly the 5 is the second significant figure and the 3 is the third significant figure.

Reading any number from left to right, the first significant figure is the first non-zero figure, the second significant figure is the next figure (which is sometimes 0) and so on.

For example, in the number 73.094

the first significant figure is 7
the second significant figure is 3
the third significant figure is 0
the fourth significant figure is 9.

To give a number correct to a certain number of significant figures, the rule is the same as we used for correcting to a given number of decimal places

i.e. look at the next significant figure; if it is 5 or more round up, otherwise round down

For example   3.17 8 = 3.18 correct to 3 s.f.
24.92 = 25 correct to 2 s.f.
0.043 72 = 0.044 correct to 2 s.f.
1.07 44 = 1.07 correct to 3 s.f.

Exercise 2k

Write each number correct to the number of significant figures given in brackets

1 34.783 (3)   **2** 1.7564 (2)
3 0.682 (2)   **4** 16.937 (3)
5 1.0837 (2)   **6** 4.666 7 (3)
7 647.88 (3)   **8** 0.096074 (3)

Estimating a result

A room is 4.375 metres long and 3.643 metres wide. Its area is found by multiplying these two distances together.

To find 4.375×3.643 using a calculator is very easy, but it is also easy to make a mistake by, for example, pressing a wrong button. It is only common sense to know roughly what answer you expect so that you can check that your calculator answer is reasonable.
If we correct each number to one significant figure

4.375×3.643 is roughly 4×4 i.e. 16.

The calculator value is 15.938125 which, compared with our estimated value, is reasonable.

Most problems do not require this degree of accuracy
Correct to 2 d.p. this answer is 15.94 square metres
and correct to 3 s.f. this answer is 15.9 square metres.

Exercise 2l

Question   Estimate the cost of 1860 books at £9.75 each. Use your calculator to find the actual cost.

Answer   Estimated cost is $2000 \times £10$ i.e. £20 000
Actual cost is $1860 \times £9.75$ i.e. £18 135.

1 Estimate a travel agent's income from selling 587 package holidays at £496 each. Compare your estimate with the exact value obtained by using a calculator.

2 Estimate the cost of 9.38 metres of cloth at £7.58 a metre. Compare your estimate with the actual cost.

3 Estimate the weight of 2834 computer components if each component weighs 4.21 grams. Compare your estimate with the value you get using a calculator.

4 The area of a room is 36.44 square metres and it is 5.29 metres wide.
   (a) Estimate its length.
   (b) Use a calculator to find its length in metres, correct to 3 s.f.

5 Paul earns £228.93 for a 39 hour week. Estimate Paul's hourly rate and compare it with the value you get by using a calculator.

6 Pete has 6700 Greek drachma and the exchange rate is: 100 drachma is equivalent to £0.288.
   (a) Estimate the value of his drachma in pounds.
   (b) Find the exact equivalent giving your answer correct to the nearest 10p.

7 A sign post in France indicates that it is 278 kilometres to Lyons. If 1 kilometre is equivalent to 0.625 miles
   (a) estimate the distance to Lyons in miles
   (b) calculate the exact value giving your answer correct to the nearest mile.

Degrees of accuracy

If you measure the length of your kitchen it is probably sensible to give it, at best, correct to the nearest centimetre. It would be a very rough measurement if given correct to the nearest metre, and an attempt to give it correct to the nearest millimetre would be absurd.

Depending on the reason for the measurement one way would be to give it correct to the nearest 10 cm.

Exercise 2m

For each measurement write down the degree of accuracy you think is reasonable. There is no single correct answer.

1 The thickness of this book.

2 The depth of tread on a tyre.

3 The length of a football pitch.

4 The distance from Edinburgh to London.

5 The distance from one Yorkshire village to the next one.

6 The weight of an aspirin tablet.

7 The amount of water you put in the kettle to make a pot of tea.

8 The area of a dairy farm.

9 The weight of a parcel you want to send by first class letter post.

10 The number of people   (i) in the doctor's surgery
   (ii) at an international match   (iii) on a train.

Multiple choice questions

In Questions 1–4 several possible answers are given. Write down the letter that corresponds to the correct answer.

1 An engine requires $8\frac{1}{2}$ pints of oil. The equivalent quantity in litres works out at 4.83055 litres. Correct to the nearest $\frac{1}{2}$ litre the rough equivalent is
   A 5 litres   B $4\frac{1}{2}$ litres
   C 4.8 litres   D 4.83 litres.

2 Kim finds the area of the office notice board by multiplying its length by its width. She finds that the board has a width of 1.5 metres and an area of 5.25 square metres. The length of the notice board is
   A 6.75 m   B 3.75 m
   C 7.875 m   D 3.5 m.

3 The cost of a one unit telephone call is 0.042 pence. An important business call uses 452 units. The cost of this call, correct to the nearest penny is
   A £189.84   B £18.99
   C £18.98   D none of these.

4 Two cars are parked bumper to bumper in a multistorey carpark. One of the cars is 4227 mm long and the other one is 3897 mm long. Which of the following answers are true and which are false?
Correct to three significant figures their combined length is
   A 8120 mm   B 8.10 m
   C 813 cm   D 8.12 m.

5 Apart from overheads a manufacturer's costs break down into $\frac{5}{12}$ labour and $\frac{1}{3}$ raw materials. Which of the following statements are true and which are false?
   A Labour costs are greater than overheads
   B Overheads cost more than raw materials
   C The cost of the overheads is three-quarters the cost of the raw materials
   D If the cost of labour could be reduced by one half, raw materials would cost more than labour.

6 In France Jean Claude's car will travel 216 km on 15 litres of petrol. He wants to make a journey of 500 miles in England and knows that 1 mile = 1.609 km. The following statements have been made:

Statement 1 Jean Claude's car travels 14.4 kilometres on one litre of petrol.
Statement 2 The distance Jean Claude intends travelling in England is about 310 km so he will need about 22 litres of petrol.
How are these two statements best described
   A True, True   B True, False
   C False, True   D False, False.

Self Assessment 2

1 The audience for a TV quiz programme is $\frac{5}{12}$ men, $\frac{7}{15}$ women and the rest children.
(a) Are there more men than women in the audience?
(b) What fraction of the audience are
   (i) adults
   (ii) children?

2 A hospital has 216 nurses, 27 of whom are male. What fraction of the nurses at the hospital are
(a) male   (b) female?

3 There are 1332 cars in an airport carpark. $\frac{4}{9}$ of them have been manufactured in the United Kingdom, $\frac{1}{3}$ in the Far East and the remainder in mainland Europe. How many cars are there in the carpark that have been made in mainland Europe?

4 How far does Mike, walking at $3\frac{2}{3}$ miles per hour, travel in $\frac{3}{4}$ hour?

5 When some bricks are laid end to end they stretch for $384\frac{3}{4}$ cm. The length of one brick is $20\frac{1}{4}$ cm. How many bricks are there?

6

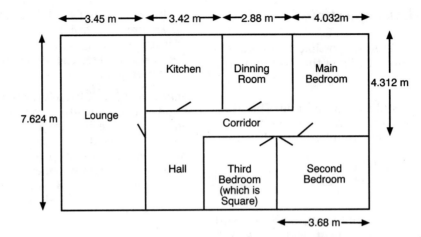

The sketch shows the plan of a three-bedroomed bungalow. Use the information on it to answer the questions that follow. All dimensions are in metres. Ignore wall thicknesses.

(a) How long is the bungalow?
(b) How wide is the second bedroom?
(c) If the corridor from the hall to the bedrooms is 1.1 m wide find the length of the dining room.
(d) What are the dimensions of the hall? (Do not include the corridor.)
(e) What is the area of the lounge? Give your answer in square metres   (i) exactly
(ii) correct to 3 s.f.   (iii) correct to 2 d.p.
(Area of a rectangle = length × breadth.)

(f) A rectangular carpet, which has an area of 13.125 m², is laid in the main bedroom. If the carpet is 3.75 m long, how wide is it?

7   Simon's motorbike travelled 337.5 miles on 5.4 litres of petrol. How far should it travel on
(a) 1 litre   (b) 2.9 litres?

8   A room is 8.926 metres long and 6.211 metres wide.
(a) By rounding each measurement to the nearest whole number estimate the area of the room in square metres.
(Area = length × width.)
(b) Use a calculator to find the exact area of the room. Give your answer correct to three s.f.

UNIT 3 Basic Measurement

After studying this unit you will be able to
- [ ] deal with length, area, volume and mass, both in metric and in imperial units
- [ ] find the perimeter of a shape
- [ ] estimate the area of an irregular shape by counting squares
- [ ] find the area of a rectangle by counting squares and by calculation
- [ ] calculate the volumes of cubes and cuboids
- [ ] solve problems involving capacity.

Length

In the *metric system* the basic unit of length is the metre (m). Other units in everyday use are the centimetre (cm), the millimetre (mm) and the kilometre (km).

The relationships between these quantities are important. They are:

$$1 \, m \quad = \quad 100 \, cm$$
$$1 \, cm \quad = \quad 10 \, mm$$

and $1 \, km \quad = \quad 1000 \, m$

To convert from the larger unit (say metres) to the smaller unit (say centimetres) we multiply by the conversion factor

e.g.   since 1 m   = 100 cm
          5 m   = 5 × 100 cm = 500 cm

and   since 1 cm = 10 mm
          3.7 cm   = 3.7 × 10 mm = 37 mm

To convert from the smaller unit (say metres) to the larger unit (say kilometres) we *divide* by the conversion factor

e.g.   since 1000 m   = 1 km

$$5900 \text{ m} = \frac{5900}{1000} \text{ km i.e. } 5.9 \text{ km}$$

and   since 100 cm = 1 m

$$7300 \text{ cm} = \frac{7300}{100} \text{ m i.e. } 73 \text{ m}$$

It is probably useful to remember that

'kilo' means 1000 times bigger
'centi' means $\frac{1}{100}$ part of

and   'milli' means $\frac{1}{1000}$ part of

The units of length used in the *imperial system* are: the inch (in), the foot (ft), the yard (yd) and the mile, where

1 ft   = 12 in (often shown as 12")
1 yd   = 3 ft (often shown as 3')
1 mile = 1760 yd

Exercise 3a

Question

(a) The distance between two villages is 3.4 km. Express this distance in metres.

(b) The depth of a kitchen unit is 672 mm. What is this in centimetres?

(c) Kate says that her garden is 9358 cm long. How many metres is this?

Answer

(a) 1 km   = 1000 m

3.4 km = 3.4 × 1000 m (large unit to small unit so multiply by 1000)

= 3400 m

The distance between the villages is therefore 3400 m.

(b) 10 mm   = 1 cm

$$672 \text{ mm} = \frac{672}{10} \text{ cm (small unit to large unit so divide by 10)}$$

= 67.2 cm

The kitchen unit is therefore 67.2 cm deep.

(c) 1 m   = 100 cm

$$9358 \text{ cm} = \frac{9358}{100} \text{ m (small unit to large unit so divide by 100)}$$

= 93.58 m

Kate's garden is therefore 93.58 m long.

1 A table is 2.3 m long. How long is this in
   (a) centimetres   (b) millimetres?

2 A picture is 1.2 m long and 0.85 m wide.
   (a) What is its length in centimetres?
   (b) What is its width in millimetres?

3 A factory site is 1.43 km long and 550 metres wide. Express:
   (a) its length in metres   (b) its width in kilometres.

4 The Humber Bridge is the longest suspension bridge in the world. It is
   1410 metres long. How many kilometres is this?

Question Penny lives in an old house. Downstairs the ceilings are 9 ft 3 in high.
(a) How many inches is this?
(b) She measures the lounge and finds that it is 257 inches long and
     171 inches wide. Give these dimensions in feet and inches.

Answer (a) Since   1 ft   = 12 in
                              9 ft   = 9 × 12 in
                                         = 108 in
              ∴   9 ft 3 in   = 108 in + 3 in
                                         = 111 in

        (b)   257 in   = $\dfrac{257}{12}$ ft = 21.4166 ... ft

            Now   21 ft   = 21 × 12 in = 252 in
              ∴   257 in   = 252 in + 5 in
                                       = 21 ft 5 in

            Similarly   171 in   = $\dfrac{171}{12}$ ft = 14.25 ft

                          14 ft   = 14 × 12 in
                                       = 168 in
              ∴   171 in   = 168 in + 3 in
                                       = 14 ft 3 in

5 The length of the Olympic marathon is 26 miles 385 yards. How many
   yards is this?

6 The oldest of the five English classics in the horseracing calendar is the
   St Leger. It takes place annually at Doncaster over a distance of 1 mile
   6 furlongs and 127 yards. How many yards is this?
   (1 furlong = 220 yards.)

7 Arthur is checking the fencing around a large field. He counts the
   number of paces he takes and finds this to be 5280. If the length of
   each pace is $\frac{3}{4}$ yd find the distance he walks
   (a) in yards   (b) in miles.

8 The *Cutty Sark* is 213 ft long, 36 ft in the beam and has a draught of 21 ft. Give each dimension
   (a) in yards   (b) in inches.

Perimeter   The distance all round a shape is called its perimeter.

Exercise 3b

Question   Find the perimeter of
   (a) the ceramic tile
       shown below

   (b) a field in the shape of a pentagon, details of which are shown in the sketch

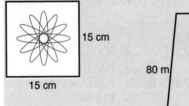

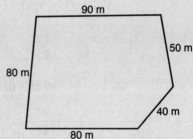

Answer   (a) The perimeter of the square tile is
       15 cm + 15 cm + 15 cm + 15 cm = 60 cm
   (b) The perimeter of the field is
       90 m + 50 m + 40 m + 80 m + 80 m = 340 m

Find the perimeter of each shape.

1 A square tile of side
   (a) 20 cm   (b) 145 mm

2 A rectangular rug measuring
   (a) 140 cm by 90 cm   (b) 1.2 m by 0.85 m

3 Find the perimeter of this room. (All the corners form right angles.)

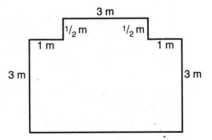

4 Find the perimeter of this field.

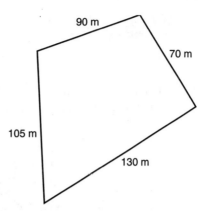

5 Find the perimeter of this section of an RSJ (reinforced steel joist). All measurements are in inches.

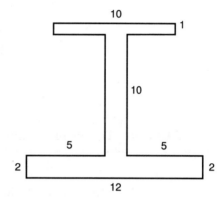

Area

The area of a shape is the amount of surface enclosed within its boundary. Area is measured in squares.

To compare areas we need to use the same size square. In the *metric system,* for small areas we usually use a square of side 1 centimetre and for larger areas a square of side 1 metre.

This square has a side of 1 cm. Its area is 1 square centimetre. We write this as 1 cm^2.

Some areas can be found exactly quite easily e.g. the area of this rectangle is 6 squares of side 1 cm i.e. its area is 6 cm^2

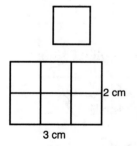

Other areas are more difficult to find exactly

e.g. the area of this metal plate can be found approximately by counting squares. If half a square or more is within the shape it is counted, otherwise it is not.

In this case the approximate area is 10 squares i.e. 10 cm^2. (The squares that are counted are marked with a ×.)

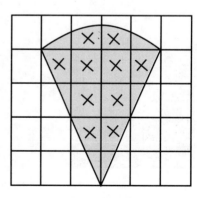

Each shape is drawn on a 1 cm grid.

Question The diagram shows the outline of the Scottish island of Mull. By counting squares find its area.

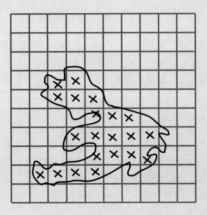

Answer The area is 21 squares.

1 Count squares to find the area of each island. Count a square if half of it or more is within its boundary, otherwise do not.

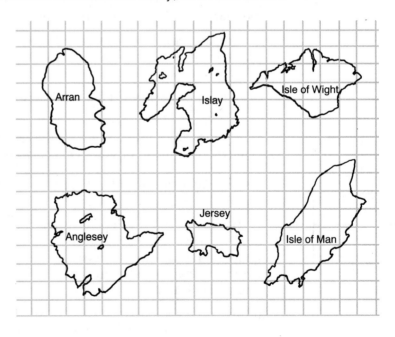

2 The sketches show the outlines of four leaves.

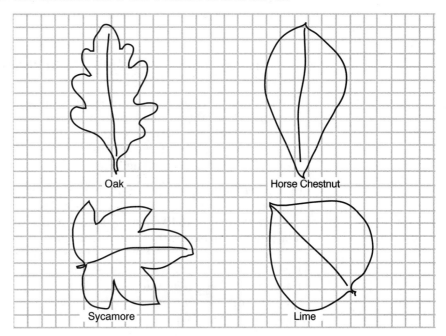

By counting squares find the approximate area of each leaf.

3 The diagrams show gaskets for different carburettors. By counting squares find the area of each.

(a)   (b)

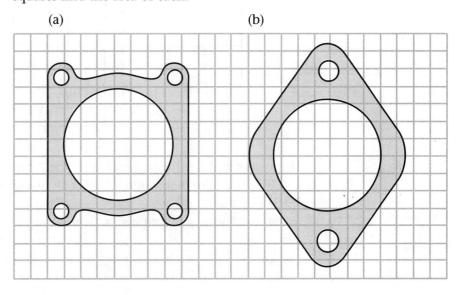

Units of area

The most common units of area in the *metric system* are the square metre (m^2), the square centimetre (cm^2), the square millimetre (mm^2) and the hectare, where

$$
\begin{aligned}
1\,m^2 &= 100 \times 100\,cm^2 &&= 10\,000\,cm^2 \\
1\,cm^2 &= 10 \times 10\,mm^2 &&= 100\,mm^2
\end{aligned}
$$

and   1 hectare = $10\,000\,m^2$

The hectare is the preferred unit for measuring the area of land on a farm or industrial site, but for countries we use square kilometres

$$
\begin{aligned}
1\,km^2 &= 1000 \times 1000\,m^2 \\
&= 1\,000\,000\,m^2 \\
&= 100 \text{ hectare}
\end{aligned}
$$

In *imperial units* the most common units of area are: the square inch (sq.in or in^2), the square foot (sq.ft of ft^2), the square yard (sq.yd or yd^2), the acre (which is 4840 square yards) and the square mile. The relationships between these quantities are:

$$
\begin{aligned}
1\,ft^2 &= 12 \times 12\,in^2 = 144\,in^2 \\
1\,yd^2 &= 3 \times 3\,ft^2 = 9\,ft^2 \\
1 \text{ acre} &= 4840\,yd^2 \\
1 \text{ square mile} &= 640 \text{ acres}
\end{aligned}
$$

Areas of squares and rectangles

The square

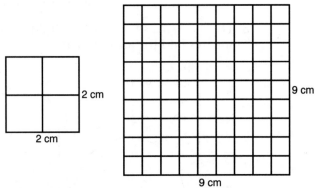

2 cm

2 cm

9 cm

9 cm

The area of a square postage stamp of side 2 cm is $2 \times 2\,cm^2$ i.e. $4\,cm^2$ and the area of a square computer disk holder of side 9 cm is $9 \times 9\,cm^2$ i.e. $81\,cm^2$.

In general, the area of a square is given by, area = (length of side)^2.

The rectangle

3 cm

The area of a rectangular card measuring 4 cm by 3 cm is $4 \times 3\,cm^2$ i.e. $12\,cm^2$.

In general, the area of a rectangle is given by, area = length × breadth.

4 cm

Note: To find an area, all dimensions need to be expressed in the same unit.

Exercise 3d

1 Find the area of a square paving slab of side 30 cm.

2 Each square on a chess board has a side of 3.5 cm and the playing area is surrounded by a border 3.5 cm wide.
   (a) How many squares are there on a chess board?
   (b) What is the area of one square on the board?
   (c) What shape is (i) the playing area (ii) the board?
   (d) What is the length of a side of (i) the playing area (ii) the board?
   (e) Find, in cm^2 (i) the playing area (ii) the area of the board.

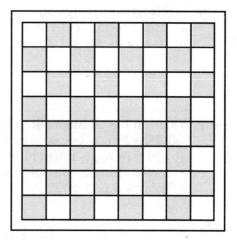

3 A door is 200 cm high and 80 cm wide. Find:
   (a) its area in cm^2
   (b) its dimensions in metres
   (c) its area in m^2.

4 The diagram shows a soccer pitch. Find:
   (a) its perimeter
   (b) its area.

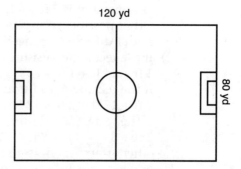

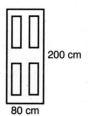

5 A postcard measures 135 mm by 85 mm. Find:
  (a) the perimeter of the card in millimetres
  (b) the area of the card in mm^2
  (c) the dimensions of the card in centimetres
  (d) the area of the card in cm^2.
      Give your answer correct to 3 s.f.

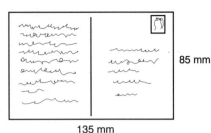
85 mm

135 mm

6 A rectangular paving slab measures 16 in by 12 in. Find:
  (a) its perimeter in   (i) in   (ii) ft
  (b) its area in   (i) in^2 (ii) ft^2.

12"
16"

Question Quentin has 24 square floor tiles each with an area of 1 ft^2.
  (a) How long is one edge of a tile?
  (b) In how many different ways can he lay them in a rectangle?
  (c) Which arrangement has the longest perimeter and which the shortest perimeter?

Answer (a) 1 ft

  (b)

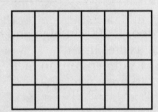

One way of arranging 24 tiles in the shape of a 6 ft by 4 ft rectangle is shown in the sketch. In this case the perimeter of the arrangement is 6 ft + 4 ft + 6 ft + 4 ft i.e. 20 ft.
Other possible arrangements are 1 × 24, 2 × 12 and 3 × 8
∴ four different arrangements are possible.
  (c) If the rectangle measures 1 ft × 24 ft the perimeter is
      1 ft + 24 ft + 1 ft + 24 ft = 50 ft
      If the rectangle measures 2 ft × 12 ft the perimeter is
      2 ft + 12 ft + 2 ft + 12 ft = 28 ft
      If the rectangle measures 3 ft × 8 ft the perimeter is
      3 ft + 8 ft + 3 ft + 8 ft = 22 ft
No other arrangement is possible without cutting some of the tiles.
The longest possible perimeter is therefore 50 ft and the shortest possible perimeter is 20 ft.

7 Darren has 12 square tiles each of side 20 cm.
  (a) In how many different ways can he arrange them in a rectangle?
  (b) Which arrangement has (i) the longest perimeter (ii) the shortest perimeter?
  (c) How much longer is the longest perimeter than the shortest?

8 Sally has 36 square tiles of side 2 in. She lays them out on a table to form a rectangle.
  (a) In how many different ways can she do this if the shortest acceptable width of the rectangle is 4 in?
  (b) Which arrangement has the longest perimeter?
  (c) Which arrangement has the shortest perimeter? What special name do we give to this shape?

Cubes and cuboids The volume of this cube is 1 cubic centimetre i.e. 1 cm^3.

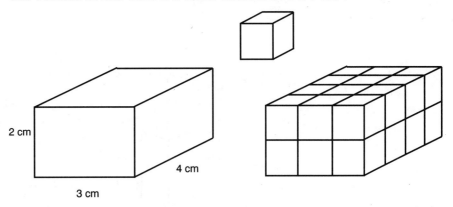

We can work out the volume of this cuboid by filling it with cubes of volume 1 cm^3 and counting the number of cubes. In this case we see that 24 cubes are needed so the volume of the given cuboid is 24 cm^3.

Volume of a cuboid = length × breadth × height.

Note that the unit used for all three dimensions must be the same.

Units of volume In the *metric system* the most common units of volume are mm^3, cm^3 and m^3 where

$$1 \text{ cm}^3 = 10 \times 10 \times 10 \text{ mm}^3$$
i.e. $$1 \text{ cm}^3 = 1000 \text{ mm}^3$$
$$1 \text{ m}^3 = 100 \times 100 \times 100 \text{ cm}^3$$

In the *imperial system* the units of volume are cubic inches (in^3), cubic feet (ft^3) and cubic yards (yd^3) where

$$1 \text{ ft}^3 = 12 \times 12 \times 12 \text{ in}^3 = 1728 \text{ in}^3$$
$$1 \text{ yd}^3 = 3 \times 3 \times 3 \text{ ft}^3 = 27 \text{ ft}^3$$

Exercise 3e

In Questions 1–4 the stack is made from cubes of side 1 cm. Find the number of cubes used to make each shape and hence write down its volume.

1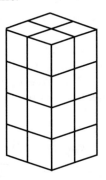

2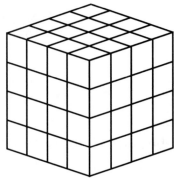

3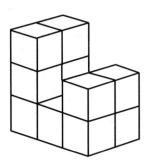

4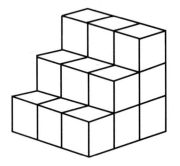

5 How many additional cubes are needed to turn the stack given in Question 4 into a cube? (You are not allowed to take the original stack apart.)

6 The cuboid in Question 1 is made from white cubes. Its outside is painted black and the cuboid then taken apart. How many of the small cubes have
(a) 3 black faces   (b) 2 black faces?

Question   How many cubes of side 2 cm are needed to fill the space inside a cuboid measuring 6 cm by 4 cm by 4 cm?

Answer

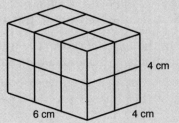

Looking down into the box 6 cubes (3 rows with 2 in each row) of side 2 cm are needed to cover the base of the box.

These cubes fill the box to a depth of 2 cm. Another layer of 6 cubes is needed to fill the box completely.

i.e. 12 cubes are needed to fill the space inside the cuboid.

7 The inside measurements of a rectangular wooden tea caddy are 22 cm by 8 cm by 10 cm. How many cubic centimetres of tea will the tea caddy hold?

8 Draw a cube of side 4 cm. How many cubes of side 2 cm would be needed to fill it?

Questions 9–12 refer to the information given below.

In a play group they have a collection of coloured cubes of different sizes and some rectangular boxes. Details are given in the table.

Solid cubes		Open rectangular boxes			
Colour	Length of side (cm)	Box	Length (cm)	Breadth (cm)	Height (cm)
Red	1	A	4	3	2
Yellow	2	B	8	4	2
White	3	C	12	6	6

9 How many red cubes are needed to fill
   (a) Box A   (b) Box B   (c) Box C?

10 How many yellow cubes are needed to fill
    (a) Box B   (b) Box C?

11 How many white cubes are needed to fill Box C?

12 Explain why Box A cannot be filled completely (so that no part of a cube is projecting above the top of the box), using either all yellow cubes or all white cubes.

13 A cuboid is to be made from cubes of side 1 cm. Every dimension (i.e. length, width and height) must be at least 2 cm.
    (a) What are the dimensions of the smallest possible cuboid? How many cubes are needed to make it?
    (b) Can an acceptable cuboid be made from
        (i) 12 cubes   (ii) 15 cubes?
    (c) Kate has 24 cubes. How many different cuboids can she make? List them.

Question | Find the volume of a rectangular room measuring 10 m by 6 m by 3 m. If 4.5 m³ of airspace is required for each person, what is the maximum number of people who should use the room at the same time?

Answer

Volume of rectangular room $\quad=$ length × breadth × height
$$= 10 \times 6 \times 3 \text{ m}^3$$
$$= 180 \text{ m}^3$$
One person needs 4.5 m³ of air space
∴ maximum number of people who can use the room is

$$\frac{\text{total airspace available}}{\text{amount of air needed by one person}} = \frac{180}{4.5}$$

$$= 40$$

i.e. the maximum number of people that should use the room at any one time is 40.

14 A cereal box for Mornwake Crunchy Cornflakes measures 12 in by 8 in by $2\frac{1}{2}$ in. How many cubic inches of cornflakes will the box hold?

15 Alf and Ena Goldthorpe each have a little box in which to keep their tablets. Alf's box measures 25 mm by 20 mm by 6 mm and Ena's measures 32 mm by 21 mm by 5 mm. Find the volume of each box in cubic centimetres. Who has the larger tablet box?

16 Find the volume of each cuboid.

(a)

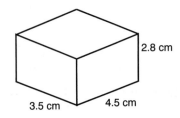

2.8 cm
3.5 cm
4.5 cm

(b)

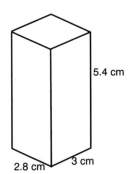

5.4 cm
2.8 cm
3 cm

(c)

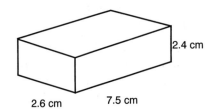

2.4 cm
2.6 cm
7.5 cm

(d) Which cuboid has
(i) the largest volume (ii) the smallest volume?

17 A classroom measuring 8 yd by 6 yd is to be used for a class of 32 students. If 5 yd^3 of airspace is required for each student, how high should the ceiling be?

Question A cabinet maker has two planks of oak from which he hopes to make a chest. Each plank is 3 m long, 36 cm wide and 65 mm thick.

Find the volume of oak in one plank in
(a) cm^3 (b) m^3

Answer (a) (Work in centimetres)

Length of plank is 3 m = 3 × 100 cm
= 300 cm

Width of plank is 36 cm
Thickness of plank is 65 mm = $\frac{65}{10}$ cm
= 6.5 cm

volume of plank = length × breadth × thickness
= 300 × 36 × 6.5 cm^3
= 70 200 cm^3

(a) (Work in metres)

Length of plank is 3 m
Width of plank is 36 cm   = $\frac{36}{100}$ m
= 0.36 m
Thickness of plank is 65 mm = $\frac{65}{1000}$ m
= 0.065 m

volume of plank = 3 × 0.36 × 0.065 m^3
= 0.0702 m^3

---

18 A swimming pool is 30 m long, 15 m wide and 2.5 m deep. It is filled with water to a level 50 cm from the top. What volume of water is there in the pool? Give your answer
(a) in m^3 (b) in litres. (1 litre = 1000 cm^3.)

19 Find the volume of a cube of sugar of side 12 mm. Give your answer in
(a) mm^3 (b) cm^3

20 Find the cost of a rectangular piece of timber measuring 20 cm by 8 cm which is 4 m long, if the price of the timber is £55 per cubic metre.

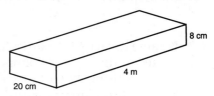

8 cm

4 m

20 cm

21 A concrete block measures 45 cm × 15 cm × 7½ cm.
   (a) Find the volume of the block in   (i) cm³   (ii) m³.
       (1 m³ = 100 × 100 × 100 cm³.)
   (b) How many such blocks can be made from 1 m³ of concrete?

22

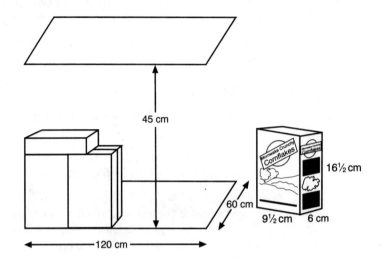

The sketch shows two supermarket shelves which are to be loaded with packets of cereal similar to the packet shown on the right.
   (a) Find   (i) the amount of space taken up by one packet   (ii) the area of one shelf.
   (b) How many packets of cereal can be stocked in one row from front to back if the largest side of each packet faces outwards?
   (c) What is the greatest number of rows that can be stacked on one shelf if all the boxes stand vertically and face outwards?
   (d) Packets are also stored horizontally on top of the packets arranged vertically. What is the greatest number of packets that can be laid horizontally in a single layer in this way? How many layers can be placed on top of the vertical packets?
   (e) What is the greatest number of packets that can be placed on one shelf?

Capacity

Many three-dimensional shapes are used for holding liquid. The volume of liquid that a container holds is called its capacity. In the *metric system* capacity is usually measured in litres (ℓ).

Small units, such as medicines, are measured in millimetres (ml), i.e. thousandths of a litre. An ordinary teaspoon holds about 5 ml.

$$1000 \text{ ml} = 1 \ell$$

Because capacity is a particular kind of volume the units of capacity are related to the units of volume we are already familiar with
           1 litre   = 1000 cm³
   and   1 millilitre = 1 cm³

In the *imperial system* the most common units of capacity are the pint and the gallon where   1 gallon = 8 pints.

Exercise 3f

In questions on capacity, assume that all the given measurements are inside measurements.

Question   (a) A medicine bottle has a rectangular cross section measuring 5 cm by 3 cm and is 11 cm high. How much medicine will it hold in (i) cm³ (ii) litres (iii) millilitres?
(b) The bottle is full of cough medicine and Sean is told to take two 5 ml teaspoonfuls three times a day. How many days should the medicine last?

Answer   (a) (i) Capacity of the bottle $= 5 \times 3 \times 11$ cm³
                                                     $= 165$ cm³
          (ii) Capacity of bottle in litres $= 165 \div 1000$ litres
              (1000 cm³ = 1 litre.)

                                                     $= 0.165$ litres
          (iii) Since 1 cm³ = 1 ml the capacity of the bottle is 165 ml.
     (b) Sean takes two 5 ml of the medicine three times a day
          i.e. he takes $2 \times 5 \times 3$ ml per day = 30 ml per day
          $\therefore$ the medicine will last $165 \div 30$ days i.e. $5\frac{1}{2}$ days.

1 An open rectangular tank is 45 cm long, 30 cm wide and 20 cm high. How much water will it hold in
(a) cm³   (b) litres?

2 How many litres of water can be poured into a rectangular tank that has an internal volume of 1 m³?

3 How many pint milk bottles can be filled from a 500 gallon tank of milk?

4 The wine glasses used at a wedding have a capacity of 10 centilitres. How many glasses can be filled from twelve litre bottles?
(1 litre = 100 centilitres.)

5 A closed wooden rectangular box has external measurements 43 cm by 35 cm by 18 cm. It is made from wood $1\frac{1}{2}$ cm thick. Find:
(a) its internal measurements
(b) the capacity of the box
(c) the amount of space that it occupies when stored on a shelf
(d) the volume of wood used to make the box.

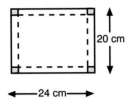

6 Four equal squares, of side 3 cm, are removed from the corners of a rectangular piece of card measuring 24 cm by 20 cm. The card is next folded about the dotted lines to form an open box.
(a) How deep is the box?
(b) What are the measurements of the base of the box?
(c) What is the capacity of the box?

Mass

When we buy meat or fruit or vegetables we usually ask for a particular weight. What we really want is a certain mass. The weight of an object depends on the pull of gravity on it, and this varies from place to place. The mass of an object is the amount of material in it.

In the *metric system* the basic unit of mass is the gram. Other units in everyday use that derive from the gram are the kilogram, milligram and tonne,

where	1 kilogram (kg)	= 1000 grams (g)
	1 gram (g)	= 1000 milligrams (mg)
and	1 tonne (t)	= 1000 kilograms (kg).

The most common units of mass in the *imperial system* are the ounce (oz), the pound (lb) and the ton, and occasionally the stone and the hundredweight (cwt)

where	1 lb	=	16 oz
	1 stone	=	14 lb
	1 cwt	=	112 lb
and	1 ton	=	2240 lb

Density

The mass of one unit of volume of material is called its density

i.e. $\text{density} = \dfrac{\text{mass}}{\text{volume}}$

A goldsmith, for example, knows that the mass of 1 cm^3 of gold is 19.3 grams i.e. the density of gold is 19.3 g/cm^3

Exercise 3g

Question (a) A goldsmith has 5.3 grams of gold. How many milligrams is this?
(b) A bag contains 864 grams of tomatoes. What is this in kilograms?
(c) 94 300 kilograms of steel needs to be moved by road. How many tonnes is this?

Answer (a) Since 1 g   = 1000 mg
                 5.3 g = 5.3 × 1000 mg (large unit to small unit so multiply by 1000)

                      = 5300 mg
i.e. the goldsmith has 5300 mg of gold.

(b) Since $1000 \text{ g} = 1 \text{ kg}$

$$864 \text{ g} = \frac{864}{1000} \text{ kg (small unit to large unit so divide by 1000)}$$

$$= 0.864 \text{ kg}$$

∴ the bag contains 0.864 kg of tomatoes.

(c) Since $1000 \text{ kg} = 1 \text{ tonne}$

$$94\ 300 \text{ kg} = \frac{94\ 300}{1000} \text{ (small unit to large unit so divide by 1000)}$$

$$= 94.3 \text{ tonnes}$$

∴ 94.3 tonnes of steel is to be moved.

1 A bag of caster sugar has a mass of $\frac{1}{2}$ kg. How many grams is this?

2 A blood pressure tablet has a mass of 5 mg. How many grams is this?

3 A mailorder firm sends advertising material to 2400 potential customers. Each one has a mass of 54 g. Find, in kilograms, the total mass of advertising material sent out.

4 A lorry, which when unloaded has a mass of 4.5 t, is loaded with 150 50 kg bags of potatoes. Find
   (a) the total mass of the potatoes, in tonnes
   (b) the mass of the loaded lorry.

5 A wine enthusiast buys three 1 kg bags of sugar to make some wine. He needs 250 g sugar to make 4 litres of sweet raisin wine. How many litres of wine can he make from the sugar he bought?

6 A chef orders 12 kg of best fillet steak. How many servings can he hope to get from this order if each steak is about 3 cm thick and weighs 200 g?

7 The instructions on a 5 kg bag of scientifically balanced puppy food which is suitable for puppies up to 18 months suggests giving a Cavalier King Charles spaniel 125 g per day. How many days should the bag last a family with one dog?

8 Find the mass of a metal bar measuring 3 m by 8 cm by 4 cm if 1 cm^3 of the metal has a mass of 9.4 g. Give your answer in
   (a) grams   (b) kilograms.

9 The diagram shows the cross-section of a girder 5.5 m long. Calculate
   (a) the volume of the girder in cubic centimetres
   (b) the mass of the girder in kilograms if 1 cm^3 of the girder has a mass of 8 g.

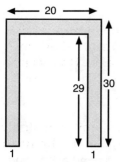

All dimensions are in centimetres

Multiple choice questions

In Question 1–4 several alternative answers are given. Write down the letter that corresponds to the correct answer.

1 A street is 1.3 kilometres long. Expressed in metres its length is
A 130 m   B 1300 m
C 13 000 m   D none of these.

2 Given that 1 mile is roughly 1.6 km, the approximate equivalent of 50 km is
A 31 miles   B 80 miles
C 45 miles   D 16 miles.

3

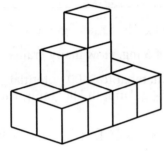

The number of cubes in this stack is
A 11   B 9   C 10   D 13.

4 The area of glass used to cover a square picture is 225 cm^2. The perimeter of the glass is
A 100 cm   B 30 cm
C 68 cm   D 60 cm

5 Niam makes up the following statements about different units of measurements. Which of the following statements are true and which are false?
A A hectare is larger than an acre
B An inch is smaller than 2 centimetres
C A yard is longer than a metre
D One litre is less than two pints.

6 The base of an open rectangular metal box measures 22 cm by 10 cm, and the box is 8 cm deep. Outside it is painted white and inside it is painted black. The following statements have been made:
Statement 1 The capacity of the box is 1760 cm^3 and the area painted white is 952 cm^2.
Statement 2 The area painted black is 732 cm^2 and 1.76 litres of water can be poured into the box when it is empty.
How are these two statements best described?
A True, True   B True, False
C False, True   D False, False.

Self assessment 3

1

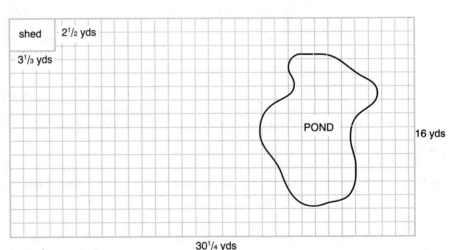

Scale: $1/2$ cm = 1 yd

The sketch shows the main features of Clay Morgan's garden. The rectangular plot has a large irregularly shaped fresh water pond at one end and a potting shed in one corner. Use the information given on the sketch to answer the questions that follow.

(a) What length of fencing is needed to enclose the plot?
(b) The fence is everywhere 6 ft high and Clay treats both sides of the fence by soaking them in creosote. What area, in square yards, does he have to treat? How many gallons of creosote does he need if 1 pint is enough to cover 15 square yards?
(c) By counting squares find the area of the pond. Each square on the sketch represents 1 yd².
(d) Find the area of the plot
(i) in yd²   (ii) as a fraction of an acre.
(e) Express the dimensions of the shed in feet.
(f) The shed has a flat roof and is everywhere 6 ft 3 in high. Find the amount of space taken up by the shed. Give your answer in cubic feet correct to 3 s.f.
(g) Clay removes 36 cubic feet of water from the pond and tips it into an empty rectangular tank which has a base measuring 2 yd by 1½ yd and which is 20 in deep. How high is the surface of the water above the base of the tank?

2

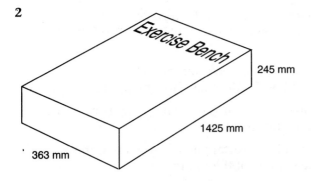

245 mm

1425 mm

363 mm

An exercise bench comes packed in a rectangular box measuring 1425 mm by 363 mm by 245 mm. A bright red label covers the whole of one of the largest surfaces. Joe orders one of these benches from a mailorder company and

one day when he comes home from college he finds it lying unopened on the garage floor.
(a) In the warehouse from which it was dispatched the benches are stored lying flat, the maximum permitted number in a stack being 8. What is the height of the highest acceptable stack of the these benches in the warehouse?
(b) Express the dimensions of a box in metres.
(c) Find the perimeter of the label in
(i) mm (ii) m.
(d) Find, in m², the area of
(i) the label
(ii) each end
(iii) each vertical side.
Hence find the total outside surface area of the box.
(e) How much space does a stack of 8 packed benches take up in the warehouse?

3   A paperback book with 480 pages has a page size measuring 185 mm by 115 mm, and is 25 mm thick including the covers. The thickness of each cover is 0.5 mm thick and the book has a mass of 241 g.
(a) Express the dimensions of a page in centimetres and hence find the area of one page in square centimetres giving your answer correct to 3 s.f.
(b) How thick is the book excluding the covers? Hence find the thickness of one leaf (one leaf is printed on both sides to give two pages).
(c) Find the total area of paper used to print the book excluding the covers.
(d) If the covers have a mass of 1 g find
(i) the mass of paper used excluding the covers
(ii) the mass of paper used for one leaf of the book.
(e) Use your answers to part (a) and part (d)(ii) to find the mass of 1 square metre of the paper used to manufacture this book.

Revision papers for units 1–3

Paper 1

1 A lorry is transporting 156 cartons of apples. Each box contains 96 apples. How many apples are there altogether?

2 An hotel in the Swiss Alps can cater for 57 skiers at any one time. If the season lasts for 19 weeks and each course lasts one week, how many skiers stay at the hotel during the whole of the season?

3 If it takes $3\frac{1}{3}$ minutes to fill $\frac{3}{8}$ of a storage tank, what fraction will be filled in 1 minute?

4 A rectangular field measures 320 m by 120 m. Find
   (a) its perimeter in kilometres
   (b) its area in   (i) m^2 (ii) hectares.

5 Glenthorpe Developments are offering building land at £50 000 per hectare. How much is this per square metre?

Paper 2

1 The doctor put Sally on a course of tablets. She was told, that if it was necessary, it was safe to continue to take the tablets for 10 000 days. Roughly, how many years is this?

2 A firm making vacuum cleaners has an order for 1344. The current rate of production is 84 per day. How many days will it take to fulfil the order?

3 A supermarket buys 720 cases of tinned tomatoes. They sell $\frac{1}{3}$ on Monday, $\frac{1}{4}$ on Tuesday and $\frac{1}{6}$ on Wednesday. How many cases remain?

4 Meg has $3\frac{1}{2}$ bars of chocolate. Each bar is $6\frac{3}{4}$ inches long. How far will they stretch if they are laid end to end?

5 A metal rod is 4.5 m long. It has a rectangular cross-section measuring 3 cm by 12 mm. Find the volume of the rod in
   (a) cm^3 (b) m^3.

Paper 3

1 A motor manufacturer needs to buy 24 000 8 mm flat steel washers. They come from the suppliers in boxes, each box containing 200 washers. How many boxes must be ordered?

2 A catalogue for stationary contains 64 pages. The firm's logo appears on every odd page but nowhere else. The company prints 5680 copies of the catalogue. How many times will the logo have been printed altogether?

3 A college has 2400 students on its three-year courses. $\frac{1}{6}$ are in the third year, $\frac{3}{8}$ are in the second year and the remainder are first year students.
   (a) What fraction of the students are in their first year?
   (b) How many first year students are there?

4 A contractor laying cables uses a mini excavator to dig a trench 180 yd long, 4 ft deep and 18 in wide. Find the amount of material excavated, giving your answer in
   (a) ft^3 (b) yd^3.

5 Tracey has a supply of square floor tiles of side 20 cm. She wants to arrange a number of them in a rectangle so that the perimeter of the rectangle is 240 cm.
   (a) Show all the different arrangements that are possible.
   (b) Which arrangement has   (i) the largest area   (ii) the smallest area?

Paper 4

1 Square paving slabs have an edge of 0.56 metres. 500 of them are laid end to end along a pavement. How long is this line of paving slabs?

2

A plank of wood is 320 centimetres long. It is cut into 4 equal lengths. If each saw cut consumes 0.16 centimetres of wood, find the length of each piece.

3 Last season a charter airline used a 96-seater aircraft to fly 4608 holidaymakers from Newcastle to Palma and back to Newcastle.
   (a) Why did the aircraft make one outward flight, and one return flight, empty?
   (b) How many fully loaded flights did the aircraft need to make between Newcastle and Palma. (Taking 96 holidaymakers in one direction counts as one flight.)
   (c) How many return flights did the aircraft make altogether?

4 A rectangular tank with a base measuring 8 ft by 5 ft has a capacity of 1000 gallons.
   (a) If 1 gallon = 277.25 in^3 find the capacity of the tank in
       (i) in^3
       (ii) ft^3.
       (Give your answers correct to 3 s.f.)
   (b) Find the depth of the tank in feet.

5 A restaurateur orders fresh trout from his supplier. He requests that each fish is about 250 g and he wants sufficient for 120 covers (i.e. servings). How many kilograms of trout should the supplier deliver? (Allow one trout per cover.)

For You To Discuss: 1

A changing world

Much has changed in British industry and commerce during the last twenty years. Not only has much of the labour force been replaced by robots but the imperial system of measurement, a system we have used for centuries, has been almost totally replaced by the metric system. We believe our future is in Europe and so joined with the other countries that were already members of the then European Economic Community (now the European Union). One of the consequences of joining was that we had to change to Europe's way of measuring.

Examples of this change are to be found everywhere. Go to the builders' merchant to buy some timber and you will find that you cannot buy lengths of 2" × 1" or 3" × 2", and you certainly won't be charged by the foot or yard. They will talk about 25 mm by 50 mm (measurements are given to the nearest 5 mm) and you will buy it by the metre. Paint is bought by the litre rather than the pint or gallon. Even the sizes of copper piping and twist drills have been altered. What about a set of twist drills ranging from $\frac{1}{32}$" up to $\frac{3}{4}$" or a length of copper tubing to repair a central heating system that was put in some years ago using $\frac{1}{2}$", $\frac{3}{4}$" and 1" piping?

I was talking to a builder at Delmo's DIY the other day. He told me he'd got used to all the changes in sizes now but that lots of other things had changed in the building trade. For example, he said, 'I wouldn't be talking to you here twenty years ago. It would have been at Axfords in our own town. They were forced out of business long ago. We have to travel six miles to this place now'. 'Do you know', he said, 'There's another thing that customers and the people you employ seem to pick up and argue about far more today than years ago, and that's the difference between what a craftsman gets paid and what his builder charges for him. Craftsmen I employ often feel hard done by when they find out how much I am charging the customer for their labour compared with the rate I pay them. It's pretty hard to convince workmen that you're not making a fortune out of them. Anyway, must dash off, these paving slabs are needed straightaway'.

Obviously he was having problems with his workmen. My thoughts moved to something else that is talked about quite a lot at the moment. A national minimum wage. I wondered how it would affect the builder when it becomes law in this country. While the national minimum wage is in the future another change is already with us. The gas, electricity and water companies are trying very hard to get customers to pay their bills by Direct Debit. The companies point out that it is far less painful to pay in ten or twelve equal instalments spread over a year, rather than to pay every quarter or even every year. My thoughts were that there must be something in it for them or they wouldn't be offering a cash incentive to customers to make the change.

When we learn to count we begin with the whole numbers. As an adult it's easy to check that you've got 2 tee shirts or 4 grapefruit or 6 magazines. However, with quantities that you weigh or measure it is more difficult to check. You ask for three pounds of new potatoes but how do you know that's what you get? Most people are satisfied if they believe they have at least three pounds. What they have is an amount which hopefully, when rounded down, is three pounds. In a similar way a large number of items is often given correct to the nearest 10, 100 or even 1000. What does '200 people killed in Mecca stampede' mean? Is it 172 or 247 or what? Can you picture what 200 people together look like? The next time you are in a small group, first make a quick estimate of how many people you think there are, then count them to see how near you are. How many groups that size would make 50 or 100 or 200?

Most people are poor estimators. Try some more estimating. How many books are there in that pile? Now count them to check. Try the same thing with the number of people on a bus or in the carriage of a train, or the number of cars in a car park. What about the number of items in a shopping trolley, or the number of paving stones on a length of pavement?

Often you think that estimating doesn't really matter, but when you sit down, do some calculations, and think things out, you find the answer is very different from your estimate. For instance, take Sam and his car. He travels about 13 000 miles a year and thought he was getting about 7 miles to the litre. He wondered how much he would save each year if he changed to a car that would give more miles to the litre. He had quite a surprise when he found out.

(a) The imperial system was based on numbers like 12 (inches in a foot), 16 (ounces in a pound) and 240 (old pence in a £) while the metric system is based on 10 (millimetres in a centimetre), 100 (new pence in a £) and 1000 (metres in a kilometre). Which is the more useful number, 100 or 240, if you want to divide the number into an exact number of equal parts? Try dividing 100 and 240 by 2, 3, 4, 5, etc.

(b) What metric sizes would you buy if you wanted to replace timber that measured 2" × 2" and 3" × 2", if the new sizes are to be too small rather than too large?

(c) You want to replace $\frac{3}{4}$" copper tube. Which metric size is
(i) nearest below
(ii) nearest above?
(New sizes go from 10 mm at 5 mm intervals.)

(d) Why should a builder, or other employer, have to charge much more for his employees' labour than he pays the employee? What expenses must the employer meet from the difference in the two rates?

(e) Some paving slabs are quite large while others are smaller than a brick. Discuss the advantages/disadvantages of different sizes of these slabs.

(f) It is quite natural that unions are interested in a national minimum wage, for this would raise the living standards of many of their members. Employers argue that this would lead to increased costs, so there would be less money for expansion and modernisation. This in turn would lead to companies becoming uncompetitive or even failing completely. Discuss both sides of the argument and suggest ways of solving it. How would you solve it? Would you have a different solution depending on whether you were an employer or an employee?

(g) What advantages are there for the customer who agrees to pay for gas and electricity by direct debit? Why are the service companies so keen for us to change to this method of payment?

(h) Discuss ways in which you can improve your ability to estimate such things as the speed of a vehicle, the size of a group of people or the weight of an object.

(i) How could Sam check how many miles his car did, on average, to the litre?

(j) Suppose his estimate was correct. Investigate how much he would save in a year, on petrol, if he changed to a car that did
(i) 9
(ii) 10, miles to the litre.
Assume that petrol costs 55p a litre. How much difference would it make if he found a petrol station where he could buy petrol 2p a litre cheaper?

(k) Milk is to be sold by the litre. How will you manage if you take three pints of milk a day? How many litres will you order? Will you end up with more or less than you take at present?

UNIT 4 | Using Percentages

After studying this unit you will be able to
- [ ] convert a fraction or a decimal into a percentage and vice versa
- [ ] express one quantity as a percentage of another
- [ ] find the percentage of a quantity
- [ ] calculate a percentage increase or decrease
- [ ] solve value added tax, income tax and other tax problems
- [ ] understand the advantages and disadvantages of different forms of saving and borrowing
- [ ] use compound growth tables
- [ ] appreciate the cost of bank loans and credit sales
- [ ] tackle problems on depreciation.

Interchanging percentages, decimals and fractions

Extra help on fractions, decimals and percentage will be found in Guidance Notes: Basic Skills, Sections **B**, **C** and **D**, p. 331.

Exercise 4a

In Questions 1–5 express each percentage as a decimal.

1 On the catering course 85% of the students are female.

2 At a rugby international 74% of the spectators are males.

3 The clear-up rate for crimes in Newborough is 34%.

4 Last year the sales of camcorders increased by 135%.

5 On a Thursday the number of customers at Sainsgate supermarket is 230% more than on a Monday.

Question	At an MOT Testing Station 60% of the cars tested pass first time. Express this as a fraction in its lowest terms.
Answer	$60\% = \dfrac{60}{100}$
	i.e. $\quad 60\% = \dfrac{3}{5}$

In Questions 6–9 express each percentage as a fraction in its lowest terms.

6 At a factory 10% of the components from the press shop failed the quality test.

7 By choosing a smaller brick a bricklayer needs to order 20% more bricks.

8 In a warehouse 43% of the potatoes are reds and 57% are whites.

9 The target for Amien Computers is to increase sales next year by 35%.

Question	(a) Out of the 20 nails in a box, 7 have round heads. What percentage is this?
	(b) On a farm 0.63 of the land is planted with cereals. What percentage is this?
Answer	(a) 7 out of 20 is $\frac{7}{20} = \frac{7}{20} \times 100\%$
	i.e. $\qquad\qquad \frac{7}{20} = 35\%$
	(b) 0.63 is $0.63 \times 100\%$
	i.e. $\qquad\quad 0.63 = 63\%$

10 Out of the 24 chocolates in a box 6 of them have hard centres. What percentages is this?

11 At a disco 0.65 of the dancers are girls. What percentage is this?

Question	Forty-five per cent of the residents in a home are men and the rest are women.
	(a) What percentage of the residents are women?
	(b) What fraction of the residents are men?
Answer	(a) If 45% of the residents are men it follows that $100\% - 45\%$
	i.e. 55% are women.
	(b) Fraction of residents that are men is $\frac{45}{100}$ i.e. $\frac{9}{20}$

12 In a library 32% of the books are reference books which are not available for borrowing. What percentage of the books can be borrowed?

13 If 72% of the cost of a cigarette is tax what percentage is not?

14 Four Seasons Travel stated that 68% of the holidays they sold were for resorts in the Mediterranean. What percentage of the holidays they sold were for resorts that were not in the Mediterranean?

15 Each Tuesday evening at a Youth Club, members have to choose one of the activities badminton, volleyball, gymnastics or dancing. If 14% choose badminton, 27% volleyball and 18% gymnastics, what percentage choose dancing?

16 Marmalade consists of 28% fruit, 58% sugar and the remainder water. Find:
(a) the percentage of marmalade that is water
(b) the fraction that is sugar.

17 The cost of running a car is 28% petrol, 35% road tax, insurance and repairs, and the remainder depreciation. What percentage accounts for depreciation?

18 In a street $\frac{2}{5}$ of the properties are bungalows.
(a) What percentage is this?
(b) What percentage of the properties are not bungalows?

19 In a factory 44 per cent of the workforce is under 24 years of age.
(a) What fraction is this?
(b) Can you say what fraction is older than 24?
(c) What fraction is older than 23?

20 The first all British nuclear submarine was HMS Valiant. She had a displacement of 4000 tons, a crew of 90, was 285 ft long and 33 ft 3 in in the beam.
(a) If 35 cubic feet of water weighs 1 ton, find the number of cubic feet of water displaced by the submarine.
(b) If 54% of the space inside the ship is unavailable for the crew, find (i) the fraction of space available for the crew   (ii) the volume of space available for the crew   (iii) the amount of space available for each member of the crew.
(c) Express the width of the submarine (the beam length) as a percentage of its length.

Expressing one quantity as a percentage of another

To express 5 m as a percentage of 25 m, we first express 5 m as a fraction of 25 m
i.e. 5 m is $\frac{5}{25}$ of 25 m
then $\qquad \frac{5}{25} = \frac{5}{25} \times 100\%$
$\qquad\qquad = 20\%$
5 m is 20% of 25 m.

Exercise 4b

In Questions 1–4 express:

1 £5 as a fraction of £10
2 60 cm as a fraction of 200 cm
3 1 pint as a fraction of 8 pints
4 50p as a fraction of 25p.

Question Express 45p as a fraction of £3.

Answer (When the given units are different, one of the units must be converted into the other before the quantities are compared. We usually change the larger unit to the smaller unit.)

£3   = 300p

45p is $\dfrac{45}{300}$ of £3

i.e. 45p is $\frac{3}{20}$ of £3.

In Questions 5–10 express the first quantity as a fraction of the second.

5 30p, £1
6 60 cm, 2 m

7 400 g, 3 kg
8 3 mm, 3 cm

9 700 kg, 1 tonne
10 4 pints, 2 gallons.

11 In a sample of 500 windscreen wipers that come off a production line, 25 are found to be faulty. What fraction is this?

12 In a box of 120 cassettes, 24 are damaged. What fraction is this?

13 At Amberley MOT Vehicle Testing Station 7 out of 10 cars pass first time.
(a) What fraction is this?
(b) What fraction fail first time?

Question Express
(a) 4 kg as a percentage of 80 kg
(b) 75p as a percentage of £2.50.

Answer (a) 4 kg is $\frac{4}{80}$ of 80 kg
But $\frac{4}{80} = \frac{4}{80} \times 100\% = 5\%$
4 kg is 5% of 80 kg.
(b) First change £2.50 to pence
£2.50 = 250p
75p is $\frac{75}{250}$ of £2.50
But $\frac{75}{250} = \frac{75}{250} \times 100\%$
     $= 30\%$
75p is 30% of £2.50

In Questions 14–21 express the first quantity as a percentage of the second.

14 £8, £10 **15** 24 cm, 50 cm

16 400 m, 1 km **17** 35p, £1.75

18 80 cm, 2 m **19** 2 pints, 1 gallon

20 650 kg, 1 tonne **21** 550 cm³, 1 litre

22 Wendy earns £180 per week and pays £30 a week at home for her keep. What percentage does Wendy
(a) pay for her keep
(b) have left after she has paid for her keep?

23 When George stood on the bathroom scales first thing one morning he weighed 11 st 6 lb. When he weighed again after lunch his weight was 11 st 8 lb. Express his lunchtime weight as a percentage of his weight first thing that morning.

24 Zena bought a second hand car for £5999 and sold it two years later for £3500. Express the price at which she sold it as a percentage of the purchase price. Give your answer correct to the nearest whole number.

Percentage of a quantity

30% of £50 is the same as finding 0.3 of £50
i.e. 30% of £50 = 0.3 × £50 = £15

Exercise 4c

Find:
1 20% of £40

2 $12\frac{1}{2}$% of a population of 20 000

3 $37\frac{1}{2}$% of 64 cm.

Question   At a village fete £3400 is raised for charity. It is decided to give 40% to Oxfam, 35% to the RSPCC and the remainder to the Church Restoration Fund.
How much goes to
(a) Oxfam   (b) The Church Restoration Fund?

Answer   (a) 40% of £3400 is $\frac{40}{100}$ of £3400
   i.e.   0.4 of £3400
Oxfam receives 0.4 × £3400 i.e. £1360.
(b) The Church Restoration Fund receives 100% − 40% − 35%
   i.e.   25% of the money raised
25% of £3400 is $\frac{25}{100}$ × £3400 = £850
The Church Restoration Fund receives £850.

4   At a wedding 85% of the guests took wine with their meal. There were 80 guests. How many guests took wine with their meal?

5   At a concert 55% of the audience are female. There are 2400 people present. How many of those in attendance are
(a) females   (b) males?

6   A shopkeeper buys 300 shirts, knowing that 10% of them are unsaleable. How many shirts can he sell?

7   Deductions from Kath's wages amount to 40%. What is her take-home pay if she earns £320?

8   The constituents of gunpowder are: nitre 75%, charcoal 15% and sulphur 10%. How many kilograms of charcoal are needed to make 12 kg of gunpowder?

9   A commercial traveller is paid 5% commission on each sale with a value up to £300. For sales above this value the commission is $7\frac{1}{2}$%.
(a) She takes two orders, one for £250 and one for £866. What commission can she expect to receive?
(b) What is her commission on a sale valued at £300?

10 A restauranteur buys 30 kg of lamb. He estimates that it loses 15% in preparation, 30% in cooking, $12\frac{1}{2}$% for bones and $2\frac{1}{2}$% for trimming and carving.
(a) How many kilograms of useful lamb remains?
(b) If 100 g is allowed per serving, how many servings should be available from 30 kg of lamb?
(c) How many kilograms of lamb should be bought to provide 160 servings at 100 g per serving?

Percentage increase and decrease

Percentage increases or decreases are very important in everyday life. For example, wages usually increase by a given percentage, but this often doesn't mean very much until it is changed into an amount of money

e.g. a 6% rise on £560 a week is worth an extra £33.60
whereas a 12% increase on £220 a week is worth only £26.40.

Exercise 4d

Question   Train fares are set to rise by 12%. Last month Nia's quarterly ticket cost £540. How much will it cost next quarter?

Answer   Increase is 12% of £540
i.e.   increase is $\frac{12}{100} \times$ £540
$$= 0.12 \times £540$$
$$= £64.80$$
∴ cost of new quarterly ticket is £540 + £64.80 = £604.80.

1 On Wednesdays a store offers a discount of 10% on all sales over £50. Find the Wednesday price of
   (a) a pair of jeans marked £35
   (b) a fireside chair marked £320
   (c) a pair of trainers marked £50.

2 My electricity bill is £76.50, excluding VAT. How much must I pay if VAT is to be added at 8%?

3 A car bought for £12 000 loses 76% of its value over a 5 year period. Find its value after 5 years.

4 After 2 years a radio bought for £24 depreciates by 65%. What is it worth when 2 years old?

5 When a length of material is washed for the first time it shrinks by $2\frac{1}{2}$%. Sally buys some new jeans which are 90 cm long. What length can she expect them to be after their first wash?

6 The doctor advises Terry, whose present weight is 125 kg, to reduce his weight by 20%. What weight should he aim to get down to?

7 A price reduction of 30% is made on a three piece suite costing £955. How much does the suite cost?

Question Phil Bellingham estimates the cost of building a new house at £56 000 of which 40% is for materials and the rest labour. By the time the house has been completed the cost of materials have increased by 15% and the labour costs by 12%. How much does the house actually cost him?

Answer

Estimated cost of materials	= 40% of £56 000
	= $\frac{40}{100} \times$ £56 000
	= 0.4 × £56 000
	= £22 400
Estimated cost of labour	= £56 000 − £22 400
	= £33 600
Increase in cost of materials	= 15% of £22 400
	= $\frac{15}{100} \times$ £22 400
	= 0.15 × £22 400
	= £3360
Increase in labour costs	= 12% of £33 600
	= 0.12 × £33 600
	= £4032
∴ actual cost of the house	= £56 000 + £3360 + £4032
	= £63 392
	= £63 400 (to the nearest £100)

8 The population of Cleartown is 50 000. Next year it is expected to rise by 10% and the following year by a further 8%.
Find the expected population of Cleartown
(a) next year
(b) the year after that.

9 Kate's weekly pay is £165 and 6% of this is deducted by her employer for pension contributions.
(a) How much is left after the pension contributions have been deducted?
(b) If Kate is given an increase of £15 per week how much additional pension contribution must she pay?

10

Year	UK	England	Wales	Scotland	Northern Ireland
1961	52 807	43 561	2635	5184	1427
1971	55 928		2740	5236	1540
1981		46 821	2814	5180	1539
1991	57 801	48 208	2891	5107	1594
2001	59 719	49 921	2964	5148	1686
2011	61 110	51 289	3010	5078	1733

The table shows the populations in thousands, including projected figures for the year 2001 and the year 2011, for the various parts of the United Kingdom at ten year intervals.
(a) Complete the blanks in the table.
(b) Find the percentage increase (or decrease) in population from 1961 to 1991 for
(i) England (ii) Wales (iii) Scotland (iv) Northern Ireland.
(c) In which region of the United Kingdom has the population from 1961 to 1991 changed by
(i) the largest percentage   (ii) the smallest percentage?
(d) In which region of the United Kingdom is the percentage of the population expected to increase most from
(i) 1991 to 2001   (ii) 1991 to 2011?
(e) For 1981 give the population of the United Kingdom and of each region, correct to the nearest million. Use these answers to find the fraction of the population that lived in   (i) England   (ii) Wales.

Buying and selling   In a business, 'mark-up' is the gross profit given as a percentage of the cost of the goods sold.

Exercise 4e

Question   Phillips & Co. buy men's Surefit shoes for £270 per dozen pairs and sells them at £33.75 a pair. Find the mark-up.

Answer

Cost price of one pair = £270 ÷ 12 = £22.50
Retail price per pair is £33.75
∴ gross profit per pair = £33.75 − £22.50 = £11.25.

$$\text{Mark up} = \frac{\text{gross profit}}{\text{cost price}} \times 100$$

$$= \frac{£11.25}{£22.50} \times 100$$

$$= 50\%$$

The mark-up is therefore 50%.

1 Rossini Computers made a gross profit of £61 600 on computer equipment costing £154 000. Find the mark-up.

2 Mclaurens (Wholesale) Ltd bought goods for £470 000 and sold them for £680 000. Find
(a) the gross profit (b) the mark-up.

3 Johnson Milnes made a profit of £3.4 m on sales of £8.8 m. Find
(a) the cost price of the goods sold (b) the mark-up.

4 At Platoni's the food cost of preparing the Speciality of the House is £4.50. What must the restaurant charge for the meal to make a gross profit of
(a) 50% (b) 60%
(c) 75% (d) 100%?

5 The table gives the cost of preparing various courses at Bellini's Restaurant as a percentage of the total bill.

Course	Dish	Approximate percentage of the total cost of the meal
First	Hors-d'oeuvre, soup	12
Main	Meat, fish, poultry	45
	Vegetables	10
	Potatoes	7
Third	Sweet, cheese, savoury	20
Sundries	Roll & fat, condiments	6
		100

Sim pays £22 for a full meal that costs the restaurant £10 for raw materials and preparation.
(a) What percentage of the cost of the meal did he pay for his main course? (Don't forget the veg!)
(b) How much did he pay for
(i) the meat (ii) his third course (iii) his main course?

(c) What mark-up did the restaurant add?
(d) If the restaurant were to add a mark-up of 100% what would the same meal cost?

6 The Lighting Department in a department store turns in the following figures for the year 1994–5:

Item	(£)
Sales	180 000
Cost of goods sold	90 000
Wages + incentive payments	73 000
Share of fixed overheads	24 000
Net profit (or loss)	

(a) Does the department make a profit or a loss? (You have to decide which figures you add together and which you subtract.)
(b) What 'mark-up' has the store used in this department?
(c) Which one figure in the list would be unchanged if the lighting department was closed?
(d) Minoli's, the well known ladies' fashion house, are interested in renting the floor area used by the lighting department at a cost of £30 000 a year. They would employ their own staff   (i) Which one of the above figures would not disappear?   (ii) Would you advise the store management to accept the offer, i.e. would it be better for Minoli's to have the space than to continue with the lighting department?   (iii) Would the space be profitable with Minoli's renting it?

7 A furniture retailer sells a chair for £144, his sales mark-up being 80%. What did the chair cost him?

Taxes

Value added tax (VAT)

Value added tax is added to most goods and services. It is a tax collected for the central government and increases the basic cost by $17\frac{1}{2}$%. Some things, for example basic foodstuffs, children's clothes, newspapers and books, are zero rated. This means that there is no tax on these items.

Income tax

Income tax is deducted from every person's income, that is, on their earnings over and above their allowances. At present (March 1995) the basic rate is 25%, but there is a reduced rate of 20% on the first £2500 of taxable income and a higher rate of 40% on taxable income above £23 700.

Other taxes

Apart from VAT and income tax the government collects other taxes e.g. inheritance tax (a tax on what you leave when you die), capital gains tax (a tax on the increase in value of an asset when it is disposed of) and numerous taxes such as those on petrol, tobacco, alcohol and the road fund licence. These are grouped together under the general heading of Excise Duty.

Exercise 4f

Question   The marked price of a camcorder is £756, plus VAT at $17\frac{1}{2}$%. What must I pay for this camcorder?

Answer   The value of the VAT is 17.5% of £756
$$= 0.175 \times £756$$
$$= £132.30$$
The price I must pay is £756 + £132.30
$$= £888.30$$
Alternatively
The price of the camcorder, including VAT, is
(100% + 17.5%) i.e. 117.5% of £756
$$= 1.175 \times £756$$
$$= £888.30$$

In Questions 1–4 find the total purchase price assuming that the rate of VAT is 17.5%.

1 A camera marked £120 + VAT.

2 A light fitting marked £68 + VAT.

3 A three course meal costing £8.50 + VAT.

4 An extension ladder marked £83.50 + VAT.

5 Meryl Darkins bought several articles which were priced exclusive of VAT at $17\frac{1}{2}$%; a bucket at 60p, a pair of steps at £14.58, a dustbin at £7.20 and a clothes line at £13.12. Calculate the total bill including the VAT.

6 A motor scooter is priced at £800 plus VAT at $17\frac{1}{2}$%.
   (a) Find the total price including VAT.
   (b) Speedstore offers a discount of 10% off the total price while Motorama offers a cash discount of £65 off the marked price. Which shop gives the better deal and by how much?

7

D. Barton (Wholesale Stationers)

110 No place
High Hope
Durham DH7 7 HJ

Invoice no: 12345   8/3/95

12 Reams photocopying paper at £2.89 per ream
VAT at 17½%
Total
5% discount for settlement within 7 days
otherwise strictly net

Copy and complete this invoice to find the amount due
(a) if the account is settled within 7 days
(b) if it is not settled within 7 days.

Question   Des paid £869.50 for a set of four alloy wheels. This price included VAT at $17\frac{1}{2}$%. Find the marked price of each wheel excluding VAT.

Answer   (We do not know the marked price of the four wheels, but we know that the VAT is 17.5% of the marked price i.e. the price Des pays is 117.5% of the marked price.)
           117.5% of the marked price is £869.50
i.e. $1.175 \times$ marked price   = £869.50
so   marked price   = £869.50 ÷ 1.175 = £740
i.e. the marked price of the four wheels is £740
Then the marked price of one wheel is £740 ÷ 4 = £185.

8 An electric typewriter costs £500.55 including value added tax at $17\frac{1}{2}$%. A businessman has the VAT refunded at a later date, whereas a private customer must pay the full price. Calculate the difference between the two prices.

9 A businessman is charged £248.16, including VAT at $17\frac{1}{2}$%, for four tyres for his van. Since he is in business he is able to claim repayment of the VAT. How much does each tyre actually cost him?

Sometimes a businessman is given a price including VAT but what he needs to know is how much the VAT is. Assuming that the rate of VAT is 17.5% this can be done using a simple formula.

$$\text{Amount of VAT} = \frac{17.5\%}{100\% + 17.5\%} \times \text{sale price including VAT.}$$

For example, if the sale price of a chair, including VAT at $17\frac{1}{2}$%, is £148

the amount of VAT $= \dfrac{17.5}{117.5} \times £148 = £22.04.$

10 How much VAT at 17½% is included in the cost of a CD retailing at £12.99? Give your answer correct to the nearest penny.

11 Piltdown Manufacturing receive a request for late payment of a bill amounting to £1468.75. This includes VAT at 17½%. Unfortunately the accounts clerk fails to find the original invoice. How much VAT does this figure include?

12 Diane Bolam runs a dating agency and buys some computer accessories at a cost of £65.80. She asks for a VAT invoice so that she can claim the VAT back as a business expense. When she checks the invoice she finds that it does not show separately the amount of VAT paid, a figure which she needs for her VAT records.
(a) How much VAT has she paid?
(b) What percentage of the total bill is this? (Assume that the rate of VAT is 17½%.) Give your answer correct to the nearest whole number.

13 At Gollams Bookstore the mark-up is 75%.
(a) Find the wholesale price of a book that retails at £17.50.
(b) They are worried that VAT will be added to books but have decided that if it is, they will absorb the cost i.e. the price of their books will remain unchanged. If the sale price of the book remains at £17.50 but now includes VAT at 17½%, find the amount of VAT included. Give your answer correct to the nearest penny.
(c) In this case how much profit do they make on this book?
(d) What is their mark-up now? Give your answer correct to the nearest whole number.

Saving

The most popular forms of saving are with building societies, banks and investing in National Savings. All these usually pay an annual percentage rate.

Question The Bradley building society pay 7% per annum for money paid into its High Interest Account, interest being paid half-yearly. If £2000 is invested in this account and the interest is not withdrawn, find the amount in the account at the end of the first year.

Answer Interest for first half-year is half of 7% of £2000
$$= 0.5 \times 0.07 \times £2000$$
$$= £70$$
The amount in the account at the end of the first half-year is £2070.
Interest for the second half-year is half of 7% of £2070
$$= 0.5 \times 0.07 \times £2070$$
$$= £72.45$$
The amount in the account at the end of the first year is
$$£2070 + £72.45 \qquad = £2142.45$$
(Note that if the interest had been added yearly it would have been $0.07 \times £2000 = £140$.)

Sometimes income tax is deducted by the building society or bank and paid directly to the Inland Revenue. At present the lowest rate of tax is 20% so that a gross interest rate of 5% gives a net interest rate of 4%, i.e. 5% reduced by 20% of 5%.

A typical building society notice reads
4% p.a. net = 5% p.a. gross.

Exercise 4g

1 Eve puts £800 into a building society that pays interest of 8% per annum. If neither capital nor interest is withdrawn, how much is in the account at the end of one year if the interest is added
(a) yearly   (b) half-yearly?

2 A lump sum of £1000 is to be invested for 2 years. Which account is the better investment either
(a) a savings account paying 4% per annum, the interest payable half-yearly or
(b) an account with a fixed charge of £7.50 and paying 5% per annum, the interest payable half-yearly?

3 Alex invests £12 000 in an income bond paying $5\frac{1}{2}$% p.a.; the income to be paid monthly. Find the monthly income.

Most accounts pay compound interest. This means that the first interest payment is added to the original amount invested, and so earns interest during the next interest period.

Question Gail puts £1200 in an account offering a fixed interest of 5% p.a. If the interest is left in the account at the end of each year find the total interest earned after 3 years.

Answer Interest for 1st year is 5% of £1200 $= 0.05 \times £1200$
                                                    $= £60$
Amount in account at end of 1st year is £1200 + £60
                                                    $= £1260$
Interest for 2nd year is 5% of £1260 $= 0.05 \times £1260$
                                                    $= £63$
Amount in account at end of 2nd year is £1260 + £63
                                                    $= £1323$
Interest for 3rd year is 5% of £1323 $= 0.05 \times £1323$
                                                    $= £66.15$
Amount in account at end of 3rd year is £1323 + £66.15
                                                    $= £1389.15$
Total interest added is £1389.15 − £1200 = £189.15
(Note that although the rate of interest is fixed the interest paid each year increases by a small amount.)

In Questions 4–6 find the compound interest earned when:

4   £1000 is invested for 2 years at 8% in the Manley and Maidstone Building Society.

5   £1000 is invested for 3 years at 4% in a Barlands Bank deposit account.

6   £3000 is invested for 2 years at $5\frac{1}{2}$% with Croxsted County Council.

In Questions 7 and 8 find the total in an account at the end of 3 years if the given amount is invested at the given rate of compound interest.

7   £1500 at $3\frac{1}{2}$% p.a. in National Savings Certificates.

8   £2500 at $4\frac{1}{2}$% p.a. in Haliabbey Investment Bonds.

Compound growth tables

From these tables we can extract a number, called a *multiplying factor*, by which we can multiply the original quantity to show what it grows into for various percentage rates over different periods of time.

The table shows the multiplying factors for rates of growth from 2% to 15% over a 10 year period.

Rate growth p.a. (%)	Number of years									
	1	2	3	4	5	6	7	8	9	10
2	1.020	1.040	1.061	1.082	1.104	1.126	1.149	1.172	1.195	1.219
3	1.030	1.061	1.093	1.126	1.159	1.194	1.230	1.267	1.305	1.344
4	1.040	1.082	1.125	1.170	1.217	1.265	1.316	1.369	1.424	1.480
5	1.050	1.103	1.158	1.216	1.276	1.340	1.407	1.477	1.551	1.629
6	1.060	1.124	1.191	1.262	1.338	1.419	1.504	1.594	1.689	1.791
7	1.070	1.145	1.225	1.311	1.403	1.501	1.606	1.718	1.838	1.967
8	1.080	1.166	1.260	1.360	1.469	1.587	1.714	1.851	1.999	2.159
9	1.090	1.188	1.295	1.412	1.539	1.677	1.828	1.993	2.172	2.367
10	1.100	1.210	1.331	1.464	1.611	1.772	1.949	2.144	2.358	2.594
15	1.150	1.323	1.521	1.749	2.011	2.313	2.660	3.059	3.518	4.046

This table shows that if a population of 10 000 increases at a constant rate of 4% for 8 years the multiplying factor is 1.369 and so the increased population is 10 000 × 1.369
i.e. 13 690.

Similarly, if £5000 is invested for 9 years at 10% the multiplying factor is 2.358 i.e. in 9 years £5000 invested at 10% compound interest grows into £5000 × 2.358 = £11 790.

Exercise 4h

In this exercise use the compound growth table on p. 89. Give answers correct to 3 s.f.

Question   The population of Kidborough is 20 000. It is projected that each year, for the next 10 years, it will grow by 8%. What is the projected population of Kidborough
(a) in 5 years' time
(b) in 10 years' time?

Answer   (a) The table shows that the multiplying factor for a growth of 8% over 5 years is 1.469
projected population in 5 years time is 20 000 × 1.469
$$= 29\ 380$$
$$= 29\ 400\ \text{(to 3 s.f.)}$$
(b) Similarly the projected population in 10 years time is 20 000 × 2.159
$$= 43\ 180$$
$$= 43\ 200\ \text{(to 3 s.f.)}$$

1 The population of Shelsdale is 3500. It is expected to increase by 5% a year for the next 5 years. What is the projected population in 5 years' time?

2 If £100 is invested for 4 years at 6% what sum will it amount to?

3 If £1800 is invested for 8 years at 6% what sum will it amount to?

4 Meazer's turnover is planned to increase by 9% a year. About how long should it be before the turnover doubles?

5 The grey squirrel population of Cotham Wood has increased steadily by 15% a year for the last 5 years. 5 years ago it was 2500.
(a) How many grey squirrels are there in Cotham Wood now?
(b) If the increase continues at the same rate how many are there likely to be in 5 years' time?

6 Trimco's sales have increased steadily by 8% a year over the last 4 years. Four years ago they sold 850 units.
(a) How many units have they sold this year?
(b) Assuming that the rate of increase remains constant how many units do they hope to sell in 6 years' time?

Borrowing   Money borrowed to buy a house or flat is usually repaid with interest over a period of 25 or 30 years. To most people the most important fact is not what the total cost will be, but how much they have to pay each month. Building societies and banks therefore quote a monthly repayment on each £1000 borrowed. This amount varies with the rate of interest and the number of years over which the loan must be repaid.

Bank loans, credit sales and credit cards

A *bank loan* is usually repaid in monthly instalments over 2 to 5 years. It is not an expensive way of borrowing money.

A *credit sale* requires a down payment followed by monthly payments over a period of up to three years. This is an expensive way of borrowing which is why, by law, the annual percentage rate – the APR – must be clearly stated.

A *credit card*, such as Access or Visa, enables us to pay for goods and services up to an agreed limit, without using money. Each month the cardholder receives a statement which shows the amount due including interest. Although $2\frac{1}{2}$% a month looks small it works out equivalent to about 34% a year. Purchases paid for when they first become due are interest free. This makes credit cards a very convenient way of buying things for cardholders who are able to clear their debt completely at the end of each month. Most credit card companies make a small yearly charge (about £15) to help cover their administration costs.

Exercise 4i

Question
A building society offers a 25 year mortgage for monthly repayments of £11.50 per £1000 borrowed.
(a) What are the monthly repayments on a mortgage of £60 000?
(b) What is the total of all the repayments during the 25 years?

Answer
(a) The monthly repayment on £1000 is £11.50
The monthly repayment on £60 000 is 60 × £11.50 = £690.
(b) The total of 12 monthly repayments over 25 years is
12 × 25 × £690 = £207 000.
(This is more than 3 times the cost of the house!)

1 The Bridgewood Building Society offers a 25 year mortgage for monthly repayments of £11 for each £1000 borrowed.
(a) What are the monthly repayments on a mortgage of
(i) £30 000
(ii) £85 000?
(b) If the monthly repayments are £726 how much is borrowed?

2 The repayments on a 30 year mortgage of £50 000 are calculated at £11.25 per calendar month for each £1000 borrowed. What amount must be paid
(a) per month   (b) per year   (c) over the full 30-year term?

3 Yearsley Building Society offer Tom Jones a 90% mortgage on a bungalow whose purchase price is £80 000.
(a) How much can he borrow?

(b) How much must he pay himself?

(c) The repayments are £12.25 per month per £1000 borrowed, for 25 years. Find (i) his monthly repayments (ii) the total repayments over the 25 years.

4 A couple decide to buy a house priced £54 400. A building society is prepared to advance 80% of the purchase price. The monthly repayments are 95p per £100 borrowed for 20 years.

(a) What is the amount borrowed?

(b) What is the total cost of the house?

Question   The cash price of a television set is £465. The credit sale terms are: a deposit of £140 followed by 36 monthly repayments of £11.95.
Find
(a) the total sale price
(b) the amount that would be saved by paying cash.

Answer   (a) Total of monthly repayments is 36 × £11.95 = £430.20
Total credit sale price   = deposit + repayments
                          = £140 + £430.20
                          = £570.20
(b) Amount saved by paying cash is £570.20 − £465
                          = £105.20

---

5 A second hand car is offered for sale at £3800. If bought on credit the terms are a deposit of 25% plus 24 monthly repayments of £145. Find:

(a) the deposit

(b) the total cost of buying the car on credit

(c) the difference between the cash price and the credit price.

6 The marked price of a video recorder is £256. A buyer who pays cash is offered a discount of 5%. For a credit sale the terms are a deposit of £75.50 plus 18 monthly payments of £11.92.

(a) How much does the cash customer pay?

(b) What is the total cost of buying on credit?

(c) How much more does it cost to buy on credit than to pay cash?

7 Sid Coleman wants to buy a motorbike costing £3500 but cannot afford to pay cash. He can either

(a) take a bank loan for £3500 repayable over 36 months at £121.60 per month, or

(b) sign a credit agreement requiring a deposit of 20% (which he can afford) plus 30 monthly repayments of £123.70.

Which is the cheaper way to buy the motorbike and by how much?

8 Amer's Access statement at the end of February shows that he has spent £374.54. He must pay either £5 or 5%, whichever is the greater, within 7 days. The rate of interest on the balance is $2\frac{1}{2}$% per month.

(a) How much must Amer pay immediately?

(b) How much interest is due at the end of March?

(c) If there are no further purchases and the minimum amount is paid at the end of March how much is due at the end of April?

(Give all amounts correct to the nearest penny.)

Depreciation

In any business operation certain assets, for example, pieces of machinery, lose value as they get older i.e. they *depreciate* in value. By finding the reduced value of depreciating assets the owners of a company can keep an eye on the company's total value. Depreciation in business is usually treated in one of two ways – either straight line depreciation or reducing balance depreciation.

Straight line depreciation

This method is frequently used and is easy to understand.

Suppose a machine, bought for £15 000, is expected to have a useful life of 4 years, at which time it is estimated to have a salvage value of £2000. The yearly depreciation using straight line depreciation is given by

$$\frac{\text{cost price} - \text{salvage value}}{\text{number of years}}$$

In the example we have given

$$\text{Yearly depreciation} = \frac{£15\ 000 - £2000}{4} = \frac{£13\ 000}{4} = £3250$$

Reducing balance depreciation

Some businesses prefer to reduce the value of a depreciating asset by a fixed percentage each year. This method is called reducing balance depreciation.

Take the same piece of machinery costing £15 000. Suppose during any year that it depreciates 40% of its value at the beginning of that year. Its value at different times is set out below.

Cost price £15 000

First year depreciation at 40% $= £15\ 000 \times \dfrac{40}{100}$

$= £6000$

Value at end of 1st year $= £15\ 000 - £6000$

$= £9000$

Second year depreciation at 40% $= £9000 \times \dfrac{40}{100}$

$= £3600$

Value at end of 2nd year	$= £9000 - £3600$
	$= £5400$
Third year depreciation at 40%	$= £5400 \times \dfrac{40}{100}$
	$= £2160$
Value at end of 3rd year	$= £5400 - £2160$
	$= £3240$
Fourth year depreciation at 40%	$= £3240 \times \dfrac{40}{100}$
	$= £1296$
Value at end of 4th year	$= £3240 - £1296$
	$= £1944$

Whichever method is used, straight line depreciation or reducing balance depreciation, the machine has reduced from £15 000 to about £2000 in four years.

Exercise 4j

1 A business car is bought for £18 000 and sold after 3 years for £3000. Use the straight line method to find the yearly depreciation.

2 A computer system costs £6000 and is written off completely after 5 years i.e. it has no value after this time.
   (a) Use the straight line method to find the yearly depreciation.
   (b) How much is the system worth after (i) 2 years (ii) 4 years?

3 Western Woodcrafts buy in an automatic tube cutting machine for £24 000. Its estimated life is 5 years, at which time it is anticipated that it will have a salvage value of £2000. Using straight line depreciation find its estimated value after
   (a) 1 year   (b) 3 years.

4 Eastern Woodcrafts buys a similar machine for the same price. They do their accounts using reducing balance depreciation at 40% a year.
   (a) What do they estimate the value of the machine to be after
       (i) 1 year (ii) 3 years?
   (b) Use your calculations for Question 3 to determine which company, and by how much, shows the machine to depreciate by the greater amount over the first two years.
   (c) What value, approximately, do Eastern Woodcrafts estimate the machine will have after 5 years? How does this compare with the value Western Woodcrafts expect it to be worth in the same time?

5 A machine costing £10 000 is to be depreciated to nil over 5 years using straight line depreciation.
   (a) How much does it depreciate each year?
   (b) What is it worth when it is three years old?

6 A car costing £40 000 is to be depreciated by 50% a year for 3 years.
(a) What will it be worth at the end of this period?
(b) How much has it depreciated in 3 years?
(c) Supposing that its value after 3 years under straight line depreciation reduces to the same value as you obtained in (a), find the yearly depreciation.

7 A van bought for £12 000 is estimated to depreciate to £1200 after 3 years. Assuming that it depreciates by the same amount each year i.e. straight line depreciation, find
(a) the yearly depreciation
(b) its value after 2 years
(c) the fraction you get, in its lowest terms, when you divide its value after 2 years by its purchase price
(d) its value after 2 years as a percentage of the purchase price.

Multiple choice questions

In Questions 1–4 several alternative answers are given. Write down the letter that corresponds to the correct answer.

1 In a local election 27% of the electorate vote Labour, 15% vote Conservative and 23% vote Liberal Democrat. There are 48 500 registered voters. The number who did not vote is
  A 13 095   B 31 525
  C 16 975   D 7275

2 The population of Westbury has increased by 5% a year for the last 5 years. Two years ago it was 1200. The population now is
  A 1300   B 1323
  C 1100   D 1452

3 A compact disc costs £11.99, including value added tax at $17\frac{1}{2}$%. The cost of the CD excluding VAT is
  A £9.89   B £14.09
  C £10.50   D £10.20

4 Ken puts £500 into his account with the Charter Building Society. The rate of interest on this account is 6% a year, payable half-yearly. He doesn't withdraw any money during the year so the amount he has in the account at the end of the year is
  A £530.45   B £30.45
  C £530   D £561.80

5 Tim and Sally agree to buy a house for £75 000. The building society agree to advance 90% of the purchase price provided they can find the remainder. The monthly repayments to the building society are £10.95 per £1000 borrowed for 30 years. Which of the following statements are true and which are false?
  A Tim and Sally must find £7500 and the building society agree to advance £67 500
  B The monthly repayments to the building society amount to £821.25
  C The repayments to the building society amount to £8869.50 a year
  D By the time they have finished paying the house will have cost them £266 085.

6 A second hand car is offered for sale at £6500. If bought on credit, the terms require a deposit of 30% plus 36 monthly repayments of £172. The following statements have been made.
Statement 1 The deposit is £1950 and the total of all the credit payments comes to £6192.
Statement 2 The total cost of the car if it's bought on credit comes to £8142 which is £1642 more than the cash price.
How are these two statements best described?
  A True, True   B True, False
  C False, True   D False, False

Self assessment 4

1   From a sample of 60 bags of crisps, 15 are found to be underweight.
(a) What fraction is this?
(b) What percentage is this?

2   When the council voted on a new by-pass road, 63% voted for the by-pass and 28% voted against it. What percentage abstained?

3   A college bought an extra 5 acres of land and so increased the area of the campus to 48 acres. Express the acreage of the campus after the purchase as a percentage of the acreage before the purchase.

4   The cost of a package holiday for an adult is £574. The cost for a child is 70% of the adult price. Two adults and three children book this holiday. How much will it cost them?

5   An employee earning £190 a week is offered an increase of either £13.50 or 7%. Which one would you advise her to take?

6   Ellaways offer a compact disc player at £150 plus VAT at 17½%. Denhams offer the identical unit at £176 including VAT. Which store offers the better deal and by how much?

7   Sally invests £20 000 in an income bond paying 4½% p.a., the income to be paid monthly. Find the monthly income.

8   Mrs Peters' Visa account shows that she owes £436.78. She must pay either £5 or 5%, whichever is the greater, within 7 days. The rate of interest on the balance is 2½% per month.

(a) How much must Mrs Peters pay within 7 days?
(b) Assuming that she made the minimum payment, how much interest is added to the account at the end of the following month?

9   A machine costing £200 000 has an estimated useful life of 5 years. The Inland Revenue agree that each yearly depreciation allowance is to be 50% of its value at the beginning of that year.
(a) Copy and complete the following table.

Cost	(£)	(£) 200 000
Year 1 – depreciation at 50%	100 000	
End of year value		100 000
Year 2 – depreciation at 50%	50 000	
End of year value		
Year 3 – depreciation at 50%		
End of year value		
Year 4 – depreciation at 50%		
End of year value		
Year 5 – depreciation at 50%		
End of year value		
Total depreciation over 5 years		
Residual value after 5 years		....

(b) Express the residual value (i.e. the salvage value) of the machine as a percentage of the purchase price.
(c) Suppose the machine had depreciated by the same amount but that the total depreciation had been divided equally over the 5 years. What would be the yearly depreciation?

UNIT 5 · Everyday Arithmetic

After studying this unit you will be able to
- [ ] work out the basic pay for people paid in different ways e.g. by the hour, on commission or an annual salary
- [ ] calculate overtime payments
- [ ] check gas and electricity bills
- [ ] interchange metric and imperial units
- [ ] calculate postage rates
- [ ] use conversion tables, conversion scales and conversion graphs.

Earning money

Hourly pay

Most people get paid an hourly rate for an agreed number of hours worked each week. They often have the option of working extra hours which are paid at a higher rate.

Commission

Representatives who sell products and services are frequently paid a fairly low basic wage plus a percentage of the value of whatever it is they sell. This percentage is called 'commission'. They are paid in this way to encourage them to sell their goods or services.

Piecework

Piecework is a form of payment that depends on the amount of work done, for example, the number of components produced on a factory production line. Workers paid in this way receive a basic wage in addition to the piecework payment.

Salaries

Many jobs pay a salary rather than a wage. A salary is an agreed payment for a given number of hours a year. It is usually paid in twelve equal monthly instalments. Employees receiving a salary do not normally get paid extra for overtime.

NUMBER	NAME	INITIAL	TAX CODE			
118086	HAMMOND	J.S.	233L	31.10.94	07	

Basic Monthly Wage	278.50	Monthly Gross Income	278.50		
				Income Tax	24.07
				National Insurance	19.51
				Total Deductions	43.58
				NET INCOME	235.14
				Analysis	
20X0514					

Gross and net wages

Your gross wage is the amount you earn before any deductions. Your net wage or take-home pay is the amount you have left after deductions for such things as income tax, National Insurance contributions, pension contributions, etc.

Exercise 5a

Question Sally Mowlan works 48 hours in a residential home in a given week, 10 hours of which is overtime. If her hourly rate is £5.20 and overtime is paid at time-and-a-half, find her gross pay for the week.

Answer
Basic working week is 48 hrs − 10 hrs = 38 hrs
Payment for 38 hrs at £5.20 per hour = 38 × £5.20
 = £197.60
Hourly overtime at time-and-a-half is £5.20 + £2.60 = £7.80
Payment for 10 hrs at £7.80 per hour is 10 × £7.80 = £78
∴ gross wage for the week is £197.60 + £78
 = £275.60

1 (a) George Whatley works as a social worker. He earns £4.80 per hour for a 38 hour week. Find his gross weekly wage.
   (b) Alma Vranch earns £5.15 per hour for a 37 hour week as a graphic designer with Golley Walker & Partners. Find her gross weekly wage.

2 Di Vincent works a basic week of 38 hours with the local solicitor. Overtime is paid at time-and-a-quarter. If her basic hourly rate is £4.40 find
   (a) her overtime rate
   (b) her basic gross weekly wage
   (c) her gross wage for a week when she does 8 hours overtime.

3 Rodney Wright works for a builder who pays £5.44 an hour for a basic week of 36 hours. Overtime is paid at time-and-a-half. How much will Rodney earn in a week when he works for 53 hours?

4 Liam Clarke's workcard for a week is shown below.

	In (a.m.)	Out (p.m.)
Mon	8.00	5.00
Tues	7.59	5.02
Wed	7.58	5.00
Thurs	8.00	6.30
Fri	8.00	1.30
Sat	8.00	12.30

Liam gets an unpaid lunch break of half an hour plus two unpaid 15 minute breaks, one in the morning and one in the afternoon. On Friday he works until 1.30 pm but takes his usual morning break. He works overtime on Thursday and on Saturday morning.
(a) What time is 'clocking-on' time?
(b) What time does he normally finish work for the day?
(c) How much overtime does he work?
(d) What is the length of the basic working week?
(e) Find his basic weekly gross wage if he is paid £4.86 per hour.
(f) How much overtime pay will he receive if overtime is paid at time-and-a-quarter?
(g) Find his gross wage for the week.

5 Debbie Allen's time-sheet for a week on days shows that she worked as follows:

	In (a.m.)	Out (p.m.)
Mon	7.28	3.58
Tues	7.30	4.00
Wed	7.34	4.01
Thurs	7.42	5.15
Fri	7.29	5.45
Sat	7.35	12.30

Debbie is due to start work each day at 7.30 a.m. and to finish at 4.00 p.m. She is not paid for arriving early but loses 15 minutes if she is more than 5 minutes late. She also loses 15 minutes if she leaves on a weekday before 4.00 p.m. but is paid time-and-a-half for each complete 15 minutes she works overtime – working on Saturday is counted as overtime.
(a) On how many days
       (i) is she more than 5 minutes late   (ii) does she leave early?
(b) How much overtime does she work?
(c) If she gets half an hour each day for lunch (for which she is not paid), find the number of hours for which she is paid.
(d) Find her gross wage for the week if her basic rate of pay is £5 per hour.

Question	Mike Pugh sells antiques. He receives a basic weekly wage of £70 plus commission at 5% on all sales over £7500 each week. Calculate his gross pay in a week when he sells antiques to the value of £16 800.
Answer	Basic wage is £70 Commission on £16 800 − £7500 i.e. on £9300 at 5% is 0.05 × £9300 $\qquad$ = £465 Gross pay for the week is £70 + £465 $\qquad$ = £535

6 Calculate the commission on
   (a) £3500 at 2%   (b) £12 500 at 5%
   (c) £34 000 at $2\frac{1}{2}$%

7 A saleswoman receives a basic wage of £50 plus commission at 2% on the value of the goods she sells. Calculate her gross wage in a week when she sells goods to the value of £14 700.

8 Carl Mantle manages a Travel Agency. Apart from a basic monthly wage of £475 he is paid commission at the following rates:
   Below £20 000   none
   From £20 000 to £40 000 $2\frac{1}{2}$%
   Above £40 000 $3\frac{1}{2}$%
   Calculate his income in a month when he sells holidays to the value of £86 000.

9 An ice-cream seller receives a basic weekly wage of £95 to which is added commission at 15% on sales over £200. Find her gross wage in a week when her total takings amount to £565.

10 Enid Jones works in a factory making windscreen wipers. She is paid a guaranteed weekly wage of £140 plus a bonus of 8p for every wiper she assembles each day after the first 650. During a particular week the number of wipers she completes are:

Mon	Tues	Wed	Thurs	Fri
752	746	782	792	722

   Calculate her wage for the week.

11 Find the monthly pay of an employee whose annual salary is
   (a) £18 000   (b) £45 840
   (c) £16 140

12 Find the annual salary of a civil servant whose gross monthly pay is
   (a) £1240   (b) £3720
   (c) £2658

13 Phil Norman is a salaried employee at an automotive factory. He receives £1472 per month gross. His brother, Chris, is employed on the same site and receives an annual salary of £19 500. Which brother is the better off and by how much?

14 Rosalyn Grant's take-home pay is £1152 per calendar month. Deductions from her gross pay amount to 40%. Find
(a) her gross monthly pay
(b) her gross annual pay.

Question Wendy Deakins earns £185.60 a week. Her deductions are: income tax £27.28, National Insurance contributions £12.40 and pension contributions £10.36. Find her take-home pay.

Answer
Total deductions   = £27.28 + £12.40 + £10.36
                   = £50.04
Take-home pay   = gross pay − deductions
                   = £185.60 − £50.04
                   = £135.56.

15 Copy and complete the following table which gives details of the weekly pay of five people employed at a Leisure Centre.

	Name	Gross pay (£)	Income tax (£)	NIC (£)	Pension (£)	Take-home pay (£)
(a)	B Jones	212	33.35	14.81	11.82	
(b)	S Brown		59.84	26.60	18.96	237.60
(c)	P Capstick	568	108.43	46.85		381.46
(d)	L Brady	290		21.83	16.08	193.97
(e)	P Lacey	198	30.47		11.96	142.02

16 Kim Forrest worked 49 hours last week. The first $37\frac{1}{2}$ hours are paid at the standard rate of £5.10 per hour, the next 5 hours is overtime that is paid at 'time-and-a-quarter' and the remainder is overtime that is paid at 'time-and-a-half'. She pays tax at 20% on her weekly income over £65, National Insurance contributions of £19.84 and pension contributions of 6% of her gross income. Find:
(a) her basic weekly wage i.e. excluding overtime
(b) the amount earned for overtime
(c) her total wage for the week
(d) the amount of income tax due
(e) her pension contribution
(f) her take-home pay.

17 A wages clerk has to prepare a coin analysis so that she has the necessary cash to pay the workforce. Copy and complete the table.

Name	Wages (£)	£20	£10	£5	£1	50p	20p	10p	5p	2p	1p
Brown	197.68	180	10	5	2	50		10	5	2	1
Martin	112.49										
O'Hare	207.37										
Hanley	254.76										

Utility costs

Collectively, the electricity, gas and water companies are called 'utilities'. In most cases commercial consumers pay different rates from domestic consumers for the products and services supplied by these companies.

Electricity bills

Electricity is measured in kilowatt hours (kWh). A kilowatt hour is the amount of electricity used in 1 hour by an appliance with a rating of 1 kilowatt. The number of units used by a company in a quarter is the difference between the meter readings at the end and the beginning of that quarter. In addition to paying for the number of units used there is a fixed or standing charge. Value Added Tax is added to the total at the current rate. A bill for Mr A. Sample is given on p. 103.

Gas bills

Gas is measured in units of 100 cubic metres. A formula is then used to convert the number of units used into kilowatt hours for the domestic consumer and/or therms for the commercial consumer. As with electricity there is a standing charge and VAT is added to the total to give the payment due. Typically a domestic consumer pays a standing charge of 11p per day plus 1.577p for every kWh used. The commercial consumer pays a standing charge of £50 a year (payable quarterly) plus a cost per therm for the gas used each quarter which is banded as follows:

Number of therms consumed	Cost per therm (p)
1–5000	45.3
5001–10 000	43.3
10 001–15 000	42.3
15 001–25 000	41.3

For amounts greater than 25 000 therms special contracts are negotiated.

LONDON ELECTRICITY

25 ECCLESTON PLACE SW1W 9NF

You can telephone us on **081-298 9898** .

London Schools Symphony Orchestra performing at Kenwood Bowl – a sponsorship of London Electricity.

MR A SAMPLE
10 SAMPLE LANE
LONDON SW10 9AT

Account Number
012.3456/789.123

Date [Tax Point]
14 JUL 94

Electricity bill

METER READINGS Present	Previous	Units Used	Unit Price (pence)	VAT Code	Amount £
26914	26334	580	7.080	1	41.06
STANDING CHARGE				1	12.22
TOTAL CHARGES (EXCLUDING VAT)					53.28
VAT 1 £53.28 @ 8.0% DOMESTIC					4.26
				TOTAL	57.54

Reading Date
14 JUL 94

Business Use
0%

VAT CHARGE THIS BILL   4.26

E = Estimated reading. If you are not happy with this reading, please phone us now.
C = Your own reading.

Balance to pay

£ **57.54**

Ways to pay shown overleaf

Exercise 5b

Question Find the cost of running a domestic 2.5 kW electric fire for 60 hours if electricity costs 8.21p per unit.

Answer Number of units used = rating in kilowatts × number of hours used
                               = 2.5 × 60
                               = 150
Cost of 150 units at 8.21 per unit is 150 × 8.21p
                               = £12.32

1 Copy and complete the table which shows the electricity meter readings for Newtown Switchgear last year.

Date	Meter reading	Number of units used in quarter
6 Nov	14563	First
10 Feb	18543	Second
4 May	20567	Third
12 Aug	22993	Fourth
8 Nov	25635	

2 How many units of electricity are used if
(a) a 150 W lamp burns for 10 hours
(b) a 2 kW fire is used for 5 hours
(c) a 3 kW kettle is boiling for 4 minutes
(d) a 250 W computer is switched on for 10 hours?

3 How many hours will each of the following appliances run on 1 unit of electricity?
(a) a 100 W light bulb   (b) a 12 W light bulb
(c) a 2 kW fire   (d) a 250 W photocopier
(e) a 2.5 kW kettle   (f) a 150 W computer.

4 Find the cost of using the following appliances for the times indicated if electricity costs 7.54p per unit.
(a) a 3 kW fire for 26 hours
(b) eight 100 W bulbs, each for 38 hours
(c) a 750 W iron for 4 hours
(d) a 350 W television set for 45 hours
(e) a 300 W dehumidifier for 84 hours
(f) a 6 kW shower heater for 5 minutes.
Give each answer correct to the nearest penny.

5 At the Holiday Express travel agency they estimate that during the course of a week they use the following electrical appliances for the times given:
  sixteen 60 W fluorescent tubes, each for 52 hours
  one 2.5 kW electric kettle for 3 hours
  four 125 W computer systems, each for 44 hours.
  Find
  (a) the number of units of electricity used by   (i) the 16 tubes
      (ii) the kettle   (iii) the 4 computer systems
  (b) the total number of units used altogether
  (c) the cost of these units at 8.35p per unit.

Question Find the cost of electricity for a quarter at Penny & James if 3263 units are consumed and the charges at commercial rates are: standing charge £16.85, first 1000 units 12.73p per unit, over 1000 units − 9.73p per unit. VAT is added to the bill at 17½ %

Answer   Standing charge   = £16.85
Cost of 1000 units at 12.73p per unit is 1000 × 12.73p
                                                            = £127.30
Cost of remaining 2263 units at 9.73p per unit is 2263 × 9.73p
                                                            = £220.19
Total cost excluding VAT   = £364.34
VAT at 17½% = 0.175 × £364.34   = £63.76
Total cost including VAT   = £428.10

Find the quarterly electric bill for each of the following businesses. Value added tax should be added at 17½%.

| | Business | Meter reading | | Number of units used | Cost per unit (p) | | Standing charge (£) |
		At beginning of quarter	At end of quarter		First 1000 units	Additional units	
6	White's Newsagents	23076	27942		12.33	7.93	15.47
7	Hodges Hardware	34947	38469		13.44	8.21	17.50
8	Mitchells Fashions	23937	26813		14.77	8.49	16.87
9	Penny's China	12896	19002		13.72	8.33	16.73
10	Sam's Jewellery	18425	25936		14.49	8.64	18.50

Question
: The gas bill for Tidal Parsons Ltd showed that they used 18 609 therms last quarter. Use the information given in the text (p. 102) to find the total cost of this gas if VAT is added at 17½%.

Answer
: Standing charge for the quarter is £50 ÷ 4 = £12.50
Cost of first 5000 therms at 45.3p per therm is 5000 × 45.3p
= £2265
Cost of next 5000 therms at 43.3p per therm is 5000 × 43.3p
= £2165

Cost of next 5000 therms at 42.3p per therm is 5000 × 42.3p
= £2115
Cost of remaining 3609 therms at 41.3p per therm is 3609 × 41.3p
= £1490.52
Total cost excluding VAT = £8048.02
VAT at 17½% is 0.175 × £8048.02 = £1408.40
Total cost including VAT = £9456.42

For Questions 9 and 10 use the information given in the text on p. 102.

11 (a) Millicent industries estimate that they will consume 13 500 therms each quarter. How much do they expect this gas to cost them?
   (b) Next year they budget that the cost of the gas they use will increase by 6.3%. How much should they allow to cover their gas bills each quarter next year?

12 A business used 16 483 therms of gas during the second quarter of the year. How much will this cost them
   (a) excluding VAT
   (b) including VAT at 20%?

Metric and imperial equivalents

Petrol is sold in the United Kingdom by the litre but to many people it doesn't mean as much to them as pricing it by the gallon. If you go to buy a carpet it will probably be priced by the square metre but it is quite likely that the width is an exact number of yards. Greengroceries are usually sold by the pound (lb) whereas most tinned vegetables are sold by their metric weights. These are but a few examples of the need to understand both metric and imperial units and to have some knowledge of their approximate equivalents. The approximate equivalents of the most frequently used units are listed below.

(We use the symbol ≈ to mean 'approximately equal to').
Length   8 km ≈ 5 miles
           1 metre ≈ 39 inches (1 m is a bit bigger than 1 yard)
           10 cm ≈ 4 inches
           1 inch ≈ 25 mm
Area   1 hectare ≈ 2.5 acres

Capacity   1 litre ≈ 1.75 pints
                    1 gallon ≈ 4.5 litres
Mass   1 tonne ≈ 1 ton (1 tonne, called a metric ton, is
                                    slightly less than 1 ton)
                    1 kg ≈ 2.2 lb
                    100 g ≈ 3.5 oz
                    1 oz ≈ 25 g

Exercise 5c

In this exercise use the approximate equivalents just given. Appreciate
that all your answers will be approximate.

Question   Sally's car is 186.5 inches long whereas Len's car is 4.443 metres. Who
has the longer car?

Answer   Since 1 inch ≈ 25 mm
Length of Sally's car is 186.5 in which is roughly 186.5 × 25 mm
= 4662.5 mm
= 4.6625 m
Len's car is 4.443 m long, so Sally's car is the longer car.

1   A petrol can holds 2 gallons. How many litres is this?

2   A caterer buys 35 pints of milk. How many litres is this?

3   The height of a building is 150 feet. How many metres is this?

4   An old dressmaking pattern states that the seam allowance is to be
$\frac{5}{8}$ inch. How many millimetres is this?

5   Petrol is 56p per litre. How much is this
(a) per pint   (b) per gallon?

6   After getting off the ferry at Cherbourg a signpost shows that it is
350 km to Ken's destination.
(a) How many miles is this?
(b) His car does 32 miles to the gallon. How many gallons should he
use for the journey?

7   The petrol tank for a Mercedes C Class holds 62 litres including a
reserve of 7 litres. If 1 gallon = $4\frac{1}{2}$ litres find
(a) the capacity of the tank in gallons
(b) the reserve in gallons
(c) the distance the car will travel on a full tank if it does 28 miles to
the gallon.

8   The engine of my car takes 5.8 litres of oil. How many pints is this?

9   A recipe requires 12 oz of fat. How many grams is this?

10 An old knitting pattern requires twenty-four 1 oz balls of knitting wool. How many 50 g balls are needed to make up this pattern?

11 A factory floor measures 185 ft by 65 ft. Give these dimensions
    (a) in yards   (b) in metres.

12 The dimensions of a new car are:
    length 4487 mm, width 1720 mm, height 1414 mm.
    If 1 inch ≈ 25.4 mm give the dimensions of the car in feet and inches, correct to the nearest inch.

13 A workshop has sets of both metric and imperial drills. The imperial sizes go from $\frac{1}{8}$ inch to 1 inch in steps of $\frac{1}{16}$ inch. The metric sizes go from 3 mm to 25 mm in steps of 1 mm. If 1 inch ≈ 25.4 mm, answer the following questions.
    (a) List the sizes of the imperial drills, giving each fraction in its lowest terms.
    (b) How many drills are there in an imperial set?
    (c) What is the next size up after   (i) $\frac{1}{2}$"   (ii) $\frac{5}{8}$"?
    (d) What is the next size down from   (i) $\frac{1}{4}$"   (ii) $\frac{3}{4}$"?
    (e) What is the size next but one up from $\frac{3}{8}$"?
    (f) What is the size next but two down from $\frac{7}{8}$"?
    (g) Which imperial drill is in the middle of the range?
    (h) How many drills are there in a metric set?
    (i) Convert $\frac{5}{8}$" into mm. Which is the nearest metric drill below $\frac{5}{8}$"?
    (j) Convert $\frac{3}{4}$" into mm. Which is the nearest metric drill above $\frac{3}{4}$"?
    (k) Which is the nearest metric drill to $\frac{3}{8}$"? Is this drill larger or smaller than $\frac{3}{8}$"?

14 Listed below are the ingredients needed to make Peppermint Squares. Copy this list and complete it to show the quantity of each ingredient if imperial measures are to be used.

Amount	Ingredient	Imperial amount
175 g	hard margarine	7 oz
175 g	soft brown sugar	
2	eggs	
150 g	self-raising flour	
25 g	cocoa	
40 ml	peppermint cordial	
40 ml	water	2 tablespoons
100 g	caster sugar	

In Questions 15 and 16 assume that 1 oz ≈ 25 g and 1 tablespoon ≈ 20 ml.

15 The ingredients required for a recipe for Steamed Chocolate Pudding are:

    4 oz   margarine
    4 oz   caster sugar

2	eggs
1 oz	cocoa
5 oz	self-raising flour

Rewrite the list of ingredients using metric quantities.

16 The ingredients for Viennese Fingers include:

150 g	butter
50 g	caster sugar
100 g	plain flour, sieved
25 g	cornflour, sieved
25 g	cocoa, sieved
	few drops of vanilla essence

and for the butter icing

150 g	icing sugar
25 g	cocoa
75 g	soft margarine
20 ml	warm water

Rewrite this list of ingredients using imperial quantities.

Postage

The Post Office offers a wide range of services, two of the most important of which are collecting and delivering letters and parcels.

The rates for sending letters and parcels within the United Kingdom in March 1995 are given below. Notice that the costs go up in steps e.g. all letters that are over 150 g but not more than 200 g cost 36p to send by second class post.

		Letters				Parcels	
weight not over	first class	second class	weight not over	first class	second class	weight not over	price
60g	25p	19p	500g	£1.25	98p	1kg	£2.65
100g	38p	29p	600g	£1.55	£1.20	2kg	£3.25
150g	47p	36p	700g	£1.90	£1.40	4kg	£4.50
200g	57p	43p	750g	£2.05	£1.45	6kg	£5.00
250g	67p	52p	800g	£2.15	not	8kg	£5.80
300g	77p	61p	900g	£2.35	admissible	10kg	£6.75
350g	88p	70p	1000g	£2.50	over 750g	30kg	£8.10
400g	£1.00	79p	each extra 250g				
450g	£1.13	89p	or part thereof 65p				

Source: The Post Office and Parcelforce.

Exercise 5d

Use the letters and parcels tables to answer the questions that follow.

Question	Find the cost of posting (a) 5 letters, by first class letter post, 4 weighing 45 g and 1 weighing 275 g. (b) 3 parcels weighing $1\frac{1}{2}$ kg, $2\frac{1}{4}$ kg and $4\frac{3}{4}$ kg.
Answer	(a) The cost of sending 1 letter not more than 60 g by first class letter post is 25p ∴ the cost of sending 4 such letters is $4 \times 25p = £1$ The cost of sending one letter weighing 275 g, i.e. not more than 300 g, by first class letter post is 77p ∴ total cost of sending the 5 letters is £1 + 77p i.e. £1.77. (b) Posting 1 parcel not more than 2 kg by parcel post costs £3.25 Posting another parcel not more than 4 kg costs £4.50 Posting a third parcel not more than 6 kg costs £5.00 ∴ total cost of posting the three parcels is £12.75

Assume that all letters are under 60 g unless it is stated otherwise.

In Questions 1–8 find the cost of posting:

1 (a) three letters by first class post
  (b) six letters by second class post

2 two letters by first class post together with three letters by second class post

3 eight letters by second class post, two of which weigh 215 g

4 four letters, each weighing 75 g, by first class post

5 five letters by first class post together with two letters weighing 235 g by second class post

6 (a) two parcels, each weighing 1.3 kg
  (b) three parcels, each weighing 3.5 kg, by parcel post

7 a parcel weighing $2\frac{1}{2}$ kg and one weighing $3\frac{3}{4}$ kg, by parcel post

8 a parcel weighing 1600 g by
  (a) parcel post   (b) first class letter post

9 What does it cost to send a small parcel weighing 725 g by
  (a) parcel post
  (b) first class letter post
  (c) second class letter post?

10 (a) How much does it cost to send a parcel weighing 2.3 kg by first class letter post?
   (b) Would they accept this parcel for second class mail?

11 (a) How much more does it cost to send a package weighing 1.3 kg by first class letter post than by parcel post?
   (b) Why do some people choose to send such a package at the more expensive rate?

12 An electronics company wants to send a package containing some components to one of its other plants. Speed is important so they decide to send it by first class letter post. If the package weighs 4.5 kg, how much more expensive does this prove than sending it at the parcel rate?

13 How much more expensive is it to send out 1200 packages, each weighing 725 g, by second class letter post than by parcel post?

14 A manufacturing company must, by law, send a copy of its annual report to every shareholder. The annual report for Duogate plc, which weighs 116 g, is to be sent to all 11 560 shareholders. How much is saved if these reports are sent by second class rather than by first class post? (In practice companies are able to negotiate lower rates for posting large amounts of mail.)

15 The postage book for BC Electronics shows that one week they sent the following mail:
   145 letters, each under 60 g, by first class post
   38 letters each under 100 g, by first class post
   88 letters, each under 60 g, by second class post
   45 letters, each under 150 g, by second class post
   6 parcels, each weighing 2.6 kg, by parcel post.
Find the post bill for the week.

Conversion tables for weights and measures

Many people find it very convenient to use conversion tables to convert from quantities measured in one unit to quantities measured in another unit. For example we may want to know how many litres of petrol is equivalent to 8 gallons or how many acres is equivalent to 160 hectares. Six of the most commonly used conversion tables are given on pp. 112 and 113.

Conversion tables for weights and measures

LENGTH			WEIGHT (MASS)		
centimetres (cm)	cm or inches	inches (in)	kilograms (kg)	kg or lb	pounds (lb)
2.54	1	0.394	0.454	1	2.205
5.08	2	0.787	0.907	2	4.409
7.62	3	1.181	1.361	3	6.614
10.16	4	1.575	1.814	4	8.819
12.70	5	1.969	2.268	5	11.023
15.24	6	2.362	2.722	6	13.228
17.78	7	2.756	3.175	7	15.432
20.32	8	3.150	3.629	8	17.637
22.86	9	3.543	4.082	9	19.842
25.40	10	3.937	4.536	10	22.046
50.80	20	7.874	9.072	20	44.092
76.20	30	11.811	13.608	30	66.139
101.60	40	15.748	18.144	40	88.185
127.00	50	19.685	22.680	50	110.231
152.40	60	23.622	27.216	60	132.277
177.80	70	27.559	31.752	70	154.324
203.20	80	31.496	36.287	80	176.370
228.60	90	35.433	40.823	90	198.416
254.00	100	39.370	45.359	100	220.462

kilometres (km)	km or miles	miles	tonnes (t)	t or UK tons	UK tons
1.609	1	0.621	1.016	1	0.984
3.219	2	1.243	2.032	2	1.968
4.828	3	1.864	3.048	3	2.953
6.437	4	2.486	4.064	4	3.937
8.047	5	3.107	5.080	5	4.921
9.656	6	3.728	6.096	6	5.905
11.265	7	4.350	7.112	7	6.889
12.875	8	4.971	8.128	8	7.874
14.484	9	5.592	9.144	9	8.858
16.093	10	6.214	10.160	10	9.842
32.187	20	12.427	20.320	20	19.684
48.280	30	18.641	30.481	30	29.526
64.374	40	24.855	40.642	40	39.368
80.467	50	31.069	50.802	50	49.210
96.561	60	37.282	60.963	60	59.052
112.654	70	43.496	71.123	70	68.894
128.748	80	49.710	81.284	80	78.737
144.841	90	55.923	91.444	90	88.579
160.934	100	62.137	101.605	100	98.421

AREA			VOLUME		
hectares (ha)	ha or acres	acres	litres	litres or UK gallons	UK gallons (UK gal)
0.405	1	2.471	4.546	1	0.220
0.809	2	4.942	9.092	2	0.440
1.214	3	7.413	13.638	3	0.660

AREA			VOLUME		
hectares (ha)	ha or acres	acres	litres	litres or UK gallons	UK gallons (UK gal)
1.619	4	9.884	18.184	4	0.880
2.023	5	12.355	22.730	5	1.100
2.428	6	14.826	27.277	6	1.320
2.833	7	17.297	31.823	7	1.540
3.237	8	19.769	36.369	8	1.760
3.642	9	22.240	40.914	9	1.980
4.047	10	24.711	45.460	10	2.200
8.094	20	49.421	90.919	20	4.399
12.140	30	74.132	136.379	30	6.599
16.187	40	98.842	181.839	40	8.799
20.234	50	123.553	227.298	50	10.998
24.281	60	148.263	272.758	60	13.198
28.328	70	172.974	318.217	70	15.398
32.375	80	197.684	363.677	80	17.598
36.422	90	222.395	409.137	90	19.797
40.469	100	247.105	454.596	100	21.997

Exercise 5e

Question

From the conversion tables given above choose the correct one and use it to find
(a) 56 inches in centimetres
(b) 168 kg in pounds
(c) 85 acres in hectares.

Answer

(a) (We need to use the cm and inches table.)
The number 56 does not appear in the table, but we can break down 56 into 50 + 6. Then go down the middle column to 50. We want to convert to cm, so we read from the left hand column of numbers
i.e.   50 inches ≡ 127 cm (≡ is the symbol we use in mathematics to stand for the words 'is equivalent to')
and similarly   6 inches ≡ 15.24 cm
∴ adding   56 inches ≡ 142.24 cm
(b) 168 breaks down into 100 + 60 + 8
then   100 kg ≡ 220.462 lb (we go down to 100 in the kg/lb table and read off from the right hand column headed lb)
                     60 kg ≡ 132.277 lb
                      8 kg ≡ 17.637 lb
                    168 kg ≡ 370.376 lb
(c) 85 breaks down into 80 + 5
then   80 acres ≡ 32.375 hectares
                     5 acres ≡ 2.023 hectares
∴   85 acres ≡ 34.398 hectares

Use the correct table to answer the questions in this exercise.

1   Convert
    (a) 60 cm into inches   (b) 80 kg into lb
    (c) 60 litres into gallons.

2   Convert
    (a) 40 miles into kilometres   (b) 70 acres into hectares
    (c) 30 inches into cm.

3   Convert
    (a) 46 inches into cm   (b) 66 kg into lb
    (c) 22 hectares into acres.

4   Convert
    (a) 73 gallons into litres   (b) 54 miles into kilometres
    (c) 28 tons into tonnes.

Question   Convert 567 tons into tonnes

Answer   (break 567 into 500 + 60 + 7, and then 500 further into 5 × 100)
The equivalent value of 100 tons in tonnes is 101.605
Then 500 tons ≡ 5 × 101.605 tonnes
i.e.   500 tons ≡ 508.025 tonnes
              60 tons ≡ 60.963 tonnes
and 7 tons   ≡ 7.112 tonnes
∴   567 tons ≡ 576.1 tonnes

---

5   Convert
    (a) 275 km into miles   (b) 550 acres into hectares
    (c) 2000 gallons to litres.

6   The Meredith family go to Normandy on holiday. They drive 246 miles
    in the UK and 459 km in Normandy. How many miles is this
    altogether? Give your answer to the nearest mile.

Conversion scales   The most likely place in everyday life that you can find a conversion
scale is on a room thermometer. Using this scale you can read
the temperature of the room either in degrees Celsius or in degrees
Fahrenheit. Given below is a Celsius/Fahrenheit conversion scale for
temperatures that range from 0° Fahrenheit to 100° Celsius.

Temperature conversion °C / °F

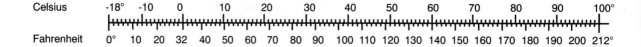

Exercise 5f

Use the temperature conversion scale to answer the questions that follow:

1 The boiling point of water is 100°C. What is this is degrees Fahrenheit?

2 The freezing point of water is 32°F. What is this in degrees Celsius?

3 A particular paraffin wax melts at 46°C. What is this in degrees Fahrenheit?

4 A different wax melts at 100°F. What is the equivalent temperature in degrees Celsius?

5 Which is the higher temperature, 55°C or 125°F?

6 Which is the lower temperature, 196°F or 90°C?

7 In the previous section we could, for example, use the appropriate conversion table to convert any number of kilograms into pounds. Could you use the Celsius/Fahrenheit conversion scale to convert 1000°C into degrees Fahrenheit?

8 You will be aware that if the barometer is rising it is likely that the weather will improve, whereas if, when it is fine and the barometer 'glass' is falling, we are likely to have rain. Have you noticed that there are usually two scales on a barometer? On the outside circle you will find 'inches' and on the inside circle 'millibars'. If you can find a barometer, use it to convert
(a) 1020 millibars (of pressure) into a pressure of 'inches of mercury'
(b) 29.5 inches of mercury into millibars.

Conversion graphs   A simple conversion graph (see p. 116) can be quite useful in certain situations. Suppose you are going to France on holiday and you are not very familiar with the value of the franc. Before going you could look up the exchange rate in the newspaper or on television. Let's say it is £1 = 8.62 French francs. From this you can work out that £20 = 172.40Ff and £100 = 862Ff.

These values can be plotted on a graph. Go across to £20 on the horizontal scale, then up to 172.4Ff, or as near as you can estimate it, on the vertical scale. Mark this position with a dot.

Similarly, go across to 100 and up to 862 and mark another dot. Join these two dots with a straight line and extend this line to pass through the point where the axes cross. It must go through this point, since £0 = 0Ff. Having 'no money' is the same whatever currency you are in! If your line does not go through this 'origin' check things again – you must have made a mistake. The correct conversion graph for the above data is given on p. 116.

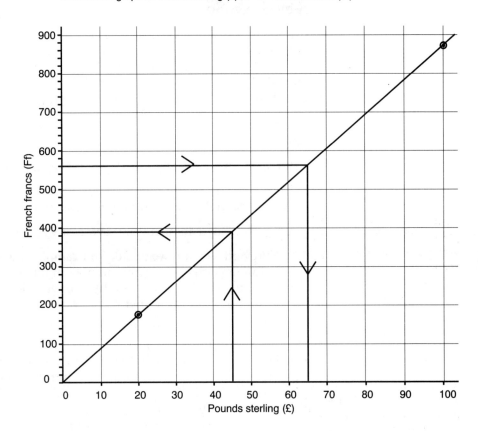

Conversion graph : Pounds sterling (£) ←—→ French francs (Ff)

From the graph we can see that:
(a) £45 is roughly 390Ff (Find 45 on the horizontal scale. Go up until you hit the graph. Now read across to find the corresponding value on the vertical scale.)
(b) 560Ff is roughly £65 (Find 560 on the vertical scale. Go across to the line. Drop down to the horizontal axis. Read off the value.)

Exercise 5g

1 Use the currency graph to find the equivalent of
(a) 750Ff in pounds   (b) £33 in French francs.

2 Leon sees a CD in a shop in France. It is marked 100f. How much is this in pounds?

3 Perhaps you would like to go to a country other than France. For a country of your choice, look up the rate of exchange for £ in terms of that currency. Work out how many units of that currency you get for, say, £50 and for £100. Use this information to plot two points as we did in the text. Join these points together and continue the line to go

through the origin. Use your conversion graph to answer questions you think you might come across on holiday.

4 You wish to draw a conversion graph to be able to change litres into gallons and/or gallons into litres. With the help of the table given on pp. 112–113, plot three points and draw a suitable graph. Use it to convert
(a) 52 litres into gallons   (b) 8 gallons into litres.

Multiple choice questions

1 Laura Russell works for an insurance firm. Her basic working week is 38 hours, for which she is paid £3.80 an hour. Any overtime is paid at time-and-a-half. Her gross pay in a week when she works for 44 hours is
A £144.40   B £167.20   C £178.60
D £174.80

2 Given that 1 kg is approximately 2.2 lb, the metric equivalent of 80 lb is about
A 176 kg   B 36 kg   C 17.6 kg
D 80 kg

3 From Jim Hatton's gross pay of £196.40 there are deductions of £31.42 for income tax, £13.80 for national insurance and £11.32 for pension contributions. Jim's take-home pay is
A £252.94   B £139.86   C £164.98
D £151.18

4 During the course of a week Sue used a 3 kW electric fire for 40 hours and a 100 W bulb for 60 hours. The cost of the electricity, at 7.5 pence per unit, that Sue is used is
A £13.50   B £54   C £8.82
D £9.45

5 My car will travel 36 miles on one gallon of petrol, and petrol costs 56 pence a litre at the local petrol station. One litre is equivalent to $1\frac{3}{4}$ pints.

Which of the following statements are true and which are false?
A My car will travel further on 4 litres than it will on 1 gallon
B The cost of 1 pint of petrol works out at 32p
C The price of petrol at the local petrol station is equivalent to £2.55 a gallon
D 5 litres is less than 1 gallon.

6 Two sisters, Sarah and Liz, are both employed by Crypto Electronics. Sarah works on the shop floor where she is paid a basic weekly wage of £146.50 plus 3p for every component over 2400 she produces in a week. Last week she produced 4100 components. Liz belongs to the sales force. She is paid a basic weekly wage of £125 plus commission at 2% on all sales over £5500. Last week her sales figures came to £9350.

The following statements have been made:
Statement 1 The combined earnings for the two sisters last week came to more than £400.
Statement 2 Sarah's piecework payments for the components amounted to £51, which was £26 less than Liz earned in commission.

How are these statements best described?
A   True, True   B   True, False
C   False, True   D   False, False

Self assessment 5

1 (a) How many hours does it take for a 100 W electric light bulb to consume 1 unit of electricity? (1 unit = 1 kilowatt hour.)
(b) How many units of electricity will a 3 kW electric fire use in 24 hours?
(c) Last quarter the reading on my electricity meter was 19 364 at the beginning of the quarter and 21 011 at the end of the quarter. How many units of electricity did I use? Apart from a standing charge of £11.27 each unit costs 7.96p, and value added tax at 8% is added to the total to give the amount due. How much should I expect to pay for electricity for the last quarter?

2 Two brothers Steve and Nick are employed by the same company but in different sections.

1   Steve is in the sales team and is paid a basic wage of £80 per week plus commission at 2% on the value of all sales over £20 000. Nick is on the assembly line. He is paid a guaranteed weekly wage of £250 plus a bonus of 15p for every component over 400 that he completes each day. The table shows Steve's sales figures and Nick's production levels one week recently.

	Mon	Tues	Wed	Thurs	Fri
Sales (Steve)	£5200	£7500	£3700	£8200	£6490
Number of components produced (Nick)	513	390	458	482	342

(a)   Calculate the gross income of each brother for the week.
(b)   Express Nick's gross income as a percentage of Steve's gross income.
(c)   Nick's deductions amounted to £113.40 and Steve's deductions amounted to £109.85. Which brother had the greater 'take-home' pay, and by how much?

3   Liz Barker's works' card shows the hours she worked last week:

	In (a.m.)	Out (p.m.)
Mon	7.30	4.30
Tues	7.28	4.31
Wed	7.30	6.30
Thurs	7.29	4.30
Fri	7.28	12.30
Sat	7.30	12.00 noon

Liz's normal working day, Monday to Thursday is from 7.30 to 4.30 with an unpaid break for lunch of 45 minutes. On Fridays she works through without a break until 12.30. Saturday work counts as overtime for which she is paid at the rate of time-and-a-half.
(a)   What is the length of her basic working week excluding overtime?
(b)   How many hours overtime did she work last week?
(c)   Her basic rate of pay is £4.76 per hour. How much is her hourly rate for overtime?
(d)   Find her basic weekly wage.
(e)   What was her gross wage last week?
(f)   Last week her deductions were: income tax £35.42, national insurance £15.37, pension

contributions £12.55. Find her take-home pay.

4   Billy May buys a new Ford car. The handbook shows that the car is 176 in long, 76 in wide and 54 in high. The tank holds $13\frac{1}{2}$ gallons and the overall fuel consumption is given as 36.4 miles per gallon. His present car, which the garage agree to accept in part exchange, is 4.365 m long and 1.362 m high.
(a)   Which car is the longer, and by how much? (1 in ≈ 25 mm.)
(b)   Find the capacity of the tank in the new car in litres. (1 litre ≈ $1\frac{3}{4}$ pints, 1 gallon = 8 pints.)
(c)   How far can Billy expect the car to travel on a full tank? Give your answer in (i) miles   (ii) kilometres (5 miles ≈ 8 km.)
(d)   Use your answers to (b) and (c)(ii) to find the number of litres required to cover 100 km.
(e)   The overall cost of running the new car is calculated to be 38.62 pence per mile. Billy travels 11 500 miles a year. How much does his motoring cost him (i) per year   (ii) per week?

5   A recipe for Pasta with Tomato and Yogurt sauce lists the following ingredients: 10 oz pasta shells, 3 tablespoons plain yogurt, $\frac{1}{2}$ oz butter, $\frac{1}{2}$ oz flour, $\frac{1}{4}$ pint beef stock, 14 oz can plum tomatoes, 1 bay leaf, sprig of thyme, parsley stalks, salt and pepper. You wish to send this recipe to a friend in France but remember that she needs the quantities in metric units. Write out the ingredients as you would send them to her (4 oz ≈ 100 g, 1 pint ≈ 600 ml. 1 tablespoon = 20 ml)

6   Use the table on p. 109 to find the cost of sending
(a)   5 letters by first class post and 4 letters by second class post, if each of them weighs less than 60 g
(b)   10 letters by second class post, 3 of which weigh 225g and the remainder each weigh less than 60 g
(c)   a parcel weighing 1550 g   (i) by parcel post (ii) by first class letter post.

7   Use the conversion tables given on pp. 112 and 113 to find the equivalent of
(a)   83 hectares in acres   (b)   182 km in miles
(c)   93 tons in tonnes   (d)   29 lb in kilograms.

UNIT 6 · Shapes and Solids

After studying this unit you will be able to
- ☐ calculate the area of compound shapes involving squares and rectangles
- ☐ calculate the area of a triangle, a parallelogram and a trapezium
- ☐ calculate the surface area and volume of a cuboid and of a prism
- ☐ calculate the circumference and area of a circle
- ☐ calculate the surface area and volume of a cylinder
- ☐ draw 2-D representation of 3-D shapes
- ☐ draw isometric drawings, plans and elevations.

Note: Help in elementary geometry will be found in Guidance Notes: Basic Skills, Section E, p. 341.

Square

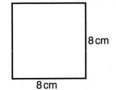

The perimeter of a square is $4 \times$ the length of one side of the square i.e. the perimeter of a square of side 8 cm is 4×8 cm = 32 cm.

The area of a square is equal to the length of a side of the square multiplied by itself i.e. the area of a square of side 8 cm is 8×8 cm^2 = 64 cm^2.

Rectangle

The perimeter of a rectangle is $2 \times$ a long side plus $2 \times$ a short side i.e. the perimeter of a rectangle measuring 12 cm by 6 cm is 2×12 cm + 2×6 cm = 24 cm + 12 cm = 36 cm.

The area of a rectangle is equal to a long side multiplied by a short side i.e. the area of a rectangle measuring 12 cm by 6 cm is 12×6 cm^2 = 72 cm^2.

12 cm

6 cm

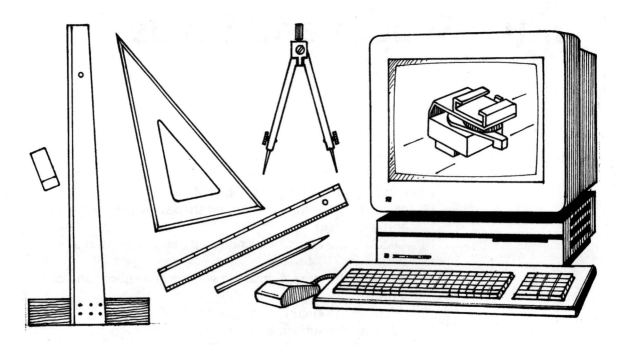

Compound shapes   In this section we find the area of shapes that can be split into squares and/or rectangles.

Exercise 6a

Unless stated otherwise, give all answers that are not exact correct to 3 s.f. This instruction applies to all the exercises in this unit.

Question   Find the floor area of the art studio shown in the diagram. All dimensions are in metres.

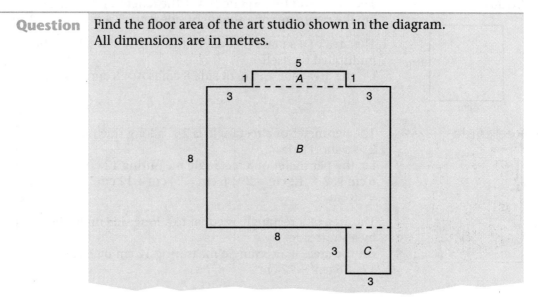

Answer (The broken lines split the room into 3 sections, marked *A*, *B* and *C*.)
Area of *A* (a rectangle) is 5×1 m² $= 5$ m²
Area of *B* (a rectangle) is 8×11 m² $= 88$ m²
Area of *C* (a square) is 3×3 m² $= 9$ m²
∴ total area of the studio is $(5 + 88 + 9)$ m² $= 102$ m².

1 Find the area of this piece of plyboard.

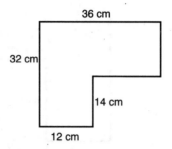

36 cm

32 cm

14 cm

12 cm

2 Find the area of this wooden cross.

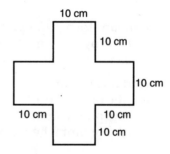

10 cm

10 cm

10 cm

10 cm

10 cm

10 cm

10 cm

3 The diagram is the plan of my lounge.
    (a) Draw your own diagram and on it mark the length of each side.
    (b) Find (i) the length of skirting board used, if there is one door
        75 cm wide
        (ii) the area that can be carpeted.

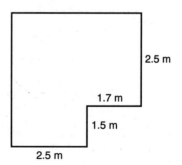

2.5 m

1.7 m

1.5 m

2.5 m

4 The diagram shows the ground floor lay-out of a hospital.
  (a) What is the distance around the outside of the building?
  (b) Find the ground floor area in (i) square metres (ii) hectares.

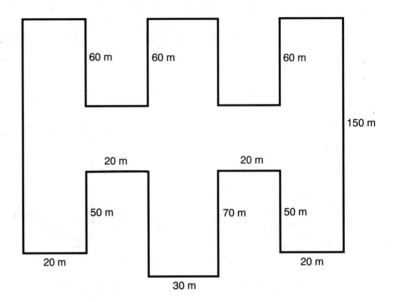

5 A mount for a photograph is in the form of a rectangle measuring 22.8 cm by 15.5 cm. A rectangular hole, 16.2 cm by 9.3 cm, is cut in the card.

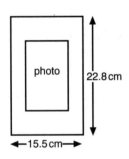

Find the area of
  (a) the original card
  (b) the photograph
  (c) the mount when it is ready to receive the photograph.

6 A wooden door has two glass panels, as shown in the diagram. Find
  (a) the area of each panel
  (b) the area of the painted surface of the door that is visible from one side.

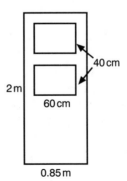

Triangle

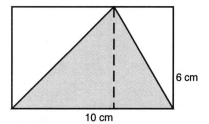

The area of the shaded triangle is equal to half the area of the rectangle that surrounds it. Area of rectangle is 10×6 cm^2 i.e. 60 cm^2 so area of triangle is $\frac{1}{2} \times 10 \times 6$ cm^2 i.e. 30 cm^2.

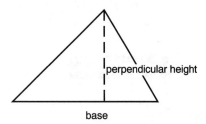

In general the area of a triangle $= \frac{1}{2} \times$ base $\times$ perpendicular height.

Parallelogram

A parallelogram is a quadrilateral with both pairs of opposite sides parallel.

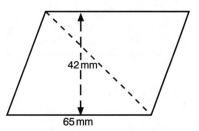

The area of a parallelogram is equal to the sum of the areas of two identical triangles
i.e. area of parallelogram is equal to the length of one side multiplied by the perpendicular distance between that side and the side opposite to it.
area of parallelogram is 65×42 mm^2
$$= 2730 \text{ mm}^2$$

Trapezium

A trapezium is a quadrilateral with just one pair of opposite sides parallel.

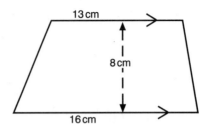

The area of a trapezium is equal to half the sum of the parallel sides multiplied by the perpendicular distance between them
i.e. area of given trapezium is $\frac{1}{2}(16 + 13) \times 8$ cm^2 = 116 cm^2.

Exercise 6b

Question Given below are the templates for four blanks that will be drilled and bent to form components used in the manufacture of a machine. Each machine requires two components made from an *A* blank, two from a *B* blank, two from a *C* blank, and six from a *D* blank. Find:
(a) the area of sheet metal used to make each blank
(b) the total area of metal required for the blanks used to make one machine. Give your answer correct to the nearest whole number.

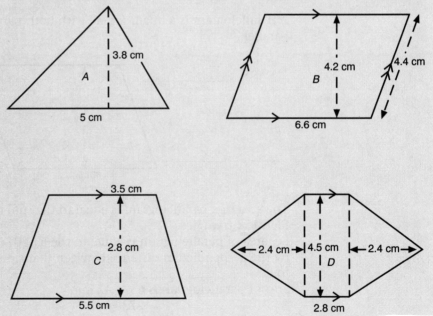

Answer (a) Area of A $= \frac{1}{2} \times 5 \times 3.8 \text{ cm}^2$
$= 9.5 \text{ cm}^2$

Area of B $= 6.6 \times 4.2 \text{ cm}^2$
$= 27.72 \text{ cm}^2$

Area of C $= \frac{1}{2}(3.5 + 5.5) + 2.8 \text{ cm}^2$
$= 4.5 \times 2.8 \text{ cm}^2$
$= 12.6 \text{ cm}^2$

Area of D $=$ area of rectangle $+ 2 \times$ area of one triangle
$= 2.8 \times 4.5 \text{ cm}^2 + 2 \times \frac{1}{2} \times 4.5 \times 2.4 \text{ cm}^2$
$= 12.6 + 10.8 \text{ cm}^2$
$= 23.4 \text{ cm}^2$

(b) Total area of sheet metal required is
$2 \times$ area $A + 2 \times$ area $B + 2 \times$ area $C + 6 \times$ area D
$= 2 \times 9.5 + 2 \times 27.72 + 2 \times 12.6 + 6 \times 23.4 \text{ cm}^2$
$= 19 + 55.44 + 25.2 + 140.4 \text{ cm}^2$
$= 240.04 \text{ cm}^2$
$= 240 \text{ cm}^2$ (to the nearest whole number)

1 Find the area of each of the following plastic shapes.

(a)

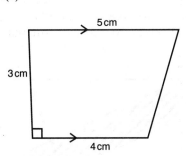

(b)

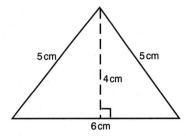

(c)

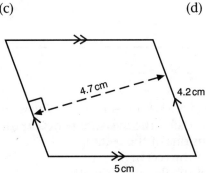

(d)

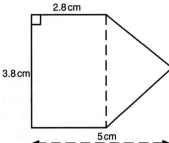

2 The diagram shows the end wall of a bungalow. Find its area

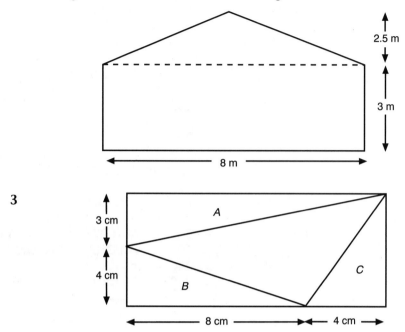

3

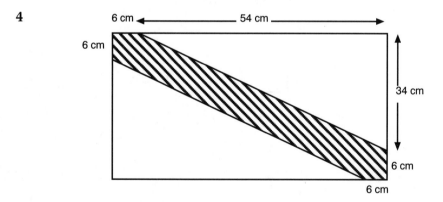

The diagram shows a rectangular sheet of card measuring 12 cm by 7 cm. The triangles marked *A*, *B* and *C* are cut off. Find:
(a) the area of each of the marked triangles
(b) the area of the triangle that remains.

4

The sketch shows a white rectangular flag which has a shaded diagonal band across it. Using the measurements on the diagram, find
(a) the dimensions of the rectangle
(b) the area of the rectangle
(c) the area of the flag that is white
(d) the area of the shaded band.

5 The diagram shows the cross-section, in the form of a trapezium, of a water trough for horses. Find the area of the cross-section.

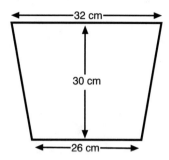

6 The diagram shows the cross-section of a hexagonal pencil. Find the area of cross-section, giving your answer correct to three s.f.

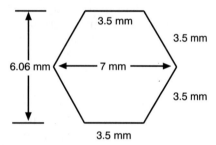

7

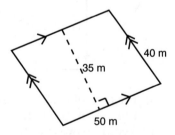

A bed that has been prepared for roses is in the shape of a parallelogram with sides 50 m and 40 m. The longer sides are 35 m apart. Find:
(a) the area of the bed
(b) the number of roses that should be bought to fill the bed if each rose requires an area of 1.5 m^2.

8 The sketch shows the side of an office desk. The facing of the side piece is a parallelogram cut from a veneered plyboard. Use the dimensions given on the sketch to find the area of plyboard used for one side.

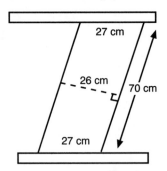

9 The area of a polygon can be found by dividing it up into rectangles and triangles. A group of agricultural students set about finding the area of a field in the shape of a pentagon. The measurements they recorded in a survey are given on the diagram. Find:

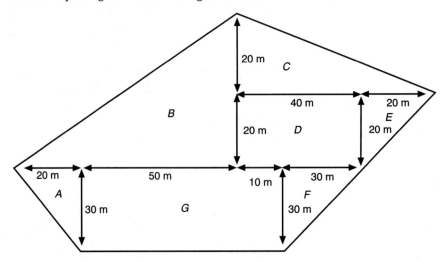

(a) the area of each shape marked by the letters *A–G*
(b) the area of the field.
Give your answer in (i) m^2 (ii) hectares.

Surface area of a cuboid

A cuboid has three pairs of identical opposite sides i.e. six faces altogether. The total surface area of a cuboid is found by adding together the areas of the six faces.

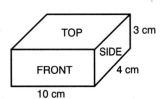

Area of the top is $10 \times 4 \text{ cm}^2 = 40 \text{ cm}^2$
∴ area of top and bottom is 80 cm^2.

Area of the front face is 10×3 cm^2 = 30 cm^2
∴ area of the front face and the back face is 60 m^2.

Area of one side is 4×3 cm^2 = 12 cm^2
∴ area of the two side faces is 24 cm^2
therefore the total area of the six faces is $(80 + 60 + 24)$ cm^2 = 164 cm^2.

Exercise 6c

Find the total surface area of
1 A brick measuring 25 cm $\times$ 12.5 cm $\times$ 8 cm.

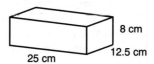

2 A rectangular room measuring 5.5 m by 4.5 m by 2.3 m.

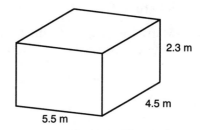

3 A rectangular box for sending wedding cake through the post measuring 65 mm by 50 mm by 18 mm.

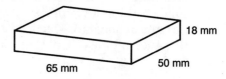

4 A book measuring 240 mm by 185 mm by 30 mm.

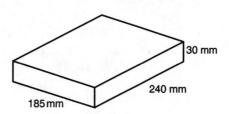

Volume

In Unit 3 we saw that the volume of a cuboid was found by multiplying its length by its breadth by its width i.e. for the cuboid shown opposite

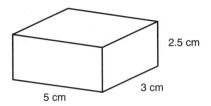

volume $= 5 \times 3 \times 2.5 \text{ cm}^2$
$\quad\quad\quad = 37.5 \text{ cm}^2$

A cuboid is an example of a solid that has a uniform cross-section, that is, wherever you slice it along its length parallel to its ends, the slice has the same shape and area. We say that a solid with this property has a uniform cross-section. Solids that have a uniform cross-section are called *prisms*.

The volume of any prism is equal to the area of cross-section × its length.

Many solids apart from cuboids have a uniform cross-section. Several different prisms are referred to in Exercise 6d.

Exercise 6d

Question   The diagram shows the cross-section of the barn at Lunghurst Farm. The barn is 12 m wide, 25 m long, 12.5 m high at the ridge and 9.9 m high at the sides. Find:
(a) the area of cross-section
(b) the volume of hay that can be stored in the barn.

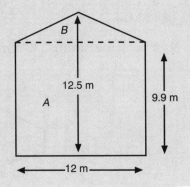

Answer (a) Area of cross-section $=$ area of rectangle A + area of triangle B
$= 12 \times 9.9 + \frac{1}{2} \times 12 \times 2.6 \text{ m}^2$
$= 118.8 + 15.6 \text{ m}^2$
$= 134.4 \text{ m}^2$
(b) Volume of hay that can be stored in the barn
$= 134.4 \times 25 \text{ m}^3$
$= 3360 \text{ m}^3$

In this exercise assume that all the solids referred to are prisms.

1 The sketch shows Tim's garage. Find:
(a) the area of the front of the garage
(b) the volume of space inside the garage.

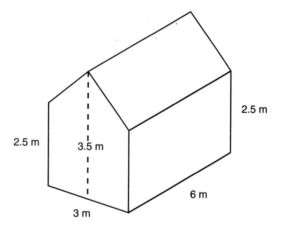

2 A ramp for a wheelchair has its upper surface covered with a non-skid material. Use the dimensions given on the sketch to find
(a) the area of non-skid material used
(b) the amount of space taken up by the ramp when it is laid against a kerb.

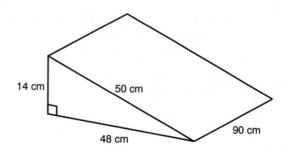

3 A foam cushion for a fireside chair is in the shape of a letter *T*. Use the dimensions given on the diagram to find the volume of material used to make it.

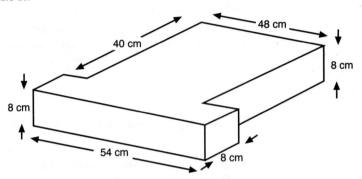

4 The diagram shows the section through a plastic ruler of length 31.6 cm. Find
(a) the area of cross-section (be careful with the units)
(b) the amount of material used to make the ruler.

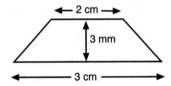

5 A gardener digs a trench in readiness for growing kidney beans. The trench is 11 metres long. Find the volume of earth that he digs out.

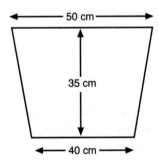

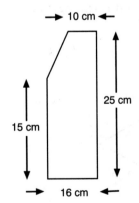

6 The diagram shows the cross-section of a concrete kerb-stone that is 1 metre long. Find its volume
(a) in cubic centimetres   (b) in cubic metres.

(Consider the cross-section as a rectangle from which a triangle has been removed.)

The circle

The *diameter* of a circle is the distance across the centre from edge to edge.

Diameter = 2 × radius.

The distance round the edge of a circle is called the *circumference*.

For any circle the circumference is just over three times the length of the diameter.

Exercise 6e

1 The top of a tin of baked beans is an example of a circle. Name other objects that have circular parts to them.

2 For this question you need a tape measure and three or four circular objects, e.g. a can of soup, a dinner plate, a bicycle wheel, a waste paper bin.
Copy the following table

Object	Diameter (mm)	Circumference (mm)	Circumference ─────────── Diameter

(a) Take your first object, for example the can of soup. Measure the distance across the top of the can in millimetres. Write it in your table.
(b) Next measure the distance round the can using your tape measure. Write this in the column headed circumference.
(c) Finally, write the value you get by dividing the value in the third column by the value in the second column. Give each value correct to 1 decimal place.

Repeat your measurements and calculations for the other objects you have available.

Do your results confirm that the distance round the object is roughly three times its diameter?

Question Find, roughly, the circumference of a circular table if its diameter is 90 cm.

Answer Circumference is roughly 3 × diameter
= 3 × 90 cm
= 270 cm

3 Find, roughly, the circumference of a bicycle wheel that has a diameter of
 (a) 50 cm   (b) 64 cm

4 A clock face has a radius of 5 inches.
 (a) What is its diameter?
 (b) What, roughly, is its circumference?

5 A car wheel is 75 cm diameter.
 (a) What, roughly, is its circumference?
 (b) About how far does the car travel forward when the wheel makes one complete turn?
 (c) Roughly, how far does the car travel forward when the wheel revolves 50 times?
    Give your answer   (i) in cm   (ii) in m.

Using π

Multiplying the diameter by 3 gives a rough value for the circumference. Multiplying by 3.14 gives a more accurate value but the easiest way is to use the value on your calculator. To avoid writing lots of figures we use the greek letter π (pi) to stand for this value. Then

$$C = \pi D$$

and $C = 2\pi r$ (since diameter = 2 × radius)

Exercise 6f

In this exercise, and the remaining exercises in this chapter, unless otherwise stated, use the value of π on your calculator and give answers correct to 3 s.f.

1 Press the π button on your calculator and write down the value in the display. Write this value correct to
 (a) 2 decimal places   (b) 3 s.f.
 (c) 3 d.p.

Question   Find the circumference of the top of a soup tin that has a diameter of 9.6 cm

Answer   Circumference $= \pi D$
           $= \pi \times 9.6$ cm   (π × 9 . 6 =)
           $= 30.2$ cm (3 s.f.)

2 A circular kitchen table, diameter 90 cm, has a plastic strip around the edge. How long is the strip?

3 The diameter of three different sizes of plates in a dinner service are 16 cm, 21 cm and 27 cm.
Find the circumference of each.

4 Insulation tape is wound on a cardboard ring. The inside diameter of this ring is 3.2 cm and the outside diameter is 3.9 cm.
(a) How thick is the cardboard from which the ring is made?
(b) The overall diameter of the roll of tape is 6.8 cm.
What depth of tape is there on the roll?

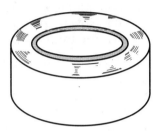

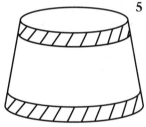

5 The sketch shows a stand which is used for displaying china figures in a department store. The top is circular with a diameter of 14 cm and the bottom is a circle of diameter 17 cm.
(a) Find the circumference of each circle.
(b) The stand is to be decorated with a metal band around the top and bottom edges. What length of strip is needed?
(c) The strip is available to the nearest 5 cm. (i) How much strip must be bought? (ii) How much is left over?

Question The distance round a circular running track is 400 m. What is the diameter of the track?

Answer Circumference = π × diameter
i.e. $C = \pi \times D$
∴ $400 = \pi \times D$

i.e. $\dfrac{400}{\pi} = D$ (4 0 0 ÷ π =)

$D = 127.32$
i.e. the diameter of the track is 127 m (3 s.f.)

---

6 Findley has a 2.4 metre length of plastic edging. What is the diameter of the largest circular table that can be edged with this length of plastic?

7 The distance round the outer edge of a soup dish is 120 cm and the distance round the inner edge of the rim is 104 cm. Find:
(a) the diameter of the outer edge
(b) the diameter of the inner edge
(c) the width of the rim.

8 A British Gas official uses a trundle wheel to check the length of a trench in which a new gas main has been laid. He pushes the wheel over the tarmaced surface after the job has been completed.
(a) If the radius of the wheel is 4 inches find its circumference.
(b) The wheel rotates 125 times. How long, in yards, is the trench?
(c) He wishes to mark out the next 100 yard section of gas main to be laid. How many rotations of his trundle wheel must he count to measure this distance?

9 The wheels of a motorbike are 60 cm in diameter.
(a) Find the circumference of a wheel in metres.
(b) How far does the motorbike move forward when each wheel makes one complete turn?
(c) How many times will each wheel revolve when the bike travels one kilometre?

10 Six circular pieces of wire are fixed to a dart board. The smallest circle encloses the bull's eye and the largest circle gives the outer edge of the doubles.
(a) If the radii of the six circles are 0.65 cm, 1.2 cm, 9.5 cm, 10.5 cm, 15.8 cm and 16.8 cm, find the length of each circular piece of wire.

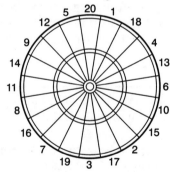

Straight pieces of wire separate one number from the next. Each piece goes from the 'outer' of the two circles near the centre of the board, to the edge of the largest circle.
(b) How long is one of the straight wires?
(c) How many straight wires are there?
(d) What is the total length of the straight wires?
(e) What is the total length of wire used to make this dart board?

Sections of a circle Half a circle is called a *semicircle*.
One quarter of a circle is called a *quadrant*.
Part of the circumference of a circle is called an *arc*.

The length of a *semicircular* arc is half the length of the circumcircle of the circle.

The length of a *quadrant* arc is one quarter the circumference of the whole circle.

Exercise 6g

Question   A semicircular protractor has a radius of 5 cm. Find the distance round the curved edge.

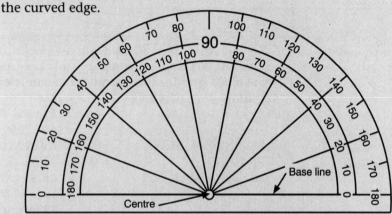

Answer   Circumference of whole circle = $2\pi r$

Distance around the curved edge is half the distance around the whole circle

∴ Distance around curved edge   = $\pi \times 5$ cm

= 15.707 ... cm

= 15.7 (3 s.f.)

1   A flower bed is in the shape of a semicircle of radius 5.6 metres. Find the length of its curved edge.

2   The diameter of a paper doiley to put on a plate under a cake is 22 cm. Find the distance round the curved edge when it has been folded
(a) once   (b) twice.

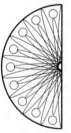

3   A fan is in the shape of a quadrant of a circle of radius 30 cm. Find the length of the curved edge.

Question   The sketch shows a shelf, in the form of a quadrant of a circle of radius 24 cm, which fits into a corner of the room and can be used for holding an ornament. Find the perimeter of the shelf.

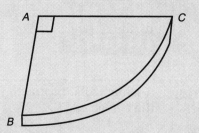

Answer   The diagram shows the shelf when viewed from above.
AB and AC are each of length 24 cm – they are both radii of the circle.
The arc BC is $\frac{1}{4}$ the circumference of a circle of radius 24 cm.

Circumference of whole circle	$= 2\pi r$
	$= 2 \times \pi \times 24$ cm
	$= 150.796\ldots$ cm
$\therefore$ length of arc BC	$= 150.796\ldots \div 4$ cm
	$= 37.69$
Perimeter of shelf	$= AB + \text{arc } BC + AC$
	$= 24 + 37.69 + 24$ cm
	$= 85.69$ cm
	$= 85.7$ cm (3 s.f.)

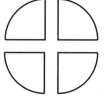

4 A metal disc, diameter 17 cm, is cut into four identical pieces. Find the distance round the edge of one of these pieces.

5 The diameter of a semicircular fire side rug is 170 cm. Find
(a) the radius of the semicircle
(b) the length of the curved edge
(c) the total distance round the
     edge of the rug.

6 The sketch shows one of the windows in the town hall. Its shape is a square, of side 140 cm, with a semicircle on the top.
(a) Write down the lengths of AB, AD and CD.
(b) Find   (i) the radius of the semicircle   (ii) the length of the arc BC.
(c) What is the distance round the outside of the window?

7 The diagram shows the inside edge of a running track which has semicircular ends. Use the dimensions on the diagram to find
   (a) the radius of each semicircle
   (b) the length of each semicircular arc
   (c) the distance once round the track
   (d) the distance run by an athlete who completes 20 laps of the track. Give your answer in kilometres.

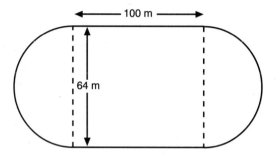

Area of a circle

It can be shown that

Area of a circle = $\pi \times$ (radius)^2

As a formula we write $A = \pi r^2$.

Exercise 6h

Question	A circular table has a diameter of 75 cm. Find its area.

Answer Diameter   = 75 cm
∴ radius   = 37.5 cm
Area   = πr^2
          = $\pi \times 37.5^2$ cm^2 ($\boxed{\pi}$ $\boxed{\times}$ $\boxed{3}$ $\boxed{7}$ $\boxed{.}$ $\boxed{5}$ $\boxed{x^2}$ $\boxed{=}$)
          = 4417.8 ... cm^2
Area of table top is 4420 cm^2 (3 s.f.)

1 The diameter of the circular top of a tin of soup is 8 cm. Find its area.

2 The radius of a circular flower bed is 22 metres. Find its area.

3 The diameter of a circular cameo brooch is 38 mm. Find its area.

4 The diameter of a 10p coin is 2.4 cm. Find the total area of both sides.

5 In soccer the diameter of the centre circle is 10 yards. Find its area.

Question   Find the area of a semicircular rose bed whose radius is 4.8 metres.

Answer   (The area of a semicircle is half the area of the whole circle.)
Area of whole circle $= \pi r^2$
   $= \pi \times (4.8)^2 \, m^2$
   $= 72.382 \ldots m^2$
Area of rose bed $= 72.382 \ldots \div 2 \, m^2$
   $= 36.191 \ldots m^2$
Area of rose bed is $36.2 \, m^2$ (3 s.f.)

---

6   A woman's cloak is made from a semicircular piece of material, the diameter of which is 90 cm. Find the area of the outside of the cloak.

7   The sketch shows a Pembroke table which has two semicircular leaves that hang vertically when the table is not wholly opened out. Find
   (a) the area of the rectangular top
   (b) the area of one semi-circular leaf
   (c) the total surface area of the table when it is opened out.

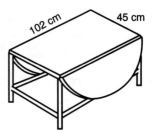

8   Sam makes a telephone shelf that fits into a corner in the hall. It consists of two quadrants of plywood supported by two rectangular pieces, each of which can be screwed to the wall. The telephone rests on the top and directories can be kept on the shelf. Use the dimensions given on the diagram to find
   (a) the area of one quadrant
   (b) the total area of plywood used to make the shelf.

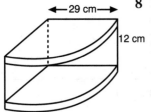

9   The stage in a rectangular concert hall is made up of a rectangle and a semicircle. Find the area of
   (a) the stage
   (b) the concert hall
   (c) the floor of the concert hall.

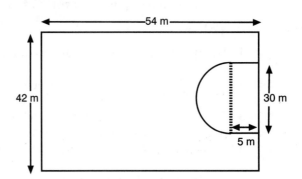

10 The shaded area shows the waste metal between four circles when circular discs, of radius 4.6 cm, are pressed from a flat sheet. Find the area of this piece of waste.

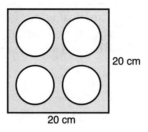

20 cm

20 cm

Cylinders

Curved surface area

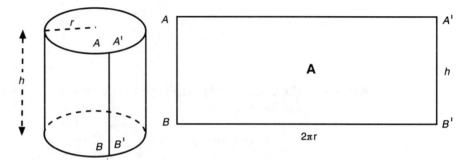

The curved surface of a cylinder, when opened out flat, gives a rectangle.

The length of the rectangle is equal to the circumference of the cylinder and the width of the rectangle is equal to the height of the cylinder.

Since the area of a rectangle is equal to its length times its width.

Curved surface area of a cylinder, A, of height h and base radius r, is given by

$A = 2\pi rh$

The area of each circular end is πr^2.

Volume

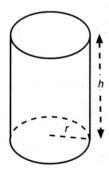

A solid cylinder has a constant cross-section and is therefore a circular prism.

The volume, V, of a cylinder of height h and base radius r is
$\pi \times (\text{radius})^2 \times \text{height}$

(height means 'width' when, for example, it is a garden roller, and 'thickness' when it is a coin)

i.e. in letters $V = \pi r^2 h$

Exercise 6i

Question   A cylindrical water tank is 1.24 m high and has a radius of 54 cm. Find
(a) the curved surface area of the tank
(b) the total surface area of the tank.

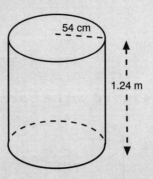
54 cm
1.24 m

Answer   (Both dimensions must be in the same unit. We shall use centimetres.)
(a) Height of cylinder   = 1.24 m
           = 124 cm
  Curved surface area   = $2\pi rh$
           = $2 \times \pi \times 54 \times 124 \text{ cm}^2$
           = $42\,072.2 \ldots \text{cm}^2$
           = $42\,100 \text{ cm}^2$ (3 s.f.)
(b) Area of one end   = πr^2
           = $\pi \times 54^2 \text{ cm}^2$
           = $9160.8 \ldots \text{cm}^2$
  Total surface area   = $9160.8 \ldots + 9160.8 \ldots + 42\,100 \text{ cm}^2$
           = $60\,421.6 \text{ cm}^2$
 $\therefore$ total surface area is $60\,400 \text{ cm}^2$ (3 s.f.)

1 A garden roller has a radius of 35 cm and is
60 cm wide.
(a) Find, in square metres, the area rolled by
 (i) one complete turn of the roller
 (ii) 100 complete turns of the roller.
(b) How many revolutions are needed to roll an
 area of 800 square metres? Give your answer
 correct to the nearest whole number.

2 A cylindrical post box is 1.5 m high and has a diameter of 63 cm. Find,
in square metres, the area that requires painting.

3 A cylindrical breakfast cup has a radius of 4 cm and is 8 cm deep. Find the surface area of the cup in contact with tea when it is filled to a distance of 0.5 cm from the top. Neglect the thickness of the cup.

4 A coin is 1.5 mm thick and has a diameter of 2.5 cm. Find the total surface area of the coin. (Take care with units.)

Question A 4-cylinder diesel engine has a bore (the diameter of each cylinder) of 89 mm and a stroke (the length of each piston stroke) of 86.6 mm. Find, correct to 4 s.f., the capacity of the engine in cubic centimetres.

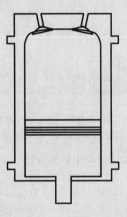

Answer (Since the answer is required in cubic centimetres we shall work in centimetres.) The radius of each cylinder is
$\frac{89}{2}$ mm = 44.5 mm = 4.45 cm
The length of each cylinder is 86.6 mm = 8.66 cm
Volume, or capacity, of one cylinder $= \pi r^2 h$
$= \pi \times 4.45^2 \times 8.66$ cm^3
∴ capacity of 4 cylinders is $4 \times \pi \times 4.45^2 \times 8.66$ cm^3
($\boxed{4}$ $\boxed{\times}$ $\boxed{\pi}$ $\boxed{\times}$ $\boxed{4}$ $\boxed{.}$ $\boxed{4}$ $\boxed{5}$ $\boxed{x^2}$ $\boxed{\times}$ $\boxed{8}$ $\boxed{.}$ $\boxed{6}$ $\boxed{6}$ $\boxed{=}$)
$= 2155$ cm^3 (to 4 s.f.)
(For an engine cm^3 is often written as cc, i.e. the capacity of this engine is 2155 cc.)

5 A hole, 30 mm diameter, is drilled in a metal plate 25 mm thick. What volume of metal is removed from the plate?

6 Copper wire is circular in cross-section with a radius of 0.4 mm. Find, in cubic centimetres, the volume of copper in a 100 m length of this wire.

7 Find the capacity of a 4 cylinder OHC petrol engine which has a bore of 84 mm and a stroke of 75 mm. Give your answer correct to 4 s.f.

8 Wooden dowel, with a diameter of 1 cm, is made from lengths of timber with a square cross-section of side 1.2 cm. Find
   (a) the area of cross-section of the original timber
   (b) the area of cross-section of the dowel
   (c) correct to the nearest whole number, the percentage of the wood wasted.

Question   A cylindrical milk bottle has a capacity of 568 cm³. If the diameter of the bottle is 8 cm find its height.

Answer   The radius of the bottle is 4 cm. If the capacity of the bottle is C cm³ and the height is h cm
Then, using $C = \pi r^2 h$ $568 = \pi \times 4^2 \times h$ ($\boxed{\pi} \times \boxed{4} \times \boxed{4} = $)
$$568 = 50.27 \times h$$

Dividing both sides by 50.27 $\dfrac{568}{50.27} = h$ ($\boxed{5}\boxed{6}\boxed{8} \div$
$\boxed{5}\boxed{0}.\boxed{2}\boxed{7} =$)
$$h = 11.29$$
∴ the height is 11.3 cm correct to 3 s.f.

---

9 A cylindrical petrol can has a capacity of 5 litres. If the height is equal to the diameter of its base find its dimensions.

10 The capacity of a drum, which is 55 cm high, is 75 litres. Find
   (a) the capacity of the drum in cubic centimetres
   (b) the area of a circular end in square centimetres
   (c) the radius of one of the ends, in centimetres.

11 The capacity of a 4-cylinder petrol engine is 1799 cm³. If the bore of the engine is 85.3 mm, find its stroke. Give your answer in mm correct to 3 s.f.

Question   The dimensions of a pipe are shown in the diagram. Calculate the volume of material used to make it.

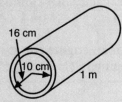

16 cm
10 cm
1 m

Answer   Area of cross-section $= \pi \times 16^2 - \pi \times 10^2$ cm² ($\boxed{\pi} \times \boxed{1}\boxed{6}\boxed{x^2} = $)
$$= 804.2 - 314.1 \text{ cm}^2 \ (\boxed{\pi} \times \boxed{1}\boxed{0}\boxed{x^2} =)$$
$$= 490.1 \text{ cm}^2$$
Volume of material used $= 490.1 \times 100$ cm³
$$= 49\,010 \text{ cm}^3$$
$$= 49\,000 \text{ cm}^3 \text{ 3 s.f.)}$$

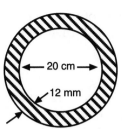

12 The diagram shows the section through a pipe. The bore of the pipe is 20 cm and the wall of the pipe is 12 mm thick. Find
(a) the area of cross-section of the bore of the pipe.
(b) the cross-sectional area of the material from which the pipe is made. (This is shown shaded in the diagram.)

13

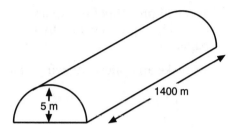

The diagram shows a semi-circular railway tunnel 1400 m long, which has been driven through a mountain side. The height of the tunnel is 5 m. Find, in cubic metres, the volume of material that has been removed to construct the tunnel.

14

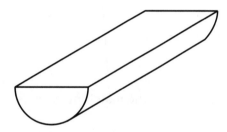

An 8 m length of guttering along the front of a house has a semi-circular cross-section of diameter 11.5 cm. If there are stoppers at the ends, calculate, in cubic metres, the maximum volume of water that the guttering will hold at any one time.

15 The diagram shows the section through a cylindrical bottle top which is everywhere 1.5 mm thick. If the external diameter is 16 mm and the external height is 16 mm, find the volume of material used to make it.

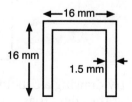

2-D representation of 3-D shapes

Drawing a three dimensional (3-D) shape on a flat sheet of paper, i.e. in two dimensions (2-D), is not easy. Two methods, each with their own advantages and disadvantages, are given below.

Oblique drawings

You will probably find squared or dotted paper helpful to start with, but you should progress rapidly to drawing most shapes easily on plain paper.

To make an oblique drawing of a cube on squared paper

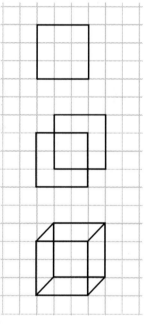

(a) Draw the front face.

(b) Draw the opposite face the same size but slightly off-set from the first.

(c) Join the matching corners.

The convention is that we use solid lines for edges we can see, but dashed lines for edges we know exist but cannot see i.e. for hidden edges.

Using this convention the cube we have drawn is redrawn below.

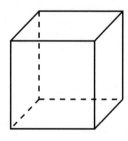

Now try drawing a cuboid, first using all solid lines, and then dashed line for the edges that you cannot see.

Isometric drawings

Isometric drawings are easier to do on isometric graph paper or on isometric dot paper, but with a little practice can be drawn effectively on plain paper.

To make an isometric drawing of a cuboid on isometric graph paper

(a) Draw the top face. The top face of a cuboid is a rectangle but is drawn here as a parallelogram.

(b) Draw the four vertical edges, all of which are parallel and equal in length.

(c) Join the matching bottom corners.

The corresponding drawing using isometric dot paper is given opposite.

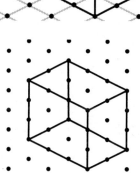

One of the big advantages of this type of drawing is that the lengths of all the edges can be drawn to the exact size.

You do not have to draw the lines in the order in which they are given above, but it is probably wise to decide on an order that is suitable for you and stick to it.

Several different oblique drawings of solids, together with their dimensions in cm, are given below.

(a) Look at each shape in turn, study it, then close the book and see if you can make your own oblique drawing of it from the picture you have in mind. (Should you find this difficult make a free-hand sketch, and put the dimensions on it, before you close the book.)

(b) Make an isometric drawing of each shape using either isometric graph paper or isometric dot paper.

1

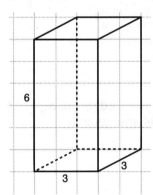

2

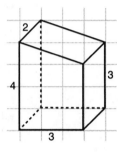

3

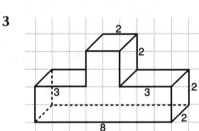

4

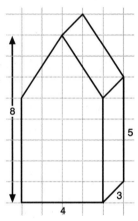

5

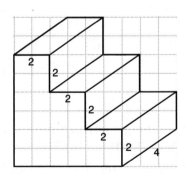

6

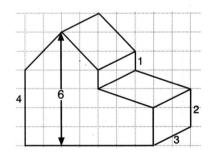

Questions 7 and 8 give isometric drawings. Sketch the corresponding oblique drawings.

7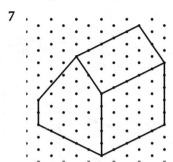

8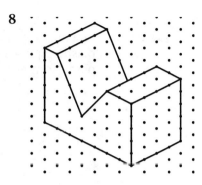

Plans and elevations

Consider this ordinary plastic beaker.

Looking directly down on it from above it appears as two concentric circles. The outer circle is the rim of the beaker and the inner circle is the bottom of the beaker.

When we look from the side the beaker looks like a trapezium.

What we see when we look at a shape from above is called its *plan*.

What we see when we look from the front is called the *front elevation*, and what we see when we look from the side is called the *side elevation*.

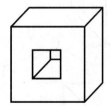

The plan, front elevation and side elevation of a cube which has a horizontal square hole cut through its centre, are given below.

Plan   Front elevation   Side elevation

(hidden edges are shown by a dashed line.)

Exercise 6k

Question The drawing shows a V-shaped block which can be used to support plastic piping so that it can be cut to the required length. Draw the plan, front elevation and side elevation.

Answer

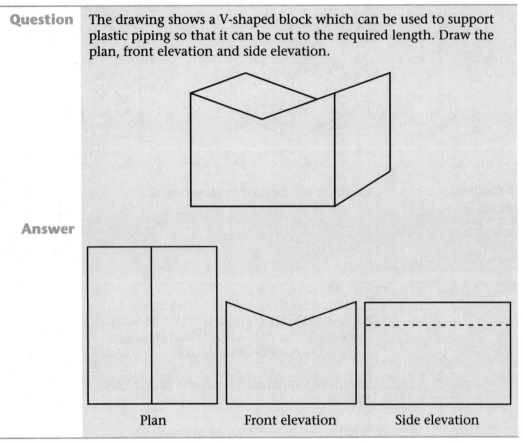

Plan   Front elevation   Side elevation

In Questions 1–6 draw the plan, front elevation and side elevation.

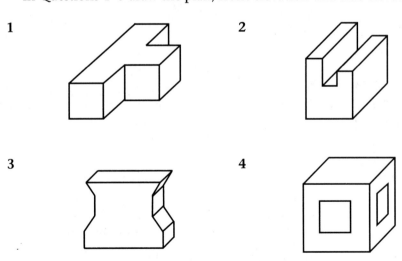

1

2

3

4

5 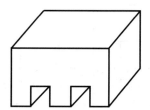   **6**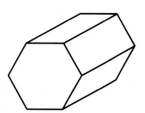

In Questions 7–10 draw the view of each solid from the direction marked with an arrow.

7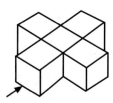

A wooden cross

8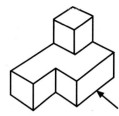

A solid made from cubes

9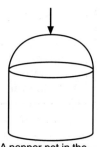

A pepper pot in the shape of a cylinder with a hemisphere on top.

10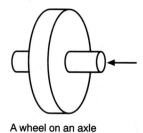

A wheel on an axle

In Questions 11–13, the plan, front elevation and side elevation for a solid are given. Sketch the solid.

11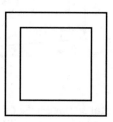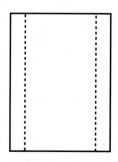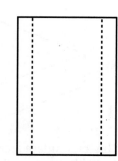

Plan   Front elevation   Side elevation

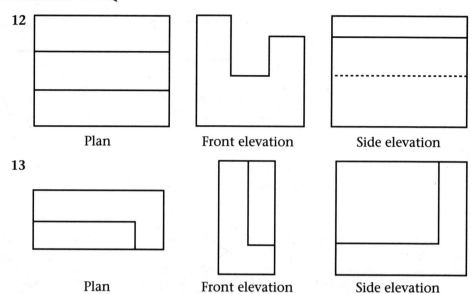

12

Plan   Front elevation   Side elevation

13

Plan   Front elevation   Side elevation

Multiple choice questions

1

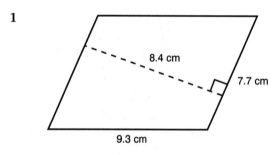

8.4 cm

7.7 cm

9.3 cm

The area of this parallelogram is
A 78.12 cm^2 B 64.68 cm^2
C 71.61 cm^2 D 39.06 cm^2

2

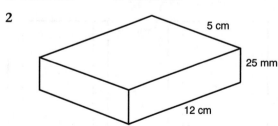

5 cm

25 mm

12 cm

The total surface area of this cuboid is
A 2050 cm^2 B 205 cm^2
C 42 cm^2 D 15 000 mm^2

3   The area of the surface of a circular table is
1 square metre. The diameter of this table, in
centimetres, correct to 3 s.f., is
A 1128 mm   B 113 cm
C 560 mm   D 56.4 cm

4

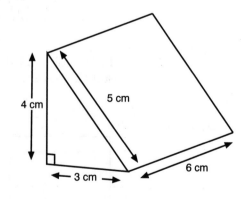

4 cm

5 cm

3 cm

6 cm

The total surface area of this prism is
A 84 cm^2 B 72 cm^2
C 60 cm^2 D 36 m^2

5

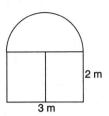

6

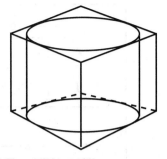

The sketch shows one of the windows in the assembly rooms at the City Hall. It is glazed using three sheets of glass – two identical rectangular sheets and one semicircular sheet. Using the dimensions given on the diagram and neglecting the thickness of any mouldings that separate the sheets, decide which of the following statements are true and which are false.

A The perimeter of one of the rectangular sheets is greater than the perimeter of the semicircular sheet.

B The area of the semicircular sheet is greater than the area of one of the rectangular sheets.

C The total area of glass used in the window is 9.53 m^2.

D The sum of the perimeters of the three sheets is 21 m.

A solid cylinder fits snugly inside a hollow metal cube, of negligible thickness, such that all six internal surfaces of the cube touch the cylinder. The length of an internal edge of the cube is 10 cm. The following statements have been made:

Statement 1 The amount of space between the cylinder and the cube is less than 200 cm^3.

Statement 2 The total surface area of the outside of the cube is more than twice the surface area of the cylinder.

How are these statements best described?

A True, True   **B** True, False
C False, True   **D** False, False.

Self assessment 6

1

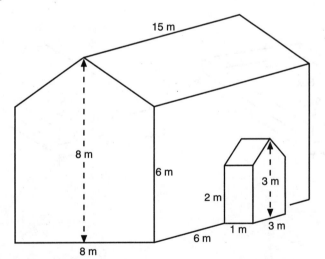

The sketch shows a detached house with a porch placed centrally on the front.
Use the information given on the sketch

(a) to make an isometric drawing of the house and porch

(b) to draw a plan, side and front elevation of the house and porch.

2

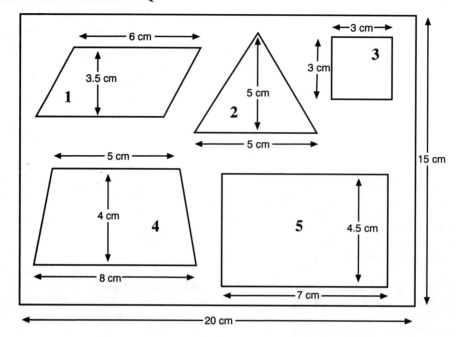

The illustration shows a child's early learning toy. The object of the exercise is for the child to fit each shape into its correct location.

(a) Name each of the shapes numbered 1–5 and find the area of each.

(b) What fraction of the base of the board is exposed when all the pieces have been withdrawn?

(c) The cardboard box in which the toy was bought is shown below. Using the dimensions given with the sketch find
(i) the area of card used to make the box
(ii) the capacity of the box.

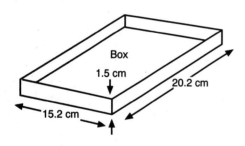

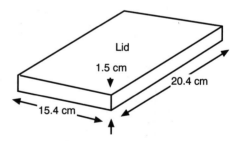

3

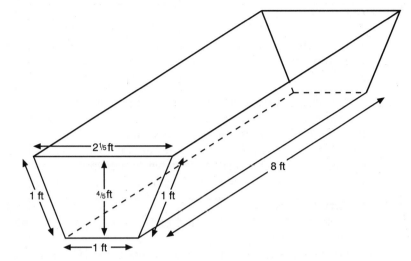

The sketch shows a water trough on a diary farm. It is constructed from three rectangular planks with pieces in the shape of a trapezium at each end. Use the measurements given on the sketch to find

(a) the area of each end piece

(b) the total area of the outside of the trough
(c) the amount of water it will hold when full. Give your answers in
   (i) cubic feet (ii) gallons, each correct to 3 s.f.
   (1 cubic foot of water is equivalent to 6.23 gallons.)

4

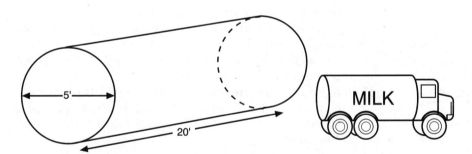

The storage container on a milk lorry is a steel cylinder 20 ft long with a diameter of 5 ft. It is made by bending a rectangular sheet of steel into an open cylinder and welding the common edge together along the top. Circular steel discs are then welded to the open cylinder at both ends. Find:

(a) the dimensions of the rectangular steel sheet from which the curved surface of the tank is made

(b) the total length that has to be welded to make the tank
(c) the total area of sheet metal used to make the tank
(d) the capacity of the tank in ft^3
(e) the weight of the milk in the tank if 1 cubic foot of milk weighs 67 lb.

Revision papers for units 4–6

Paper 5

1 A good quality stainless steel knife weighs 80 g. It contains 18% chromium and 8% nickel. Find the weight of each metal in a set of 12 knives.

2 Government figures show that a typical person earning over £300 a week is likely to spend 18½% of their income on leisure time activities, whereas a typical person earning less than £200 per week is likely to spend 12% of their income in a similar way. Sally, who earns £350 a week, and John, who earns £175 a week, are both typical. How much more is Sally likely to spend on leisure activities than John?

3 (a) Barry Crooks is employed in a plastics factory. He works a basic week of 37½ hours and is paid £5.85 an hour. What is his gross weekly wage?
   (b) Barry is paid time-and-a-third for overtime. How much extra does he earn in a week when he does 7½ hours overtime?

4 The simplified cross-section of a domestic radiator is shown opposite. It shows a rectangle with a square at each end. If the radiator is 1.5 m long find
   (a) the area of cross-section
   (b) the volume of water, in litres, inside the radiator when it is full. (1 litre = 1000 cm³.)

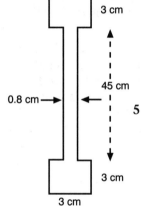

3 cm

3 cm

45 cm

0.8 cm →

3 cm

3 cm

5 The radius of a bicycle wheel is 28 cm.
   (a) What is the circumference of the wheel?
       Give your answer correct to the nearest whole number.
   (b) How far does the axle of the wheel move forward for one complete turn of the wheel?
   (c) The bicycle moves forward a distance of 264 metres. How many times has the wheel revolved?
   (d) In a certain gear one revolution of the pedals produces 3 revolutions of each wheel. How many revolutions of the pedals are needed for the bicycle to travel forward a distance of 132 metres?

Paper 6

1 Recent figures show that last year there were 2229 reported injuries to hotel and catering staff. Of these 1858 led to staff being off work for 3 days or more.
   (a) What percentage of the reported injuries led to staff being off work for 3 days or more?
   (b) The Health & Safety Executive estimate that only 17% of injuries are reported. Estimate, to the nearest 50, the total number of injuries to hotel and catering staff last year.

2 A sandwich loaf (800 g) yields 22 slices and requires 100 g of creamed butter. A caterer is to supply midday sandwiches for a conference gathering of 260 people. They allow 3 slices of bread per person when they prepare sandwiches.
  (a) How many loaves do they need? (Round up to the nearest whole number.)
  (b) How much butter do they need? (Round up to the nearest 250 g.)
  (c) Find, in kilograms, the total weight of this order, if the weight of all the fillings used comes to 16.4 kg.
  (d) What weight of sandwiches is allowed for each person?

3 A Senior Railcard costs £18 and gives a 30% discount to people over 60. Ann Whittaker, aged 67, buys a card and uses it for the first time to go to London with her son.
  (a) The cost of a ticket for her son is £45.60. How much does Ann pay?
  (b) Assuming that she does not take another train journey during the year, how much has she gained or lost by buying a railcard?
  (c) However, she makes a second rail journey, this time to Edinburgh and, using her rail card, pays £67.48 for her ticket.
  (i) How much would her son have to pay for a ticket to travel to Edinburgh with her?
  (ii) Taking the two journeys together, how much has she saved by buying a railcard?

4 Mr and Mrs Buxton have three children aged 6, 7 and 14. The family credit due to them, because they are on a low income is: adult credit (£45.00 maximum), £11.40 for each of their younger children and £17.80 for the eldest child. However, the maximum adult credit is reduced by 70% of the amount that their net income exceeds £70. Mrs Buxton does not work and Mr Buxton has a net income of £105 a week. Find
  (a) the weekly reduction in their adult credit allowance
  (b) the total family credit due
  (c) Mr and Mrs Buxton's total weekly income.

5 At Chartwell plc the allowable stay away expenses for salespersons are: £42 a night for bed and breakfast, £7.50 for lunch, £12.50 for an evening meal and a mileage allowance of 42p a mile. Ben Walden's expenses for a week are indicated below.

Day	Mileage	Lunch	B&B	Evening meal
Mon	54	✓	✓	✓
Tues	82	✓	✓	✓
Wed	67	✓	✓	✓
Thurs	95	✓		
Fri	52	✓		

Use the details given above to calculate Ben's expenses for the week.

1 Lean topside of beef with no visible fat contains about 4.4% fat. How much fat, correct to the nearest gram, can be expected in four pieces of lean topside, each weighing 359g?

2 Alf Compton is soon to have his 65th birthday. If he decides to take his pension at 65 he will receive £200 per week. However, if he wishes, he can continue working and so put off taking his pension, in which case the pension due to him is increased by $7\frac{1}{2}$% on each birthday until he decides to take it.

How much weekly pension will be due to him if he decides not to take his pension at 65 but to wait until he reaches
(a) his 67th birthday   (b) his 70th birthday?

3 The recreational facilities at a Georgian mansion, now used as a hotel, include an indoor swimming pool (12 m × 4 m), an outdoor swimming pool (25 m × 15.5 m) and 2 tennis courts (96 ft × 31 ft 8 in).
If 1 ft ≈ 0.308 m, find
(a) the dimensions of the tennis courts in metres
(b) the dimensions of the swimming pools in feet.
Give each dimension correct to one decimal place.

4 The diagram shows the cross section, *ABCD*, through a length of bull-nose skirting board. The arc *BC* is a quadrant of a circle. Find
(a) the length of   (i) *AB*   (ii) *BC*
(b) the perimeter of the cross-section.

5 A cylindrical tin of jam has a volume of 600 cm³. If the diameter of its base is 9 cm find
(a) its height
(b) the area of the label that completely covers the curved surface of the tin if the label is held in position by a 1 cm overlap.

1 New books appear in ever-increasing numbers. In 1960 there were 29 000 new titles and by 1990 the number of new titles had increased to 62 500.
(a) Find, correct to the nearest whole number, the percentage increase in new titles from 1960 to 1990.
(b) It is anticipated that the increase in new titles from 1990 to the year 2000 will be 15% and that from the year 2000 the number of new titles will increase by 17.5% every 10 years. Estimate to 2 s.f. the number of new titles in the year   (i) 2000 (ii) 2010 (iii) 2020.

2 The partly completed table summarises the expenses one week of the 6 employees at Space Electronics who have expense accounts

Name	Mileage	Hotel accom. (£)	Hotel meals (£)	Casual meals (£)	Total (£)
B. Ayola	116.55	56.72	28.70	18.17	
C. Love	82.95	123.14		24.84	283.12
L. Draigo	64.50	none	none	36.42	100.92
P. Lineen	108.92		34.40	16.42	249.58
R. Dence	136.87		78.50		499.67
M. Hayes	109.64	213.36	59.20	18.78	
		725.18			1754.41

(a) Copy and complete the table.
(b) By how much did the total hotel costs (for accommodation and evening meals) exceed the other costs?
(c) Express, correct to the nearest whole number, Pat Lineen's mileage costs as a percentage of her total costs.

3 The adult population of Roxford consists of 350 000 men and 375 000 women. The table shows the percentage of men and women taking part in outdoor and indoor sports in 1990, together with the projected percentages for the year 2000.

Year	Percentage participating			
	Outdoor		Indoor	
	Men	Women	Men	Women
1990	43.2	30.7	37.8	29.8
2000 (projected)	46.8	36.3	40.1	35.8

(a) How many men were participating in
   (i) outdoor activities
   (ii) indoor activities, in 1990?
(Give these answers, and those for parts (b)–(d), correct to the nearest 1000.)
(b) How many women were participating in
   (i) outdoor activities
   (ii) indoor activities, in 1990?
(c) Which of the four categories shows
   (i) the largest
   (ii) the smallest, projected increase from 1990 to the year 2000?
(d) By 1995, i.e. halfway through the ten year period, the number of women participating in outdoor activities had risen to 128 000.
   (i) What percentage increase is this since 1990?
   (ii) Does this figure suggest that the hoped-for increase is on track?

4

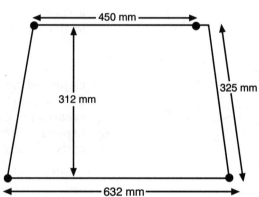

The sketch shows a walking frame which rises to height of 700 mm above the floor. The positions and distances apart of its four feet, are shown in the diagram.

(a) Find, in centimetres, the dimensions of the smallest rectangular box that can be used to pack this frame. Sketch it.

(b) If an extra 0.1 m² is required to allow for overlapping at the corners and flaps for the lid, find, correct to the nearest tenth of a square metre, the area of card needed to make the box.

(c) What space, in m³ correct to 2 decimal places, would be needed inside a lorry to carry 6 similar boxed walking frames?

5 The Cod War of 1972 arose from Iceland's decision to extend her territorial waters from 12 miles to 50 miles

(a) Assuming that Iceland is a circular island of diameter 226 miles, find the additional area of open sea that was claimed as a result of this action.

Give your answer correct to the nearest thousand square miles.

(b) How much larger (or smaller) is this extra area of sea than the area of Iceland?

For You To Discuss: 2

Trouble in store

Joanne Collier has ideas of setting up a business of her own one day, but at the moment she is working in a large department store to try to learn as much as she can about the problems of running a business. She has moved around from one department to another and often sits in on departmental meetings. Sometimes she has been asked to contribute. There was a very interesting case some time ago when inflation was quite high. Prices were increasing every few months. At one meeting a problem about the price of trainers was discussed. The head of section reported a conversation he had had with Gemma, one of his sales assistants. Gemma was aware that the shop was buying a certain brand of trainers for £16 a pair and was selling them for £24 a pair. When a new price list arrived, which increased the cost to the store from £16 to £24, the selling price of their existing stock was immediately put up from £24 to £36. Gemma thought that this was very unfair. The argument the head of section put to her was this: 'If we sell the first pair of trainers for £24 we certainly make a profit of £8, but we must put the extra capital immediately to buy-in a new pair to replace the stock we have sold. We must pay £24 for them, and so we will be in exactly the same position as we were before the sale. That is, we will have originally paid out £16, made a sale, but made no profit since we had to spend all the income immediately on another pair of trainers to replace the pair we had sold. We can't carry on in business if we don't make a profit.'

On another occasion Joanne sat in on a meeting of the Food Department. They were discussing proposals for new packaging that had recently been received from one of their cereal manufacturers. The manufacturer was proposing to change the shape of the packaging from rectangular boxes to packaging that was cylindrical or oval in cross-section. They wanted to get away from straight lines and straight edges because they thought they were uninteresting. Curves they suggested were far more interesting. One of the senior sales assistants pointed out that it was most unlikely that sales would be increased by changing the shape of the packaging. The public would always buy cereals so they should keep the packaging as it is, and in any case rectangular packets were much easier to handle than any other shape. Another member of staff pointed out that since cereals were so bulky all the available space should be used most effectively and this meant using rectangular boxes as they always had. It would be better for the manufacturer to reconsider the size of the box, perhaps they could reduce its height since. 'There always appears to be empty space in the top of a packet when you open it'. A third member of staff thought that the store could give far more attention to different widths of shelves, different distances between the shelves and things like that. He pointed out that a top priority is how much profit the company makes from each square foot of floor space and he thought that on this point alone rectangular boxes were best.

The third meeting Joanne sat in on was one to decide at what price they should sell a new line and how many they should buy in for the launch. It was obvious that the more they bought the better price they could get. In theory the better the price they bought at, the more profit they could make, but she soon discovered that it wasn't quite as simple as that. The best price they can sell at would not necessarily come from buying the largest possible number. Some of the problems they had to consider were: If we buy too many where do we store them until they are sold? What if we buy a large number and find that they do not sell? We'll have lost a lot of money. What is the lead time – i.e. how quickly can we get additional deliveries if we need them? How much money can we afford to put into this launch? How much do we spend on promoting it? A market research team had also done some work for them. They had showed that lowering the price would probably increase sales but increased sales would not, above a certain figure, lead to increased profits. The longer the meeting went on the more questions seemed to be asked and the more uncertain everybody seemed of the answers.

Many more interesting problems have come up since Joanne has been working at the department store, but perhaps we can come back to those at some other time?

Questions and points for discussion

(a) Joanne could see that the argument put forward for increasing the price of the trainers immediately, that is increasing the price of the old stock, was a sound one, but Gemma had not been convinced. Was it a fair thing to do? What do you think? Discuss other possible solutions.

(b) Why are cereals usually sold in rectangular boxes?

(c) Why do you find unused space at the top of a packet of cereal when it is opened?

(d) Can you add anything to the discussion on packaging? Maybe you could do some research to see how your local department store or supermarket arranges cereals on its shelves. Would you change the width of the shelving or the distance between the shelves? Take some measurements. Make some calculations. Can you improve things for the company and/or the customer? Are the shapes of the cereal packets influenced by the shapes of the larger boxes (called 'outers') in which the packets arrive at the store?

(e) Can you suggest a reason why some items are available in shops for a short time and then never seen again?

(f) Joanne soon realised that one of the biggest problems with most businesses is 'cash flow'. This is caused because too many bills come in at the same time or because customers take too long to pay their bills. Do you have these problems with your personal finances? Make out a detailed list of your income and expenditure for a week or a month or a year. When are the pressure points? What can you do to ease them? Can some problems be avoided by planning well ahead? Once you've made a plan it is important to stick to it?

UNIT 7 Time and Travel

After studying this unit you will be able to solve problems involving
- [ ] The calendar
- [ ] a.m./p.m. time
- [ ] the 24-hour clock
- [ ] bus, train and air timetables
- [ ] movement between time zones
- [ ] distance tables
- [ ] distance, speed and time
- [ ] package holidays
- [ ] foreign exchange
- [ ] travel insurance.

The calendar

The calendar is the division of years into months, weeks and days and the method of ordering the years. For our calendar every month has either 30 or 31 days, except February which has 28 days in an ordinary year but 29 every fourth year (called a leap year). Century years that are not divisible by 400 e.g. 1700, 1800, 1900, are the exception to this rule.

Exercise 7a

January								February								March							
M	T	W	T	F	S	S		M	T	W	T	F	S	S		M	T	W	T	F	S	S
						1			1	2	3	4	5				1	2	3	4	5
2	3	4	5	6	7	8		6	7	8	9	10	11	12		6	7	8	9	10	11	12
9	10	11	12	13	14	15		13	14	15	16	17	18	19		13	14	15	16	17	18	19
16	17	18	19	20	21	22		20	21	22	23	24	25	26		20	21	22	23	24	25	26
23	24	25	26	27	28	29		27	28							27	28	29	30	31
30	31

April								May								June							
M	T	W	T	F	S	S		M	T	W	T	F	S	S		M	T	W	T	F	S	S
					1	2		1	2	3	4	5	6	7				1	2	3	4
3	4	5	6	7	8	9		8	9	10	11	12	13	14		5	6	7	8	9	10	11
10	11	12	13	14	15	16		15	16	17	18	19	20	21		12	13	14	15	16	17	18
17	18	19	20	21	22	23		22	23	24	25	26	27	28		19	20	21	22	23	24	25
24	25	26	27	28	29	30		29	30	31						26	27	28	29	30

July								August								July							
M	T	W	T	F	S	S		M	T	W	T	F	S	S		M	T	W	T	F	S	S
					1	2		1	2	3	4	5	6						1	2	3
3	4	5	6	7	8	9		7	8	9	10	11	12	13		4	5	6	7	8	9	10
10	11	12	13	14	15	16		14	15	16	17	18	19	20		11	12	13	14	15	16	17
17	18	19	20	21	22	23		21	22	23	24	25	26	27		18	19	20	21	22	23	24
24	25	26	27	28	29	30		28	29	30	31					25	26	27	28	29	30
31

October								November								December							
M	T	W	T	F	S	S		M	T	W	T	F	S	S		M	T	W	T	F	S	S
						1			1	2	3	4	5						1	2	3
2	3	4	5	6	7	8		6	7	8	9	10	11	12		4	5	6	7	8	9	10
9	10	11	12	13	14	15		13	14	15	16	17	18	19		11	12	13	14	15	16	17
16	17	18	19	20	21	22		20	21	22	23	24	25	26		18	19	20	21	22	23	24
23	24	25	26	27	28	29		27	28	29	30					25	26	27	28	29	30	31
30	31

The questions that follow refer to the calendar given above.

1 How many days are there in
   (a) February   (b) November?

2 Is this a calendar for a leap year?

3 Which month is
   (a) three months after May   (b) 5 months before October?

4 How many weekends are there between 1 June and 1 September?

5 How many Fridays are there in
   (a) March   (b) April?

6 In how many months of the year are there five Saturdays?

7 Today is 27 May.
   (a) What day of the week is it?
   (b) What was the date last Saturday?
   (c) What will be the date a week next Wednesday?

8 Yesterday was the second Thursday in September.
   (a) What is the date today?
   (b) What was the date a week yesterday?
   (c) What will be the date next Monday?

9 Terri leaves on 25 August for a ten-night holiday in Majorca. What date is she due to return?

10 Mandy Black goes on holiday on 27 August and returns on 11 September. How many nights will she be away?

11 Todd's first term in college starts on 11 September and finishes on 15 December.
(a) How many weeks is this?

He is given his first project on the second Tuesday of term. It is to be completed and handed in so that the lecturer has two weeks to mark it and can return the project to him on the last Tuesday of term.
(b) On what date is Todd given his project?
(c) How long does Todd have to work on it before he is due to hand it in?

12 Steve injures his leg playing soccer in an evening match played on 8 February. He is off work until 20 March and cannot resume playing soccer for a further three weeks. Assuming that he works a 5-day week and that matches are played every Wednesday and Saturday:
(a) How many days work does he miss?
(b) For how many matches is he unavailable for selection?

Time

Each day is divided into hours, each hour into minutes and each minute into seconds, where
    1 day = 24 hours
    1 hour = 60 minutes
  1 minute = 60 seconds.
Using the 12-hour clock we denote times before midday by the letters a.m. and times after midday by the letters p.m.

For example, 3 a.m. means 3 hours after midnight, i.e. in the 12-hour period before noon, whereas 3 p.m. means 3 hours after midday.

Exercise 7b

1 How long is it
(a) from 7.15 a.m. to 10.00 p.m.
(b) from 10.28 a.m. to 12.36 p.m.
(c) from 10 a.m. to 6 p.m. the next day?

2 Neale starts work at 8 a.m. He takes 25 minutes to travel to work and needs 15 minutes to get ready. What time should he aim to get up?

3 Lynne went to work on Saturday morning to do some overtime. She clocked in at 8.18 a.m. and clocked off at 12.22 p.m.
(a) How long did she work?
(b) She is paid for complete periods of 15 minutes only. At what time could she have clocked off but still receive the same pay?

4 Given below are the television programmes for BBC1 and ITV one evening.

BBC1	ITV
6.00 Dad's Army	**6.00** Gladiators
6.30 Big Break	**7.00** Blind Date
7.00 Noel's House Party	**8.00** New Murder She Wrote
8.00 Casualty	**8.50** News
8.50 News and Sport	**9.20** Regional News and
9.10 Film: Planes, Trains	Weather
and Automobiles	**9.35** Film: The January Man
10.40 Match of the Day	**11.20** The Big Fight
11.40 Golf	**12.20 a.m.** The Champ of the
1.10 - 1.15 a.m. Weather	Casbah

(a) How long is it   (i) from the end of Dad's Army to the beginning of Match of the Day   (ii) from the end of Blind Date to the beginning of The Big Fight?

(b) How many minutes is
(i) News and Sport on BBC1   (ii) the ITV News?

(c) Which film is the longer, and by how much: Planes, Trains and Automobiles or The January Man?

(d) Sam saw the last 10 minutes of Blind Date and remained televising until the end of The January Man. How long was this?

(e) When Planes, Trains and Automobiles finished Janice turned over to watch what remained of The January Man. How much of this film   (i) did she see   (ii) had she missed?

The 24-hour clock
Rail, bus and aircraft timetables usually use the 24-hour clock, since the companies that run these services believe that the 24-hour system leads to fewer mistakes than would occur using the more familiar a.m./p.m. times.

In the 24-hour clock, four figures are always used. The first two give the number of hours after midnight, and the last two the number of minutes past that hour.
In the 24-hour system 7.30 a.m. is written as 0730 or 07.30. The same time in the evening, 7.30 p.m., is written 19.30 i.e. we add 12 to the hours number.

Similarly 9.15 p.m. converts to 21.15.

Most digital clocks use the 24-hour system. It is therefore important that we understand both systems and can convert quickly from one system to the other.

Exercise 7c

Question Gavin Lawlor rings Inquiries to find the times of the early evening trains to London for his father. He finds that the most suitable train leaves at 18.53 and arrives in London at 20.22. His father does not understand the 24-hour clock very well so he has to convert these times for him.
(a) What times does he tell his father
    (i) the train leaves (ii) the train is due to arrive in London?
(b) How long, in minutes, is the train journey supposed to take?
(c) His father wants to return home at 1.15 p.m. the following day.
    (i) What time would the timetable show as the time that the train is due to leave? (ii) If the homeward journey takes exactly the same time as the outward journey what time is it due at the local station?
Give your answer in a.m./p.m. time.

Answer (a) (i) 18.53 is 6.53 p.m. (18.53–12.00)
      (ii) 20.22 is 8.22 p.m. (20.22–12.00).
(b) From 6.53 p.m. to 7.00 p.m. is 7 minutes
    from 7.00 p.m. to 8.22 p.m. is 1 hour and 22 minutes
    ∴ total time is (7 + 60 + 22) minutes i.e. 89 minutes.
(c) (i) 1.15 p.m. is 13.15 in the 24-hour system
      (ii) Homeward journey takes 89 minutes i.e. 1 hr 29 min.
If the train leaves at 1.15 p.m., it will arrive at the local station at
1.15 p.m. + 1 hr 29 min
i.e. at 2.44 p.m.

1 Sally Tranter left work for home at twenty-five to six in the afternoon. Write this
(a) in a.m./p.m. time
(b) as it would appear on a 24-hr clock.

2 How many minutes are there
(a) from 08.27 to 20.19
(b) from 03.44 to 18.27
(c) from 22.16 to 08.41 the next morning?

3 One day last winter, lighting up time started at 16.54 and ended at 07.25 the next day. How long was this?

4 What time is it
(a) 25 minutes after 15.45
(b) 54 minutes before 10.20
(c) 4 hr 18 min after 20.55
(d) 6 hr 55 min before 03.45

Question Part of the time table for buses between Brixford and Chatley is shown below.

Brixford	dep	08.34	09.15	11.04	12.48
Canley	dep	08.46	09.27	11.16	13.00
Durseley	arr	09.00	09.41	11.30	13.14
	dep	09.02	09.43	11.32	13.16
Ganton	dep	09.21	09.58	11.51	13.35
Jenwood	dep	09.34	10.08	12.04	13.48
Chatley	arr	09.46	10.20	12.16	14.04

(a) At what time should George leave Canley to get to Jenwood by 11 a.m.?

(b) How long does the 11.04 from Brixford take to travel from Durseley to Chatley?

Answer (Try to use a straight edge, such as a ruler, to read across a table. In this table there are four columns of times; each column refers to a different bus. Reading down any column shows the times at which that bus will arrive at, or depart from, the place named.)

(a) The latest time before 11 a.m. that George can arrive in Jenwood is 10.08. This bus leaves Canley at 9.27
∴ George must leave Canley at 9.27
(When the departure time only is given in a timetable, assume that this is also the arrival time. The bus will arrive, put down and pick up any passengers, then leave immediately.)

(b) The 11.04 from Brixford departs from Durseley at 11.32 and arrives in Chatley at 12.16
Time taken is the time from 11.32 to 12.16
i.e. 28 minutes (up to 12.00) + 16 minutes (after 12.00) = 44 minutes.

5 For this question use the table given in the worked example.
(a) At what time should Sophie leave Brixford to make
(i) the quickest journey to Chatley
(ii) the slowest journey to Chatley?
(b) How long does it take to travel from Canley to Durseley?
(c) Ross Telfer misses the 09.15 from Brixford by 3 minutes
(i) How long must he wait for the next bus?
(ii) What time should he then arrive at Ganton?
(iii) How much later is this than if he had caught the bus he had intended to catch?
(d) Bryn lives in Canley and has an appointment in Jenwood at 11.45. If it takes him 10 minutes to walk to the bus stop, what is the latest time he can leave home to keep his appointment?

6

Bristol Parkway – Cardiff – Swansea
London →
Bath – Bristol Temple Meads
SATURDAYS

	RR	IC	IC	IC R	IC R	IC	IC R	iC H	iC J	IC R	IC R	IC R	IC R	IC R	IC	IC R
London Paddington d	—	—	0715	0800	0815	0900	0915	0925	0945	1000	1015	1100	1115	1200	1215	1300
Slough d	—	—	0703	0753	0804	0853	0930	—	1000	—	1030	1053	1104	1153	1204	1253
Heathrow Airport ; ‡ d	—	—	—	0715	0715	0815	0815	0845	0845	0915	0915	1015	1015	1115	1115	1215
Gatwick Airport d	—	—	0545	0626	0626	0726	0726	—	0826	0826	0826	0926	0945	1026	1026	1126
Reading d	—	—	0741	0826	0841	0926	0945	0954	1015	1026	1045	1126	1141	1226	1241	1326
Didcot Parkway d	—	—	0756	—	0856	—	—	—	1030	—	1100	—	1156	—	1256	—
Swindon a	—	0705d	0816	0857	0916	0957	1016	—	1050	1057	1120	1157	1216	1257	1316	1357
Chippenham a	—	0721	0830	—	0930	—	1030	—	—	—	1134	—	1230	—	1330	—
Bath Spa a	—	0736	0844	—	0944	—	1044	—	—	—	1148	—	1244	—	1344	—
Bristol Parkway a	0713d	—	—	0925	—	1025	—	—	1118	1127	—	1225	—	1325	—	1425
Bristol Temple Meads a	—	0752	0855	—	0955	—	1055	—	—	—	1159	—	1255	—	1355	—
Weston-super-Mare a	—	0830	0920	—	1020	—	1120	—	—	—	1225	—	1320	—	1420	—
Newport a	0736	—	—	0948	—	1048	—	—	1141	1150	—	1248	—	1348	—	1448
Hereford a	—	—	—	1044	—	1143	—	—	—	1244	—	1343	—	1444	—	1543
Cardiff Central a	0751	—	—	1001	—	1101	—	1120	1156	1203	—	1301	—	1401	—	1501
Bridgend a	0811	—	—	1023	—	1123	—	—	—	1225	—	1323	—	1423	—	1523
Port Talbot Parkway a	0822	—	—	1034	—	1134	—	—	—	1236	—	1334	—	1434	—	1534
Neath a	0830	—	—	1042	—	1142	—	—	—	1244	—	1342	—	1442	—	1542
Swansea a	0842	—	—	1055	—	1155	—	—	—	1258	—	1358	—	1458	—	1558

Source: British Rail Intercity Great Western.

The timetable shows some of the scheduled train services between London and Swansea, and between London and Bristol, on Mondays to Friday. Times in light print indicate a connecting service, whereas times in **heavy type** show direct journeys.

(a) How long does the 0815 from Paddington take to get to
  (i) Swindon   (ii) Bristol Temple Meads?

(b) How many of the listed trains travel non-stop from Paddington to Reading?

(c) Which train must Erin Sherrin catch from Paddington to get to Cardiff by 1340?

(d) How long does it take   (i) to go from Swindon to Newport on the 0900 from Paddington   (ii) from Reading to Swansea on the first available train after 1015?

(e) Phil needs to get to Bristol Parkway by 1200. What is the latest time he can leave Paddington?

(f) Sam and Liz leave Gatwick Airport on the 0826 train that connects with the main London to South Wales train at Reading.   (i) What time are they due to catch their connection at Reading?   (ii) What is the earliest time they can hope to reach Swansea?   (iii) How long is their journey from Gatwick to Swansea?

Time zones

If you fly to Spain for a holiday, leaving the United Kingdom at 0800 you may find that you arrive in Spain at 1200, even though your flight has taken just 3 hours. On the other hand if you leave Spain at 1500 and again enjoy a 3 hour flight you will arrive back in the United Kingdom at 1700. The reason for this apparent contradiction is that *local time* in Spain is one hour ahead of local time in the United Kingdom.

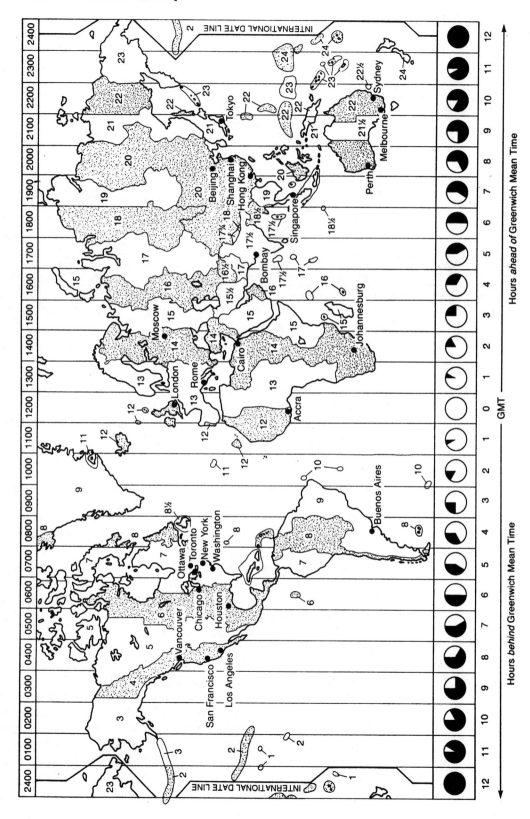

When it is 12 noon in London it is midnight in New Zealand, 8 p.m. in Singapore and 6 a.m. in Chicago. So that we all know how local time in one part of the world is related to local time in another part, we divide the Earth's surface into twenty-four time zones. Local time or clock time in all these zones is related to Greenwich Mean Time (GMT). Greenwich was the site of the Royal Observatory just outside London. In countries to the east of Greenwich the sun rises earlier, so their time is *ahead* of GMT. In countries to the west of Greenwich the sun rises later, so their time is *behind* GMT. The map on p. 170 shows the time in each zone when it is 1200 GMT. The figures beneath this map show the number of hours each zone is ahead or behind GMT.

The zig-zag line drawn from the north pole to the south pole through the Pacific Ocean so that it doesn't pass through any land mass is called the International Date Line. If you cross this imaginary line from east to west (for example if you fly from America to China) you lose a day, that is, if it is 23 August as you approach the line from the American side the date changes to 24 August once you have crossed it. On the other hand, if you cross the date line in the opposite direction i.e. if you go from west to east, then you move the date back one day and hence gain a day.

Exercise 7d

Question Sid and Evelyn Dobson leave London Heathrow at 11.30 a.m. to fly to Vancouver. The flight takes 9 hours. If the time in Vancouver is 8 hours behind the time in London
(a) what time, London time, will they arrive
(b) what time, local time, will they arrive?

Answer (a) (It is probably easier to answer a question like this using the 24-hour clock.) When they arrive in Vancouver the time in London is 11.30 a.m. + 9 hours
$$= 11.30 + 9.00$$
$$= 20.30$$
i.e. they arrive in Vancouver at 8.30 p.m. London time.
(b) When it is 20.30 in London the time in Vancouver is 8 hours behind
i.e. $20.30 - 8.00 = 12.30$
∴ they arrive in Vancouver at 12.30 p.m. local time.

Use the information on the map on p. 170 to answer Questions 1–5.

1 How many hours is each of the following places ahead of Greenwich Mean Time (GMT)?
(a) Cairo   (b) Hong Kong
(c) Sydney   (d) Tokyo.

2 How many hours is each of the following places behind London time i.e. GMT?
   (a) New York   (b) Vancouver
   (c) Houston   (d) Buenos Aires.

3 When it is 12 noon in London, i.e. 1200 GMT, what time is it in
   (a) Johannesburg   (b) Perth
   (c) Washington   (d) San Francisco?

4 When it is 2 p.m. in London what time is it in
   (a) Rome   (b) Beijing
   (c) Toronto?

5 When it is 10 a.m. in London what time is it in
   (a) Los Angeles   (b) Melbourne
   (c) Accra?

   For the remaining questions in this exercise, the map may be found useful, but each problem can be solved without it.

6 The time in New York is 5 hours behind the time in London. What time is it
   (a) in New York when it is noon in London
   (b) in London when it is 8 p.m. in New York?

7 Moscow time is 3 hours ahead of London time while the time in Ottawa is 5 hours behind London. What time is it
   (a) in Moscow when it is 8 a.m. in Ottawa
   (b) in Ottawa when it is midnight in Moscow?

8 The distance from London to Bombay is approximately 4500 miles. A jet leaves London for Bombay at 10 a.m. and flies at an average speed of 500 miles per hour.
   (a) Approximately, how long does the journey take?
   (b) If the time in Bombay is $5\frac{1}{2}$ hours ahead of London time what time will it be in Bombay when the plane arrives?

9 During the summer months, the United Kingdom uses British Summer Time (BST) which is one hour ahead of GMT. When it is 8 a.m. BST in London what time is it
   (a) in Shanghai, which is 8 hours ahead of GMT
   (b) in Chicago, which is 6 hours behind GMT?

10 What happens to the date as
   (a) you fly from Sydney to San Francisco, thereby crossing the International Date Line from west to east
   (b) you fly from Los Angles to Tokyo and cross the International Date Line from east to west?

Distance tables

Many books of road maps give tables that enable us to find out quickly how far it is from one place to another.

Exercise 7e

Use the following table to answer the questions that follow.

Distances are in miles

	London	Birmingham	Cardiff	Edinburgh	Leeds	Manchester	Sheffield
Birmingham	111						
Cardiff	155	101					
Edinburgh	378	286	365				
Leeds	190	111	212	199			
Manchester	192	81	172	209	40		
Sheffield	162	75	176	235	36	64	
York	196	134	242	186	24	103	56

1 How far is it
 (a) from London to Manchester   (b) from Edinburgh to York?

2 Which two cities are
 (a) nearest together   (b) furthest apart?

3 Which city is
 (a) nearest to Edinburgh   (b) furthest from Sheffield?

4 How much further is Birmingham from Edinburgh than Manchester is from Cardiff?

5 How far is it
 (a) from Cardiff to York via Manchester
 (b) from London to Sheffield via Birmingham?

Speed, distance and time

Speed compares distance with time. It is the distance travelled in one unit of time. Speed is frequently measured in metres per second (m/s), kilometres per hour (km/h) or miles per hour (m.p.h.)

Suppose a train travels 150 miles in 2 hours. This journey may include times when the train is moving slowly or even stopped because of a red signal. The steady speed that allows the train to travel the same distance in the same time is called the *average speed*. In this case, if the train travels 150 miles in 2 hours we say that the average speed of the train is 75 m.p.h.

$$\text{average speed} = \frac{\text{total distance travelled}}{\text{total time}}$$

from which we also have

$$\text{total distance travelled} = \text{average speed} \times \text{total time}$$

and

$$\text{total time} = \frac{\text{total distance travelled}}{\text{average speed}}$$

Exercise 7f

1 A car travels 160 miles in 4 hours. Find its average speed.

2 Georgina takes 3 hours to pedal 45 kilometres. Find her average speed.

3 An aeroplane travels at an average speed of 450 m.p.h. for 3 hours. How far does it travel?

4 A middle distance runner takes 4 minutes to run 1500 metres. Find his average speed in metres per minute.

Question   In training, a long distance runner takes 2 hours 20 minutes to run 14 miles. Find his average speed in miles per hour.

Answer

20 minutes	$= \frac{20}{60}$ hours $= \frac{1}{3}$ hr
∴ time taken	$= 2$ hr $+ \frac{1}{3}$ hr
	$= 2\frac{1}{3}$ hr

$$\text{average speed} = \frac{\text{total distance}}{\text{total time}}$$

$$= 14 \div 2\tfrac{1}{3} \text{ miles per hour}$$
$$= {}_2\!14 \div \tfrac{7}{3} \text{ m.p.h.}$$
$$= \cancel{14} \times \tfrac{3}{\cancel{7}} \text{ m.p.h.}$$

i.e. his average running speed is 6 m.p.h.

---

5 An intercity express travels the 32 miles from Dingeston to Lexley in 20 minutes. Express this speed in
(a) miles per minute   (b) miles per hour.

6 An international sprinter ran 100 metres in 10 seconds dead. Give his average speed in
(a) metres per second   (b) metres per minute
(c) metres per hour   (d) kilometres per hour.

Question   A college student returned from London to her home in the north. She travelled for 1 hr at an average speed of 35 m.p.h. followed by 3 hr at an average speed of 55 m.p.h. Find her average speed for the whole journey.

Answer

Distance travelled	= average speed × time taken
Distance travelled in 1 hr at 35 m.p.h.	= 35 × 1 miles = 35 miles
Distance travelled in 3 hr at 55 m.p.h.	= 55 × 3 miles = 165 miles

∴ total distance travelled = 35 miles + 165 miles = 200 miles
and total time taken = 1 hr + 3 hr = 4 hr

$$\text{average speed} = \frac{\text{total distance}}{\text{total time}} = \frac{200 \text{ miles}}{4 \text{ hr}}$$

$$= 50 \text{ m.p.h.}$$

7 An aircraft travels for 3 hours at an average speed of 400 m.p.h. but then a headwind reduces its average speed to 340 m.p.h. for the remaining hour of the journey. Find
(a) the total distance travelled
(b) the total time taken
(c) the average speed for the whole journey.

8 Neal walks the $\frac{1}{2}$ mile from his home to the bus stop at an average speed of 4 m.p.h. and immediately catches the bus that takes him the 10 miles to college at an average speed of 20 m.p.h. Find his average speed for the whole journey.

9 Andy wanted to make the 110 kilometre trip to Birmingham in 2 hours. He travelled the first 60 kilometres at an average speed of 45 km/h, and the next 30 kilometres at an average speed of 90 km/h. What must be the average speed for the final 20 kilometres if he is to arrive on time?

10 *Canberra* sails from Southampton at 6 p.m. one Saturday and returns at 6 a.m. the following Saturday. During the time she is away she is in foreign ports for a total of 48 hours, but apart from her time in these ports she is cruising at a steady speed of 22 knots.
(a) How many hours is it from the time she leaves Southampton until she returns?
(b) For how many of these hours is she cruising?
(c) How many nautical miles has she travelled?
(d) How many land miles is this given that 1 nautical mile is equivalent to 1.15 land miles?
      (1 knot = 1 nautical mile per hour.)

Package holidays

Most people find it easier to buy a package holiday from a travel agent than to make all the arrangements themselves.

On p. 176 some typical information from a travel brochure is reproduced. The details refer to package holidays in Corfu, either on half-board at the Aloe Hotel or self-catering at Paleo Village. The flight details from various UK airports are given in a separate table. In addition there is a bar chart that shows the amount of sunshine that can be expected during the holiday period.

You will need these tables to answer the questions in Exercise 7g.

Exercise 7g

Questions 1–5 refer to the bar chart.

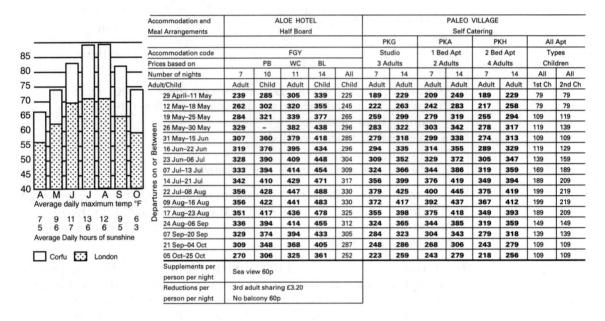

85
80
75
70
65
60
55
50
45
40

A M J J A S O
Average daily maximum temp °F

7 9 11 13 12 9 6
5 6 7 6 6 5 3
Average Daily hours of sunshine

☐ Corfu   ⬚ London

Accommodation and Meal Arrangements	ALOE HOTEL Half Board					PALEO VILLAGE Self Catering							
						PKG Studio 3 Adults		PKA 1 Bed Apt 2 Adults		PKH 2 Bed Apt 4 Adults		All Apt Types Children	
Accommodation code	FGY												
Prices based on		PB	WC	BL									
Number of nights	7	10	11	14	All	7	14	7	14	7	14	All	All
Adult/Child	Adult	Child	Adult	Adult	Child	Adult	Adult	Adult	Adult	Adult	Adult	1st Ch	2nd Ch
29 April–11 May	239	285	305	339	225	189	229	209	249	189	229	79	79
12 May–18 May	262	302	320	355	245	222	263	242	283	217	258	79	79
19 May–25 May	284	321	339	377	265	259	299	279	319	255	294	109	119
26 May–30 May	329	–	382	438	296	283	322	303	342	278	317	119	139
31 May–15 Jun	307	360	379	418	285	279	318	299	338	274	313	109	109
16 Jun–22 Jun	319	376	395	434	296	294	335	314	355	289	329	119	129
23 Jun–06 Jul	328	390	409	448	304	309	352	329	372	305	347	139	159
07 Jul–13 Jul	333	394	414	454	309	324	366	344	386	319	359	169	189
14 Jul–21 Jul	342	410	429	471	317	356	399	376	419	349	394	189	209
22 Jul–08 Aug	356	428	447	488	330	379	425	400	445	375	419	199	219
09 Aug–16 Aug	356	422	441	483	330	372	417	392	437	367	412	199	219
17 Aug–23 Aug	351	417	436	478	325	355	398	375	418	349	393	189	209
24 Aug–06 Sep	336	394	414	455	312	324	365	344	385	319	359	149	149
07 Sep–20 Sep	329	374	394	433	305	284	323	304	343	279	318	139	139
21 Sep–04 Oct	309	348	368	405	287	248	286	268	306	243	279	109	109
05 Oct–25 Oct	270	306	325	361	252	223	259	243	279	218	256	109	109
Supplements per person per night	Sea view 60p												
Reductions per person per night	3rd adult sharing £3.20 No balcony 60p												

CORFU (Corfu Airport)

Departure Airport	No. of Nights	Day of Dept.	Time of Dept.	Day of Return	Time of Return	Departures	Flight Code	27 APR-30 MAY	31 MAY-6 JULY	7 JULY-21 JULY	22 JULY-8 AUG	9 AUG-28 OCT
GATWICK (3 hrs)	7/14	FRI	06.45	FRI	13.45	29 APR-21 OCT	32200	£27	£27	£27	£29	£29
	11	FRI	06.45	TUE	14.15	29 APR-21 OCT	32200	£19	£19	£19	£21	£21
	7/14	FRI	14.45	FRI	22.00	29 APR-28 OCT	32201	£17	£17	£17	£19	£19
	7/14	SUN	22.45	MON	06.00	1 MAY-23 OCT	32202	£3	£3	£3	£5	£5
	7/14	TUE	07.00	TUE	14.15	3 MAY-25 OCT	32203	£24	£21	£21	£26	£23
	10	TUE	07.00	FRI	13.45	3 MAY-18 OCT	32203	£12	£12	£12	£14	£14
	7/14	TUE	23.45	WED	07.15	3 MAY-25 OCT	32204	£0	£0	£0	£0	£0
LUTON (3¼ hrs)	7/14	FRI	21.00	SAT	04.15	29 APR-21 OCT	32208	£7	£5	£5	£7	£7
	11	FRI	21.00	WED	02.30	6 MAY-21 OCT	32208	£0	£0	£0	£0	£0
	7/14	TUE	19.15	WED	02.30	3 MAY-25 OCT	32209	£0	£0	£0	£0	£0
	7/14	TUE	21.00	SAT	04.15	3 MAY-25 OCT	32209	£0	£0	£0	£0	£0
STANSTED	7/14	TUE	21.00	WED	04.15	3 MAY-25 OCT	32212	£0	£0	£0	£0	£0
NORWICH	7/14	SUN	08.15	SUN	15.45	1 MAY-23 OCT	32213	£55	£49	£25	£32	£46
BRISTOL	7/14	TUE	21.15	WED	04.45	3 MAY-25 OCT	32214	£11	£11	£11	£13	£13
CARDIFF	7/14	FRI	15.15	FRI	23.00	3 MAY-25 OCT	32216	£28	£28	£12	£49	£30
BIRMINGHAM (3¼ hrs)	7/14	TUE	07.30	TUE	15.00	3 MAY-25 OCT	32218	£29	£29	£14	£41	£32
	10	TUE	07.30	SAT	05.00	3 MAY-18 OCT	32218	£5	£5	£0	£12	£7
	7/14	FRI	21.30	SAT	05.00	6 MAY-21 OCT	32219	£19	£19	£0	£34	£21

Departure Airport	No. of Nights	Day of Dept.	Time of Dept.	Day of Return	Time of Return	Departures	Flight Code	27 APR-30 MAY	31 MAY-6 JULY	7 JULY-21 JULY	22 JULY-8 AUG	9 AUG-28 OCT
BIRMINGHAM	11	FRI	21.30	TUE	15.00	6 MAY-21 OCT	32219	£25	£25	£10	£37	£27
	7/14	SUN	22.15	MON	05.45	1 MAY-23 OCT	32220	£12	£9	£0	£11	£11
EAST MIDLANDS (3¼ hrs)	7/14	FRI	07.30	FRI	15.00	6 MAY-21 OCT	32223	£39	£39	£33	£37	£37
	11	FRI	07.30	WED	00.30	6 MAY-21 OCT	32223	£25	£25	£15	£22	£22
	7/14	TUE	06.45	WED	00.30	3 MAY-25 OCT	32224	£25	£25	£16	£23	£23
	10	TUE	06.45	FRI	15.00	3 MAY-18 OCT	32224	£21	£21	£21	£23	£23
MANCHESTER (3¼ hrs)	7/14	FRI	21.00	SAT	05.00	29 APR-21 OCT	32227	£24	£24	£26	£26	£23
	7/14	FRI	08.45	FRI	16.30	6 MAY-21 OCT	32228	£42	£42	£42	£44	£44
	11	FRI	08.45	TUE	22.45	6 MAY-21 OCT	32228	£29	£29	£29	£31	£31
	7/14	SUN	08.00	SUN	15.45	1 MAY-23 OCT	32229	£42	£42	£42	£44	£44
	7/14	SUN	17.15	MON	01.00	1 MAY-23 OCT	32230	£19	£19	£19	£21	£21
	7/14	TUE	15.15	TUE	22.45	3 MAY-25 OCT	32231	£33	£33	£33	£31	£31
	10	TUE	15.15	FRI	16.30	3 MAY-18 OCT	32231	£25	£25	£25	£27	£27
LEEDS BRADFORD	7/14	TUE	16.45	TUE	14.30	3 MAY-25 OCT	32235	£43	£31	£17	£23	£33
TEESSIDE	7/14	SUN	19.45	SUN	18.30	1 MAY-23 OCT	32237	£39	£39	£33	£41	£41
NEWCASTLE	7/14	FRI	07.45	FRI	15.45	29 APR-21 OCT	32239	£44	£44	£59	£46	£46
	7/14	SUN	10.30	MON	03.45	1 MAY-23 OCT	32240	£32	£32	£17	£44	£34
GLASGOW	7/14	TUE	21.45	WED	05.45	3 MAY-25 OCT	32243	£12	£45	£59	£27	£27

1 Which months in Corfu are the hottest?

2 On an average day in July
   (a) how much hotter is it in Corfu than in London
   (b) how many more hours sunshine are there in Corfu than in London?

3 In September Sharon and Don have booked to spend 12 days in Corfu. In total, how many more hours sunshine can they expect than if they stay in London?

4 (a) In a single day in October how many more hours sunshine should there be in Corfu than in London?
   (b) During the month of May how many more hours sunshine should there be in Corfu than in London?

5 In which months is the difference in temperature between London and Corfu
   (a) greatest
   (b) least?
   Estimate these differences.

Question Find the cost of a 14-night holiday for 4 adults in a two-bedroomed apartment at the Paleo Village, leaving home on 30 August.

Answer (We go down the first column as far as the entry 24 Aug–06 Sep, since this includes 30 Aug, which is the date of departure. From here we move across until we come to the heading for a 2 Bed Apt for 4 adults for 14 nights at Paleo Village. The figure in the table is 359.)
∴ the cost for four adults is 4 × £359 = £1436.

Do not add any flight supplements for Questions 6–9.

6 What is the cost of a 14-night holiday for two adults in a one-bedroom apartment at Paleo Village, leaving on 18 May?

7 Len Sutton, together with his wife and three children, leave on 26 July for a 10-night holiday at the Aloe Hotel. How much will it cost them?

8 (a) What is the latest date on which a couple can leave the UK to get the cheapest rate for a 7-night holiday at the Aloe?
   (b) How much more is it to stay at the Aloe than to book a one-bedroom apartment at Paleo Village for the same week?

9 Ted and Meg Bray book a 14-night holiday for themselves and their two children in a two-bedroomed apartment at Paleo Village. How much will the holiday cost them
   (a) if they leave on 23 June?
   (b) if they leave on the last day of July?

Question   The Jarret family (husband, wife and three children) book a 10-night holiday at the Aloe Hotel. They plan to fly from Gatwick on Tuesday 12 July.
(a) How much, in total, must they pay the travel agent if, in addition to the brochure price, £85.50 is added to cover insurance?
(b) The travel agent requires a deposit of 10% of the brochure price plus the cost of insurance, at the time of booking. How much is this?

Answer   (a) (Go down to 07 Jul–13 Jul (their departure date is 12 July) then across to the column headed Aloe Hotel for 10 nights. The entry in the table is 394. The cost for a child is found on the same line in the next column but three. It is headed 'Child'.)
Brochure price for one adult spending 10 nights at the Aloe leaving on 12 July is £394 and the cost for one child is £309
∴ the cost for 2 adults is 2 × £394   = £788
and the cost for 3 children is 3 × £309   = £927
Flight supplement from Gatwick on a Tuesday for a 10-night holiday between 7 and 21 July is £12 per person.
∴ total for the flight supplements is 5 × £12
                    = £60
Total brochure price   = £788 + £927 + £60
                    = £1775.
Total due to travel agent = total brochure price + cost of insurance
                    = £1775 + £85.50
                    = £1860.50.
(b) Deposit due is 10% of the brochure price i.e. £1775 × $\frac{10}{100}$ = 177.50
∴ amount due at time of booking   = deposit + cost of insurance
                    = £177.50 + £85.50
                    = £263.

The remaining questions require details found in the flight information on p. 176.

10 Jo and James go to the travel agent to book a 14-night holiday in Corfu. They wish to fly out on a Friday or a Saturday. From which airports can they fly?

11 From which airports can you take an 11-night holiday in Corfu. What choice of weekday do you have?

12 Write down the flight supplement, i.e. the extra you have to pay, for
(a) a 7-night holiday from Gatwick leaving on Friday 5 August
(b) a 14-night holiday from Bristol leaving on Tuesday 12 July
(c) a 10-night from Luton leaving on Tuesday 19 July
(d) a 7-night holiday from Glasgow leaving on Tuesday 3 May.

13 How much extra do the flight supplements come to for a family of four, 2 adults and 2 children, if they fly from Newcastle on a Sunday in June?

14 Four couples book a 14-night holiday in Corfu. They wish to fly from Birmingham.
   (a) When should they fly to have the lowest flight supplement?
   (b) Eventually they find it impossible to arrange the holiday during the cheapest time. Instead they decide to fly out on the first Tuesday in August. How much, in total, will it cost them in flight supplements?

15 Jake and Nia book a room with a sea view for a 14-night holiday at the Aloe Hotel. They leave Gatwick on the early morning flight (06.45) on Friday 24 June.
   (a) What is the basic brochure cost?
   (b) How much extra do they pay for a room with a sea view?
   (c) What do the flight supplements come to?
   (d) Find the total cost of the holiday if they take £400 for spending money.

Foreign currency If you have been abroad you know that you cannot spend pounds and pence freely in a foreign country – you have to use the currency of the country in which you find yourself, e.g. pesetas in Spain, drachmas in Greece or dollars in the United States. The number of units of a foreign currency you get for £1 is called the *exchange rate*. You can buy foreign currency from a bank, from some travel agents or through a building society. If you return home, from Spain say, with unspent pesetas, you will have to give more pesetas for every £ you receive than you were given for each £ when you bought them. By offering different buying and selling rates the company exchanging currency for you is able to make money to meet its operating costs. Apart from using different rates they also charge commission, typically 1%, when you convert from one currency to another.

Exercise 7h

Question If £1 is equivalent to 210 Spanish pesetas convert
(a) £75 into pesetas   (b) 8400 pesetas into pounds sterling (£).

Answer (a) £1   = 210 pesetas
           ∴ £75   = 75 × 210 pesetas
           i.e.   £75 = 15 750 pesetas
       (b) (pesetas are often abbreviated to pta.)
           210 pta   = £1
           1 pta   = £$\frac{1}{210}$
           8400 pta   = 8400 × £$\frac{1}{210}$
           i.e. 8400 pta = £40

For Questions 1–6 use the exchange rates given in the following table.

Pound sterling	French franc	Spanish peseta	US dollar	German Deutschmark
£ 1	(Ff) 8.70	(pta) 210	($) 1.50	(DM) 2.50

1   Sara needed French francs to go on holiday.

   (a) How many francs did she get for £250?
   (b) At the end of the holiday she was left with 1740 Ff. What was this worth in pounds?

2   Emma is going to Spain on holiday. What is the value of
   (a) £120 in pesetas   (b) 9660 pta in pounds?

3   Phil and Jen are going to Disneyland for a holiday. Some of the optional tours can be booked before they go. They sit down and work out the cost of the tours of their choice. If they book before they go it will cost them £268; if they wait until they get there the cost is $395. What advice would you give them? Do they book before they go or wait till they get there?

4   Sue has always wanted a good camera. While on holiday she sees the camera she wants in a German shop at DM 380. She is aware that she can buy the same camera at home for £155 and decides against buying in Germany. Later in the holiday she is in France where she sees a similar camera again. It is priced 1400 Ff. She decides to buy. Did she get the best available deal?

5   Ross has heard that it is much cheaper to buy his Christmas drinks in France than locally. He and his wife take the car to France and load up with bottles of wines and spirits for which they pay 1268 Ff. At home they work out that the same goods would have cost £184. If the cost of the ferry trip was £35 how much did they save?

6   What is the exchange rate if a tourist receives
   (a) 124 US dollars in exchange for £80
   (b) 7800 Spanish pesetas in exchange for £40
   (c) 635 Deutschmarks for £250.

7   Paula Blake buys a bottle of perfume in a shop at Rome airport for 85 500 lire. If £1 is equivalent to 2512 lire, how much does she save if a similar bottle costs £30.50 in London?

8   While Harry was on holiday in the United States he saw a Lincoln car priced $28 000. He was told that the car was available in the United Kingdom but that it would cost him 20% more there. Find its UK price if the exchange rate is £1 = $1.491. Give your answer correct to the nearest £10.

9 A tourist changed £500 into French francs when she entered France and the exchange rate was £1 = 8.72 Ff. She did not spend anything in France and when she crossed into Spain her francs were changed into pesetas at the rate of 1 f = 24 pta. Once again she found it unnecessary to spend anything and so, when she returned to Manchester she changed her pesetas into pounds at the rate of 204 pta to the pound. Compared with when she left the UK how much had she gained or lost as a result of the exchanges?

10 Before setting out on a European tour Amjun and Sabina changed £1200 into Belgian francs at a rate of 53 francs to the pound. They spent four days in Belgium, spending 1680 Bf a day on food and accommodation, plus 1260 Bf altogether on other expenses. On the fifth day they crossed into Germany, changing the Belgian francs they still had into Deutschmarks at the rate of DM1 = 20.8 Bf. They stayed in Germany for nine days. Food and accommodation worked out at DM120 a day and they spent an additional DM760 between them on other things. The unspent Deutschmarks were exchanged into pounds when they returned home at a rate of £1 = DM2.58. How much did they receive?

Travel insurance

To lose your luggage or be ill on holiday can, apart from the inconvenience, be very expensive. Most travellers attempt to put their minds at rest by taking out travel insurance.

Like most things the cost of insurance and the extent of the cover varies from one policy to another. Most policies cover lost luggage, hospital and medical expenses, loss of money and tickets, delays, personal accident and personal liability.

The table gives typical premiums for different amounts of cover.

Premium per person for European countries and other countries bordering the Mediterranean	(£)
Up to 9 days	19.95
10–17 days	22.95
Each additional 8 days	3

For countries other than those included above the rates are doubled. The rates are halved for children under 16 on the date of departure. Children under 2 on the day of departure are free.

Exercise 7i

Use the table in the text to answer the questions in this exercise.

Question   Jeff and Judy Berger, together with their two children, Francis aged 12 and Keith aged 16 are going on holiday to Majorca for 14 nights. How much will travel insurance cost them? How much extra would it have cost them if they had gone to America instead?

Answer   Since Keith is 16 the insurance costs for him are the same as those for an adult.
Cost of insurance for one adult for 14 nights in the Mediterranean is £22.95
∴ the cost for two adults plus a child of 16 is 3 × £22.95 = £68.85.
Since the cost of insurance for a child under 16 is half that for an adult, the cost of insurance for Francis is $\frac{1}{2}$ × £22.95 = £11.48 to the nearest penny
∴ total cost for the family of 2 adults and 2 children is £68.85 + £11.48
= £80.33
Since the premiums are doubled for countries outside Europe the cost of travel insurance for the family to go to America is 2 × £80.33
= £160.66

1   How much does travel insurance cost for a family of three (father, mother and child aged 14 years) to go on a 12-day holiday to France?

2   Pete and Dorothy Wells and their children George (aged 12), Max (aged 10) and Adele (aged 7) propose taking a 14-night holiday in Malta. What would the insurance premiums come to?

3   Bill and Sandra Winifred are taking their 14 year old daughter to the United States for a three-week holiday. How much will the insurance premium come to?

4   What are the insurance costs for three adult couples plus four children, all under 16, to go on a twenty-one day holiday to Australia?

5   Ben and Susan George do not like the British winter so they have decided to go to the Spanish resort of Benidorm next winter. They plan to spend 10 weeks there.
(a) How much will travel insurance cost them?
(b) How much is this per person per day?
(c) What would travel insurance cost, in total, if they spend the same amount of time at a resort in Florida instead?

Multiple choice questions

1 Gemma went to see a film at the Odeon. As soon as the film had finished she went home. She took 3 minutes to get to the bus stop, where she waited for 8 minutes before the bus arrived. The bus journey took 26 minutes and she took a further 15 minutes before she arrived home at 23.15. The film finished at

A 22.21   B 22.23

C 22.33   D 22.17

2 Yesterday was Wednesday 16 July. My next visit to the dentist is a week tomorrow. This appointment is on

A Thursday 24 July   B Friday 24 July

C Friday 25 July   D Thursday 23 July

3 The time in London is 10 hours behind the time in Sydney. When it is 6 p.m. in London the time in Sydney is

A 4 a.m.   B 8 a.m.

C 8 a.m. the next day   D 4 a.m. the next day

4 Karen takes 3 minutes to run 600 metres. In kilometres per hour her speed is

A 12 km/h   B 20 km/h

C 18 km/h   D 2 km/h

5 Phil and Meryl book to take their young son Thomas, aged 5, for a 10-night holiday in Spain. The brochure price is £370 per adult, with a 40% reduction for their son. To this price is added 60p per person per night for a sea view and insurance costs which are £22 per adult, children being charged half the adult rate. Which of the following statements are true and which are false?

A The total cost of the insurance for the three of them comes to £57.20

B If they did not take their son the cost of the holiday would be £239 cheaper

C The amount they must pay to the travel agent is £1035

D If they had decided against a sea view the total would be less than £1000

6 Before Melanie went to France she changed £350 into francs at the rate of 8.50 francs to the pound. While on holiday she spent 2575 francs. When she got back home she changed her unspent francs into pounds at the rate of 8.82 francs to the pound. The following statements have been made:

Statement 1 When she returned home the exchange rate had changed in her favour so she got more pounds than she expected for her unspent francs.

Statement 2 The French francs Melanie had spent cost her £302.94 so when she changed back her unspent francs she had £47.06.

How are these statements best described?

A True, True   B True, False

C False, True   D False, False

Self assessment 7

1 (a) How long is it from 2140 tonight to 0715 tomorrow morning?

(b) Sally is due in college by 9.00 a.m. She needs 20 minutes to get ready and 35 minutes to drive to college. What time should she aim to get up if she is to get to college 10 minutes early?

2 Julie leaves home on 23 June for a 14-night holiday in Hong Kong.

(a) What date does she return?

(b) Her non-stop flight leaves London at 11.35 and arrives in Hong Kong at 08.50 local time the next day. If the time in Hong Kong is 8 hours ahead of the time in London, how long was her flight?

(c) The flying distance from London to Hong Kong is given as 5990 miles. Find the average flying speed, giving your answer correct to three significant figures.

(d) On the return flight she leaves Hong Kong at 02.40. The plane encounters a headwind which reduces its average speed to 440 m.p.h. How long should the return flight take?

(e) At what time should she arrive in London?

3 The extract given below shows the costs of various package holidays at the Fiesta Hotel in Tenerife.

Accommodation and Meal Arrangements	FIESTA HOTEL Half Board			
Number of Nights	7	10	11	14
Adult/Child	Adult	Adult	Adult	Adult
01 May – 11 May	299	343	364	424
12 May – 18 May	307	357	378	438
19 May – 25 May	324	368	389	450
26 May – 30 May	352	395	—	463
31 May – 15 Jun	320	377	398	436
16 Jun – 22 Jun	325	405	426	463
23 Jun – 06 Jul	335	416	437	475
07 Jul – 13 Jul	351	425	445	484
14 Jul – 21 Jul	378	440	462	501
22 Jul – 08 Aug	388	466	487	528
09 Aug – 16 Aug	383	453	474	515
17 Aug – 23 Aug	382	445	466	507
24 Aug – 06 Sep	366	440	460	498
07 Sep – 20 Sep	361	437	457	496
21 Sep – 04 Oct	355	419	440	484
05 Oct – 23 Oct	355	419	440	478

Source: Thomson Holidays.

Children under 16 are charged at $\frac{2}{3}$ the adult rate.

(a) Use this extract to find the brochure price of a holiday at the Fiesta for Tim Saxton, his wife and two children, aged 6 and 10, if they leave on Friday 22 July for 14 nights.

(b) To the brochure price must be added £26 per person because they wish to fly from Manchester. At the time of booking the travel agent requires a 10% deposit plus the full cost of insurance which is £26.95 per adult and £16.50 per child. The balance is to be paid eight weeks before they leave. (i) How much must Tim pay when he books the holiday? (ii) How much remains to be paid eight weeks before they leave?

(c) While in Tenerife they change £550 into pesetas at the rate of 210 pta to the pound. They spend 99 000 pta and when they return home, change the pesetas that remain into pounds at the rate of 215 pta to the pound. How much do they receive for the unspent pesetas?

(d) In addition they spend £130 in English money. (i) Find the total cost of the holiday. (ii) How much does this work out per person per night?

4 Given below is a typical timetable for Barry's working day.

Time	Action
7.10 a.m.	Get up
7.25	Leave home
7.55	Arrive in work (5 minutes early)
10.20–10.30	Morning break
12.30–1.00 p.m.	Lunch break
2.50–3.00	Afternoon break
5.00	Finish work
5.35	Arrive home
6.30–7.00	Main meal
8.30	Go out
11.30	Return home
11.45	Go to bed

(a) How long is it from the time Barry gets up until he is due to start work?
(b) How long is it from the time he gets up until he goes to bed?
(c) How long is he at home after work before he goes out?
(d) How much sleep does he normally get from one working day to the next?
(e) What is the length of his normal working day (i) including breaks (ii) excluding breaks?
(f) How much longer does he work in the morning than in the afternoon?
(g) How long does he spend at home, apart from the time he is in bed?
(h) Assuming that he is not paid for his breaks and that the above timetable is for each day from Monday to Thursday, how long must he work on Friday so that the length of his working week is $37\frac{1}{2}$ hours? (He gets a 10-minute unpaid break on Friday morning, just the same as any other day.)

UNIT 8

Organising Numbers: Statistics

After studying this unit you will be able to
☐ design and use an observation sheet to collect data
☐ design and use a questionnaire to survey opinions
☐ tabulate data that you have collected by observation, or from questionnaires
☐ tell the difference between discrete and continuous data
☐ interpret and draw various types of bar charts
☐ construct and interpret pie charts
☐ find the mean, mode, median and range of a set of data.

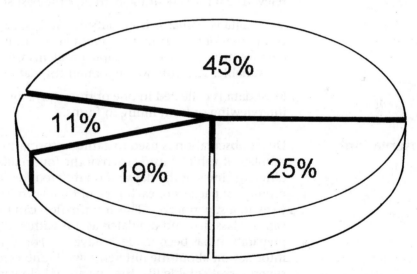

Statistics and data   Statistics is the subject that tries to make sense of a large amount of information, called data, which is given in the form of numbers.

We become aware of a problem, often because of some startling, unexpected or unacceptable event. Maybe it is a problem that is big enough to make headlines in a newspaper, like the example on the next page.

Mother with pram waits 20 minutes to cross Westgate Street.
The residents of the Pilton Vale Estate are fed up with the time they have to wait to cross Westgate Street to get to the shops. This was brought to a head last Saturday morning when Vera Benfield, with her twins in a pushchair, had to wait 20 minutes before it was safe for them all to cross. . .

Faced with such a problem we set about gathering as much information as we can that will help us to solve it. We must know how many people need to cross the road, how long on average they have to wait, are there just a small number of problem times or is it always difficult to cross? If you are aware of a similar problem in your area there could be lots of other factors you think are relevant in trying to solve it.

When data has been collected it must be organised and represented clearly and precisely so that it can be analysed. Finally we draw conclusions and, looking at all the facts and consequences, we act on them. The solution to the problem of crossing Westgate Street could be to introduce full-time or part-time traffic lights, install a zebra or panda crossing, erect a bridge or an underpass, put an island in the middle of the road, or even to do nothing, because the problem is no where near as serious as was at first thought. One thing is certain, without the relevant data we are unlikely to find the best solution.

Some data is available from outside sources, such as market research companies or Government departments, but it is more likely that the data we need to solve the simple problems we are interested in is unavailable. The only way to obtain this data is to collect it.

Most data is collected in one of three ways: by observation, by interviewing or from filling in forms.

Observation

Direct observation is used to gather information on, for example, the number of vehicles using each of the four roads off a roundabout at different times of the day and on different days of the week, or the number of packets of each type of their own-brand cereal sold each week in a supermarket. This information can be found by counting and can be classified and tabulated as it is gathered provided adequate preparation has been made in advance. For example, in collecting information about the different own-brand cereals sold in a supermarket, a table like the one given below would be useful.

Type of cereal					
Day/Date	Flakes	Fruit & Fibre	Muesli	Rice crispies	Oat bran
Mon 20 Jun Tues 21 Jun Wed 22 Jun	⊬⊬ ⊬⊬	⊬⊬	⊬⊬ IIII	III	⊬⊬ II

Exercise 8a

Draw up an observation sheet that would help you to collect data to solve the following problems.

1 A local bus company wants to buy some new buses but is uncertain whether to order 12-seater, 15-seater, 24-seater or 35-seater buses to replace the existing 35-seaters on the route from Dolmand to Cripton.

2 A manufacturer sells three products. The board would like to increase profits without introducing any new products. To do this they have to decide whether or not to increase or decrease the production of each of their products.

3 Kim's Boutique needs to order dresses from Omega Fashions for next season. They have records of their sales for the last five years.

4 A market gardener wants to run trials this year to decide which type of kidney bean plant he will grow on a commercial basis next year.

5 A main road runs north south through the town of Croxton. Within the town four other roads lead off in different directions. The local county council wish to build a by-pass, either on the east side of the town or on the west side. (They cannot afford both!) They wish to find out which side to build it so that traffic within the town is reduced as much as possible.

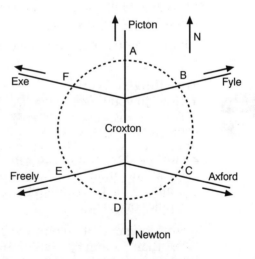

Questionnaires

Information about people and their opinions that cannot be observed directly or cannot be measured, can often be found by asking questions. You can either ask people questions in a face to face interview or you can get them to fill in a form.

An *interview* is an example of a type of questionnaire. It can be formal or informal. In a formal interview only agreed, previously prepared questions are asked. In an informal interview, such as a job interview, the first few questions asked can lead to other questions which will vary from person to person.

The answers to the questions asked during an interview must be realistically available. A man interviewed at his front door will know which daily newspaper he reads or that he is not in favour of shops opening on Sundays, but he is unlikely to know exactly how many shirts he has or how many estate agents or building societies there are in the local High Street. When a person is interviewed he is far more likely to think carefully about his answer if he thinks that his opinion is valued or will influence events.

A *questionnaire* is a list of questions intended to discover particular information. A questionnaire is relatively easy to construct, and is comparatively cheap to produce. While an advantage of handing out a questionnaire is that people have time to think about their answers before they give them, many people put off replying to them unless there is some incentive.

The questions in a questionnaire must be worded so that they

- are short and easy to understand
- do not suggest a particular answer
- are likely to be answered truthfully
- allow for all possible answers
- can preferably be answered 'yes' or 'no' or by ticking one of several suggested answers.

A simple questionnaire on Travelling To Work is given below

Travelling To Work
1 How do you travel to work?
   Public transport ☐   Car ☐   Walk ☐   Motor cycle ☐
   Cycle ☐   Other ☐

2 How far do you travel to work?
   less than 1 mile ☐   1 mile–less than 2 miles ☐
   2 miles–less than 3 miles ☐   3 miles–less than 5 miles ☐
   5 miles or over ☐

3 How long does it take you to get to work?
   less than 15 min ☐   15 min–less than 30 min ☐
   30 min–less than 45 min ☐   45 min–less than 60 min ☐
   1 hour or more ☐

The easiest way to gather information expressing people's opinion about some matter is to make a statement and measure the reaction to it. The person interviewed is asked to indicate the box that is nearest to his/her opinion. For example

1 Pop stars are paid too much
  strongly agree ☐   agree ☐   neither agree nor disagree ☐
  disagree ☐   strongly disagree ☐

2 AC Milan are the best football team in Europe
  strongly agree ☐   agree ☐   don't know ☐   disagree ☐
  strongly disagree ☐

3 A sound knowledge of number is needed to get the best out of life
  in the modern world
  strongly agree ☐   agree ☐   don't know ☐   disagree ☐
  strongly disagree ☐

Exercise 8b

Comment on each of the following questions which have been
extracted from some actual questionnaires.

1 How do you rate the in-flight meals?
excellent ☐   good ☐   average ☐   poor ☐   very poor ☐
(Please tick one box)
(A question taken from an airline questionnaire to be filled in by
passengers on their journey home.)

2 How much do you spend each week on leisure?
(Taken from a students' survey on leisure.)

3 Which political party do you think would be best for Britain?
(Taken from a newspaper questionnaire two weeks before a general
election.)

4 At your local branch, how long, on average, do you have to wait
before you are served?
less than 1 minute ☐   1–2 min ☐   2–3 min ☐   3–5 min ☐
over 5 min ☐   (Please tick one box)
(Included in a questionnaire from a bank to its customers.)

5 How often do you wash your hair?
less than once a week ☐   once a week ☐   twice a week ☐
3–6 times a week ☐   every day ☐
(From a survey on hair shampoos conducted by a market research
company.)

6 Which of these questions are likely to get honest answers?
(a) Are you generous to your friends?   yes ☐   no ☐
(b) How old are you?
   under 18 ☐   18–21 ☐   22–40 ☐   over 40 ☐
(c) Do you always pay attention to what the teacher is saying?
   yes ☐   no ☐
(d) Do you always drive within the speed limit?   yes ☐   no ☐
(e) Do you care enough about your family to take adequate
   insurance cover when you go on holiday?   yes ☐   no ☐

7 What's wrong with these questions?
(a) Would you prefer not to eat in a non-smoking restaurant?
(b) What do you think about the size and shape of this container?

8 A research and marketing company was engaged to find out what owners of new Ford Mondeos liked/disliked about their new car. They asked the following questions to 5000 people, chosen at random, in town centre car parks. The numbers opposite each answer show the percentage of those responding that gave each answer.

1 Have you bought a car in the last year?   yes 10%   no 90%
   (if 'yes' go to question 2)
2 Was this a new car?   yes 20%   no 80%
   (If 'yes' go to question 3)
3 Was it a Ford?   yes 20%   no 80%
   (If 'yes' go to question 4)
4 Was it a Mondeo?   yes 10%   no 90%
   (If 'yes' go to question 5)

Numerous other questions followed.
(a) How many positive respondents did they have by the time they got
   down to those that had bought   (i) a Ford   (ii) a Mondeo?
(b) What was wrong with this survey?
(c) How could it have been done differently so that the information
   obtained would have been more useful?

9 Design a short questionnaire to find out
(a) How many times a week the students in your group read
   newspapers, which newspapers they read, and how long they spend
   reading them.
(b) How often the teenagers in your street have an alcoholic drink,
   where they drink, how much they drink and how much they spend
   on drink.

Frequency tables

The list of numbers that follows shows the number of occupants, including the driver, in each car entering a multistorey car park from 10 a.m. to noon one morning.

2	3	1	4	2	3	2	2	2	1	2	4	1	6	2
1	2	3	2	1	3	5	1	2	2	1	3	1	2	1
2	1	3	2	1	2	2	2	2	1	3	1	4	2	3
1	4	5	2	1	2	4	1	3	2	1	2	2	1	2
3	2	1	2	2	3	3	2	1	5	2	1	1	1	2
3	2	1	1	2	2	3	1	1	2	1	2	1	1	4

This is raw data and needs to be sorted into categories.

Number of occupants per car	1	2	3	4	5	6
Tally	II	II	II			
Frequency						

(Remember to work down the columns, making a tally mark in the tally column next to the appropriate group. The tallies for the first column of numbers have been entered for you.)

This is called a *frequency table*. It would have saved time if this table had been prepared previously so that the data could have been entered as the cars entered the car park

Discrete and continuous data

The data given above was collected by counting. It is an example of *discrete data*. Discrete data can take only particular values: we cannot have $\frac{1}{2}$ or $\frac{1}{3}$ of a person in a car! Discrete data values are usually whole numbers but it is possible to have fractions, for example $3\frac{1}{2}$ and $8\frac{1}{2}$ are shoe sizes.

While discrete data is obtained by counting, other data can be found by measuring. For example, the heights and weights of a group of people can be found by measuring. Such values can lie anywhere between certain limits. This kind of data is called *continuous data*.

Grouping of data

When discrete data, such as the number of people queuing at a cash machine, is being collected, it is quite clear that if the data is grouped the groups 0–4, 5–9, 10–14, . . . are acceptable. The next possible value after 4 is 5 so the fact that there is a gap between the end of one group and the beginning of the next group does not matter.

For continuous data we must consider all the possible values from the lowest to the highest, leaving no gaps between.

If we have a list of the weights of a group of adults that vary from 51 kg to 96 kg, suitable groups would be $50 \leq w < 60$, $60 \leq w < 70$, and so on up to $90 \leq w < 100$, where the weight of a given adult is w kg. (The symbol $\leq$ means 'is less than or equal to' and $<$ means 'is less than' so

$50 \leqslant w < 60$ means that 50 is less than or equal to the value of w (i.e. w is greater than or equal to 50) but w is less than 60.)

In this way there is no doubt as to which group a given weight belongs. For the group $50 \leqslant w < 60$, 50 is called the lower boundary and 60 the upper boundary. The difference between these two values is the width of the group. In this case the group width is 10.

When you have to choose the number of groups yourself do not choose too many or too few. Between 5 and 8 is usually satisfactory.

Exercise 8c

In Questions 1–12 state whether the data is discrete or continuous.

1 The number of telephone calls made by an office in a day.

2 The length of a telephone call.

3 The volume of detergent in a container as it leaves the factory.

4 The lengths of peas picked in an allotment.

5 The number of cans of beer produced by a brewery in one week.

6 The number of letters in a postman's bag.

7 The weight of the letters in a postman's bag.

8 The length of a machined part produced by several similar machines in a factory.

9 The number of compact discs in a music store.

10 The time that patients have to wait before they are seen by the doctor.

11 The amount of money in a pensioner's purse.

12 The amount of money in Tim's building society account.

In Questions 13–16 the first two groups to be used for a set of data are given. Suggest the next three groups.

13 The number of rejects per 100 in a manufacturing process
0–9, 10–19, . . .

14 The number of passengers on an Inter City train between stations
0–49, 50–99, . . .

15 The height, h cm, of the adults at an international match
$150 \leqslant h < 155$, $155 \leqslant h < 160$, . . .

16 The weight, w gms, of the screws produced by the same machine
$8.85 \leqslant w < 8.90$, $8.90 \leqslant w < 8.95$, . . .

17 The groups for the heights, h cm, of some plants after 10 weeks are
$0 \leqslant h < 10$, $10 \leqslant h < 20$, $20 \leqslant h < 30$, $30 \leqslant h < 40$
Into which class interval would you put a plant whose measured height after 10 weeks is
(a) 9.9 cm   (b) 20.3 cm
(c) 29.3 cm   (d) 19.5 cm?

18 The number of letters in a postman's bag can be anything up to 500. Suggest 5 groups that would be suitable for grouping this data.

19 A sample of 100 bottles of wine were checked by measuring the amount of wine, v ml, in each bottle. The contents ranged from 696 ml to 724 ml. Suggest 6 equal groupings that would be suitable to group this data.

Bar charts

The following frequency table shows the number of elderly people admitted to residential care each month by Anderson Borough Council in 1994. It was compiled from returns that gave the date on which each resident was admitted.

Month	Jan	Feb	Mar	Apr	May	Jun	Jul	Aug	Sep	Oct	Nov	Dec
Number of residents admitted	16	25	14	8	6	4	6	6	8	12	16	22

Data can be illustrated very clearly on a bar chart. The bar chart for the given data is shown below.

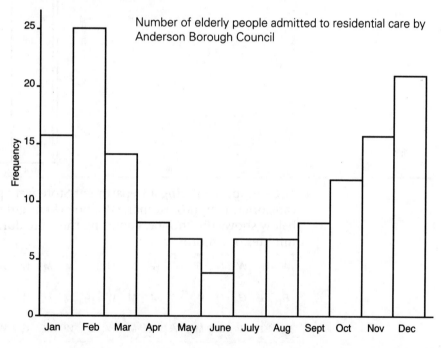

We mark the months of the year along the horizontal axis and frequency along the vertical axis.

Each bar gives the number for one month; all the bars are the same width. The height of the bar shows the frequency for that month.

We could use horizontal bars.

Exercise 8d

Question A recent return on the number of children, by age, on the Child Protection Register gave the following details:

Age	Number
1–4	150
5–8	135
9–12	75
13–16	50

Show this information on a bar chart.

Answer Number of children on the Child Protection Register

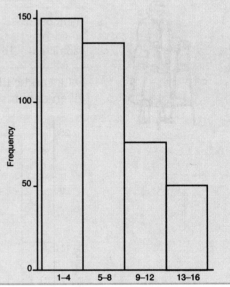

1 The shoppers entering a Department Store were put into one of four categories: man (*M*), woman (*W*), boy (*B*) or girl (*G*). The list given below shows the shoppers entering the store during the first ten minutes one morning.

W	W	W	G	B	W	W	M	G	G	M	M	W	W	W	W	G	B	M	W
B	G	G	M	W	W	M	M	W	W	W	M	W	B	W	G	M	W	W	W
W	G	W	M	M	W	W	M	W	G	W	M	G	W	M	·M	B	G	G	W

(a) Copy and complete this frequency table.

Person	Man	Woman	Boy	Girl
Tally				
Frequency				

(b) Draw a bar chart to illustrate it.
(c) How many more women than men entered the store to shop?
(d) How many more girls than boys were there?
(e) How many shoppers were there altogether?

2 An automated manufacturing process makes pearl, 60W bayonet cap electric light bulbs and puts them in packs of five. A small number of packs are selected at random and the number of defective bulbs in each pack noted. The results for one morning shift are shown in the bar chart.

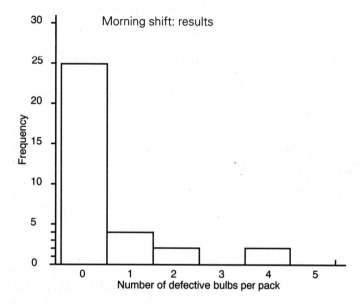

(a) How many packs contained
   (i) no defective bulbs   (ii) 2 defective bulbs?
(b) How many packs were checked?
(c) How many defective bulbs were there altogether?
(d) What percentage of the bulbs checked were defective?

3 The following list gives the age, in years, of 100 people taken into residential care by a local authority.

99	82	87	85	81	87	83	73	82	77	83	90	72	84	78	92	84	87	83	92
84	74	80	65	93	84	89	87	81	94	84	67	85	80	94	84	74	78	80	81
82	87	83	77	89	80	88	66	72	77	91	98	77	88	87	83	94	88	94	85
86	75	72	80	94	82	95	70	92	81	89	78	87	76	72	86	77	68	86	83
87	92	84	67	89	91	76	84	78	93	74	68	71	75	96	72	83	79	74	88

(a) What is the age of
   (i) the youngest   (ii) the oldest, person in this list?

(b) Copy and complete the following frequency table.

Age	65–69	70–74	75–79	80–84	85–89	90–94	95–99
Tally							
Frequency							

(c) Draw a bar chart to represent this data.
(d) How many of the new residents were at least 80?
(e) Which age group has the largest number of people?

Other types of bar charts

The business interests of a major national company are divided into three main areas: shipping, building and road transport. The profit from each area, over a four year period, is shown in the table.

Year	Shipping (£)	Building (£)	Road transport (£)
1991	24m	42m	12m
1992	27m	36m	36m
1993	32m	29m	18m
1994	38m	26m	42m

This information can be represented in a bar chart is several different ways.

Compound or multiple bar chart

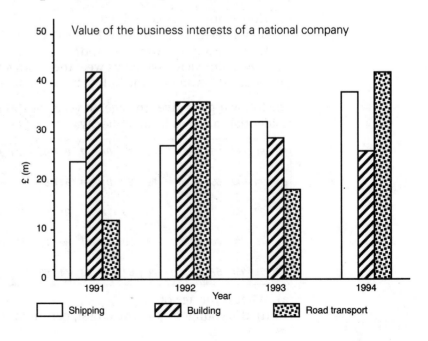

This type of bar chart is useful for comparing a number of features within a year, as well as comparing these features for different years.

Component Bar Chart

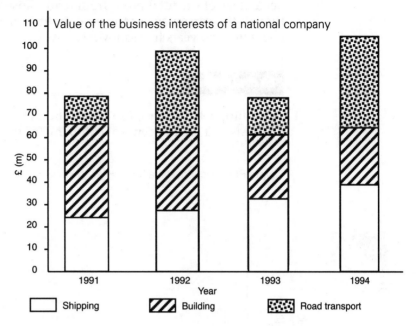

A component bar chart shows the division of the whole into its separate parts.

Percentage component bar chart

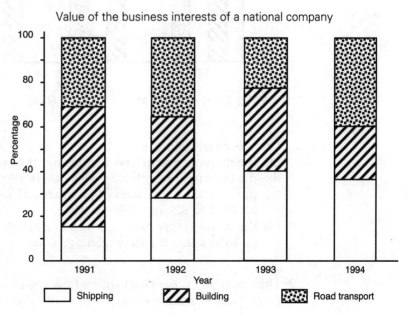

Each bar is the same length since it represents the total profit for each year. The component parts show the percentage profit originating from each of the three areas. This form of representation shows clearly that the percentage of the total profit from building is decreasing, that the percentage of the total profit from road transport is erratic and that though the percentage of the total profit from shipping is probably going up, two years have shown slight falls.

Exercise 8e

1 The multiple bar chart given below shows the annual sales in the three divisions of a pharmaceutical company for the period 1991–94.

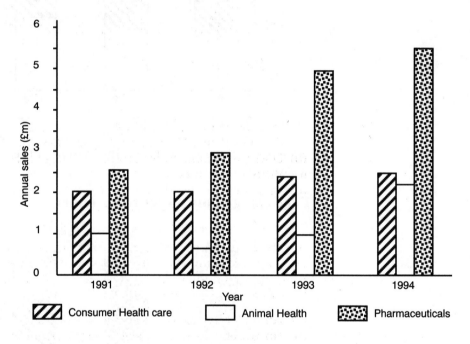

Crypto Pharmaceuticals: annual sales, by division

Use this chart to find:
(a) the division that always contributes the largest sales
(b) the consumer health care sales in   (i) 1991   (ii) 1993
(c) the increase in the sales of pharmaceutical products from
   (i) 1991 to 92   (ii) 1993 to 94
(d) the division that has improved most from 1991 to 1994 in
   (i) total sales   (ii) in percentage sales.

2 This component bar chart shows how the income of Alma Airways, from its three main routes, has been divided over a period of years.

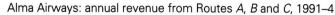

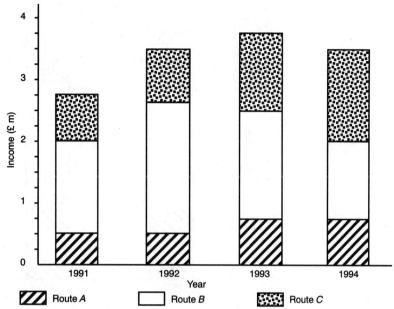

(a) What was the income from
(i) route *A* in 1991 (ii) route *B* in 1993 (iii) route *C* in 1994?
(b) Does the income from route *C* get bigger each year?
(c) Which route produced the most income in (i) 1991 (ii) 1992?
(d) Can you see any possible trends in the income from these routes?
If you were the managing director would this information give you
(i) any cause for concern (ii) satisfaction?

3 A college runs three GNVQ courses: Business, Health & Social Care and
Tourism & Leisure. The percentage bar chart given on p. 200 shows
how the total number of GNVQ students are divided between the three
courses for the years 1992, 1993 and 1994.

(a) For which course is the percentage of students rising?
(b) For which course is the percentage of students dropping?
(c) Altogether 170 students followed these courses in 1992. How many
were there on the Health & Social Care course?
(d) There were 280 students on these courses in 1993 and 300 students
on them in 1994. Had the number of students taking GNVQ Business
gone up or down (i) from 1992 to 1994 (ii) from 1993 to 1994?
(e) Which of the following statements are true and which are false?
A The numbers in Health & Social Care more than doubled from
1992 to 1994
B The numbers in Business have gone down from year to year.
C All three courses have increased numbers in 1993 compared with
1992

Foxborough College: percentage of GNVQ students following three GNVQ courses

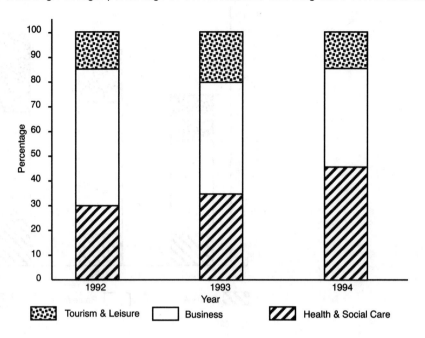

D It is possible that the percentage of students taking each course next year will show an increase compared with this year.

Continuous data

The number of students in a class is a whole number but their heights are likely to be anywhere between 140 cm and 200 cm. Because height can be anywhere on a continuous scale the heights of the students are an example of continuous data.

167	172	185	175	174	174	188	178	179	172
173	169	175	172	169	177	167	172	188	179
182	174	184	168	153	176	172	197	173	189
172	179	165	175	174	193	165	187	162	172
165	172	151	176	186	167	171	176	152	179

This is a list of the heights of 50 students. It was found using a computer data base. Each height has been rounded down to the nearest whole centimetre, so that a height of 152 cm means any value, h cm, that is in the range $152 \leqslant h < 153$. This data shows a shortest height of 151 cm and a tallest height of 197 cm.

We can sort the data into five class intervals as follows:

Height (h cm)	Frequency
$150 \leqslant h < 160$	3
$160 \leqslant h < 170$	10
$170 \leqslant h < 180$	27
$180 \leqslant h < 190$	8
$190 \leqslant h < 200$	2

Another way of giving this information in a table is:

Height (h cm)	150–	160–	170–	180–	190–200
Frequency	3	10	27	8	2

150– means 'all values from 150 cm up to but not including 160 cm'.

In each case the width of the class interval is 10 cm.

The bar chart for this data is shown below

50 students: Bar chart for their heights

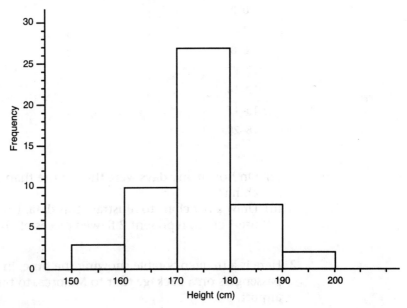

50 students:
The horizontal axis gives the height on a continuous scale. No gaps are allowed between the bars.

Exercise 8f

1 In a china factory a sample of 100 pieces of china is selected at random each day to test for flaws. The number of flaws found on 60 consecutive days is listed below.

13	6	4	10	7	3	6	4	7	11
8.	12	7	9	0	7	13	11	14	3
10	8	7	2	0	8	5	16	14	6
3	17	8	5	16	1	11	7	0	10
0	7	7	9	8	11	6	4	13	11
4	9	11	15	2	5	6	3	10	7

(a) Is this data discrete or continuous?
(b) Copy and complete the following frequency table.

Number of flaws	Tally	Frequency
0–2		
3–5		
6–8		
9–11		
12–14		
15–17		
18–20		

(c) On how many days were there more than 11 flawed pieces of china?
(d) Draw a bar chart to illustrate this data. For the heights of the bars use 1 cm to represent 2 flawed pieces of china.

2 Here is a frequency table showing the time, in minutes, taken by the passengers on a package tour to Majorca, to travel from home to the airport.

Time (t min)	$0 \leqslant t < 20$	$20 \leqslant t < 40$	$40 \leqslant t < 60$	$60 \leqslant t < 80$	$80 \leqslant t < 100$
Frequency	21	33	56	40	18

(a) Copy and complete this bar chart

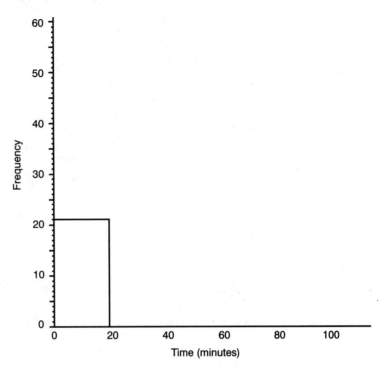

(b) How many passengers travelled on the aircraft?

(c) How many passengers had a journey to the airport that took less than an hour?

3 Each year from 1992 to 1994 a group of 100 people were asked 'What is your main source for world news?' Their replies were recorded and are reproduced below.

Year	Radio	TV	Newspapers
1992	37	52	11
1993	42	50	8
1994	47	47	6

(a) Illustrate this information using
(i) a multiple bar chart (ii) a component bar chart.

(b) How does the bar chart you got in (a)(ii) differ from the appropriate percentage bar chart?

4 Given below is a list of the amount, each correct to the nearest millilitre, of the vinegar in a batch of bottles that are said to contain 500 ml. The quantities are given in ascending order.

487	489	490	491	491	492	492	492	493	495
495	496	496	496	496	497	497	498	498	498
498	498	498	499	499	500	500	500	501	501
501	501	501	502	502	503	503	503	503	504
504	504	504	504	504	504	504	504	504	504
505	505	505	505	506	506	506	507	507	507
508	508	508	508	508	508	508	509	509	509
510	510	511	511	512	512	512	513	514	514

(a) What is the smallest quantity recorded?
(b) If a recorded amount is 498 ml what is the range within which the actual amount lies?
(c) Copy and complete the following frequency table.

Amount (v ml)	Tally	Frequency
$484.5 \leqslant v < 489.5$		
$489.5 \leqslant v < 494.5$		
$494.5 \leqslant v < 499.5$		
$499.5 \leqslant v < 504.5$		
$504.5 \leqslant v < 509.5$		
$509.5 \leqslant v < 514.5$		
$514.5 \leqslant v < 519.5$		

(d) How many of the sample contain 499.5 ml or more?
(e) Explain why it is not possible to find out from the table the number of bottles containing more than 500 ml.

5 The table shows the workforce in employment, together with the number of people unemployed, in the United Kingdom at 4-yearly interval from 1974.

Year	Workforce in employment (thousand)	Number unemployed (thousand)
1974	25 676	599
1978	26 358	1299
1982	26 677	2904
1986	27 791	3312
1990	26 918	1623

(a) Draw a bar chart for   (i) the workforce in employment
(ii) the number of unemployed, from 1974 to 1990.
(b) Illustrate this data on a compound percentage bar chart.

Line graphs   Line graphs are drawn by plotting points, then joining the points in order with straight lines.

Exercise 8g

Question   Lena was admitted to hospital as an emergency. Her temperature was taken at 4-hourly intervals and a record kept on a chart. The chart is shown below

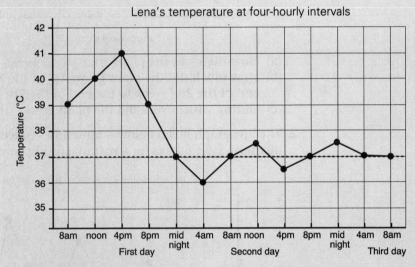

Lena's temperature at four-hourly intervals

(a) What was Lena's
(i) lowest temperature   (ii) highest temperature?
(b) Was her highest recorded temperature necessarily her highest temperature?
(c) By the third day Lena was feeling much better. What do you think the dashed line represents?

Answer   (a) (i) Her lowest recorded temperature was 36°C at 4 a.m. on the second day.
(ii) Her highest recorded temperature was 41°C at 4 p.m. on the first day.
(b) No. Her temperature could have been higher at some time between 12 noon and 4 p.m.
(c) Since Lena was feeling much better it is probably her normal temperature.

1 Joyce measured the height of a plant at the end of each week for 8 weeks. Her values are shown on the graph.

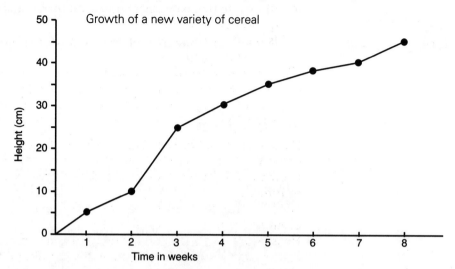

(a) How high was the plant after   (i) 2 weeks   (ii) 3 weeks?
(b) How much did the plant grow   (i) in the 3rd week   (ii) from the end of the 2nd week to the end of the 7th week?
(c) During which week did the plant grow   (i) most   (ii) least?

2 The line graph given below – sometimes called a time series – shows the quarterly sales figures for a manufacturing company.

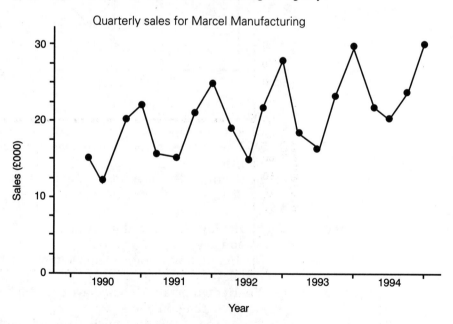

(a) What were the 1st quarter sales in   (i) 1990   (ii) 1994?
(b) What were the 3rd quarter sales in   (i) 1991   (ii) 1993?

(c) Find the difference between the 2nd quarter sales and the 4th quarter sales in (i) 1990 (ii) 1994

(d) In which year was there the greatest difference between the poorest quarter and the best quarter?

(e) Is there a sales pattern in these figures? If you were the boss, would you be satisfied?

(f) Can you think of a product that could give a sales pattern like this?

(g) Sketch a similar graph for (i) an ice cream seller at a seaside resort (ii) the sales of a company distributing school and college textbooks (iii) holiday bookings at your local travel agent.

3 Darren Eastman works a 5-day week in a factory. He gets up early every day because he has to be in work by 7 a.m. Over the weekend he enjoys a few glasses of beer, each pint containing $2\frac{1}{2}$ units of alcohol. His usual routine is:

Friday evening – 3 pints, Saturday lunchtime – 2 pints and Saturday evening – 4 pints.

He is aware that 1 unit of alcohol results in a blood alcohol concentration (BAC) of 15 milligrams per 100 millilitres; that 5 units is about the legal limit for driving (it is 80 mg/ml) and that the body can filter through about 1 unit each hour.

(a) What, approximately, is his BAC when he is about to go home on Friday evening?

(b) Copy the axes drawn below and on them plot his blood alcohol concentration at hourly intervals from Friday evening to noon on Sunday.

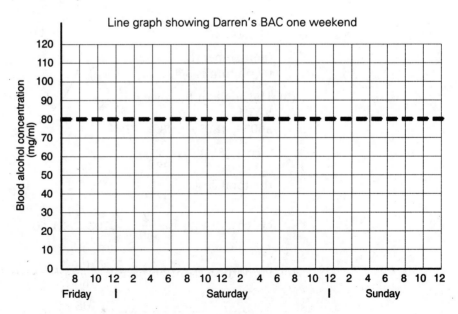

(c) When is his blood alcohol concentration highest?

(d) Should he drive home on Friday or Saturday night?

(e) It is recommended that men ought to consume no more than 21 units a week. Does he keep within this limit?

Pie charts

Earlier in this unit we used compound bar charts and percentage compound bar charts to show how something was shared out. We now show how pie charts can be used to do the same thing.

Note: If you need help in using a protractor, see Guidance Notes: Basic Skills, Section E, p. 343.

Exercise 8h

Question   The pie chart shows the breakdown of a bill of £108 for a 6000 mile service of my car.
(a) What fraction of the bill was for labour?
(b) How much was the charge for VAT?
(c) What percentage of the bill was to pay for parts?

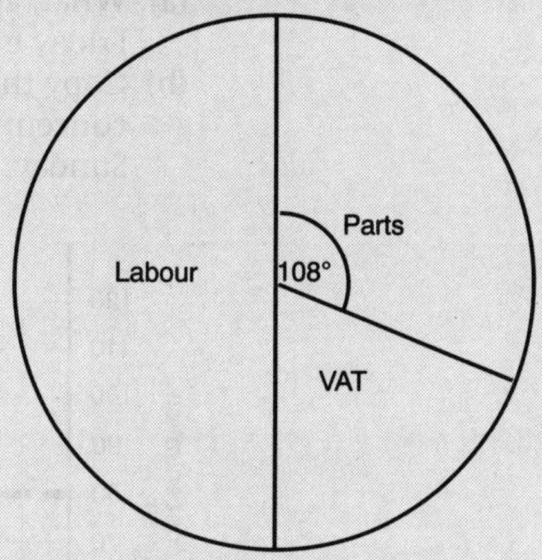

6000 mile service : cost breakdown

Answer   (a) The angle in the slice for labour is 180°

∴ fraction of bill for labour

is $\dfrac{180°}{360°} = \frac{1}{2}$

(Remember that 1 revolution is 360°.)

(b) The angle in the slice for VAT is
360° − 180° − 108° = 72°
∴ cost of VAT is $\dfrac{72}{360}$ of

the total cost

i.e. cost of VAT is $\dfrac{72}{360} × £108 = £21.60$.

(c) Proportion spent on parts is $\dfrac{108}{360}$ of the total

Percentage spent on parts is $\dfrac{108}{360} × 100\% = 30\%$

1   Oat cereal: proportion of nutrients, by weight

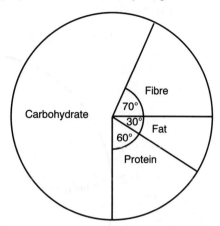

This chart shows the proportion, by weight, of various nutrients in a packet of oat cereal.
(a) What fraction of the nutrients is (i) fat . (ii) fibre (iii) carbohydrate?
(b) How many grams of protein are there in a serving of
     (i) 100 g   (ii) 36 g?
(c) How many grams of carbohydrate are there in a serving of
     (i) 100 g   (ii) 36 g?

2   180 adults were weighed and placed into one of four categories: underweight, average, overweight, obese (i.e. grossly overweight). The pie chart shows the proportion of adults falling into each category.
(a) What fraction of the group were
     (i) overweight (ii) obese (iii) above average?
(b) How many of these adults were (i) underweight (ii) either above average weight or below average weight?
(c) What percentage of the group were
     (i) obese (ii) not above average weight?

180 adults: weight categories

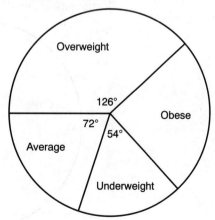

3 The pie chart shows how all the land in the world was being used in the early 1990s.

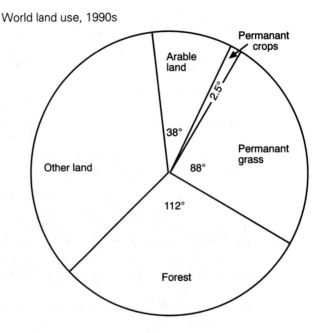

World land use, 1990s

If the total area of the land mass in the world is 200 million square kilometres find how many million square kilometres was
(a) forest   (b) being used as arable land.

4 Scotto's total income of £5m is divided between costs, taxes and profits as shown in the pie chart.
(a) What fraction of the income is allocated to   (i) taxes   (ii) costs?
(b) What is the ratio of the profit to the costs?
(c) How much do Scotto's pay in taxes?
(d) If taxes are reduced by one third and the costs remain unchanged, what is the ratio of profits to taxes?

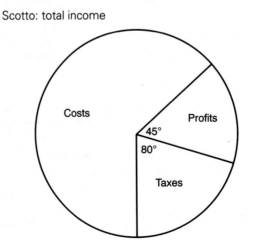

Scotto: total income

Constructing a pie chart

Question   The sales of petrol from five petrol outlets are shown in the table.

Petrol Station	Adcot	Burley	Crossway	Deighton	Eden
Sales (thousands of litres)	85	30	120	130	35

Construct a pie diagram to illustrate this data.

Answer   The total sales, in thousands of litres, is
$85 + 30 + 120 + 130 + 35 = 400$.

The total angle of 360° at the centre of the pie chart must be divided according to the proportion of the sales at each station.

The angle representing the sales at Adcot petrol station is given by

$\dfrac{85}{400} \times 360° = 77°$ (to the nearest whole number).

The values for the other stations are given in the table.

Petrol station	Angle at centre
Burley	$\dfrac{30}{400} \times 360° = 27°$
Crossway	$\dfrac{120}{400} \times 360° = 108°$
Deighton	$\dfrac{130}{400} \times 360° = 117°$
Eden	$\dfrac{35}{400} \times 360° = 31°$ (rounded down so that the total is 360°)

The resulting pie chart is given below.

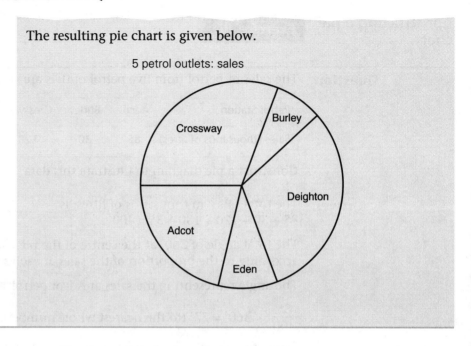

5 petrol outlets: sales

1 Each £1 received from sales at Busicom Industries is divided as follows: raw materials 28p, wages 33p, plant and machinery 8p, advertising 9p, the remainder being profit. Construct a pie chart to illustrate this information.

2 The populations, in millions, of India, China and the United States in 1991 are given as: India 844, China 1116 and the United States 253.
   (a) Draw a pie chart to illustrate this data.
   (b) During the decade to the year 2001 it is anticipated that the population of India will grow by 170 m, the population of China will grow by 100m and the population of the United States will grow by 20m. Draw a pie chart to illustrate the populations of the three countries in the year 2001.

3 The table shows the known oil reserves in 1993.

Region	Number of barrels (thousand million)
America (North and South)	160
Middle East	660
Former Soviet Union	60
Africa	60
Asia and Australasia	50
Europe	10

Construct a pie chart to illustrate this data.

4 The table shows the average daily sales of the four leading tabloid newspapers, together with the estimated total daily readership, in 1991.

Newspaper	Circulation	Readers per copy	Total readership (thousands)	Percentage (%)
Daily Express	1 541 680	2.4	3643	
Daily Mail	1 701 794		4303	
Daily Mirror	2 918 947		8035	
The Sun	3 678 897		9857	
Total				

The number of readers per copy is found by dividing the total readership by the number of papers sold, e.g. for the Daily Express,

$$\text{readers per copy} = \frac{3\,643\,000}{1\,541\,680} = 2.4 \text{ (1 d.p.)}.$$

(a) Copy and complete the table. In the last column express the circulation of each newspaper as a percentage of the total sales of the four newspapers.
(b) Construct a pie chart to show the circulations of the four papers as a fraction of their combined circulations.
(c) Draw a bar chart to illustrate the numbers of readers per copy.
(d) Draw a multiple bar chart showing, for each paper, the circulation and the total readership.

Averages

The *mean* of a set of numbers is found by adding all the numbers together and dividing by the number of numbers,

e.g. the mean of 5, 5, 2 and 12 is

$$\frac{5 + 5 + 2 + 12}{4} = \frac{24}{4} = 6$$

and the mean of 1.2, 3.7, 9.2, 16.3 and 8.7 is

$$\frac{1.2 + 3.7 + 9.2 + 16.3 + 8.7}{5}$$

$$= \frac{39.1}{5}$$

$$= 7.82$$

The *mode* of a set of numbers is the number that occurs most often,

e.g. the mode of 5, 7, 8, 8, 11, 11, 11, 14, 14, 16 is 11, since 11 occurs three times and the most any other number occurs is twice.

A set of numbers can have more than one mode,

e.g. the set of numbers 1, 1, 2, 2, 2, 3, 4, 5, 5, 6, 6, 6, 7, 9, has two modes, namely 2 and 6.

The *median* of a set of numbers is the middle number when the numbers have been arranged in order of size

e.g. the median of 3, 9, 11, 20, 32, 47 and 53 is 20.

There are seven numbers. The middle number of seven is four, and the fourth number is 20. To find the median the numbers are usually placed in increasing order, but they do not have to be. If they are placed in decreasing order the median is still the middle number,

e.g. the median of 21, 20, 18, 17 and 2 is 18.

If there is no middle number the median is the average of the two middle numbers,

e.g. the median of 5, 9, 12 and 16 is $\dfrac{9+12}{2} = \dfrac{21}{2} = 10.5$.

Range

The range of a set of data is the difference between the highest value and the smallest value,
e.g. the range of the numbers 5, 2, 8, 40, 45, 32, 31, 17 and 29 is $45 - 2$ i.e. 43.
Similarly if, over a period of ten years the largest profit a company makes is £546 000 and the smallest profit it makes is £65 000 the range is
£546 000 − £65 000 i.e. £481 000.

Exercise 8j

Question The nurses on one table in a hospital canteen were asked to turn out their purses and count the number of coins in them. The results are listed below
12, 8, 9, 16, 24, 0, 7 and 8.
For this data find
(a) the mean   (b) the mode
(c) the median   (d) the range.

Answer (a) mean = $\dfrac{12 + 8 + 9 + 16 + 24 + 0 + 7 + 8}{8}$

$= \dfrac{84}{8}$

$= 10.5$

(b) The only number that occurs more than once is 8.
The mode is therefore 8.

(c) First arrange the numbers in order. We will choose ascending order.
0, 7, 8, 8, 9, 12, 16, 24.

There are 8 numbers, so there is no middle number.
The two middle numbers of eight numbers are the 4th and the 5th.
The median is therefore the average of 8 and 9, i.e. 8.5.
The range of this data is 24 − 0 i.e. 24.
(Note that in this question the mean, mode and median are all different.)

1 Viv watches his fellow workmates arriving by car one morning as they enter the car park. He counts the number of occupants in each car and obtains the following list
1, 2, 2, 2, 1, 1, 4, 3, 2, 1, 2, 1, 1, 5, 2, 1, 2, 3, 1, 1.
(a) How many cars are there in the survey?
(b) How many workmates does he count altogether?
(c) What is the mean number of occupants per car?
(d) What is the modal number of occupants per car?
(e) What is the median number of occupants per car?
(f) Find the range.

2 Over the space of one year the days-off sick by the staff in a factory computer centre were
4, 23, 0, 1, 0, 10, 0, 3, 18, 35.
(a) (i) How many staff are employed in the computer centre?
    (ii) Find the total number of days lost.
(b) Find (i) the mean (ii) the modal (iii) the median,
    number of days-off sick taken by the staff of this centre.

3 Some of the patients who attend a doctor's surgery one morning have their blood pressure taken. The diastolic blood pressures recorded are:
82, 88, 69, 76, 84, 90, 75, 62, 80, 84, 93, 79 and 88.
(a) How many patients have their blood pressure taken?
(b) Find the mean diastolic blood pressure for the group.
(c) What is the modal diastolic blood pressure?
(d) What percentage of the group have a diastolic blood pressure greater than 80?
(e) Find the median diastolic blood pressure.
(f) Find the range.

4 A small business employs 10 people. The basic weekly wages of the three senior employees are £500, £420 and £400, and the basic wage for the remainder is £256.
(a) How many employees receive a basic weekly wage of £256?
(b) Find the total cost of the basic weekly wages.
(c) What is the mean basic weekly wage?
(d) What is the modal basic weekly wage?
(e) Which is the fairest average to use if you were telling a friend about the level of wages paid by the business?

Question The mean weight of the 15 players in a rugby team, i.e. the forwards and the backs, is 84 kg. If the mean weight of the 8 forwards is 91 kg, find
(a) the total weight of the 15 players
(b) the total weight of the forwards
(c) the total weight of the backs
(d) the mean weight of the backs.

Answer (a) Total weight of the 15 players is 84 × 15 kg = 1260 kg.
(b) Total weight of the 8 forwards is 91 × 8 kg = 728 kg.
(c) If there are 15 players, 8 of whom are forwards, there are 7 backs. Total weight of the 7 backs is 1260 kg − 728 kg = 532 kg.
(d) Mean weight of the 7 backs is $\dfrac{532}{7}$ kg = 76 kg.

5 The mean weight of the 13 players in a rugby league side is 84 kg. If the mean weight of the 6 forwards is 91 kg find
(a) the total weight of the 13 players   (b) the total weight of the forwards
(c) the total weight of the backs   (d) the mean weight of the backs.

6 In a game of darts, three throws make one turn. On 12 turns Sid has a mean score of 22. How many does he need to score on his next turn to raise his mean score to 26?

7 Over a four week period the mean number of rejects per day from an automatic lathe is 12. This is considered to be unsatisfactory, so the lathe is serviced ahead of schedule. As a result, during the next seven weeks, the mean number of daily rejects is reduced to 2.5.
(a) Find the total number of rejects during (i) the first four week period (ii) the next seven week period (iii) the full period of the study.
(Assume that the lathe runs for 6 days each week.)
(b) What is the mean number of daily rejects for the period of the study?
(c) Estimate the number of potential rejects that have been 'saved' as a result of the service.

8 Every day, at Sonpo Electronics, a sample of 1000 components is selected at random from the thousands produced by machine *A* on a production line. These are tested and it is found that the mean number of defective components is 5 and the range of defects 10. Similar figures for machine *B* give a mean of 3 and a range of 7.
(a) Which machine appears to be the more reliable?
(b) Is it possible that when the tests are run tomorrow there will be more defective items from machine *B* than machine *A*?

Question The bar chart shows the number of television sets rejected each day on an assembly line e.g. 4 sets were rejected on each of 8 days.

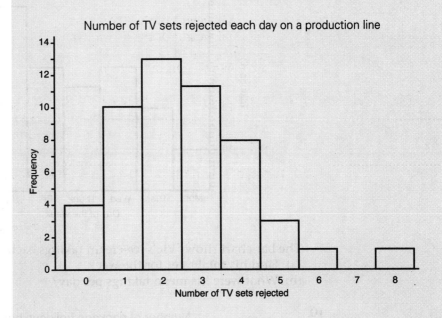

Number of TV sets rejected each day on a production line

Find the mean number of TV sets rejected per day.

Answer First we must find the total number of TV sets rejected and the total number of days over which the data was collected. This is best done using a table

Number of rejected sets per day	Number of days Frequency	Number of rejected sets
0	4	0
1	10	10
2	13	26
3	11	33
4	8	32
5	3	15
6	1	6
7	0	0
8	1	8
Total	51	Grand total 130

From the table the records refer to 51 days during which time 130 TV sets were rejected

$\therefore$ mean numbers of sets rejected per day is $\frac{130}{51}$ = 2.55 (to 3 s.f.)

9

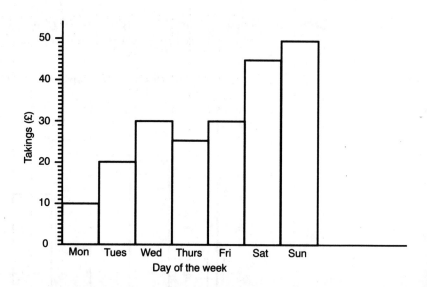

The bar chart shows Vic's ice-cream takings each day for a week.
(a) Find his total sales for the week
(b) What were his mean takings per day?

10

Number of package holidays booked

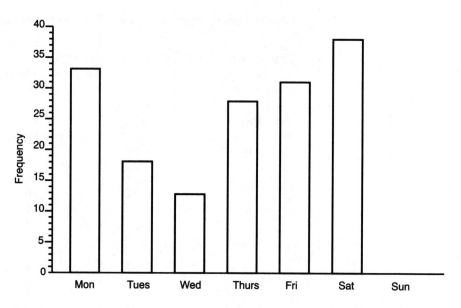

The bar chart shows the number of package holidays booked each day
at All Seasons Travel during a two-week period last January.
(a) How many package holidays were booked altogether?
(b) What was the mean number of package holidays booked per day?

11 The table shows the numbers of below-standard oranges per case in a consignment of oranges delivered to a cruise ship when taking on stores at Southampton.

Number of bad oranges	0	1	2	3	4
Number of boxes Frequency	5	10	19	12	4

(a) How many boxes of oranges were there in the consignment?
(b) Find the mean number of below-standard oranges per box.

Mean, mode and median for grouped data

The table shows the number of bottles of wine broken each week in the cellar of a large restaurant.

Number of broken bottles	0–3	4–7	8–11	12–15	16–19
Frequency	9	23	12	6	2

We do not know the number of bottles broken on every single day, so we cannot give the mode as a single figure. However, between 4 and 7 bottles were broken on 23 different days – we call this group the *modal group*.

Similarly, since the data refers to 52 days, the median is the average of the number of breakages on the 26th and 27th days, when arranged in order of size.
There are 9 in the 0–3 interval and 9 + 23 i.e. 32 in the intervals 0–3 and 4–7.
The 26th and 27th values are both in the interval 4–7.
The median number of breakages is therefore in the class interval 4–7.

To find the mean we assume that the mean number of breakages per class interval is the value half-way through that interval.
This means that we assume that the mean value for the class interval 0–3 is $1\frac{1}{2}$

(i.e. $\dfrac{0+3}{2}$)

and the mean for the second interval is 5.5

(i.e. $\dfrac{4+7}{2}$)

We can set this information out in a table

Number of breakages	Frequency (f)	Mid-way values (x)	(fx)
0–3	9	1.5	13.5
4–7	23	5.5	126.5
8–11	12	9.5	114
12–15	6	13.5	81
16–19	2	17.5	35
Total	52		370

$\therefore$ mean number of breakages per week is $\frac{370}{52}$ = 7.12 (to 3 s.f.).

For continuous data the calculation is similar.

The frequency table shows the weights of 53 pigs when they were taken to market.

Weight (w kg)	Frequency (f)	Halfway value (x)	(fx)
$84 \leqslant w < 86$	4	85	340
$86 \leqslant w < 88$	7	87	609
$88 \leqslant w < 90$	12	89	1068
$90 \leqslant w < 92$	16	91	1456
$92 \leqslant w < 94$	14	93	1302
	53		4775

Mean weight when taken to market is $\dfrac{4775}{53}$ kg = 90.1 kg.

In your own work you may well have to decide which average to use. To help you to make this decision some of the advantages and disadvantages of each average are listed below.

Type of average	Advantages	Disadvantages
Mean	Is the best known average Uses all the data and can be found exactly. Is used a great deal in further work.	Can give impossible values for discrete data e.g. a shoe size of 5.13, and is affected too much by extreme values.
Median	Is not affected by extreme values. Can be an actual value from the given data.	May not be a good representative of the given data when the number of items is small.
Mode	Usually quick and easy to find. Unaffected by extreme values.	There may be no mode or even more than one.

1 The table shows the number of rejects per day from the two machines in a factory that are used for pressing panels.

Number of rejects	0–4	5–9	10–14	15–19	20–24	25–29
Frequency for Machine A	4	11	13	19	32	21
Frequency for Machine B	8	13	16	18	27	18

(a) Estimate the mean number of daily rejects for
(i) Machine A (ii) Machine B.

(b) Which machine, on average, gives the larger number of daily rejects?

2 A pack of 24 cans of beer were checked carefully for quantity. The table shows the number of millilitres by which these cans exceeded 500 ml.

Excess (v ml)	$0 \leqslant v < 5$	$5 \leqslant v < 10$	$10 \leqslant v < 15$	$15 \leqslant v < 20$
Number of cans	12	6	4	2

Estimate
(a) the mean value by which the contents of the cans exceeds 500 ml
(b) the mean quantity of beer per can.

3 The table shows the lengths, in seconds, of the telephone calls made from a building society office one morning.

Time (h sec)	Frequency (f)	Halfway value (x)	(fx)
$0 \leqslant h < 100$	12	50	600
$100 \leqslant h < 200$	7		
$200 \leqslant h < 300$	7		
$300 \leqslant h < 400$	11		
$400 \leqslant h < 500$	8		
Total		Grand total	

(a) How many calls were made?
(b) What, approximately, was the mean length of telephone call that morning?

4 The table shows the number of patients seen at the Outpatients department of a hospital over a period of 100 consecutive days.

Number of patients	80–99	100–119	120–139	140–159	160–179	180–199
Frequency	14	8	14	21	25	18

(a) The mid-value for the class interval 80–99 is $\dfrac{80 + 99}{2}$ i.e. 89.5. Write down the mid-values for the remaining class intervals.

(b) Estimate the mean number of outpatients per day attending the hospital.

Multiple choice questions

In Questions 1–4 several alternative answers are given. Write down the letter that corresponds to the correct answer.

1 A shoe manufacturer exporting to Malaysia needs to know the size of the 'average' person's feet. The most useful single average is

    A the mean   B the mode

    C the median   D none of these.

2 There are several different types of bar charts. The type in which all the bars have the same height is

    A a compound bar chart

    B a component bar chart

    C a multiple bar chart

    D a percentage component bar chart.

3 Listed below are several different types of data

    1 The weights of the potatoes I harvested this year in my allotment

    2 The number of cards Kim received last Christmas

    3 The shoe sizes of the students in my group

    4 The distances that the workforce at a factory travel to work.

Of these, the number that refer to continuous data is

    A 1   B 2

    C 3   D all of them.

4 In a rugby team the mean weight of the 8 forwards is 13st 10lb and the mean weight of the 7 backs is 11st 8lb. It follows that the mean weight of the 15 players in the team is

    A 12st 11lb   B 12st 10lb

    C 12st 9lb   D 12st 8lb.

5

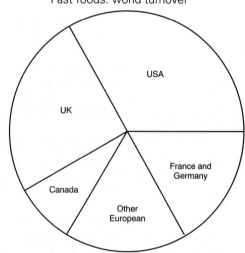

Fast foods: world turnover

The pie chart shows the turnover of a large food producer in the different parts of the world where it operates. The turnover in Canada is about £300m. The following statements have been made:

Statement 1 The turnover in mainland Europe exceeds the turnover in North America.

Statement 2 The turnover in the United States is about £1200m which means that the total turnover of the company is about £3600m.

How are these statements best described?

    A True, True   B True, False

    C False, True   D False, False.

6 A horticulturist planted 6 seeds in each of 50 pots and when the seeds had germinated she

noted the number of seedlings in each pot. These are recorded in the following table.

Number of seedlings	0	1	2	3	4	5	6
Number of pots (Frequency)	0	1	5	13	14	13	4

Which of the following statements are true and which are false?

A The mean and modal number of seeds germinating per pot is 4
B The mean number of seeds germinating per pot is 3.9
C For this data the mean, mode and median are all different
D The mean number of seeds per pot failing to germinate is 2.1.

Self assessment 8

1 (a) Design a simple observation sheet that will enable you to collect the data necessary to find out how long children in different age-groups spend watching television or videos each week.
  (b) A government spokesman has suggested that everybody should carry an identity card with their photo on it. Design a short questionnaire to test people's reaction to this suggestion.

2 A unit trust company divides its investments between three sectors – companies that produce capital goods, companies that produce consumer goods and companies that provide financial services. The table shows the amount invested in each of these sectors over a four year period.

Year	Capital goods	Consumer goods	Financial services
1991	12	22	7
1992	13	18	18
1993	16	16	10
1994	29	14	22

Represent this information on
(a) a multiple bar chart
(b) a component bar chart
(c) a percentage component bar chart.

3 Paramount Car Auctions: sales, 1994

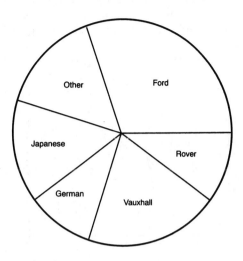

The cars that pass through Paramount Car Auctions are placed in one of six categories for record purposes. The pie chart given below shows the number of cars in each category for sales that took place in 1994.

(a) What fraction of the cars sold were
  (i) Fords
  (ii) Japanese
  (iii) German?
(b) If 340 German cars went through these auction rooms, how many of the cars auctioned were
  (i) Vauxhalls (ii) Japanese?
(c) By 1996 the total number of cars passing through these auction rooms had increased to 4420 and the percentage in each category had changed to: Rover 15%, Ford 25%, Vauxhall 20%, German 12% and Japanese 20%.
  (i) What percentage were there in the 'other' category?
  (ii) Draw a pie chart to represent this data.
(d) Comparing 1996 with 1994, which category had
  (i) held its market share steady
  (ii) increased its market share?
(e) In which category had the number of cars sold increased even though the market share had decreased?

4 The number of people sitting in the lounge of a residential home was counted at hourly intervals one Sunday and the results recorded on a line graph. A copy of this graph is given below.

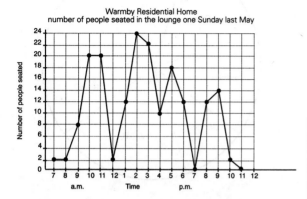

Warmby Residential Home
number of people seated in the lounge one Sunday last May

(a) How many people were sitting in the lounge at (i) 10 a.m. (ii) 11 p.m.?
(b) Can you say how many there were at (i) 11.30 a.m. (ii) 3.35 p.m.?
(c) Can you explain the pattern?
(d) Would you expect to find a similar pattern
  (i) in this lounge on the following day
  (ii) for a lounge in an hotel that has a similar number of beds to the residential home?

5 At the Duxborough Residential Home they keep a record of the number of times each resident is taken out by friends or relatives for the day. Last quarter the recorded number of times were:
20, 8, 3, 5, 0, 12, 0, 5, 3, 6, 3, 0, 18, 0, 2, 0, 6, 0, 3, 5, 14, 10, 5, 2, 0, 3, 0, 4, 5, 1, 12.
(a) How many residents live in the home?
(b) Find the mean, mode, median and range of the number of day trips taken.

6 The table shows the weights, in kilograms, of the bags of potatoes loaded on a lorry. Each bag is supposed to contain at least 50 kg.

Weight (w kg)	Frequency (f)	Halfway value (x)	(fx)
$49 \leqslant w < 50$	12	49.5	594
$50 \leqslant w < 51$	120		
$51 \leqslant w < 52$	55		
$52 \leqslant w < 53$	13		

(a) How many bags are there on the lorry?
(b) What fraction of the bags are underweight?
(c) Find the mean weight of the bags on the lorry.
(d) The maximum weight permitted on the lorry is 10 000 kg.
  (i) Is the lorry likely to be overloaded?
  (ii) If so, by approximately how much?

UNIT 9 Equations and Formulae

After studying this unit you will be able to
☐ use formulae expressed in words
☐ solve simple equations in words and in letters
☐ collect like terms
☐ solve a problem by forming an equation
☐ remove brackets
☐ solve equations by trial and improvement.

Formulae in words   Many people regularly use formulae that are expressed in words rather than in letters.

Note: If you find difficulty in solving simple algebraic equations you will find it useful to look at Guidance Notes: Basic Skills, Section F, pp.348–350.

Exercise 9a

Question   An electricity bill is calculated using the formula
Amount to pay (excluding VAT)
      = standing charge + number of units used × price of each unit
How much is there to pay if the standing charge is £12.36 and 1645 units have been used at a cost of 7.96p each?

Answer
Amount to pay (excluding VAT)   = £12.36 + 1645 × 7.96p
                                = £12.36 + 13 094.2p
                                = £12.36 + £130.94 (to the nearest penny)
                                = £143.30

1 The displacement of an engine is given by the formula

Displacement in cc = number of cylinders $\times \pi \times \left(\dfrac{\text{bore in cm}}{2}\right)^2 \times$ stroke in cm

(a) Find the displacement of 4-cylinder diesel engine which has a bore of 87.0 mm and a stroke of 84.0 mm

(b) Find the displacement of a 6-cylinder petrol engine which has a bore of 89.9 mm and a stroke of 86.6 mm.

2 The annual sales growth of a company is defined as
$\dfrac{\text{increase in sales}}{\text{previous year's sales}} \times 100\%$.

(a) Find the annual sales growth over the last five years for a company whose sales figures are those given in the table

Year	1991	1992	1993	1994	1995
Sales (000)	145	167	190	214	240

(b) Comment on what is happening to
(i) the annual sales growth (ii) the annual sales.

3 The annual birth rate of a population is defined as

$\dfrac{\text{registered number of births}}{\text{total population}} \times 1000$

and the annual death rate is

$\dfrac{\text{registered number of deaths}}{\text{total population}} \times 1000$.

Find
(a) the birth rate   (b) the death rate,
for a population of 68.5 million for which there were 895 536 registered births and 767 983 registered deaths.

4 The 'density' of a cruise ship is the gross registered tonnage divided by the number of passenger berths. Find the density of
(a) the *QE2* which has a gross tonnage of 66 450 tons and can carry 1877 passengers
(b) *Canberra* which has a gross tonnage of 43 975 tons and can carry 1706 passengers
(c) the yacht *Ocean Islander* which has a gross tonnage of 5000 tons and can carry 260 passengers.

5 The cutting speed of a twist drill, in metres per minute, is given by

$$\frac{\text{Diameter of twist drill in millimetres} \quad \times \quad \text{number of revolutions per minute of the twist drill}}{1000}$$

A high speed steel twist drill, with a diameter of 20 mm, revolves at 475 revolutions per minute.
Find its cutting speed.

6 The amount of value added tax included in the purchase price of an article is given by

$$\frac{\text{sales price including VAT} \times \text{rate of VAT as a percentage}}{100\% + \text{rate of VAT as a percentage}}$$

How much value added tax is included in the price of
(a) a chair costing £156 when the VAT rate is 20%
(b) an album costing £18.80 when the VAT rate is 17½%
(c) a car costing £17 580 when the VAT rate is 20%
(d) a motorbike costing £564 when the VAT rate is 17½%?

7 A person's mean blood pressure is calculated using the formula
Mean blood pressure =

$$\text{diastolic pressure} + \frac{(\text{systolic pressure} - \text{diastolic pressure})}{3}$$

Use the information given in the table to find the mean blood pressure for each person

	Systolic pressure (mm of mercury)	diastolic pressure (mm of mercury)
Mel	140	80
Wendy	160	86
Bina	176	90
Hank	120	75

8 The dividend yield on a share is defined by the formula

$$\text{Dividend yield} = \frac{\text{gross dividend in pence}}{\text{quoted share price in pence}} \times 100\%$$

(a) Find the dividend yield on Marks and Spencer Ordinary shares if the gross dividend per share is 10.4p and the price of each share is 413p
(b) Find the dividend yield on Thorn/EMI shares if the gross yield is 23p a share and the price of the share is £10.78.

9 The gross yield on a Government stock is calculated using the formula

$$\text{Gross interest yield} = \frac{\text{interest rate}}{\text{stock price}} \times 100$$

Find the gross interest yield on
(a) Exchequer Gas 3% stock priced at 98
(b) Treasury $12\frac{3}{4}$% stock priced at 111.

A market trader started the day with a certain number of battery operated radios. Three of them were broken so had to be thrown away, and of the good ones he sold 21. At the end of the day he still had 9 left. How many did he start with?

From this information we can form an equation.

The number he had to start with − 3 (those he had to throw away) − 21 (the number he sold) = 9 (the number he had left).

Equations involving words

More simply

Number he had to start − 3 − 21	= 9
i.e. Number he had to start − 24	= 9
Add 24 to each side Number he had to start	= 9 + 24
	= 33

We were able to form a simple equation from which we found that he had 33 radios to start with.

Many problems can be expressed as a simple equation, involving numbers and words, which can then be solved.

Exercise 9b

Question Kay bought a packet of used postage stamps in a car boot sale. She went through the stamps carefully and decided to keep 13 of them for her collection. The remainder she divided equally among her three sons. If each son received 18 stamps how many stamps were there in the packet?

Answer The number she had to divide between her three sons was: the number in the packet − 13.
But each son received 18 stamps
i.e. the sons had 18 × 3 = 54 altogether between them
∴ number in the pack − 13 = 54
Adding 13 to each side gives: Number in pack = 54 + 13
                     = 67

There were 67 stamps in the packet.

1 Any product that is manufactured needs components such as screws, nuts, bolts or washers. Inevitably some of the components are faulty so cannot be used. The following equations have arisen in calculating the number of components needed in different situations. In each case find that number.
(a) Number of components − 5   = 245
(b) (Number of components − 3) ÷ 4 = 63
(c) (Number of components + 7) ÷ 3 = 146
(d) Number of components × 2 − 7   = 159.

2 In this question study each set of statements carefully and then write down an equation similar to those given in Question 1. Once you are satisfied that your equation is correct solve it to answer the question asked.
(a) Nicki started with a box of components. After using 512 of them she had 27 left. How many did she have to start with?
(b) Cliff began the shift with a basket of components. He used 387 of them but had 13 left over at the end of the shift. How many were in the basket to start with?
(c) Alan needed another 5 bolts to complete the assembly of 65 electric motors. If each motor required 4 bolts how many bolts did Alan need to assemble that batch of motors?
(d) Each of the units Sharon assembled required 7 washers. She started with a box of washers that was sufficient to assemble 54 units, with 4 washers left over. How many washers did she have at the beginning?

3 An operator on the production line for front disc brakes was given a basket containing a quantity of identical components. He used the components, 2 to a brake, until all that remained in the basket were 5 faulty components. A check showed that he had assembled 43 front disc brakes. Form a suitable equation and use it to find the number of components in the basket when he started.

In the questions that follow form an equation and solve it to answer the question asked.

4 A fuse box takes 8 identical fuses. How many fuses does Madge need to draw from the stores if she completes an order for 144 fuse boxes and in the process comes across 3 faulty fuses?

5 Six bolts are needed to assemble an electric light fitting. How many bolts did Tim start with if he was able to assemble 176 light fittings and had 27 bolts left over?

6 A washing machine needs 12 of a particular size of Philips screw. Dave starts with a box of 288 screws, 3 of which he finds to be faulty. How many washing machines can he complete from his stock of screws? How many usable screws remain?

7 Sid has a stock of 514 self-tapping screws which can be used with plastics. Each unit he assembles requires 8 screws. When he has completed the order 146 screws remain. How many plastic units were there in the order?

Using letters in equations

Frequently it is convenient to use a single letter to stand for a word or descriptive phrase.

For example, instead of writing
(number of bolts $- 5) \div 3 = 52$
we could write

$(n - 5) \div 3 = 52$ where n stands for 'the number of bolts'.
We can then proceed as we did in the questions in 9b using n (or any other letter we care to choose) instead of the words that it represents.

$$
\begin{aligned}
\text{Then } (n - 5) \div 3 &= 52 \qquad \text{(Multiply both sides by 3)} \\
n - 5 &= 52 \times 3 \\
n - 5 &= 156 \qquad \text{(Add 5 to each side)} \\
n &= 161
\end{aligned}
$$

This shows that the number of bolts is 161.

The only rule that you need remember when solving equations of this type is:

whatever you do to one side you must do to the other

Now we will consider solving simple equations increasing the degree of difficulty as we progress. In any question, if it helps, you can think of the letter in the equation as standing for a word. Let it mean 'the number of screws, or people, or CDs', or whatever else the problem involves.

Exercise 9c

Question   Solve
(a) $b - 10 = 12$ (b) $a + 4 = 10$

(c) $3c = 24$ (d) $\dfrac{p}{4} = 5$

Answer
$$
\begin{aligned}
\text{(a) } b - 10 &= 12 \qquad \text{(Add 10 to each side)} \\
b &= 12 + 10 \\
\text{i.e.} \quad b &= 22 \\
\text{(b) } a + 4 &= 10 \qquad \text{(Subtract 10 to each side)} \\
a &= 10 - 4 \\
\text{i.e.} \quad a &= 6 \\
\text{(c)} \quad 3c &= 24 \qquad \text{(Divide both sides by 3)} \\
c &= 24 \div 3 \\
\text{i.e.} \quad c &= 8
\end{aligned}
$$

(d) $\quad\dfrac{p}{4} = 5 \qquad$ (Multiply both sides by 4)

$$p = 5 \times 4$$
i.e. $\quad p = 20$

In this exercise solve the equations. In each case say what you have done.

1 $p - 5 = 21$	**2** $y - 7 = 2$
3 $q - 10 = 12$	**4** $a + 6 = 58$
5 $x - 16 = 4$	**6** $b - 19 = 34$
7 $b + 8 = 25$	**8** $x + 11 = 21$
9 $2a = 16$	**10** $3b = 24$
11 $7x = 49$	**12** $4y = 48$

Question Solve the equation $\frac{1}{2}a = 6$.

Answer $\frac{1}{2}a$ is another way of writing $a \div 2$, so the given equation can be written

$$\dfrac{a}{2} = 6 \qquad \text{(Multiply both sides by 2)}$$

$$a = 6 \times 2$$
i.e. $\qquad\qquad\quad a = 12$

---

13 $\frac{1}{3}x = 15$		**14**	$\frac{1}{2}b = 24$
15 $\frac{1}{4}c = 23$		**16**	$\frac{1}{10}p = 4$

Sometimes the answers are not exact.

Question Solve $3x = 7$.

Answer $\qquad 3x = 7 \qquad$ (Divide both sides by 3)
$\qquad\quad\ x = 7 \div 3$
i.e. $\quad x = 2\frac{1}{3}$ or 2.33 (correct to 2 d.p.)

---

17 $a + 3.5 = 5$	**18** $b - 2.7 = 7.9$
19 $z + \frac{1}{4} = \frac{3}{4}$	**20** $w - \frac{1}{2} = 2\frac{3}{4}$
21 $p + \frac{1}{3} = 3\frac{1}{3}$	**22** $q - \frac{2}{3} = 7\frac{1}{3}$
23 $4c = 6$	**24** $5p = 12$
25 $\dfrac{p}{2} = 2.8$	**26** $\dfrac{q}{3} = 3.1$
27 $\dfrac{x}{5} = 14.2$	**28** $\dfrac{y}{7} = 6.7$

29 $\dfrac{x}{4} = \frac{1}{2}$ **30** $\dfrac{a}{2} = \frac{1}{4}$

31 $\dfrac{b}{3} = \frac{2}{3}$ **32** $\dfrac{c}{5} = \frac{3}{10}$

Some equations require two operations.

Question	Solve $3x - 4 = 23$.
Answer	$\begin{aligned} 3x - 4 &= 23 \quad \text{(Add 4 to each side)} \\ 3x &= 23 + 4 \\ 3x &= 27 \quad \text{(Divide both sides by 3)} \\ x &= 27 \div 3 \end{aligned}$
	i.e. $\qquad x = 9$

33 $2a - 7 = 13$ **34** $5x - 9 = 6$
35 $7p - 11 = 17$ **36** $9q + 1 = 10$
37 $4y + 3 = 15$ **38** $2x + 7 = 10$
39 $6x - 5 = 15$ **40** $12z + 3 = 13$

Like and unlike terms

$3a$ and $5a$ are examples of like terms. They can be added together to give $8a$. On the other hand $3a$ and $5b$ are unlike terms. They cannot be simplified in any way.

Exercise 9d

Question	Simplify where possible (a) $2a + 3 + 7a - 4$ (b) $2b + 4c - 5$
Answer	(a) $\begin{aligned} 2a + 3 + 7a - 4 &= 2a + 7a + 3 - 4 \\ &= 9a - 1 \end{aligned}$ (b) $2b + 4c - 5$ are unlike terms and so cannot be simplified.

Simplify where possible.
1 $a + a + a + 6$ **2** $2a + 4c$
3 $2a + 3a + 4a$ **4** $5a - 2 + 7a - 4$
5 $8p + 2q - 5p + 3q$ **6** $9p - 3p - 2p - p$

Question	Simplify the equation $3p + 2p = 25$ and hence solve it.
Answer	$\begin{aligned} 3p + 2p &= 25 \\ 5p &= 25 \end{aligned}$ i.e. $\qquad p = 5$

Simplify the following equations and hence solve them.

7 $b + 2b = 12$ 8 $a + 2a + 3a = 24$

9 $8p - 3p + p = 36$ 10 $5q + 2q - q = 27$

11 $3y - y = 7$ 12 $8x - 4x + x = 5$

Question   Solve the equation $7p - 2 + 5p - 7 = 27$.

Answer

$$7p - 2 + 5p - 7 = 27 \quad \text{(Collect like terms)}$$
$$7p + 5p - 2 - 7 = 27$$
$$12p - 9 = 27 \quad \text{(Add 9 each side)}$$
$$12p = 27 + 9$$
$$12p = 36 \quad \text{(Divide both sides by 12)}$$
$$p = 36 \div 12$$

i.e. $\qquad\qquad p = 3$

Solve the equations

13 $3b + 2b + 8 - 3 = 15$ 14 $4c + 3 - 2c - 5 = 4$

15 $p + 2p + 5p - 7 = 1$ 16 $5q - 2q + 4 = 10$

17 $7x - 2 + x + 6 = 36$ 18 $a + 7 + 2a = 25$

Question   The Peacock family take 2 pints of milk a day and an extra pint on Saturday and on Sunday. They pay every Monday when they get 4p change from a £5 note. If the price of one pint of milk is q pence form an equation in q and solve it to find the price of a pink of milk.

Answer   The Peacock family take 2 pints of milk a day, Monday to Friday, plus 3 pints on Saturday and 3 pints on Sunday.

Altogether they take $5 \times 2 + 3 + 3$ pints i.e. 16 pints

If 1 pint costs q pence, 16 pints cost $16 \times q$ pence i.e. $16q$ pence

The amount they pay is £5 $-$ 4 pence = 500 pence $-$ 4 pence
$$= 496 \text{ pence}$$

We now know how much they pay in two different ways, namely $16q$ pence and 496 pence. These two quantities must be equal

so $\qquad 16q = 496$

i.e. $\qquad q = \frac{496}{16}$

$\qquad\qquad = 31$

The cost of a pint of milk is therefore 31 pence.

---

19 A fishing rod, consisting of three pieces, is 450 cm long. Measuring from one end, the first piece is h cm long, the second piece is 15 cm longer than the first piece, and the third piece is 15 cm longer than the second piece. Form an equation in h and solve it to find

(a) the length of the shortest piece

(b) the lengths of the other two pieces.

(As a check, the sum of your three lengths should be 450 cm.)

20 A chelsea bun costs x pence and a cream doughnut costs $2x$ pence. Find, in terms of x, the cost of
(a) 3 chelsea buns (b) 4 cream doughnuts.
If the total cost of these 7 cakes is £2.75 form an equation in x and solve it to find the cost of
(c) a chelsea bun (d) a cream doughnut.

21 Sandra orders a cup of coffee, costing n pence, and a jacket potato, costing $4n$ pence. She pays with a £5 note and receives £2 change. Form an equation in n and solve it. Hence find the price of
(a) a cup of coffee (b) a jacket potato.

22 On a 420 acre farm there are five times as many acres of wheat as there are acres of barley; there are three times as many acres of grassland as there are acres of barley and as many acres are unused due to 'set aside' as are used to grow barley. Assuming that there are x acres of barley form an equation in x and solve it to find the number of acres
(a) put to 'set-aside' (b) of wheat
(c) of grassland.
Note: In an attempt to prevent surplus food production the European Parliament has decreed that a certain percentage of farm land must not be used for producing food. This land is called 'set aside'.

23 For a concert at the village hall the Amberley Operatic Society are able to sell 70 tickets at £a each and 148 tickets at £$2a$ each. If the total receipts are £1464 form an equation in a and solve it to find the price of each ticket.

24 An artist sells three sizes of prints – small, medium and large. She charges £10 for the small size, £25 for the medium size and £75 for the large. Last year, of the 133 prints she sold, twice as many were medium compared with large and twice as many were small compared with medium.
(a) Form an equation and solve it to find how many of each size of print were sold.
(b) What was the total income from the sale of the 133 prints?

Simplifying, including the removal of brackets

When a bracket has a number immediately in front of it that number multiplies everything that is inside the bracket.
e.g. $7(4a - 3) = 7 \times 4a - 7 \times 3$
$= 28a - 21$

Exercise 9e

Question (a) Simplify $5 \times 4p$ (b) Remove the brackets in the expression $3(2q + 5)$.

Answer
(a) $5 \times 4p = 20p$
(b) $3(2q + 5) = 3 \times 2q + 3 \times 5$
$= 6q + 15$

1 Simplify
(a) $2 \times 3x$ (b) $5 \times 2p$
(c) $3 \times 8q$ (d) $12 \times 5y$

2 Write, without brackets
(a) $4(3p - 4)$ (b) $5(6 - 3b)$
(c) $7(p + 2)$ (d) $3(2x + 7)$

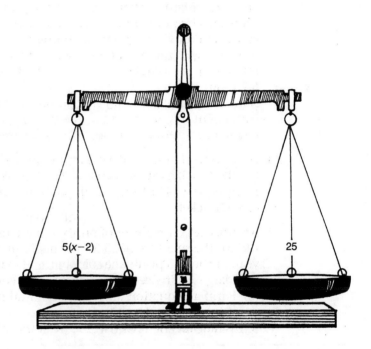

Question   Write the equation $5(x - 2) = 25$ without brackets and hence solve it.

Answer

$5(x - 2)$	$= 25$	(Remove the brackets)
$5x - 10$	$= 25$	(Add 10 to each side)
$5x$	$= 35$	(Divide both sides by 5)
x	$= 7$	

In Questions 3–8 remove the brackets and hence solve the equation.

3   $2(a + 5) = 14$ 4 $3(x - 2) = 42$
5   $4(p + 6) = 44$ 6 $5(q - 3) = 25$
7   $2(3 + a) = 25$ 8 $3(5 + b) = 18$

Solving equations by 'trial and improvement'

Sometimes, a real life problem leads to an equation which we cannot solve easily. When this happens we guess the solution, and then substitute the guess into the equation to see how well it fits. This should enable us to make a better guess second time than we did first time.

Exercise 9f

Question

The area of a small metal plate, which is used in the assembly of a lawnmower, is 21 cm^2. This plate is 1 cm longer than it is wide. The width of the plate can be found by finding the value of x that satisfies the equation $x^2 + x = 21$. Find, correct to 1 d.p., two positive values, between which the width of the plate lies.

Answer

x^2, x and 21 are unlike terms so the equation cannot be simplified
Try $x = 3$ in the left hand side of the equation
$x^2 + x = 3^2 + 3 = 9 + 3 = 12$ (too small i.e. less than 21)
Try $x = 4$ $\quad x^2 + x = 4^2 + 4 = 16 + 4 = 20$ (too small – a little less than 21)

Trying 5 would be much too big so we try 4.5
If $x = 4.5$ $\quad x^2 + x = 4.5^2 + 4.5$
$\qquad\qquad\qquad = 20.25 + 4.5$
$\qquad\qquad\qquad = 24.75$ (still too big – larger than 21)
Try $x = 4.1$ $\quad x^2 + x = 4.1^2 + 4.1$
$\qquad\qquad\qquad = 16.81 + 4.1$
$\qquad\qquad\qquad = 20.91$ (a little too small – less than 21)
Try 4.2 $\quad x^2 + x = 4.2^2 + 4.2$
$\qquad\qquad\qquad = 17.64 + 4.2$
$\qquad\qquad\qquad = 21.84$ (a little too big – more than 21)
$\therefore x$ lies between 4.1 and 4.2.

The equations that follow have arisen in solving problems – some of these problems are referred to in brackets. Find, correct to 1 d.p., two positive numbers between which the solution of the given equation lies.

1 $x^2 = 20$ (x cm is the side of a square that has an area of 20 cm^2)

2 $a^2 = 30$ (a m is the side of a square that has an area of 30 m^2)

3 $r^2 = \dfrac{8}{\pi}$ (r cm is the radius of a circle which has an area of 8 square centimetres. Use the value of π on your calculator)

4 $x^2 + x = 32$ (x m is the shorter side of a rectangular flower bed that has an area of 32 m^2)

5 $y^2 - y = 18$ (y cm is the length of the longer edge of an oblong piece of plastic that has an area of 18 cm^2)

6 $h^2 + 4h = 106$ (h cm is the height of a triangle that has an area of 106 cm^2)

7 $b^2 + 4b = 87$ (b cm is the distance between two parallel sides of a parallelogram that has an area of 87 square centimetres)

8 $c^2 - 4c = 2$

9 $z^2 + 5z = 16$

10 $x^3 = 18$ (x mm is the length of the side of a small cubical metal block that has a volume of 18 cubic millimetres)

11 $x^3 = 40$ (x cm is the length of an edge of a cubical cardboard box that has a capacity of 40 cubic centimetres)

12 $x^3 = 62$ (x m is the length of the side of a cubical Egyptian burial chamber that has 62 cubic metres of space inside it.)

Multiple choice questions

1 The solution of the equation $3x = 15$ is
A $x = 12$ B $x = 3$
C $x = 5$ D $x = 18$

2 If $p - \frac{3}{4} = 2\frac{1}{2}$ it follows that the value of p is
A $1\frac{3}{4}$ B $3\frac{1}{4}$
C $2\frac{3}{8}$ D $2\frac{2}{3}$

3 When $2b + 3b + 5b$ is simplified the answer is
A $10b$ B $10b \times b \times b$
C $30b$ D $30b \times b \times b$

4 A rectangular lawn, which has an area of 70 m^2, is 2 m longer than it is wide. If the lawn is p metres wide the value of p can be found by solving the equation $p^2 + 2p = 70$. Trial and improvement methods show that the value of p lies between
A 7.2 m & 7.3 m   B 7.3 m & 7.4 m
C 7.4 m & 7.5 m   D 7.5 m & 7.6 m

5 Karl is p years old and his father, Len, is five times as old as Karl. In 18 years' time Len will be twice as old as Karl.
Which of the following statements are true and which are false?
A Len's present age is $p + 5$ years
B In 18 years time Karl will be $p + 18$ years old and Len will be $5p + 18$ years old

C The equation we can form from the given information is $5p + 18 = 2p + 36$
D In 5 years' time Karl will be 11 and Len will be 33.

6 Brace Electronics make a 1 for 5 rights issue of their ordinary shares. This means that for every 5 shares an investor owns 1 new share will be offered at a favourable price. Fractions of a share are discounted. Goff Morgan has 473 ordinary share in Brace Electronics. The following statements have been made:
Statement 1 If he takes up the rights issue Goff will have exactly 20% more shares than he had to start with.
Statement 2 If Goff does not take up the rights issue he will have 94 fewer shares than if he had taken them up.
How are these statements best described
A True, True   B True, False
C False, True   D False, False.

Self assessment 9

1 A small component for a car requires 3 rubber washers. How many washers must be taken out of stock to manufacture 175 components if 12 washers are broken during assembly and have to be replaced?

2   Solve the equations

(a) $a + 7 = 36$ (b) $b - 9 = 21$

(c) $8c = 56$ (d) $\frac{1}{4}d = 4$

3   The Body Mass Index (BMI) for a person is

$$\frac{\text{weight in kilograms}}{(\text{height in metres})^2}.$$

(a) Find the BMI for the four brothers whose heights and weights are listed below

Height (m)	Weight (kg)
Alf	1.74	82
Ben	1.92	93.7
Cliff	1.84	74.5
Dave	1.57	95.2

(b) Find Eddy's Body Mass Index if he is 5 ft 3 in tall and weighs 14 st 6 lb.
(2.2 lb = 1 kg and 1 inch = 2.54 cm.)

4   Solve the equations

(a) $3p - 4 = 20$ (b) $2q + 9 = 12$

(c) $\dfrac{x}{10} = \dfrac{7}{5}$ (d) $y + \frac{1}{4} = 3\frac{1}{2}$

5   Simplify the following equations and hence solve them

(a) $5x - 3x + 6x = 48$

(b) $7y + 3 - 2y + 8 = 26$

6 (a) Simplify   (i) $5\,(2p + 9)$ (ii) $3(7q - 3)$

(b) Solve the equation $3(2m - 3) = 39$.

7   Georgina has two wooden boxes, one of which is three times as heavy as the other. 3 kg of potatoes are put into the heavier box and 12 kg of carrots into the other box. When the partially filled boxes are put on the opposite sides of a scales they balance.

(a) If the weight of the lighter box is x kg, how heavy, in terms of x, is the other box?

(b) Form an equation in x and solve it to find the weight of each box.

Paper 9

1 An Arts Centre employing several staff is open from 09.00 to 18.00, 6 days a week.
   (a) How many hours is the centre open each week?
   (b) Members of staff work a 36 hour week and at any one time 6 of them must be on duty. What is the minimum number of staff they must employ?
   (c) Due to an upsurge in interest the Leisure Committee decide to open the centre from 09.00 to 21.00 every day, including Sunday. How many extra staff do they need to take on assuming that 6 staff are always on duty and the length of the working week remains unchanged?

2 The number of bedrooms in the hotels listed in a Heart of England tourist brochure are given below.

26	27	53	10	23	10	12	23	12	14
20	49	12	81	14	40	50	8	25	25
11	15	25	20	8	12	15	72	30	27
20	10	96	15	85	10	16	20	10	15
11	6	7	9	10	24	9	31	9	14
39	18	38	17	23	20	41	60	22	48
34	94	23	20	33	78	12	5	17	10

   (a) What is
      (i) the highest   (ii) the lowest, number of bedrooms available?
   (b) Copy and complete the following frequency table

Number of bedrooms	Tally	Frequency
1–20		
21–40		
41–60		
61–80		
81–100		

   (c) Draw a bar chart to illustrate this information. For the heights of the bars use 1 cm to represent 4 bedrooms.
   (d) Which group contains the greatest number of hotels?
   (e) How many more hotels are there in the largest group than in the smallest group?

(f) How many bedrooms are there altogether? (You need the raw data to answer this question.)

(g) Do the hotels with more than 80 bedrooms provide more bedrooms than all the other hotels put together?

3

Pilkinborough: how each £1 is spent

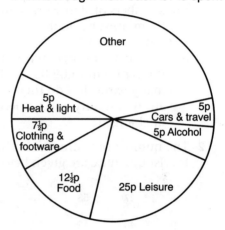

A survey among the population of Pilkinborough was conducted to find out how the average person spends each £1. The results are given on the diagram.

(a) (i) How much in the £ does the average person spend on 'other'?
    (ii) Give some examples of what this could be.

(b) If an accurate pie chart was drawn to illustrate this data what would be the angle at the centre for
    (i) leisure   (ii) food   (iii) clothing & footwear?

(c) John has £180 a week to spend. Use the above information to decide how much he spends on   (i) cars and travel   (ii) leisure.

4 The temperature required to harden steel which contains up to 0.8% carbon is given by the formula
Temperature in degrees celsius = $950 - 250 \times$ percentage of carbon
Find the temperature required to harden a plain steel which has a carbon content of 0.4%.

5 (a) Simplify $5p - 7p + 2p + 4p$.
(b) Hence solve the equation $5p - 7p + 2p + 4p = 12$.
(c) Find, correct to 1 d.p., two positive values, between which lies a solution of the equation $x^3 = 90$.

Paper 10

1 The 90 players in the first round of a golf competition go out in groups of three, the first group teeing off at 08.00. The other competitors follow at 8 minute intervals. If each group takes $3\frac{1}{4}$ hr to complete a round find
(a) the time at which the last three tee off
(b) the time at which the last group complete their round

(c) how long the 12th group have been playing when the 1st group complete their round

(d) the time it takes to complete the first round of the competition.

2 An analysis of a copy of the *Silverbridge Argus* shows that the percentage of space allocated to the various sections is: News 35%, Sport 20%, Business and Commerce 5%, Features 10%, Advertisements 25%, other 5%.

The paper has 26 pages and each page is divided into 8 columns.

(a) How many columns are there altogether?

(b) How many columns are devoted to each of the given sections? Illustrate this information on a bar chart.

(c) Construct a pie chart to illustrate this information.

3 Today is Friday 25 March.

(a) What will be the date   (i) next Tuesday   (ii) next Friday
(iii) a week on Wednesday?

(b) What date was it
(i) a week yesterday   (ii) a week last Wednesday?

(c) What day of the week will it be on   (i) 30 March   (ii) 6 April?

4 The average weight of the oarsmen in a rowing eight is 13 st 2 lb and the average weight of the crew, including the cox, is 12 st 6 lb. How heavy is the cox?

5 The brochure for Travel Abroad includes details of the following cancellation charges.

42	days or more before departure	deposit
29 – 41	days before departure	30%
15 – 28	days before departure	45%
8 –14	days before departure	60%
1 – 7	days before departure	90%
departure date or after		100%

Sid and Esther Bonnie have already paid Travel Abroad £1256 which is the full cost of their holiday to Cyprus. They are forced to cancel 3 weeks before they are due to leave.

(a) How much will they lose?

(b) How much will they get back?

(c) How much more would they have lost if they had waited until the tenth day before departure before cancelling?

1 Meubles Français wish to purchase 36 refectory tables and 216 dining chairs from Goldsborough Furniture, Walsall. Prices are quoted in pounds sterling and are: £156.50 for a table and £46.75 for a chair. There is a discount of 5% for orders over £10 000 and a further discount of $2\frac{1}{2}$% if payment is made within 7 days of delivery.

(a) If £1 ≈ 8.711 French francs convert these figures so that the total cost and the cash discounts can be placed before the purchasing manager at Meubles Français.

(b) Meubles Français accept the quotation as stated in francs, but before payment is due the rate of exchange has become £1 ≈ 8.728 Ff. How much do Goldsborough Furniture gain or lose as a result of the change in the exchange rate?

2 One of Mike's jobs at Rowley Motors is to carry out all the PDIs (pre-delivery inspections) on the new cars they sell. He keeps careful records which include, for each vehicle, the number of slack or missing bolts. For the vehicles he checked last week the figures were:

3, 2, 0, 2, 3, 7, 4, 6, 0, 1, 0, 2, 5, 2, 3, 0, 0, 4, 9, 10, 2, 4

(a) How many PDIs did he do last week?

(b) How many slack or missing bolts did he find?

(c) Find the mean number of slack or missing bolts per vehicle.

3 Travelworld has three travel agencies in three different towns. One week the first 100 callers at each agency were asked to fill in a questionnaire about holidays. One of the questions asked them to tick the appropriate box to show where they had spent their main holiday last year (if they took one). The results are listed below.

	Agency		
	Knoxton	Droyden	Wegglley
Holiday abroad	16	43	15
Seaside in the U.K.	7	26	12
Other in the U.K.	9	32	14
No holiday	3	8	10

For the people who took a holiday, illustrate the above information on

(a) a multiple bar chart   (b) a compound bar chart

(c) a percentage component bar chart.

4 Solve the equation

(a) $2p - 9 = 15$ (b) $3q + 5 = 23$

(c) $4(a + 3) = 36$

5 A company decides how many seats it needs in the canteen by using the formula

Number of seats = (Number of employees + 30) ÷ 2

(a) How many seats do they need for 350 employees?

Paper 12

(b) How many extra seats do they need if they increase the workforce by 100?

(c) They have 350 seats. What is the largest number of workers they should employ?

1 Sue Edgar keeps careful records of the total number of tomatoes she harvests from each of the plants in her greenhouse. Last season they were:

49, 55, 36, 43, 51, 57, 42, 29, 47, 51, 60, 46 and 55.

(a) How many tomato plants did she have in her greenhouse?

(b) Find the mean number of tomatoes per plant.

(c) What is the modal number of tomatoes per plant?

(d) Find the median number of tomatoes per plant.

2 In a manufacturing process at Cunicliffe plc, a group of 5 is withdrawn at random from the work force each day to perform a task requiring a greater than average degree of concentration. The table shows the number of females chosen each day.

Number of females chosen	0	1	2	3	4	5
Frequency	2	4	8	12	6	1

(a) How many days does the information in the table refer to?

(b) How many (i) females (ii) males, were selected altogether?

(c) Find the mean number of females selected per day.

(d) What is the mean number of males chosen per day.
    (Very little calculation is needed to do this!)

3 In Miami the clocks are 5 hours behind the clocks in London. What time is it

(a) in Miami when it is 12 noon in London?

(b) in London when it is 9 a.m. in Miami

(c) in Miami when it is midnight in London?

4 In 1991 the percentage of a publisher's book sales through the different outlets were: Retail bookshops 20%, Book Clubs 17.5%, Library & Institutional suppliers 22.5%, Schools & Leisure market 15%, Supermarkets 10%, other 15%. Illustrate this data on a pie chart.

5 The table shows the weight, in grams, of a random selection of the two varieties of potato Harry grew in his allotment.

Weight (w grams)	$0 \leqslant w < 100$	$100 \leqslant w < 200$	$200 \leqslant w < 300$	$300 \leqslant w < 400$
King Edward	8	13	23	16
Majestic	5	9	25	21

(a) Estimate the mean weight of (i) King Edwards (ii) Majestics.

(b) Which variety, on average, provides Harry with the heavier potato?

For You To Discuss: 3

Going places

It is more than a year now since Julie was appointed as the manager of a new branch of Going Places. When they planned the layout of the office she was asked what furniture she thought they needed, what equipment should be installed, and she helped to choose the carpet and decide on the colour scheme.

The carpet gave her a particular problem. She had a lot of trouble in convincing her boss which quotation to accept. They chose a very good quality, hard wearing carpet, and got three quotations. The one from Bisco Carpets quoted £35 a square yard plus £1.50 a square yard for underlay and fitting, VAT to be added at $17\frac{1}{2}$%. The amount of carpet to be supplied to be found by calculating the area in square yards, then rounding it up to the next whole number. The second quotation was from Deanley Floorcoverings. They wanted £44 a square metre but this included VAT. Underlay and fitting was free. The amount of carpet they would charge for is found by calculating the area in square metres, also rounding it up to the next whole number. The final quotation came from Newmann Bros. Their price was £38 a square metre, plus £1.75 a square metre for underlay and fitting. All prices inclusive of VAT. Measurements are rounded up to the nearest 5 cm and the area of carpet, in square metres, rounded up to the nearest tenth of a unit. Careful measurement of the office showed that, correct to the nearest inch, it is 33 ft 9 in long and 26 ft 4 in wide. Eventually Julie was able to explain clearly to her boss which quotation was the best and this was swiftly accepted.

After they had been open for little under a year Julie was told that the firm was going to allow her to spend £10 000 on advertising and promotion. She was very satisfied with the amount of business the branch was doing and thought that this offer showed that the company directors were pleased with her achievements so far. One of the ways she thought of spending some of the money was to conduct a survey. There were lots of questions she would like to ask and here was an opportunity to be able to answer some of them. Hopefully these answers would help her to increase turnover.

Julie was very keen on staff training. Two problems that arose, which good training helped to solve, are worth recording. One day last summer, Sarah, one of her assistants, had great difficulty in satisfying a client. The client arrived to collect his tickets for a holiday in the Mediterranean. Before he left he checked them and noticed that the flight times showed that he left Gatwick at 10.25 and was due to arrive at his destination at 12.40 whereas the flight times home showed that he left the resort at 16.52 and arrived back in Gatwick at 21.07. The client understood this to mean that the flight time out was $2\frac{1}{4}$ hours and the flight time home was $4\frac{1}{4}$ hours. He thought that the flight time should be the same both ways. Eventually Sarah succeeded in convincing him that the times on the tickets were correct and the flights times were the same both ways.

There was also a problem with currency. Nick had to explain to another client the ins and outs of currency exchange. That client had changed several hundred pounds, including two £50 notes, into pesetas. She had bought the currency at the rate of 185 pesetas to the £. The pesetas she exchanged for the two £50 notes she kept separately for emergencies. She didn't spend any of this money so when she got home, she changed it back into pounds for which she was paid £1 for every 190 pesetas she sold. She didn't get £100 back and found this difficult to accept especially as the rate of exchange had gone up from 185 pesetas to the £ to 190.

Another thing that clients often complain about to the office staff is that they see the same holiday advertised in different brochures at very different prices. They say 'You get the same hotel, the same facilities and the same service – why is the price so different?' Julie explains that different prices usually mean that you are not buying exactly the same holiday package. It is always worth looking carefully at the small print. Sometimes it takes her a long time to explain the differences and so justify why the brochure costs are so different from one travel company to another.

A more recent problem involved a discussion with a client who wanted to take his wife on a cruise but was convinced that he couldn't afford to. Before Julie and the client had finished their conversation she had

convinced him that he was spending more per person per day when he went to an expensive hotel in Bournemouth than if he took his wife on a cruise. She pointed out that he was forgetting about all the extras – things like mid-day meals, daytime and evening entertainment, morning coffee, afternoon teas, trips to the cinema, visits to the fitness centre, etc. As he walked out, convinced and satisfied that a cruise was good value for money, she felt that she'd given him a great deal of help and she certainly hoped he would return soon to boost her business.

An exercise that was attempted at one of the staff training sessions was to see if anyone could come up with a formula, using either words or letters, which could be used to find the total cost of a holiday, given all the separate costs. The idea was to be able to read off brochure prices, for an adult and/or a child, put in the number of adults and the number of children, the insurance costs and the flight supplements depending on the airport. If each of these values was put into the formula it would give the full cost of the holiday immediately. Angela finally constructed a very simple formula.

Questions and points for discussion

(a) Discuss how Julie could have convinced her boss that one quotation was cheaper than the others.

(b) Which carpet supplier did they choose?

(c) What questions do you think would be useful for Julie to ask in her survey? How would you go about getting these questions answered by potential customers?

(d) Apart from the survey, what other ways does Julie have of promoting Going Places?

(e) How could Sarah explain satisfactorily the apparent difference in the two flight times?

(f) Show that there is a simple way of working out the length of the flight by using both pairs of arrival and departure times. How long was this particular flight?

(g) For flying longer distances, for example to the pacific coast of America or to Australia, what other advice could Sarah give travellers?

(h) When travellers go abroad they have a choice. Money can be taken either in pounds sterling or in the currency of the country visited. As an alternative a person can take Travellers' Cheques. Discuss the advantages and disadvantages of each. Are there other ways of paying for something when you are abroad?

(i) The total costs of a holiday are often very different from the brochure costs. Discuss the advantages and disadvantages of self-catering, half-board, full-board and fully inclusive holiday packages. What hidden expenses can there be?

(j) Can you construct a formula that would be similar to Angela's?

UNIT 10 Ratio and Proportion

After studying this unit you will be able to
- ☐ find and simplify the ratio of two quantities
- ☐ compare the sizes of different quantities whether in the same or different units
- ☐ increase or decrease a quantity in a given ratio
- ☐ divide a quantity in a given ratio
- ☐ solve simple problems in direct and inverse proportion

Ratio

A factory that assembles motor cars needs, among other things, roadwheels and front headlamp units. If they assemble 5 cars they need 25 wheels and 10 headlamp units. If they assemble 50 cars they need 250 wheels and 100 headlamp units. In all cases the number of wheels compared with the number of headlamp units is the same as 5 compared with 2. We say that the ratio of wheels to headlamps is 5 compared with 2 and write this as 5:2.

When 6 buckets of sand are mixed with 2 buckets of cement, the ratio of sand to cement is 6:2.

A ratio can be simplified by dividing each part by the same number. For example 20:15 is the same as 4:3 because both 20 and 15 can be divided by 5.

Similarly 12:3 is the same as 4:1 and 18:27 is the same as 2:3.

Exercise 10a

In Questions 1–4 simplify the ratio.

1 20:30   2 35:21
3 12:18   4 56:72.

Question   At Waterstones Financial Services there are 12 male staff and 21 female staff. What is the ratio of males to females?

Answer   Ratio of males to females is 12:21
                = 4:7 (Dividing by 3)

5 In a residential home there are 35 women and 14 men. What is the ratio of
   (a) women to men   (b) men to women?

6 It is expected that by the year 2011 the population of Wales will be 3 000 000 and the population of Scotland will be 5 000 000. What is the expected ratio in 2011 of the population of Scotland to the population of Wales?

7 Two shafts, connected by a belt, rotate at 150 revs per minute and 250 revs per minute. What is the ratio of the speed of the slower shaft to the speed of the faster shaft?

8 Last week at Holiday Travel they took 30 bookings for holidays in America and 105 bookings for holidays in Europe. What is the ratio of the number of holiday bookings for America to the number of holiday bookings for Europe?

9 To make sweet apple wine Linda uses 2 lb white sugar to 11 lb mixed apples. Find the ratio of
   (a) the weight of sugar to the weight of apples
   (b) the weight of apples to the weight of sugar.

10 On a farm of 371 acres, 106 acres are used to grow cereals and the remainder is put down to grass. Find the ratio of
   (a) the acreage used for cereals to the acreage used for grass
   (b) the acreage used for grass to the acreage used for cereals.

Comparing the sizes of quantities

Question 25 m compared with 15 m is the same as 5 compared with 3. Use the symbol : to write this sentence as an equation.

Answer 25 m : 15 m = 5:3

1 Using the symbol : write each sentence as an equation.
  (a) 30 lorries compared with 10 vans is the same as 3 compared with 1.
  (b) 675 red posters compared with 540 yellow posters is the same as 5 compared with 4.
  (c) 3738 seated spectators compared with 534 standing spectators is the same as 7 compared with 1.

2 Write each equation as a statement
  (a) 42 p : 105 p = 2:5
  (b) 80 beds empty : 440 beds occupied = 2:11
  (c) 364 shopfloor workers : 312 office workers = 7:6

Question Maggie has £5 and John has 175 p. What is the ratio of the amount of money Maggie has to the amount of money John has?

Answer (The units of money must be the same, so we change the larger unit to the smaller unit i.e. we change pounds to pence.)
  £5 = 500 p.
  Ratio of amount of money Maggie has to amount of money John has is £5 : 175 p
  = 500 p:175 p
  = 500:175
  = 20:7 (Dividing by 25)

3 A fruit cake costs £2.55 and a loaf of bread costs 85 p. What is the ratio of the cost of a fruit cake to the cost of a loaf of bread?

4 One piece of wood is 80 cm long and a second piece is 2 m long. the ratio of the length of the first piece to the length of the second.

5 To make sweet marrow wine Glenys uses 1 ounce whole ginger to every 4 lb sugar. Find the ratio of the weight of whole ginger to the weight of sugar.

The ratios we have considered so far have been simplified by dividing by a common factor. To simplify ratios that include fractions we multiply both parts by the same number.

Question	Simplify (a) $3:\frac{3}{4}$ (b) $\frac{2}{3}:\frac{3}{5}$
Answer	(a) $3:\frac{3}{4} = 12:3$ (Multiplying by 4) $= 4:1$ (b) $\frac{2}{3}:\frac{3}{5} = 10:9$ (Multiplying by 15, the common denominator of 3 and 5)

6 Express each ratio in its simplest form
  (a) $2:\frac{1}{3}$ (b) $5:\frac{3}{8}$
  (c) $\frac{2}{3}:\frac{3}{4}$ (d) $2:3\frac{1}{2}$

7 A recipe for blackberry jam includes $3\frac{1}{2}$ lb blackberries and 2 lb sugar. Find the ratio of the weight of blackberries to the weight of sugar.

8 Out of his working day of $10\frac{1}{2}$ hours, a salesman spends $3\frac{1}{2}$ hours driving. Find the ratio of
  (a) the time he is driving to the time he is not driving
  (b) the time he is not driving to the time he is driving.

Question	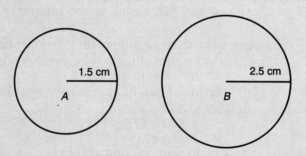 The radii of two metal plates, A and B, are 1.5 cm and 2.5 cm respectively. Find the ratio of (a) the radius of A to the radius of B (b) the area of A to the area of B.

Answer	(a) The ratio of the radius of A to the radius of B is 1.5 cm : 2.5 cm
	                                  $= 1.5:2.5$ (Multiply by 10)
	                                  $= 15:25$
	                                  $= 3:5$ (Divide by 5).

(b)   The area of $A = \pi \times 1.5 \times 1.5$ cm^2
and   the area of $B = \pi \times 2.5 \times 2.5$ cm^2.
The ratio of the area of A to the area of B is
$\pi \times 1.5 \times 1.5$ cm$^2 : \pi \times 2.5 \times 2.5$ cm^2
$$= 2.25\pi : 6.25\pi$$
$$= 2.25 : 6.25 \text{ (Dividing by } \pi)$$
$$= 225 : 625$$
$$= 9 : 25 \text{ (Dividing by 25)}$$
(Note that the ratio of the areas is the same as the squares of the ratio of the radii.)

Simplify each ratio

9 (a) 1.5:5.5   (b) 13:7.8
     (c) 1.05:0.42   (d) 44.8:39.2

10 (a) 2 kg:1.5 kg   (b) 12 m:4.8 m
      (c) 5.4 kg:7.2 kg   (d) 1.75 litres:4.5 litres

11

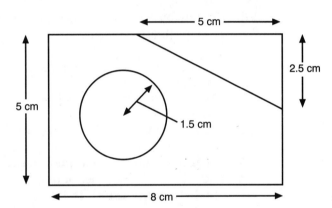

The diagram shows a metal component for a washing machine. It has been made from a rectangular plate by cutting off a triangular corner and drilling out a circular hole. Use the dimensions given on the diagram to find the ratio of
(a) the width of the rectangular plate to its length
(b) the area of the triangular piece that has been removed to the area of the original plate
(c) the area of the hole to the area of the triangular piece (take $\pi = 3$).

12 In a business the Acid Test ratio is defined as

$$\frac{\text{current assets} - \text{stock}}{\text{current liabilities}}$$

Find the acid test ratio for a business that has assets of £148 000, stock of £50 000 and liabilities of £80 000. Give your answer
(a) as a fraction in lowest terms   (b) in the form n:1.

Exercise 10c

Question A recipe that will make 24 Swedish tea cakes requires

    8 oz margarine
    3 tablespoons cream
    8 oz plain flour
    1 egg
    2 tablespoons crushed walnuts
    2 tablespoons sugar
    3 oz raspberry jam

If a larger number of tea cakes is made,
(a) How much margarine would be required to mix with 24 oz plain flour?
(b) How many tablespoons of crushed walnuts would be required to mix with 5 eggs?
(c) How many tablespoons of sugar would be required to mix with 12 oz raspberry jam?

Answer (a) The ratio of the weight of plain flour to the weight of margarine is 8 oz : 8 oz i.e. 1:1
∴ if 24 oz plain flour is used the required weight of margarine is also 24 oz.
(b) The ratio of the number of eggs to the number of tablespoons of crushed walnuts is 1:2
∴ 5 eggs require 10 tablespoons crushed walnuts.
(c) The ratio of the number of ounces of raspberry jam to the number of tablespoons of sugar is 3:2
∴ 12 oz raspberry jam requires 8 tablespoons of sugar.

1 A recipe for 4 servings of beef stew includes the following ingredients:

    1 lb stewing beef
    3 tablespoons lard
    2 medium onions
    $\frac{3}{4}$ pint water
    4 carrots
    one 8 oz packet frozen peas.

If a larger quantity of beef stew is made,
(a) How many onions would be needed to go with 6 carrots?
(b) How much beef would be needed to go with 3 pints of water?
(c) What weight of frozen peas would be needed to go with $3\frac{1}{2}$ lb stewing beef?

2 A builder makes compo by mixing sand and cement in the ratio 3:1.
(a) How much sand is required to mix with 40 kg cement?

(b) How much cement is required to mix with 150 kg sand?
(c) How many shovels of cement are needed to mix with 9 shovels of sand?

3 The ratio of males to females at a factory is 2:3.
  (a) If there are 120 male employees, how many females are there?
  (b) If there are 120 female employees, how many males are there?

4 A businessman visits the bank for change. He needs 20 p coins and 50 p coins in the ratio 4:1. If he collects £20 in 20 p coins
  (a) How many 20 p coins does he collect?
  (b) How many 50 p coins does he collect?
  (c) What is the total value of the 50 p coins?

Question   In Jason's pay the ratio of £10 notes to £20 notes is 2:3. What fraction of the notes he receives are £10 notes?

Answer   For every 2 £10 notes there are 3 £20 notes
i.e. for every 5 notes he receives 2 of them are £10 notes and 3 of them are £20 notes.
So fraction of notes that are £10 notes is $\frac{2}{5}$.

5 In a soccer squad the ratio of attackers to defenders is 8:7. What fraction of the squad are
  (a) attackers   (b) defenders?

6 The ratio of boys to girls in a brass band is 4:3.
  What fraction of the players are girls?

7 Pat O'Connell is an artist. He works in watercolours and in oils.
  If $\frac{3}{10}$ of his pictures are watercolours and the remainder are oils find the ratio of watercolours to oils.

8 Seven-eighths of a small holder's land is devoted to vegetables and the remainder to flowers.
  Find the ratio of the area used for vegetables to the area used for flowers.

Division in a given ratio   **Exercise 10d**

Question   Share £250 between David and Jonathan in the ratio 3:2.

Answer   (One share is made up of 3 portions and the other share is made up of 2 portions. There are therefore 5 portions altogether.)
1 portion is £$\frac{250}{5}$ i.e. £50
David's share is 3 × £50, i.e. £150
and Jonathan's share is 2 × £50, i.e. £100.
(Check: £150 + £100 = £250.)

1 Share 36 chocolates between Dick and Ann in the ratio 4:5.

2 Share £84 between Jo and Mel in the ratio 4:3.

3 Two sisters Carol and Diane are given £50 between them by an aunt for Christmas. They are to share the money in the ratio of their ages. Carol is 11 years and Diane is 14 years.
How much does Carol get?

4 A 48 acre field is to be divided into two parts in the ratio 7:5.
What is the area of the smaller part?

5 The record of admissions to a hospital shows that the ratio of those that need surgery to those that do not is 1:4. Over the next three months they estimate that there will be about 18 000 admissions.
How many of these patients are likely to need surgery?

6 A national housebuilder builds houses and bungalows in the ratio 5:2. Last year they built 10 300 properties.
How many houses did they build? Give your answer correct to the nearest 10.

Direct proportion

'Proportion' is another word for comparison. We say that two quantities are in proportion if they are always in the same ratio, e.g. if one quantity is doubled, so is the other.

When we buy bread rolls the total cost is proportional to the number of rolls we buy, e.g. if we treble the number of rolls we treble the cost.

Exercise 10e

1 If 5 cups of tea cost £3.50 what is the cost of
(a) 1 cup   (b) 3 cups?

2 It costs £3.30 to buy 3 cups of coffee. How much does it cost to buy
(a) 1 cup   (b) 4 cups?

Question It costs £115 for 5 adults to take the coach from their home town to Heathrow airport. What does it cost for 7 adults to make the same trip?

Answer   5 fares cost £115
               1 fare costs £$\frac{115}{5}$
                   = £23
               7 fares cost 7 × £23 = £161.

---

3 Three copies of *Good Woodworking* cost £5.85.
Find the price of 5 copies.

4 The amount of plain flour required to make 24 biscuits is 8 oz.
How much plain flour is required to make 42 biscuits?

5 5 coaches can carry 235 passengers.
   How many passengers can 13 similar coaches carry?

6 A car travels 171 km on 15 litres of petrol.
   How many litres are required for a journey of 285 km?

7 An invoice from a computer centre lists the total cost of 8 boxes of
   3½" diskettes as £41.76. This was an error, the requested order was for
   18 boxes.
   How much do 18 cost?

8 In an Olympic swimming pool there is seating all the way round.
   Section *A* has 30 rows, with 12 seats in each row.
   (a) How many seats are there in this section?
   (b) Section *B* has the same number of seats but they are arranged in
       24 rows. How many seats are there in each row?
   (c) In Section *C* there are the same number of seats as in each of the
       other two sections. There are 18 seats in each row.
       How many rows are there?

Inverse proportion In the previous section we considered quantities that were in direct
proportion i.e. quantities where if one increases so does the other. This
is not always the case. Sometimes when one quantity is increased the
other decreases.

For example, suppose we have £5 to spend on oranges. If they are 20 p
each we can buy 25, but if the price is raised to 25 p each we can buy
only 20.
The number of oranges × the cost of one orange is a constant.

The result of multiplying together two inversely proportional quantities
is a constant.

Exercise 10f

Question The manager at a cattery has sufficient food to feed 12 cats for 15
days. If she takes in another 6 cats today how long will the food last?

Answer   12 cats can be fed for 15 days
               1 cat can be fed for 15 × 12 days
               18 cats can be fed for $\dfrac{15 \times 12}{18}$ days
             i.e. for 10 days.

1 A business allocates a fixed sum to spend on new machinery. Two
   machines are considered. If the managers opt for the cheaper machines,
   which cost £3500 each, they can buy 7 of them.
   (a) How much money did they set aside for new machinery?

(b) The more expensive machines cost £4900 each. How many of these could they afford?

2 A sub-contractor agrees to build a large stone retaining wall which is needed as part of a new by-pass. He estimates that if he uses 15 men he can complete the work in 60 days.
(a) How long would 25 men take to do the job?
(b) If the work must be completed in 20 days how many men should he allocate to the job?

3 A borough council agrees to supply, free of charge, 'wheelie' bins to all the properties from which it collects refuse. It is far too expensive to make the change immediately so they agree to set aside a fixed amount each year until the changeover has been completed. If they chose a bin that costs £34 they can buy 1900 bins in the first year.
(a) How much money do they set aside for wheelie bins each year?
(b) How many bins can they buy for the same sum of money if they go for more expensive bins costing £38 each?

4 The owners of a small factory have a meeting to decide their targets for next year. They decide that they cannot afford to spend any more next year on wages than they spend this year. At present they employ 112 workers who are paid £240 per week each.
(a) What is the total weekly wage bill?
(b) If they agree to increase the weekly wage per person to £256 by how many must they reduce the size of the workforce?
(c) They decide that they should have 120 workers. What is the most they can afford to pay them?

Multiple choice questions

In Questions 1–3 several alternative answers are given. Write down the letter that corresponds to the correct answer.

1 The airfare between two American cities is $545 during the high season and $436 during the low season. The ratio, in its lowest terms, of the fare during the high season to the fare during the low season is
A 545:436 B 1:1¼ C 5:4 D 4:5

2 A lorry is 8.64 metres long and a model of the same lorry is 12 cm long. The ratio of the length of the model to the length of the lorry is
A 1:72 B 72:1 C 1:0.72 D 1:36

3 If 4 jars of bramble jelly cost £3.44 the cost of 7 similar jars is
A £6.88 B £6.02 C £5.95 D £6.08

4 The accountant at Speed Electronics found that the profits this year compared with last year are in the ratio 5:4 and the costs of production this year compared with last year are in the ratio 7:10. Last year the costs of production were £5m and this year the profits are £½m. After some calculations the accountant presented the following statements to the board:
Which of these statements are true and which are false?

A The profit last year was £400 000
B The ratio of the profit last year to the costs of production last year was 2:25
C This year the ratio of the profits to the production costs is exactly the same as it was last year
D Comparing this year with last year the costs and the profits have both gone up.

5 A recipe that will make 12 tarts includes 4 oz sugar, 1 tablespoon flour, 1 egg and 6 oz raisins. Eve has half a dozen eggs.
The following statements have been made:
Statement 1 If Eve uses half the eggs she has she will also need 18 oz raisins, 12 oz sugar and 2 tablespoons flour.
Statement 2 If Eve has enough ingredients to use all the eggs she can make 72 tarts and has 12 oz of raisins left after opening a 3 lb bag.
How are these statements best described?
A True, True   B True, False
C False, True   D False, False.

Self assessment 10

1 On a Health & Social Care course there are 35 students, 21 of whom are female.
What is the ratio of
(a) females to males   (b) males to females?

2 A ship is 350 m long and a model of it is 1750 cm long. Find the ratio of the length of the model to the length of the ship.

3 The ingredients required for 7 kg marmalade are: 2 kg oranges, 4 kg sugar, 1 lemon, 1 litre water.
What quantities are needed to make 63 kg marmalade?

4 At a bank the ratio of the number of customers having to wait less than 4 minutes to the number of customers having to wait 4 minutes or more is 7:2. During one day there were 747 customers.
How many had to wait at least 4 minutes?

5 The ratio of the gross profit to sales for firms manufacturing/selling similar products is expected to be fairly constant from year to year and from one company to another. Any large difference from the expected ratio (expressed as a percentage) is a cause for concern for authorities such as the Inland Revenue. Given below are figures for five drapery companies, for which the ratio of gross profit to sales is normally about 18%.

Company	Sales (£000)	Cost (£000)	Gross profit (£000)	Gross profit as a percentage of sales
Axford Bros	80	66	14	$\frac{14}{80} \times 100 = 17.5$
Besleys	120	100		
Croxley & Son	1750	1420		
Denhams	2500	2200		
Esther & Co	950	780		

(a) Copy and complete the table.
(b) Presented with these figures, which company do you think would be of greatest interest to the Inland Revenue?

UNIT 11 Maps and Networks

After studying this unit you will be able to
- [ ] use a map for which the scale is given, to find the actual distance between two places on it.
- [ ] use a map to find a suitable route
- [ ] understand such mathematical terms as odd and even nodes, traversable and non-traversable networks
- [ ] determine mathematically whether or not a network is traversable
- [ ] use networks to solve simple everyday problems, e.g. traffic flows, shortest routes, etc.

Maps

Maps are scale drawings of selected areas of the surface of the earth.

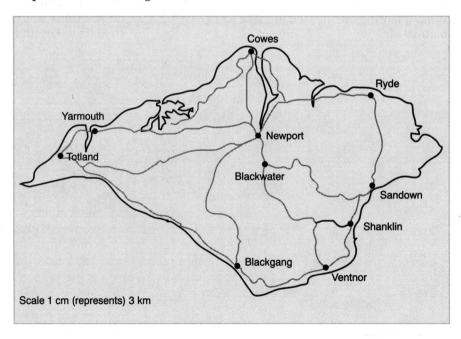

This map represents the Isle of Wight. It shows the network of main roads on the island and is drawn to a scale of 1 cm to 3 km. This means that the actual straight line distance from, say, Newport to Ventnor, is found by measuring the distance between them on the map (3.9 cm) and multiplying the number of centimetres by 3. This gives the actual distance in kilometres

i.e. the distance from Newport to Ventnor is 3.9×3 km
$$= 11.7 \text{ km}$$
$$= 12 \text{ km correct to the nearest kilometre.}$$

(The best we can expect by measuring distances from this map is that we are able to give distances on the island correct to the nearest kilometre.)

The scale of this map could also have been given as the ratio 1:300 000 or 1 to 300 000.
When written like this it means that the ratio of the distance on the map to the actual distance is 1:300 000,

so 1 cm represents 300 000 cm

i.e.   1 cm represents $\dfrac{300\,000}{100}$ m = 3000 m (Divide by 100 to change cm to m)

i.e.   1 cm represents $\dfrac{3000}{1000}$ km = 3 km   (Divide by 1000 to change m to km).

Exercise 11a

Question   (a) On the map of the Isle of Wight, measure the distance in a straight line from Ventnor to Cowes.
        (b) What is the distance, in kilometres, as the crow flies from Ventnor to Cowes?
        (c) Estimate the distance, in kilometres, along the road from Blackgang to Newport and on to Ryde.

Answer   (a) The straight line distance from Ventnor to Cowes is 6.1 cm.
        (b) Since 1 cm represents 3 km, the actual straight line distance from Ventnor to Cowes is 6.1×3 km = 18.3 km = 18 km (nearest km).
        (c) If a pair of dividers (or a pair of compasses) is set at $\frac{1}{2}$ cm and then walked along the road from Blackgang to Newport and on to Ryde the approximate distance is 8.1 cm. Therefore the distance along the road from Ventnor to Ryde via Newport is about 8.1×3 km i.e. 24 km.

Use the map of the Isle of Wight to answer Questions 1–4

1 (a) How many centimetres is it on the map in a straight line
   (i) from Newport to Totland   (ii) from Cowes to Blackgang?
   (b) How far is it in kilometres in a straight line
   (i) from Cowes to Shanklin   (ii) from Sandown to Totland?

2 Use a method of your own choice to estimate the distance along the roads for a circular tour from Cowes visiting Ryde, Sandown, Shanklin, Ventnor, Blackwater and Newport, before returning to Cowes.

3 Lyn Beresford takes the ferry from Southampton to Cowes. She sets off from Cowes in her car with the intention of visiting all the places on the map that are named.
   Is it possible for her to do this without passing through any one of them more than once and without travelling along any road on the island more than once? Justify your answer.

4 Cam Bennett also lands at Cowes. His wish is to travel along all the marked roads once and only once before he returns to Cowes.
   Is his proposed trip possible? If it is, give details; if it is not, justify your answer.

5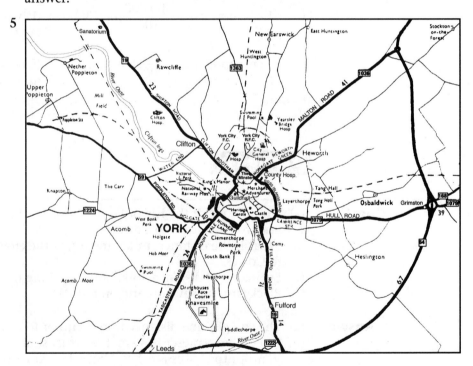

This map of York is drawn using a scale of 1:90 000. A number on a road, e.g. ⌐64⌐ shows that the road is the A 64.
(a) What actual distance, in kilometres, is represented by 1 cm on the map?

    (b) What is the actual straight line distance (i) from the Grimston exit of the A 64 to the Guildhall (ii) between the grounds of York City F C and York R F C?

    (c) How far is it from the sanatorium, along the A 19 to the end of Clifton Bootham nearest to the Minster?

    (d) A minibus is travelling west from Bridlington on the A 168, and has to drop off passengers at seven different addresses, namely Fulford, Tadcaster Road, the County Hospital on Ross Islands Road, a guest house half way along Hull Road, Nunnery Lane, Clifton and the north end of Malton Road, before continuing south to Leeds.

Suggest a possible route that does not travel over the same section of road more than once. Is this necessarily the shortest way of making this detour?

(Assume that all the roads are passable in both directions.)

Networks

The word *network* is quite common in everyday life. We often hear reference in the newspapers and on television to a television network or a rail network or a road network. In school and college we also have computer networks.

A network looks like several pieces of string knotted together in a number of places. The knots represent the objects and the strings the connections between the objects. In a mathematical form a network is an *arrangement or pattern of intersecting lines*.

It's quite possible that at some time you have tried this puzzle. Draw the shape of the back of an envelope without picking your pencil off the paper and without going over any line twice, starting and finishing at the same point. If you have never tried to do this, try it now.

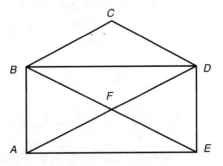

If you fail, try again, starting at a different point.

- Does it matter where you begin?
- Can you start and finish at the same point?
- Is there more than one way of doing it?

If a network can be copied without taking the pencil off the paper and without going over any line more than once the network is said to be *traversable*.

The two lines that meet at C are called *arcs*.
The lines in a network are called arcs whether they are straight lines or curved lines.

A point where arcs intersect is called a *node*.
On the above diagram the nodes are marked by letters.
To make it easier to follow a node is often marked by a dot(•).
(You may find it easier to think of arcs as *pieces of string* and nodes as *knots* in the string.)

The number of arcs coming together at a node gives the *order* of that node.

In the envelope diagram   C is a node of order 2
A and *E* are nodes of order 3
B, D and *F* are nodes of order 4.

If the number of arcs intersecting at a node is even the node is called an *even node*. If the number of arcs intersecting at a node is odd the node is called an *odd node*.
B, C, D and *F* are even nodes; *A* and *E* are odd nodes.

Lots of problems on networks can be solved without knowing anything at all about nodes and arcs. However some questions are much easier to solve using them.

Exercise 11b

Question Copy the following network without taking your pencil off the paper and without going over any line more than once.

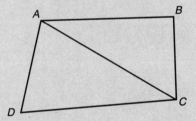

Give the order of each node and say whether it is an even node or an odd node.

Answer

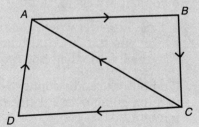

The sketch shows how to copy the network by starting at *C* and finishing at *A*.
(There are several possible ways of drawing it, but you must start either at *A* or at *C*.)
The nodes at *A* and *C* are of order 3
The nodes at *B* and *D* are of order 2.

1 (a) What is the order of the node at   (i) *A*   (ii) *B*   (iii) *C*?
(b) How many nodes are there of order 4?

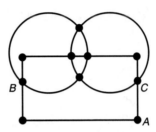

2   In this question copy each network without picking your pencil off the paper and without going over any line more than once. If you fail to draw a network, try again starting from a different point. For each diagram state the number of odd nodes and the number of even nodes.

A

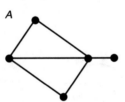

B

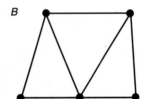

C

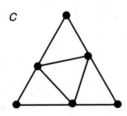

D

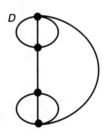

3 Draw a network that has
(a) four nodes each of order 2
(b) two nodes each of order 3
(c) four nodes, two of order 2 and two of order 3
(d) three nodes, two of order 3 and one of order 2
(e) four nodes, one of order 3 and three of order 1.

4 Use the networks given in Question 2 to complete the following table.

Network	Number of even nodes	Number of odd nodes	Is the network traversable?
A B C D			

5 Complete the table for the networks given below.

Network	Number of even nodes	Number of odd nodes	Is the network traversable?
(a) (b) (c) (d) (e) (f)			

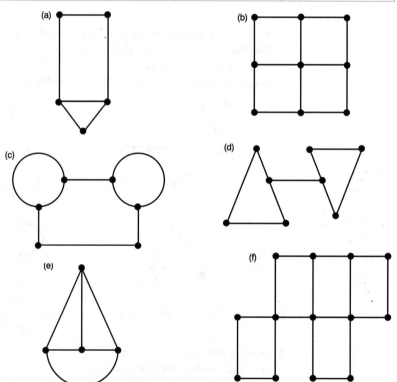

6 Draw six networks of your own choice. Now draw and complete a table similar to the one given in Question 5. Try to include some networks that are traversable and some that are not.

7 Use your results from Questions 4, 5 and 6 to answer the following questions.
   (a) Is a network traversable if it has two odd nodes?
   (b) Is a network traversable if it has all even nodes?
   (c) If a network is traversable what can you say about the number of odd nodes it has?
   (d) If a network is traversable, starting and finishing at the same point, what can you say about the number of odd nodes it has?
   (e) Do your answers to parts (a)–(d) support the fact that a network is traversable if   (i) there are no odd nodes or   (ii) there are no more than 2 odd nodes?

Using networks to solve problems

First we look at some questions that do not need any knowledge of nodes and arcs.

Traffic flow

Networks can often help us to solve traffic problems

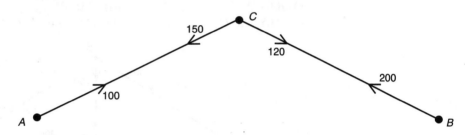

The diagram shows a road from A to B via C. Each number gives the maximum traffic flow per hour from the point which it is placed nearest to. For example, the maximum traffic flow from A to C is 100 vehicles per hour whereas the maximum flow from C to A is 150 vehicles per hour.

We can use a simple network to answer such questions as: what is the maximum traffic flow from
(a) A to B (b) B to A?

(a) The maximum flow from A to C is 100 vehicles. Even though the road from C to B will take 120 vehicles per hour we cannot get more than 100 from A to C. The maximum traffic flow from A to B is therefore 100 vehicles per hour. (Remember that a chain is as strong as its weakest link – i.e. the best possible flow is only as good as the flow in the slowest section.)
(b) For the reasons given in (a) the maximum traffic flow from B to A is 100 vehicles per hour.

Exercise 11c

1 The diagram shows the maximum number of vehicles per hour that can travel along the roads of a network.

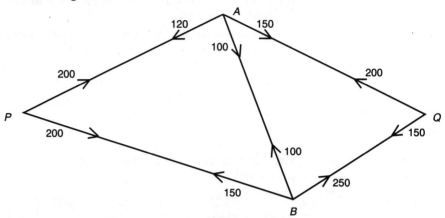

What is the maximum hourly traffic flow from
(a) *P* to *A*   (b) *A* to *B*
(c) *B* to *Q*   (d) *B* to *P*
(e) *P* to *A* to *Q*   (f) *Q* to *B* to *A* to *P*?

2

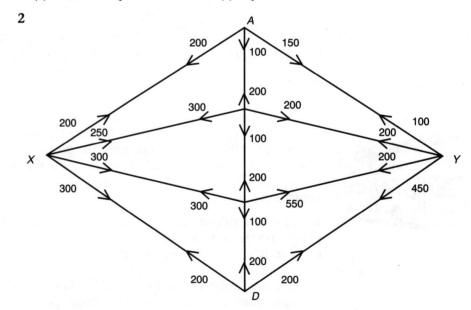

The diagram shows the principal roads between two cities. The numbers show the greatest number of vehicles that can travel along a road from the point marked by a capital letter to the point at the other end of that road and marked with another capital letter.
(a) What is the largest number of vehicles per hour that can   (i) leave *X* and travel directly to *C*   (ii) leave *Y* and travel directly to *D*?

(b) What is the largest number of vehicles per hour that can (i) leave X (ii) leave Y (iii) leave X and drive to Y (iv) leave Y and drive to X?

Production problems

A network can also be used to put together the different stages necessary to do a job. If Chris wants to have beans on toast he must open the tin and warm the beans as well as make the toast. To get the beans ready to pour over the toast at the right time he needs to know how long it takes to perform each task. If the toast takes longer to prepare he should see to that first; if the beans take longer to heat than the bread takes to toast then he should start to heat the beans before cutting the bread and putting it in the toaster. We can illustrate these two events with a simple network.

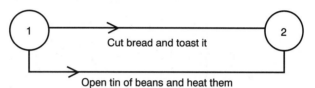

Industry and commerce wish to use their employees in the most effective ways. Consider a process that has 4 distinct stages, let's call them A, B, C and D. Stage A takes 9 minutes, Stage B 6 minutes, Stage C 5 minutes and Stage D 3 minutes. Suppose B must be finished before C can start, and that A, B and C must all be completed before D can start. We can show this information on a network.

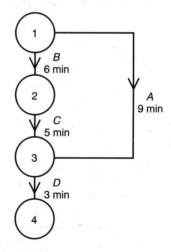

From this network we see that

1 There are 2 routes through the network, namely ① ② ③ ④ and ① ③ ④. The first route takes 6 + 5 + 3 i.e. 14 minutes and the second route takes 9 + 3 i.e. 12 minutes

2 the shortest time if all the stages are to be completed is 14 minutes
3 stage *A* and stage *B* do not have to begin at the same time e.g. it is possible to start stage *A* two minutes after the start of stage *B*, the whole job can still be completed in 14 minutes
4 if there is a delay in either stage *B* or *C* or *D*, the whole job takes longer
5 if Dennis is responsible for stage *A* and Colin for stages *B* & *C*, during any 11 minute period Dennis has 2 minutes with nothing to do while Colin is working all the time: profitable and competitive industry depends on reducing non-productive time to a minimum.

Exercise 11d

1 The various stages in manufacturing a product are shown on the network. Each number shows the time, in minutes, for the stage marked by a capital letter.

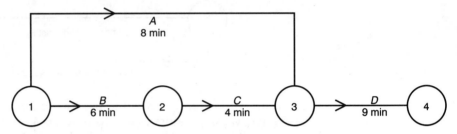

(a) How many different stages are there?
(b) Which stages must be completed before   (i) stage *C*   (ii) stage *D*, can be started?
(c) What is the shortest time it takes to manufacture the product?

2 This network shows the different stages in assembling a radio.

(a) How many stages are there?
(b) How many different routes are there through this network?
(c) What stages must be completed before stage *F* can begin?
(d) Is it necessary to complete stage *E* before stage *F* can begin?
(e) What is the shortest time it takes to assemble a radio?

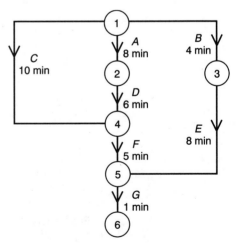

Using network theory to solve problems

We have seen in Exercise 11b that a network is traversable if it has either two odd nodes or all even nodes.

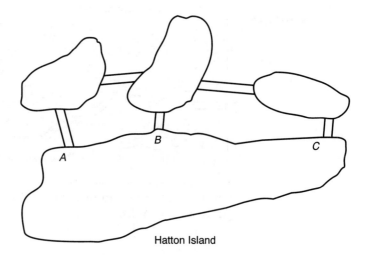

Hatton Island

The diagram represents four islands which are joined by five bridges. Is it possible to take a walk, starting at A, that crosses every bridge once only?

In this case the islands can be taken as nodes and the bridges as arcs. A simplified diagram is given below.

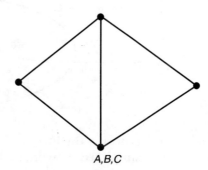

A,B,C

Three bridges (arcs) meet at Hatton Island (a node) so this node is of order 3.
Altogether there are 2 nodes of order 2 and 2 nodes of order 3.

This satisfies the condition for a network to be traversable i.e. there are just two odd nodes, so it is possible to take a walk crossing all five bridges once and only once. Such a walk is possible by starting on Hatton Island at A or B or C.

Exercise 11e

Question

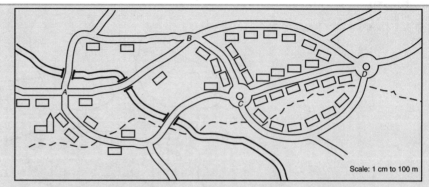

Scale: 1 cm to 100 m

This map shows buildings, paths, side roads and bridges.
(a) Draw a simplified network showing only the roads that are unshaded. Mark the points A, B, C, D and the estimated distances between them.
(b) Is it possible to enter the town at A, drive along every road in the network, and leave the town at D? If so, describe your route and give the length of it.
(c) A motorist entering the town at A wishes to call at B and C before leaving the town from D.
What is the length of her shortest possible route?

Answer (a)

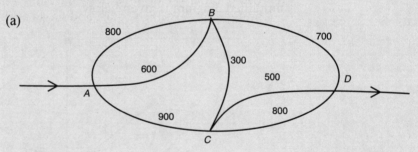

(b) Ignoring the incoming road at A and the outgoing road at D the simplified network looks like this

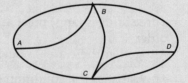

This network has 2 odd nodes, all the other nodes are even.
The network is therefore traversable.
One possible route is $A \rightarrow B \rightarrow A \rightarrow C \rightarrow B \rightarrow D \rightarrow C \rightarrow D$
(c) The shortest route from A to D passing through B and C is
$A \rightarrow B(600m) \rightarrow C(300m) \rightarrow D(500m)$ i.e. a distance of 1400m.

1

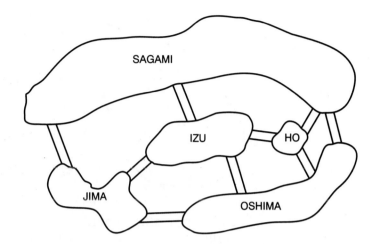

The diagram shows the position of five small Japanese islands which are connected by 9 bridges as shown.

(a) Draw a simplified network of this layout with each island represented by a dot (a node).

(b) Is it possible to plan a route that would allow tourists to cross every bridge just once?

If it is possible, draw such a route. If not, show where you could build another bridge that would make it possible.

(c) Using either the original network or the network with your added bridge, is it possible to start and finish at the same point?

2

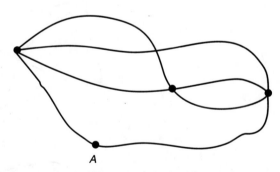

The diagram shows the layout in a country garden.

(a) By counting the number of odd and even nodes find out whether or not this layout is traversable.

(b) Is it possible to start at A, walk along every path once and only once, and to end your walk at A?

If your answer is 'yes', show a possible route.

If your answer is 'no', suggest where a path could be added to make it possible.

3

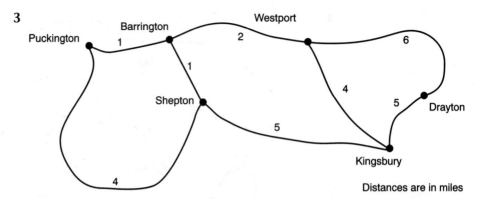

Distances are in miles

(a) The main post office is at Kingsbury.
Find the shortest distance for a post office van to travel if the postman must call at all of the other villages and return to Kingsbury.

(b) An inspector of roads lives at Shepton. He wishes to travel along every road shown on this network to inspect the road surfaces.
Find his shortest route if he starts from, and finishes at, home.

(c) Could he find a shorter route if he lived at Puckington?

4 Starting at *A* find the shortest distance for a cyclist who wishes to cycle along every road in the network at least once, and return to *A*. The numbers on the networks refer to distances in kilometres.
Remember – if a network is traversable all you have to do is add up all the distances.

(a)

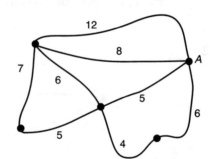

(b)

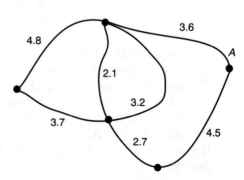

5 Find the shortest distance from A back to A if every place must be visited. Each dot (•) (or node) represents a place. (Distances are in miles)

(a)

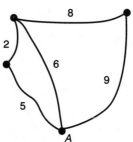

(b)

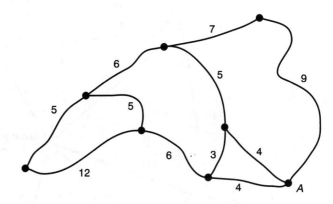

6

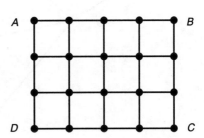

A van service, delivering parcels, wishes to call at all the businesses on an industrial estate.

The layout of the estate is shown on the diagram. Dots represent businesses and lines represent roads.

(a) Starting at A, plan a route for the van so that every business is visited once. The van must not travel along any road more than once, but need not travel along every road.

(b) If the distance between adjacent businesses is 200 metres what is the length of the shortest satisfactory route?

(c) Would the distance be longer or shorter if the van started at one of the other three corners of the estate but still visited every business?

7

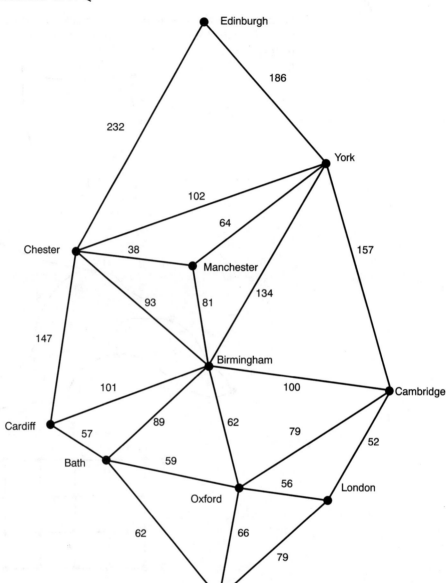

Edinburgh

186

232

York

102

64

Chester   38

Manchester

157

93   81

134

147

Birmingham

101   100   Cambridge

Cardiff

89   62

79

57   52

Bath   59

56   London

Oxford

62   66

79

Southampton   Distance in miles

A tourist arrives at Southampton by ship and wishes to visit the places marked on the diagram. She hires a car and plans a route that will take her to each place once and only once.

(a) Suggest a possible route.

(b) Is this the shortest route?

(c) If her car averages 40 miles per gallon find the number of gallons of petrol used and the total cost of fuel if petrol costs £2.50 per gallon.

8

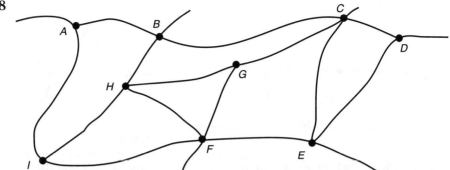

(a) Represent the road system given above by a simple network showing only whether or not there are roads between the villages. Each village is indicated by a capital letter. Neither directions nor distances need be preserved.

(b) Ignoring the incoming roads, is the network traversable? What kind of person is interested in the answer to this question?

(c) Is it possible, without using any road more than once, to enter this system at village *A*, visit all the other villages, and leave the system from village *D*?

Multiple choice questions

In Questions 1–3 several alternative answers are given. Write down the letter that corresponds to the correct answer.

1 The scale of a map is 1:50 000. This means that 1 cm on the map represents

A 50 m   B $\frac{1}{2}$ km   C 5000 m   D 2 km

2

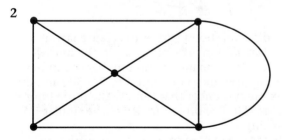

This network has

A 5 odd nodes

B 4 odd nodes and 1 even node

C 3 odd nodes and 2 even nodes

D 2 odd nodes and 3 even nodes.

3 The figures on the lines of this network show the time, in minutes, to perform the various tasks necessary to make a saucepan.

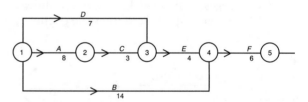

The shortest time in which the saucepan can be made is

A 17 min   B 21 min   C 20 min   D 28 min

4 Which of the following statements are true and which are false?

A It is possible to draw a network with 2 even nodes and 1 odd node

B Every network is traversable

C A network with 3 odd nodes is traversable

D It doesn't matter where you start, a network without any odd nodes is always traversable.

5

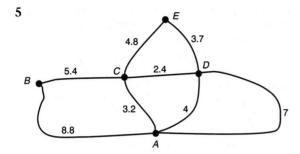

This network shows the roads and distances, in miles, between 5 villages in the Cotswolds. The following statements have been made:

Statement 1 This network has 2 odd nodes and therefore it is possible to take a route, starting at *A* and returning to *A*, that travels along every road once but only once.

Statement 2 The shortest journey, starting at *A*, that travels along every road at least once is 26.1 miles long.

How are these two statements best described?

A True, True   **B** True, False
C False, True   **D** False, False.

Self assessment 11

1 (a) The scale of a map is 1:20 000. How far apart are two places that are 5.6 cm apart on the map?
  (b) Two villages, that are 40 km apart, are shown on a map 5 cm apart. Find the scale of the map.

2

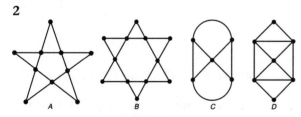

For each of the networks given above find
(a) the number of odd nodes
(b) the number of even nodes
(c) whether or not the network is traversable.

3

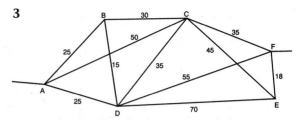

This network is marked with the time it takes in minutes for a commercial traveller to travel from one client to another.

(a) What is the shortest possible time to travel from *A* to *F*?
(b) Find (i) the fastest route (ii) the slowest route, from *A* to *F* that calls on every client once but does not travel along any road more than once.
(c) The commercial traveller wishes to call on his clients, starting at *A* and finishing at *A*. Plan a route for him that reduces his total travelling time to a minimum.
(d) (i) Is this network traversable?
    (ii) A post office van enters the network at *A* and leaves it at *F*. Is it possible for the postman to drive along every road just once?
    (iii) Plan a route that takes this postman over every road.
    (iv) How long will it take?

4

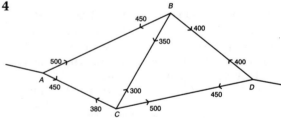

The diagram shows part of the course layout for a half-marathon. The numbers on the line *AB* indicate that the maximum number of runners that can use the route from *A* to *B* is 500 and the maximum number that can use the route from *B* to *A* is 450. The other numbers have similar meanings.

What is the maximum number of entries the organisers can accept if they decide to run the marathon
(a) from *A* to *D*   (b) from *D* to *A*?

5

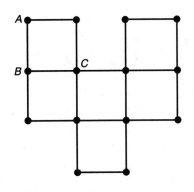

The diagram shows part of the road layout in an American city. Post Office collection boxes are placed at every road intersection. The distance between any two adjacent collection boxes is 100 yards.

(a) Is it possible to start at A or B or C and cover the complete road system without driving along any road more than once?

(b) (i) Starting at B, what is the shortest distance that a van can travel to visit every box and return to B?

(ii) Does the van have to pass any box more than once to make this shortest trip?

UNIT 12 The Laws of Chance

After studying this unit you will be able to
- [ ] understand the meaning of common everyday words used in probability e.g. random, equally likely, certainty, impossibility
- [ ] express a probability as a number between 0 and 1
- [ ] find the probability that an event does or does not happen
- [ ] draw and use a possibility space
- [ ] use probability to find the expected number of times an event is likely to occur.

Randomness

When we say that an event will happen 'at random', we mean that there is no certain way of predicting where and when it will happen. For example, it is fairly certain that at least one team in the football league will lose 2–0 at home on the last Saturday before next Christmas, but we cannot predict which team it will be. It is also fairly certain that every team in the league will lose 2–0 at home on some future occasion but, once again, we cannot say when. If an event happens 'at random' other possibilities are also implied. For example, if we toss a coin we know that it will come down either heads or tails.

When we say that a letter is chosen from a word *at random* we mean that each letter in the word is equally likely to be chosen, that is, it has the same chance of being chosen as any other letter. When you see the word 'random' it means that all the possibilities are *equally likely*.

Probability is the study of unpredictable events, which may or may not happen. It is possible, though unlikely, that sometime in the next year, you will receive a million pounds from someone in their will. On the other hand it is as certain as anything can be that the sun will rise tomorrow.

Equally likely events

How often have you heard people say: 'It's an even chance – there are two possibilities: either we'll win or we won't.'

It is usually quite wrong to suppose that because there are two possibilities they are both equally likely. If you roll a dice it is certain that either you will roll a 6, or you will roll some value other than 6, but the two possibilities are not equally likely. The two chances are not the same. The face showing 6 is but one of six possible scores when the dice is rolled. You are just as likely to score 1, 2, 3, 4 or 5 as you are to score 6.

When you cross the road you also have two chances – you will either get to the other side safely or you will not. The chances are that you will cross the road safely thousands of times. When you cross the road the chance that you will not cross safely is quite small.

However, some events do have even chance of happening. Suppose you toss an unbiased coin. It can land heads up or it can land tails up. In this case there are two possible outcomes, each of which is equally likely.

Tossing a coin is called an *experiment*, the result is called an *outcome* or *event*.

Exercise 12a

1 Neale saved £100 and used the money to buy 100 Premium Bonds. Would he be equally likely to win a prize with any of them?

2 Callum and Sandy decided to spend the evening playing darts. Callum won the first seven games. As Sandy stood to throw his first dart of the eighth game he said to himself: "I've lost the first seven games, so I'm bound to win this one."
Was he right? Give reasons for your answer.

3 Manchester United, who have won their last ten games play Kidderminster United who have also won their last ten games, in the FA Cup next weekend.
   Do you agree that each team is equally likely to win?

4 Before a test match between England and Australia a coin is tossed to decide which side can choose whether or not to bat.
   Is the captain who tosses the coin as likely to win as the captain who does not?

5 When someone is chosen from a group of boys and girls there is an even chance that the person is a girl.
   What does this tell you about the number of boys and the number of girls in the group?

6 Can you think of some events that have a 50–50 chance of happening? Discuss these events with a partner.

Probability

If you toss a coin, it will land head up or tail up. Landing head up is one of two equally likely events, so the chance of throwing a head is 1 out of 2, i.e. $\frac{1}{2}$.

Expressing the chance as a fraction is a way of measuring that chance, but it is often more convenient to give this value as a decimal, e.g. the chance of getting a head when a coin is tossed is 0.5.

The word we use to measure chance is *probability*.

When a dice is rolled there are six equally likely possibilities so, the probability or chance of rolling a two is 1 out of 6 i.e. $\frac{1}{6}$.

Exercise 12b

In this exercise, assume that all the possible outcomes are equally likely.

1 What is the probability of rolling a dice and getting a 3?

2 What is the probability of tossing a coin and getting a tail?

3 If one letter is chosen at random from the letters in the word BIKE what is the probability that the letter is E?

4 If one letter is chosen at random from the letters in the word FIGURE what is the probability that the letter is G?

5 One coin is chosen at random from the six different coins that were issued in a boxed set in 1970 in readiness for the introduction of decimal coinage on 15 February 1971.
   What is the probability that the value of the chosen coin is
   (a) 50 p   (b) 10 p   (c) 5 p?
   (The coins in a 1970 boxed set are one each of 50 p, 10 p, 5 p, 2 p, 1 p, $\frac{1}{2}$ p.)

**Events that can
happen more than
once**

The word QUEEN has 5 letters, including 2 Es.

There are 2 equally likely ways of choosing a letter E and there are 5
equally likely ways of choosing a letter.
2 out of these 5 equally likely ways give a letter E, so the probability
that if one letter is chosen it is a letter E is $\frac{2}{5}$.

To take another example, look at the word SEPTEMBER. This word has
9 letters, 3 of which are E. If I choose a letter from this word the
probability or chance that it will be a letter E is 3 out of 9 i.e. $\frac{3}{9}$ which
simplifies to $\frac{1}{3}$.

In general, the probability that an event will happen is the fraction

$$\frac{\text{number of ways in which the event can happen}}{\text{total number of equally likely events.}}$$

Exercise 12c

Question

Anna empties the coins in her purse on the counter of her local
newsagent because she is not sure whether or not she has enough
money to pay for some magazines. She finds that she has five £1
coins, three 50 p pieces, four 20 p pieces and six 10 p coins. One coin
is picked up from the counter at random. What is the probability that
it is
(a) a £1 coin   (b) a 10 p piece
(c) a silver coin?

Answer

(a) She has 5 + 3 + 4 + 6 i.e. 18 coins altogether, 5 of which are £1
coins.
The probability of choosing a £1 coin is 5 out of 18 i.e. $\frac{5}{18}$.
(b) She has 18 coins altogether, 6 of which are 10 p pieces.
The probability of choosing a 10p piece is 6 out of 18 i.e. $\frac{6}{18} = \frac{1}{3}$.
(c) Of the 18 coins, 13 of them are silver, namely three 50 ps, four
20 ps and six 10 ps.
Therefore probability of choosing a silver coin is 13 out of 18 = $\frac{13}{18}$

1 A hardware store sells fluorescent tubes. The present stock is given in
the table.

Length (ft)	2	3	4	5	6	8
Number	5	12	10	4	3	2

A tube is chosen at random from this stock.
What is the probability that the length of the chosen tube is
(a) 4 ft   (b) 3 ft
(c) at least 4 ft.

2 At the end of a day a market trader has a wad of bank notes. He counts them and finds he has two at £50, twenty-eight at £20, thirteen at £10 and nine at £5. He takes one note at random from this wad to pay his assistant.
   (a) Is the note more likely to be a £20 note than any other?
   (b) What is the probability that the value of the note he gives is
       (i) £10 (ii) £50 (iii) not £20?

3 The sketch shows the pictures on the wheels of a fruit machine.

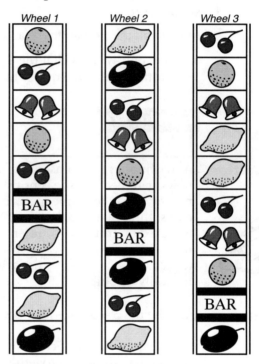

   (a) Find the number of times each fruit appears on the display.
   (b) Find the probability of getting
       (i) a bar on the first wheel
       (ii) a lemon on the second
       (iii) cherries on the third.

4 A class of business studies students is made up of 5 male students and 10 female students. Sue Powell, the lecturer, has the habit of going round the class at random asking different students questions.
   What is the probability that the next student she asks is
   (a) male   (b) female.

5 38 old age pensioners, 24 of whom are women, go on a day trip to London to see *Phantom of the Opera*. The tickets for the show are given out at random on the coach.
   What is the chance that the ticket for the best seat goes to a man?

Impossibility and certainty

Some events are impossible. For example, it is impossible to take a tin of beans from a kitchen cupboard if there are no tins of beans in the cupboard. If an event is impossible, the probability that it happens is 0.

On the other hand, some events are certain. If a cashier in the supermarket takes a coin from a bag of 10 p coins that has just been collected from the bank, its value will be 10 p.
If an event is certain to happen the probability that it happens is 1.

Exercise 12d

Questions 1–4 refer to the picture which shows the staff in an office.

1 How many women are there in the office in the picture?

2 How many men are there in the picture?

3 What fraction of the people in this office are
   (a) female   (b) male?

4 You choose a person at random from this office. What is the probability that the chosen person is
   (a) a male   (b) a female?

5 What is the probability?
   (a) of choosing the letter R from the letters in the word AUGUST?
   (b) that it will get dark tonight?
   (c) that you will live to be 150?
   (d) that a baby will be born in London tomorrow?

If an event is impossible the probability that it happens is 0, but if an event is certain to happen the probability that it happens is 1.

For most events the probability that they occur lies between these two extremes.

The scale given below, which is given in fractions and in decimals, shows the complete range of possibilities.

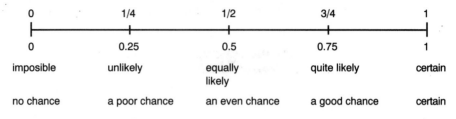

```
    0              1/4            1/2            3/4             1
    ├───────────────┼──────────────┼──────────────┼──────────────┤
    0              0.25           0.5            0.75            1

 imposible        unlikely       equally       quite likely    certain
                                 likely

 no chance      a poor chance   an even chance  a good chance   certain
```

Exercise 12e

1 Use words such as 'unlikely', 'quite likely', etc. to describe the probability of the given events happening.
  (a) The sun rises tomorrow morning.
  (b) You will live for 100 years.
  (c) The first person I'll see when I switch the television set on will be a female.
  (d) I get a head when I spin a coin.
  (e) Next year will have at least 365 days.
  (f) You will represent your country in a sport.
  (g) Value Added Tax (VAT) will be reduced in the next budget.
  (h) You will successfully complete this GNVQ course.
  (i) It will still be dark when you get up tomorrow.

2 (a) Write a sentence to show that you understand each of the following words/phrases: (i) even chance, (ii) less than an even chance, (iii) no chance, (iv) a certainty, (v) most unlikely, (vi) very likely.
  (b) Which of the words/phrases do you think best describes a probability of (i) 0 (ii) 0.01 (iii) 0.45 (iv) 0.5 (v) 0.9 (vi) 1?

3 How many different possible outcomes are there if you
  (a) choose a first course from a menu that has six different first courses on it
  (b) decide to buy a car from a second hand car dealer who has 45 cars for sale
  (c) telephone a friend at her home?

Probability that an event does not happen

If Tim promises he will give you a ring one day within the next week, with any day equally likely, the probability that he will ring tomorrow is $\frac{1}{7}$.

If he does not ring tomorrow the probability that he will ring on one of the other six days is $\frac{6}{7}$

$\therefore$ probability of ringing tomorrow + probability of ringing on some other day is $\qquad \frac{1}{7} + \frac{6}{7}$

$$= \frac{7}{7} = 1$$

i.e. the probability that he rings tomorrow + probability that he does not ring tomorrow = 1.

In general terms

probability that an event happens + probability that the event does not happen = 1

i.e. probability that an event happens = 1 − probability that the event does not happen

and probability that an event does not happen = 1 − probability that the event happens.

Exercise 12f

Question The sketch shows some brochures on the shelf in a Travel Agents. A brochure is chosen at random. What is the probability that the selected brochure is
(a) for Florida   (b) is not for Florida?

Answer (a) There are 7 brochures on the shelf and 2 of them are for Florida so the probability that the selected brochure is for Florida is $\frac{2}{7}$.
(b) The probability that the brochure is not for Florida is $1 - \frac{2}{7} = \frac{5}{7}$.

1   The probability that I will get home before 6 p.m. tonight is ¾.
    What is the probability that I will not get home before 6 p.m. tonight?

2   The probability that it will rain tomorrow in Cairo is 0.008.
    What is the probability that it will not rain in Cairo tomorrow?

3   The probability that Jen will pass her driving test is 0.68.
    What is the probability that she will not pass?

4   A team is chosen at random from the 22 teams in the Premier League.
    What is the probability that it is
    (a) Arsenal   (b) a team other than Arsenal?

5   You buy 10 tickets in a raffle.
    If 450 tickets are sold altogether what is the probability that you will
    not win first prize?

6   Recently the Blood Transfusion Service held a session at the Grenford
    Park Industrial Estate. The table shows how the donors were divided
    into different blood groups.

Blood Group	Number of donors
O	75
A	51
B	17
AB	10

    If a donor is chosen at random what is the probability that the donor's
    blood group is
    (a) A   (b) AB   (c) not O?

7   A box contains a set of snooker balls. They consist of 15 reds and one
    each of white, yellow, green, brown, blue, pink and black.
    If one ball is removed at random from the box what is the probability
    that it is
    (a) red   (b) not red
    (c) blue   (d) neither red nor black?

8   On a certain day at Renstor College of Further Education, 518 students
    are registered as present. 111 are on a GNVQ course, 185 are on an A
    level course and the remainder are on other courses.
    (a) How many of those attending are not taking either a GNVQ course
         or an A level course?
    (b) One student is selected at random.
         What is the probability that the chosen student
         (i) is on a GNVQ course   (ii) is not on an A level course?

Bookmaker's odds   If a horse is quoted at 10–1 it means that if you are prepared to stake
£1, the bookmaker is willing to stake £10 i.e. the total stake is £11, the
winner to take all. Odds of 10–1 therefore imply that you have 1

chance of winning and 10 chances of losing i.e. the probability of winning is 1 out of 11 i.e. $\frac{1}{11}$.

If 'Laura's Joy' is '2–1 on' it means that for every £2 you stake the bookmaker stakes £1 i.e. the chance of it winning is $\frac{2}{3}$. 'Evens' i.e. 1–1 implies a 50–50 chance of winning i.e. the probability of winning is $\frac{1}{2}$.

Exercise 12g

1 What is the probability of winning if the starting price of a horse is
   (a) 5–1   (b) 9–1
   (c) 7–2   (d) 5–2?

2 A bookmaker quotes odds of 20–1 on West Ham winning the FA Cup next year.
   What does the bookmaker believe to be West Ham probability of winning?

3 The odds that 'Ardent Hope' will win the 2.30 at Cheltenham are 3–2 on. Sam puts £5 on the horse.
   (a) What does the bookmaker think is the probability that 'Ardent Hope' will win?
   (b) How much will Sam collect if it does win?

Possibility space for two events

The light switches in Sally's hall and on her upstairs landing have never operated as intended. Although other combinations for the positions of the two switches are possible, both switches must be in the 'down' position for the landing light to be on. All the possible combinations can be listed in a table called a *possibility* space. The possible positions for the hall switch are written along the top and the possible positions for the landing switch are written down the side.

	Landing switch	
	up (U)	down (D)
Hall up (U)		
Switch down (D)		

The table shows that there are 4 different possible combinations:

	Landing switch	
	up (U)	down (D)
Hall up (U)	U,U	D,U
Switch down (D)	U,D	D,D

Note that the first entry of each pair refers to the hall switch which is listed along the top while the second entry refers to the landing switch which is listed down the side. From this table it is easy to see that only one of the four possible combinations gives two *D*s i.e. the combination to put the landing light on.

Exercise 12h

1 Nicki and Phil each have a bag with 3 compact discs and 2 cassettes. Liz chooses one item from Nicki's bag and one from Phil's.
Complete the following possibility space to show the possible combinations of two items. A compact disc is denoted by *D* and a cassette by *C*.

First bag

		D	D	D	C	C
	D	D,D	D,D	D,D	C,D	
Second	D					
bag	D					
	C	D,C				
	C				C,C	

2 In the ladies' fashion department of a department store the size 10 coats, for a particular style of Jules Vere coat style, hang on two rails. On one rail hang 2 blue coats, 2 red coats and 1 yellow coat while on the other rail hang 3 blue coats and 2 yellow coats. The sales assistant selects one coat at random from each rail.
(Blue, red and yellow are denoted by the letters B, R and Y.)
(a) Copy and complete the following possibility space.

First rail

		B	B	R	R	Y
	B		B,B			Y,B
Second	B					
rail	B			R,B		
	Y				R,Y	

(b) How many entries are there in the table altogether?
(c) How many of these entries include a red coat?
(d) How many of these entries do not include a blue coat?

3 Lindsay and Vicki look into their purses. Lindsay's purse contains three
   £1 coins and two 20 p coins whereas Vicki's purse contains one £1 coin
   and one 20 p coin. A coin is removed at random from each purse.
   (a) Complete the following possibility space

		Lindsay's purse				
		£1	£1	£1	20p	20p
Vicki's purse	£1				20p, £1	
	20p					

(b) How many different possible outcomes are there?
(c) How many of these outcomes give one £1 coin and one 20 p coin?
(d) How many of these outcomes give two coins of the same value?

Using a possibility space

We can use a possibility space to find a probability since we can count
all the possible outcomes and we can count the number that satisfy the
particular condition we are interested in.

Exercise 12i

Question Tracy has 3 chocolates with hard centres and two chocolates with soft
centres, while Kevin has 2 chocolates with hard centres and 4
chocolates with soft centres. Nigel is asked to close his eyes, then
choose one of Tracy's chocolates and one of Kevin's chocolates.
(a) Construct a possibility space to show the different ways in which
he can make his choice.
(b) What is the probability that
  (i) the two chocolates he chooses both have hard centres
  (ii) one chocolate he chooses has a hard centre and the other a
  soft centre
  (iii) at least one of the chocolates he chooses has a hard centre?

Answer (a) In the possibility space given below H denotes a chocolate with a hard centre and S one with a soft centre. The first letter in each box refers to Tracy's chocolates.

		Tracy's chocolates				
		H	H	H	S	S
	H	H,H	H,H	H,H	S,H	S,H
Kevin's	H	H,H	H,H	H,H	S,H	S,H
chocolates	S	H,S	H,S	H,S	S,S	S,S
	S	H,S	H,S	H,S	S,S	S,S
	S	H,S	H,S	H,S	S,S	S,S
	S	H,S	H,S	H,S	S,S	S,S

(b) (i) The table shows that there are 30 different ways in which Nigel can make his choice
In 6 of these both chocolates have hard centres
∴ probability that Nigel takes 2 chocolates with hard centres is $\frac{6}{30} = \frac{1}{5}$.
(ii) There are 16 boxes with one H and one S
∴ probability that Nigel chooses one chocolate of each type is $\frac{16}{30} = \frac{8}{15}$.
(iii) There are 22 boxes with either one or two Hs
∴ probability that there is at least one chocolate with a hard centre is $\frac{22}{30} = \frac{11}{15}$.

In the questions that follow assume that all the possible outcomes are equally likely. Give probabilities as fractions or as decimals correct to 2 d.p.

1 Use the possibility space in the worked example to find the probability that Nigel gets
(a) a chocolate with a hard centre from Tracy and one with a soft centre from Kevin
(b) two chocolates with soft centres
(c) one chocolate with a hard centre and one chocolate with a soft centre.

2 Use the possibility space for Question 2 of Exercise 12h to find the probability that the two coats selected by the sales assistant
(a) are both blue   (b) are of different colours
(c) include at least one yellow coat.

3 Copy and complete the following possibility space which shows the total score when two dice are rolled together.

		First dice					
		1	2	3	4	5	6
	1	2	3	4	5	6	7
Second	2	3					8
dice	3	4					9
	4	5					10
	5	6					11
	6	7	8	9	10	11	12

(a) How many entries are there altogether?
(b) (i) Which score is most likely? (ii) How many times does it occur?
(c) How many times is the score (i) greater than 10 (ii) less than 10?
(d) Use your possibility space to find the probability that the score
    (i) is greater then 10 (ii) is less than 10 (iii) is 6 or more.

4 Barrie keeps dogs. She has 3 alsatians and 2 corgis. Eddie also keeps
dogs. He has 1 alsatian and 4 labradors.
One dog is chosen at random from each owner. Draw a possibility
space to show the different combinations possible.
What is the probability that
(a) both dogs are alsatians
(b) the dogs are of different breeds
(c) at least one dog is an alsation.

5 Sue and Andy apply for jobs in residential homes and in nursing homes.
Sue applies to 3 residential homes and to 2 nursing homes. Andy applies
to 2 residential homes and to 3 nursing homes. Draw a possibility space
to show the various combinations in which they might be offered jobs.
Use your possibility space to find the probability that
(a) they might both be offered jobs in a residential home
(b) one gets a job in a residential home while the other gets a job in a
    nursing home.

Expected values

We can use probability to estimate the expected number of times an
event is likely to happen.

If I toss a 10 pence coin the probability of getting a head is $\frac{1}{2}$.
On 1000 tosses I can therefore expect to get $1000 \times \frac{1}{2}$ heads i.e. 500
heads.

If a student is chosen at random out of a group of 3 male students and
6 female students the probability of choosing a female student is $\frac{6}{9}$ i.e. $\frac{2}{3}$.

Suppose that on every one of the 180 days of the college year a student
is chosen at random from these nine. The number of times a female
student can be expected to be chosen is $180 \times \frac{2}{3}$ i.e. 120 times.

Exercise 12j

1 In Barsetshire the probability of passing your driving test at the first attempt is $\frac{5}{8}$. Next week 160 learner drivers are booked in to take their test.
(a) How many of them would you expect to pass?
(b) How many are likely to fail?

2 10 per cent of the 80-year-olds in Sufford are expected to reach their ninetieth birthday.
(a) What is the probability that Jim, who is 80 today, will reach his ninetieth birthday?
(b) At present there are 9870 eighty-year-olds in Sufford.
How many of these can expect to celebrate their ninetieth birthday?

3 A car manufacturer knows from experience that the probability that the electrical system on any car they manufacture will fail during the first three years is 0.002. This year the company has produced 527 000 cars. How many of these are likely to have an electrical breakdown at some time during the next three years?

4 The probability that I will have to wait for a game when I go to the skittle alley is 0.6.
I intend going to play skittles twice a week for the next thirty weeks.
On how many occasions should I be able to play straightaway?

5 Henri's restaurant offers a choice of four first courses at lunchtime. Over the years they have got to know the probabilities that a given customer will select any one of them. They are:
French Onion Soup – $\frac{1}{4}$, Duckling Pâté – $\frac{1}{3}$, Bacon Stuffed Tomatoes – $\frac{1}{5}$ and Pineapple Mint Cocktail – $\frac{13}{60}$.
They expect to serve 240 lunches. What is the minimum number of
(a) Pineapple Mint cocktails
(b) Duckling Pâté, they should prepare?

6 If I post a first class letter at my local post office the probability that it will arrive at its destination the following morning is 0.95. The firm I work for sends out about 150 first class letters every week.
In a year how many of these letters would my firm expect to fail to be delivered the next morning?

7 At Clegg's Nursery the probability that a geranium cutting will become a saleable plant the following season is 0.82.
(a) How many saleable plants can be expected if 850 cuttings are taken?
(b) How many cuttings should prove unsatisfactory?

8 A firm of motor insurers knows from experience that 10% of its policyholders will make a claim during a year's driving. At present it has 14 540 policyholders. How many claims does the firm expect will be made on these policies during the forthcoming year?

9 The probability that a person in Swidenshire, which has a population of 350 000, will suffer a fatal attack of influenza next winter is stated to be 0.00008. How many deaths do they expect next winter which are caused from influenza?

10 The probability that the occupants of a house fitted with a smoke alarm will escape unharmed in the event of a fire is 0.96 whereas the probability that the occupants of a house not fitted with a smoke alarm will escape unharmed is one-sixth of this.

(a) What is the probability that, Geoff, who lives in a house in which a smoke alarm has not been fitted, will escape unharmed in the event of a fire?

(b) During the next year in the county of Redfordshire it is estimated that there will be 650 fires in homes fitted with smoke alarms. In how many of these is it anticipated that the occupants   (i) will escape unharmed   (ii) will suffer some kind of injury?

(c) During the same period it is estimated that the number of fires in houses not fitted with smoke alarms will be 1250. In how many of these fires is it estimated that the occupants will be injured?

Multiple choice questions

In Questions 1–3 several alternative answers are given. Write down the letter that corresponds to the correct answer.

1 If one letter is chosen at random from the letters in the word INTERESTED the probability that it is the letter E is

A $\frac{1}{10}$ **B** $\frac{2}{10}$ **C** $\frac{3}{10}$ **D** $\frac{2}{5}$

2 When Norman plays darts the probability that he will score a treble 20 with any dart is $\frac{1}{10}$. He throws a single dart 300 times.

The number of times he does not expect to score 60 is

A 30   **B** 250   **C** 280   **D** 270

3 A taxi company, which has 3 red cabs and 2 yellow cabs, employs 2 female drivers and 3 male drivers. When a call comes in it is answered at random by any one of the 5 drivers, and the colour of the cab that the driver takes is also selected at random. Kilmer rings for a taxi. The probability that the cab he gets is yellow and driven by a female is

A $\frac{6}{25}$ **B** $\frac{9}{25}$ **C** $\frac{4}{25}$ **D** $\frac{3}{25}$

4 On a coach trip 250 tickets are sold in a raffle. Each person, including Jane, buys 5 tickets. Which of the following statements are true and which are false?

A Every person has exactly the same chance of winning and that chance is $\frac{1}{50}$

B If every person had bought one ticket Jane would have had exactly the same chance of winning as when everybody bought 5 tickets

C There were fewer than 50 people on the coach

D If Jane had bought 10 tickets but everybody else bought 5 Jane's chance of winning would have increased from $\frac{1}{50}$ to $\frac{1}{25}$.

5 Sophie put £5 on 'Pitman's Boy', a horse that was running in the 3.30 at Doncaster. Sophie had a good day because the horse won at odds of 7–1. The following statements have been made:

Statement 1 The chance of winning is $\frac{1}{8}$ and since the horse wins Sophie makes a profit of £35.

Statement 2 Sophie wins £35 so she is £40 better off than if the horse had lost.

How are these statements best described

A True, True   **B** True, False

C False, True   **D** False, False.

Self assessment 12

1 A letter is chosen at random from the word EASTENDERS. What is the probability that the letter is
(a) D   (b) S   (c) E?

2 Kelly has twelve CDs. Seven of them include hit songs by The Shamen while the remaining five include hit songs by Take That but none by The Shamen. Hank chooses a CD from Kelly's collection.
    What is the probability that the CD he chooses includes a hit song by
(a) The Shamen   (b) Take That?

3 On any working day the probability that I will get stuck in a traffic jam on the way to work is 0.1.
(a) What is the probability that the next time I go to work I will not get stuck in a traffic jam?
(b) At present I work a 5-day week forty-eight weeks a year. How many times in a year do I expect to get to work without getting stuck in a traffic jam?

4 One box on a shelf in a shop contains five 100W bulbs and two 60W bulbs. Another box contains four 100W bulbs and three 60W bulbs.
Complete the following possibility space to show all the different possible combinations if one bulb is chosen at random from each box. For each combination the first entry refers to the first box and the second entry refers to the second box.

		First box					
		100W	100W	100W	100W	100W	60W	60W
	100W	100W,100W					60W,100W	
	100W							
	100W							
Second	100W							
box	60W							
	60W	100W,60W						
	60W							

Use your possibility space to find the probability that
(a) two 60W bulbs are chosen
(b) one 60W bulb and one 100W bulb are chosen.

5 Estimate the probability that
(a) you will get an 8 if you roll an ordinary six-sided dice
(b) the sun will rise tomorrow
(c) you will get a head or a tail if you toss a coin
(d) the next person who comes through the door is a male.

6 Mitsushoni Electronics make TV sets. The probability that a particular set will break down within three years is 0.002. Last year the company made 347 500 sets.
How many of these would you expect to break down during the first three years?

7

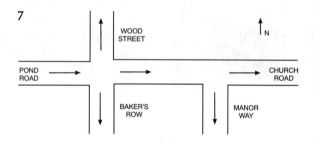

The sketch shows part of the one-way road system in Milchester. Experience shows that for a vehicle travelling east along Pond Road the probability is $\frac{1}{4}$ that it turns left along Wood Street, $\frac{3}{20}$ that it turns right down Baker's Row, otherwise it goes straight on. At the next junction on Pond Road the probability that a vehicle turns down Manor Way is $\frac{7}{20}$, otherwise it continues straight on along Church Road.
(a) What percentage of the vehicles travelling along Pond Road are expected to
    (i) turn left
    (ii) turn right
    (iii) go straight on?
(b) What is the probability that a vehicle on Pond Road will go straight on at the first junction?
(c) Between 9 a.m. and 12 noon 1800 vehicles are predicted to enter Pond Road travelling east towards the Wood Street/Baker's Row junction. How many of these vehicles are expected
    (i) to turn left into Wood Street
    (ii) to go straight ahead at the first junction?
    (iii) to turn right down Manor Way?

Revision papers for Units 10–12

Paper 13

1 (a) On a map 1 cm represents $\frac{1}{4}$ km. What is the scale of the map?
(b) The distance between two cities is 150 km. How far apart will they be on a map whose scale is 1:2 000 000?

2 From past experience the probability that it will rain in Puddleton on a Saturday in August is $\frac{3}{4}$. Next August has four Saturdays.
On how many of them would you expect it to rain?

3 The probability that a car fitted with Durman tyres will have a puncture before the tyres reach there legal limit is 0.006. A company buys 170 cars, all fitted with Durman tyres.
How many of these cars can be expected to have a puncture before their tyres reach the legal limit?

4 When a newspaper is bought for 35 p, one-fifth of the purchase price is profit.
Find the ratio of the production and distribution costs to the profit.

5

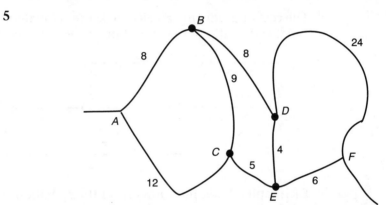

In this road system the distances between the towns are marked in kilometres.
(a) Find (i) the shortest distance from *A* to *F* that visits every town
(ii) the longest route from *A* to *F* that does not use any road more than once.
(b) (i) Is this network traversable? (ii) If it is, where do you start? Show your route. (iii) If it is not, where do you think an additional road could be laid to make the resulting network traversable? Show this on your network and use the capital letters to give a traversable route.

Paper 14

1 Weather records at Northford show that it has snowed on New Year's Day on 20 out of the last 50 years.
(a) What is the probability that it will snow on next New Year's Day?
(b) During the next 10 years how many times would you expect it to snow on New Year's Day?

2

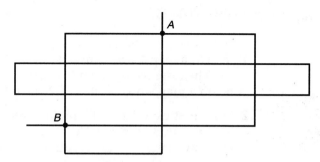

The diagram shows the layout of streets on an estate. Can you find a route for the milkman, who enters the network at *A*, needs to travel along every road in it, preferably only once, and wishes to leave the network from *B*?

3 (a) There are twelve horses in a race. Is each horse equally likely to win?

(b) Jo puts £1, at odds of 5–1, on the horse that wins.
How much better off is he than if the horse had lost?

4 The cost of producing an electric kettle is $\frac{1}{3}$ materials and $\frac{2}{3}$ labour. What is the ratio of the cost of materials to the cost of labour?

5

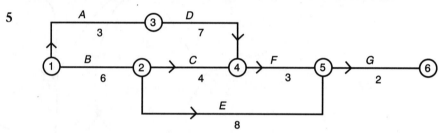

Each capital letter indicates one of the operations necessary to assemble a food processor.

The numbers adjacent to each letter, give the time, in minutes, to carry out that operation e.g. operation *A* takes 3 minutes and operation *D* takes 7 minutes.

(a) How many different operations are there?

(b) Which operations must be completed before
    (i) operation *C* (ii) operation *F*, can be started?

(c) What is the shortest time it takes to assemble one of these food processors?

Paper 15

1 The Post Office states that the probability that a First Class letter is delivered the next day is 0.95, and the probability that it will be delivered within two days is 0.99. A motor insurance company posts 740 letters on Monday using first class post. How many does it expect to be delivered

(a) on Tuesday   (b) before Thursday

(c) after Wednesday?

2 In a factory making coffee percolators two cells share a bonus of £780 in the ratio of the number of units they produce. The first cell produces 14 490 units and the second cell produces 1890 units. How much bonus does each cell get?

3 A lorry travels 100 km on 20 litres of diesel.
   (a) How far will this lorry travel on 55 litres of diesel?
   (b) How many litres of diesel are required for the lorry to travel 550 km?

4

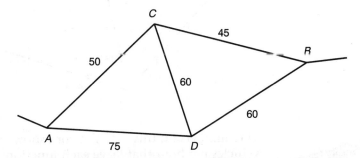

The network shows the layout of a system of pipes in a chemical factory that is used to transport a liquid from A to B. The numbers show the number of gallons per minute that can be pumped along each pipe. An advantage of this system is that the liquid can still be pumped from A to B even if any one pipe in the network breaks down.
Find the greatest possible rate of flow
   (a) from A to B (b) from B to A
   (c) from A to B if AC is out of action.

5 Last year Purley Transistors made a profit of £1.5 m on sales of £14 m. It is anticipated that the sales this year to sales last year will increase in the ratio 7:9 and that profits will increase in the ratio 1:2. Find
   (a) the costs of production last year   (b) the expected sales this year
   (c) the expected profits this year   (d) the predicted costs this year
   (e) the ratio this year of the profits
       to the costs.

Paper 16

1 Wendy and Alan agree to collect some holiday brochures on the way home from work. Wendy comes home with 5 brochures for America and 2 for Australia while Alan has 2 for America and 1 for Australia. They sit down that evening to look through them. Draw a possibility space to show which brochures they could each be reading at any one moment. Use this to find the probability that at a particular moment
   (a) they are both looking at a brochure advertising holidays in America
   (b) they are looking at brochures for different countries
   (c) at least one of them is looking at a brochure for Australia.

2

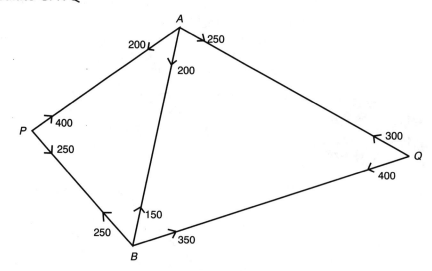

The numbers on this road network show the maximum number of vehicles per hour that leave each junction in a given direction. For example, 400 vehicles an hour can leave *P* for *A* but only 200 an hour can leave *A* for *P*.

What is the maximum number of vehicles per hour that this road system can carry

(a) from *P* to *Q* passing through *A*   (b) from *P* to *Q*
(c) from *Q* to *P*?

3 A factory with 150 machinists has enough material to keep them employed for 16 days. If 30 machinists are made redundant how many days will the available material employ those that remain?

4 The table shows the costs and income from sales for 5 factories in a group whose main business is manufacturing ladies' dresses.

Company	Costs (£m)	Sales (£m)	Gross profit (£m)	Ratio of gross profit to costs expressed as a percentage
Cranford	1.51	1.74	0.23	$\frac{0.23}{1.51} = 15.2\%$
Bishton	2.13	2.67		
Danely	2.81	3.94		
Frensham		4.03	0.81	
Rusford	2.59	3.18		

(a) Copy and complete this table to show, for each company, the ratio of the gross profit to costs and express each ratio as a percentage.
(b) If you were the Managing Director of the group which companies would you show particular interest in? Give reasons for your choice.
Which company would you need to take a very close look at
(i) because it was unsatisfactory   (ii) to find the reason for its success?

5

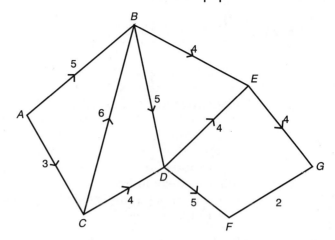

Distances in kilometres

(a) How many different routes are there through this network from *A* to *G*?

(b) Which route is (i) the shortest (ii) the longest?

(Acceptable routes are those that move from left to right across the page, e.g. *C* to *D* is acceptable, but *E* to *D* is not.)

For You to Discuss: 4

An ageing population

The average female born in 1900 could expect to live for 51 years and the average male for 46 years. It is a startling fact that by 1940 these figures had increased to 68 and 63 and are about 79 and 73 today. Such progress, in increasing the number of years we can expect to live, also creates problems. These facts prompted student Lee Curtiz to do a little investigating. He found out that by the year 2001 the expected population of the United Kingdom would be about 56 million, 10 million of whom would be people of retirement age (65 for men, 60 for women – though this is going to change), 4 million would be over 75 and 1 million over 85.

Many of these retired people would spend their twilight years in a residential home. Some would have to pay a great deal for this privilege while others would not have to contribute at all. A visit to the Beatrice Webb Home in Lee's area revealed that they had 55 beds. All of them were taken. In fact there was a long waiting list. At the time of his visit the ratio of men to women was 4 to 7.

He soon got chatting to some of the residents. There was Edna Broad. She told him that when she was born she weighed $7\frac{1}{2}$ pounds and was 20 inches long. By the time she was 65 she weighed 70 kilograms and was 170 centimetres tall. "They changed the way you measure things compared with when I was a child", she chuckled. Now that she's in her late seventies she's lost a lot of that weight and she is certainly a few inches shorter. She also explained to Lee that before a new resident is accepted a social worker calls to discuss the move. 'The person moving into the home is asked all manner of questions – How much

money do you have? What's your income? Would you like to spend some of your money to make the room you're going to have more like home? What small items would you like to bring with you? Do you have any relatives? Where do you live? Would you like to know how much you will have to contribute? In particular the social worker will show you a plan of the layout of the room you have been allocated. You are told about the furniture fittings in the room, and about the decor and colour scheme. My bedroom measures about 12 feet by 9 feet. Most of the others are about the same size.' Quietly she leaned across and whispered 'People are touchy when they're asked how much they have. Most people don't like to show they are poor and if they've got money they want it to be kept a secret.'

Inquiries at the office suggested that public transport in the area is quite good for those pensioners fit enough to take advantage of it. There is a special agreement with the bus company that pensioners will be charged $\frac{2}{5}$ of the full fare and taxis cost £1.50 for any metered fare up to £8 plus the full amount by which the fare is more than £8. On the trains, OAPs can buy a Railcard for £20 a year and this card allows the pensioner to go anywhere by train at 30% discount.

During the year Lee visited the Beatrice Webb many times and had lots of interesting conversations with the residents. He learned how life had changed comparing the period before the First World War with today. The old folk told him about the sizes of the houses they used to live in, how many brothers and sisters they had and how their parents took in lodgers to make more money. There were few radios and no television sets. They couldn't travel very far and so had to make their own entertainment. Although life is very much better for most people today than it was more than seventy years ago there are still problems. Today one in five of the population has an income that is below the poverty line. The present average weekly wage is about £300 a week and, according to the EU, the poverty line is half this figure. 33% of those below the poverty line are OAPs. In the community as a whole, over the last 10 years, the total number who are below the poverty line has increased from 7 m to 10 m.

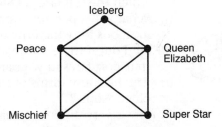

On his last visit Lee took a walk in the garden with one of the residents. The paths in the rose garden, which is placed in the middle of a large lawn, are laid out in the form of the back of an opened out envelope. There are standard roses at each of the five corners. Going round the outside, starting at the 'point' of the envelope they are called Iceberg, Peace, Mischief, Super Star and Queen Elizabeth. The old lady Lee was with said that she saw quite different things if she walked along the same path but in opposite directions. Her comment made him think. By the time Lee had completed his project he knew that things had got a lot better over the years, but there was still a long way to go.

Questions and points for discussion

(a) What is the ratio of the life expectancy for men in 1900 to the life expectancy today?
What is the equivalent ratio for women?

(b) In the year 2001 what fraction of the population is expected to be (i) of retirement age (ii) over 75?

(c) Discuss some of the financial problems that can arise in the future because we have an ageing population. Where does the money come from to pay pensions? How many people contribute to the state pension scheme now, compared with the number that receive pensions? Find out what the ratio is. Will this ratio change? Will it go up or down? Are there going to be problems?

(d) How many men are there at the Beatrice Webb?

(e) What is the probability that a resident chosen at random from the Beatrice Webb Home is a man? Use this probability to discuss how many of the next 100 residents that come into the home are likely to be (i) male (ii) female.

(f) Can you convert Ena Broad's weight and height at birth into metric units? Why do we use different units today from those used by our grandparents? Are the changes for the better? Is it easier to work things out using the new units rather than the old?

(g) Mark six or eight places at random on a map of your local area. Now plan a route from your home so that you visit all these places and return home, using the shortest possible route.

(h) How much do residents in Old People's homes have to contribute to the costs? Collect some literature to find out.

(i) How much will a pensioner with a railcard have to pay for ticket for which the full fare is £66?

(j) What will a pensioner pay for (i) a £12 taxi fare (ii) a ride on the local bus for which the full fare is £1.50?

(k) Find out if there are any local agreements for subsidised public transport fares in your area.

(l) Are there any forms of transport in your area that cater solely for older people?

(m) Life is very different today compared with seventy years ago. Draw up a simple questionnaire that allows you to collect some data to compare the two periods.

(n) How many people are estimated to be living below the poverty line? What fraction of the population is this? How many of these are pensioners?

(p) Lee wanted to give routes through the rose garden that allows a stroller to visit every standard rose and walk along every path once but only once. Can you help him? Discuss the different places a person could start. How many different routes are there?

General Revision Papers

1 (a) Lee Ann wishes to order envelopes for her company. She finds the following details in different catalogues:

Norse Direct			
12" x 10" Manilla envelopes (250 per box)			
Price per box			
1 Box £	3 Boxes £	5 Boxes £	10 Boxes £
29.99	18.49	17.49	16.49

(She understands this to mean that if she orders 5 boxes each box will cost £17.49 while if she orders 4 boxes the price will be at the next higher rate i.e. £18.49 per box.)

W. H. Deakin	
12" x 10" Manilla envelopes (100 per box)	
Number of boxes purchased	Price per box £
0–50	6.99
51–100	5.99
101–500	4.49
over 500	3.99

She needs 3 months' supply which she estimates to be 5000 envelopes. Which supplier should she order from, assuming that delivery charges and delivery dates are identical?

(b) Tim Benson has the same two catalogues. He wants to order 1000 envelopes. Where should he place his order? How much does he save by making the correct choice?

2 Part of a catalogue for a forthcoming property auction is shown on p. 305. The figure against each **LOT** number is the price the auctioneer expects the property to be sold for.
Use this information to answer the following questions:
(a) **LOT 1** sold for £2500 above its estimated sale price.
How much did the buyer pay per acre?
(b) **LOT 2** was sold for 20% more than the highest estimated sale price.
How much was this?

```
┌─────────────────────────────────────────────────────────────┐
│              AUCTION OF COMMERCIAL AND                        │
│                RESIDENTIAL PROPERTY                           │
│                                                              │
│   LOT 1  Land at Hunter Street, Nr Heath          £27 500   │
│          1/3 acre, outline planning                          │
│          permission                                          │
│                                                              │
│   LOT 2  57 Princess Street, Camden         £15 000–£17 000 │
│          Three bedroomed semi–detatched                      │
│          house                                               │
│                                                              │
│   LOT 3  Unit 2 City Business Park          £28 000–£32 000 │
│          4200 sq ft–modern industrial                        │
│          premises                                            │
│                                                              │
│   LOT 4  26 Freehold ground rents in                         │
│          Westpool Significant reversionary        £50 000   │
│          sale                                                │
│                                                              │
│   LOT 5  5 Victoria Terrace, Crosslands           £12 000   │
│             Two bedroomed mid–terrace house                  │
│                                                              │
│   LOT 6  38 Commercial Road, Bridgeside           £42 000   │
│          Mixed commercial & residential                      │
│          investment                                          │
└─────────────────────────────────────────────────────────────┘
```

(c) The sale price of **LOT 3** was exactly in the middle of the price range given in the catalogue.
How much was this per square foot?

(d) Two people were very keen to buy **LOT 4**. This pushed the price up to 70% above the catalogue estimate.
What was the mean (average) cost of purchasing a ground freehold?

(e) The reserve price for **LOT 5**, i.e. the lowest price at which the vendor (seller) was prepared to sell, was seven-eighths of the catalogue estimate. **LOT 5** was eventually sold for £450 more than the reserve price.
How much was this?

(f) (i) **LOT 6** was sold for 15% more than the catalogue estimate.
How much was this? (ii) The commercial part of the property was considered to be twice as valuable as the residential part.
How much did this mean that the buyer paid for the commercial part of the property?

(g) **LOTS 1–6** were sold for the same seller. (i) Find the gross proceeds from the sale. (ii) If the expenses of the sale cost the seller £23 475 find the net proceeds from the sale and express this as a percentage of the gross sale price.

3 The table shows the number of available beds and listed facilities for a well known UK holiday resort, at ten year intervals.

Year	Number of hotel rooms	Number of rooms with private bath
1973	1420	652
1983	1363	821
1993	1292	974

(a) What was the increase in the number of hotel rooms with a private bath (i) from 1973 to 1983 (ii) from 1973 to 1993?

(b) Find the percentage decrease in the number of available hotel bedrooms from 1973 to 1993.

(c) Find the increase, from 1973 to 1993, in the percentage of hotel bedrooms with a private bath.

4 (a) A 4-cylinder OHC petrol engine has a bore of 82.5 mm and a stroke of 92.8 mm.
Find its displacement, i.e. the total capacity of the four cylinders.

(b) A 4-cylinder engine has a bore of 79.5 mm and a displacement of 1896 cubic centimetres.
Find its stroke.

(The *bore* is the diameter of the cylinder, the *stroke* is the length of the piston stroke i.e. the length of the cylinder.)

Paper 18

Mike and Sue have ideas of going into business together. In order to come to grips with cash flow problems they decide to see what they can learn by estimating their personal financial position each month for the present year.

Study their estimates and answer the questions that follow.

Notes: The Opening balance at the start of the year is £0. The Closing balance at the end of January is the amount by which the income exceeds the expenditure i.e £271. This is the Opening balance for February. A monthly balance is placed in brackets e.g. (£925) if what is paid out is greater than the income for that month.

1 Make out a table to show
(a) their 'cash in' each month
(b) their 'cash out' each month
(c) their monthly balance i.e. income − expenditure.

2 Find
(a) their total estimated income for the year
(b) their total estimated expenditure for the year.
(c) Should their income be more than their expenditure?

3 In which months is their 'cash out' greater than their 'cash in'?

(a)

Cash in	Jan	Feb	Mar	Apr	May	Jun	Jul	Aug	Sep	Oct	Nov	Dec
Mike	1220	1220	1220	1260	1260	1260	1260	1260	1260	1260	1260	1260
Sue	850	850	850	850	850	940	940	940	850	850	960	960
Total	2070											
Cash out												
Mortage	750	750	750	750	750	750	750	750	750	750	750	750
Food	300	300	300	300	300	300	300	300	300	300	300	350
Clothes	100	50	50	50	50	50	100	50	50	50	50	100
Gas	38	38	38	38	38	38	38	38	38	38	38	38
Electricity	42	42	42	42	42	42	42	42	42	42	42	42
Phone			95			95			95			95
Water				286								
Council tax			450									
House Ins							284					
Car loan	190	190	190	190	190	190	190	190	190	190	190	190
TV licence						120						
Car tax				65						65		
Car Ins				485								
Petrol	45	45	45	45	45	45	45	45	45	45	45	45
Life Ins	35	35	35	35	35	35	35	35	35	35	35	35
Credit cds	65	65	65	65	65	65	65	65	65	65	65	65
Bank loan	84	84	84	84	84	84	84	84	84	84	84	84
Hols							1200					
Christmas											450	
Reg saving	100	100	100	100	100	100	100	100	100	100	100	100
Misc	50	50	50	50	50	50	50	50	50	50	50	50
Total cash out	1799											
Monthly balance	271											
Opening bal	0	271	1002									
Closing bal	271											

4 Find their Opening and Closing balance each month.

5 Do they have any cash flow problems i.e. are there any months when their income plus their closing balance at the end of the previous month is not enough to meet their expenditure?

6 (a) How much does the car cost them for the year?
  (b) Express this as a percentage of their total income.

7 How much, in total, do they spend on gas, electricity, telephone and water?

8 Next year Mike's income is expected to rise by 5% and Sue's income is expected to rise by 6%.
  Estimate their total income next year.

9 Next year they expect their expenses to rise by 8%.
  Should their income exceed their expenditure?

10 If they are to start a business they must accumulate some capital. Suggest where they could cut their expenses in order to save more.

11 What is the ratio of the amount their mortgage costs to the amount they spend on food?

12 Express their mortgage payments as a percentage of their total income.

13 Next year they will be able to pay their car insurance, council tax, house insurance and water bill, in twelve equal monthly amounts, each payment beginning in the same month as they pay the full amount this year.
(a) Assuming that all other entries remain unchanged make out financial estimates for the following year.
(b) Does this new arrangement solve their cash flow problems? (Monthly payments that are not an exact number of £ should be rounded up to the nearest whole number.)

14 The annual expenses for the car are under four headings: car loan, car tax, car insurance, petrol. Show this information on
(a) a bar chart   (b) a suitable pie chart.

15 The 'cash out' information can be summarised under the headings–mortgage, household expenses (food, gas, electricity, phone, water, council tax, house insurance, TV licence), car expenses and other.
Construct a pie chart to show how the total 'cash in' is divided between these four areas.

Paper 19

1

INVOICE

Wally's Food Importers
24 Butler Street
London SE14 0HQ

CUSTOMER
Adams Wholesale
148 Mirror Street
Birmimgham B2 1QR   5/5/95

Invoice No.	Customer Ref.	Invoice Date.

Quantity (Kg)	Description	Unit price (£)	Total (£)
250	Apricots	2.45	612.50
450	Walnuts	3.65	
300	Prunes	1.62	
500	Bran Oats	0.86	
350	Sultanas	1.32	

(a) Copy and complete this invoice to show the total amount due

(b) Wallys offer a 2½% discount if the account is paid within 7 days. How much should Adams Wholesale send if they pay 5 days after delivery?

2 The management of Byfleet Engineering meet to agree the price for their new MK16 drilling machine. They have engaged a market research company who supplied the information given in the first two columns of the table. Their accounts department has supplied the data given in column 3. Estimate sales and unit profits for MK16 drilling machines sold at various prices.

Price (£)	Estimated sales (000)	Net profit per machine (£)	Total estimated profit (£)
540	35	140	
525	38	128	
515	42	119	
505	48	108	
490	53	94	
475	60	82	

(a) What figures should be entered in the 4th column of the table?

(b) Which of the proposed selling prices gives the maximum profit if the expected sales figures materialise?

3 An ordinary pint of beer contains about 300 calories and a single measure of whisky about 90 calories. It is estimated that 10 000 surplus calories can produce 3 pounds of body weight.

(a) (i) How much weight is Mickey likely to gain from drinking 5 pints of beer a week for a year?

(ii) Would he put on less weight if he drank 6 whiskies a week instead?

(b) How much weight could Peg expect to put on if she drank a whisky and pep twice a day for a year?

4 (a) Find q given that $q + 7 = 30$

(b) Simplify $8a + 3a - 4a - a$ and hence solve the equation $8a + 3a - 4a - a = 36$

(c) Find, correct to 1 d.p., two positive numbers between which lies a solution of the equation $x^2 + 5x = 60$.

5 A second hand car is offered for sale at £5595. If bought on credit the terms are: a deposit of 25% plus 36 monthly repayments of £148.50. For cash there is a discount of 2½%. Find

(a) the cash price

(b) the deposit

(c) the total cost of the car if bought on credit

(d) how much more it costs to buy on credit than to pay cash

(e) the credit price as a percentage of the cash price.

(Give answers correct to the nearest £)

6

This map shows the central area of Blackpool. Roads whose edges are marked with a solid edge are called *through routes*. Arrows on certain roads tell us that they are one-way streets. For streets without arrows assume that traffic flows in both directions. The scale given on the map shows that 1.5 cm represents 300 metres.

(a) Give this scale in the form 1:*n*.

(b) How far is it along the promenade from the entrance to the Central Pier to the entrance to the North Pier?

(c) Estimate the length of Church Street from the Opera House to the junction with Devonshire Road.

(d) A lorry driver driving into Blackpool on the A 5099 is approaching Chapel Street. He wants to deliver several heavy electrical units to the ballroom beneath Blackpool tower. Suggest a through route so that as he approaches the tower it is on his side of the road.

Paper 20

1 A recipe for lemon marmalade gives the ingredients as 2 lb lemons, 4 lb sugar and 2 pints of water.

(a) If 1 pint of water weighs 1.25 lb find the total weight of the ingredients.

(b) The recipe states that these ingredients will make 7 lb of lemon marmalade.

What percentage of the ingredients are lost during the making of the marmalade?

2 The table shows several facts, including some prices, for the people of Oxbridgeshire, in the years 1964, 1984 and 1994.

Item	1964	1984	1994
Average house price	£4000	£32 000	£72 000
Family car	£1000	£5000	£10 000
TV set	£100	£250	£350
Loaf of bread	8p	24p	66p
Gallon of petrol	20p	160p	250p
Average weekly wage	£20	£190	£340

We see that the cost of the average house went up 8 times from 1964 to 1984 (i.e. from £4000 to £32 000) and by 2.25 times from 1984 to 1994 (i.e. from £32 000 to £72 000).

(a) How many times did the price of a TV set increase (i) from 1964 to 1984 (ii) from 1984 to 1994 (iii) from 1964 to 1994?

(b) Copy and complete the following table which shows the number of times the cost of each item increased between the given dates.

Item	1964–84	1984–94	1964–94
Average house price	8		18
Family car			
TV set			
Loaf of bread			
Gallon of petrol			

(c) Work out similar figures for the increase in the average wage and add this information below the last line of the table.

(d) How many weeks would a person earning the average wage have to work to buy an average house in (i) 1964 (ii) 1984 (iii) 1994? (iv) When was the best time for the average person to buy an average house?

(e) The average wage in 1964 was based on a 40 hour week. (i) What was the average hourly pay in 1964? (ii) In 1964 how many minutes would the average person have to work to *a.* buy a loaf of bread *b.* pay for a gallon of petrol?

(f) In 1984 the average wage was based on a 38 hour week and in 1994 it was based on a 37 hour week (i) Find, correct to the nearest penny, the hourly pay of the average person in *a.* 1984 *b.* 1994. (ii) For each

year find the number of minutes (correct to the nearest whole number) a person on the average wage has to work to buy a gallon of petrol.
(iii) In real terms, is petrol cheaper now than it was in *a.* 1964 *b.* 1984?

(g) (i) Find the percentage increase in the cost of a TV set from 1964 to 1994.   (ii) How does this compare with the percentage increase in the average wage over the same period?

3 An estate agent charges fees of $2\frac{1}{2}$% on the first £20 000 and $1\frac{1}{2}$% on the rest.
What would be his fees on a house sold for £95 000?

4 The main office of the Pitteville Assurance Company measures 34 ft by 125 ft and requires a new floor covering. Pitteville were quoted £30 a square metre for the carpet of their choice by Goodeal Carpets and £26.50 a square yard by Wearhard Floor Coverings for the same carpet. Each supplier will round up the area to be covered to the nearest whole number before calculating the cost.
(a) Find the area of the office   (i) in square yards (1 yd^2 = 9 ft^2)
(ii) in square metres (1 yd^2 = 0.836 m^2).
(b) What is the quoted cost of the carpet from
(i) Goodeal Carpets   (ii) Wearhard Floor Coverings?
(c) Assuming that there are no hidden extras, which is the better deal and by how much?

5 Clair's heart rate is 64 beats a minute while Jon's is 84 beats a minute. How many more beats does Jon's heart make than Clair's in
(a) a week   (b) a year
(c) a lifetime of 70 years.
Give your answers to (b) and (c) correct to 3 s.f.

Paper 21

1 (a) Triplegate Dairies are interested in exporting some of their other drinks to the continent and so decide to change their machines from imperial to metric. The Neot family take 2 pints of milk a day and 2 extra at the weekend. How many litres a week should the Neot family order so that they get approximately the same amount of milk as before the change? (1 litre = 1.76 pints.)
(b) Triplegate Dairies distribute 22 500 pints of milk a day. Correct to the nearest 10 litres, how many litres is this?

2 The results of the 1992 General Election are given in the table

Party	Number of seats	Percentage of votes cast	Percentage of seats in the House of Commons
Conservatives	336	41.9	51.6
Labour	271	34.5	41.6
Liberal Democrats	20	17.9	3.1
Scottish Nationalists	3	1.9	0.5
Plaid Cymru	4	0.5	0.6
Other	17	3.3	2.6

(a) What was the Conservative government's majority over all other parties?
(b) In a vote, 32 Conservative backbenchers voted against the government, the Liberal Democrats plus 6 of the 'other' members voted with the government and of those that failed to record a vote, 2 were Conservative, 3 Labour and 1 a Liberal Democrat. What was the result?

3

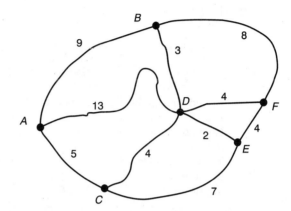

The diagram is a simplified map showing the distances (in kilometres) between the components factories in a group.
(a) What is the length of the shortest route from factory A to factory F?
(b) Starting at A, what is the shortest route that enables an engineer to visit all the other factories and return to A?
(c) Is it possible to start a A, travel along every road in the network exactly once, and end up at A?

4 Ashford Woodworking Products are interested in buying four milling machines from a German machine tool company. The German company can supply the machines at a cost of 25 000 Deutschmarks (DM) each, the cost to be paid in Deutschmarks using the exchange rate on the day of delivery.
When the machines are ordered the exchange rate is £1 = DM 2.56 but by the time they are delivered it has changed to £1 = DM 2.62.
(a) Do the machines cost Ashford Woodworking products more or less than they anticipated?
(b) (i) Find, in pounds, the difference between the price at which the machines were ordered and the price for which they are delivered.
(ii) Is this change good or bad for Ashford Woodworking Products?

5 A Boeing 737–100 is 27.6 m long, has a wingspan of 28.3 m, a fuel capacity of 17 900 litres, a range of 4800 km and a maximum speed of 874 km/h. If 1 m = 3.281 ft, 1 km = 0.621 miles and 1 litre = 0.2200 gallons, convert this data from metric units into imperial units. Give the lengths correct to the nearest inch and the other values correct to 3 s.f.

1 On four consecutive Fridays last summer Kerry sold eggs on a stall in the local market. She sold $12\frac{1}{2}$ dozen the first week, $15\frac{3}{4}$ dozen the second week and $14\frac{3}{4}$ dozen the third week. In all she sold 63 dozen. How many did she sell
   (a) on the first three Fridays
   (b) on the last Friday?

2 The table shows the surface area and population of several European countries.

Country	Surface Area (000 km²)	Population (million)
United Kingdom	244	56.7
France	544	55.3
Germany	356	78.0
Italy	301	57.3
The Netherlands	41	14.5
Belgium	31	10.0
Ireland	70	3.5

   (a) Illustrate these facts on a compound bar chart.
   (b) Find the population density for each country, i.e. the number of thousands of population for each 1000 km². Which country is
      (i) the most densely populated   (ii) the most sparsely populated?
   (c) If you were planning to increase your exports in these countries, in which country would you reach most people most easily?

3 The table gives the pump price of petrol, in pence per litre, in the world's leading industrial countries. It also shows the amount per litre that is included as a tax for the government.

Country	United Kingdom	France	Germany	Italy	Japan	United States
Cost per litre in pence	54	60	55	60	76	20
Amount of tax per litre	36	45	40	44	35	6

   (a) Show this information on a multiple bar chart.
   (b) (i) For each country find the tax as a percentage of the pump price.
      (ii) In which country does the highest percentage of the cost of a litre of petrol go to the government as tax?
   (c) Find the price of petrol in each country before tax is added.
   (d) Which European country has the cheapest petrol before tax is added?
   (e) Excluding Japan, which country has the dearest petrol before tax is added?

4 When bending a conduit to carry electrical cable the smallest acceptable internal radius of the bend is 2.5 × the diameter of the conduit.

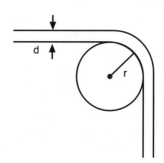

(a) Find the smallest internal radius for a conduit of diameter
(i) 8 mm (ii) 25 mm.
(b) What is the diameter of the conduit if the smallest acceptable radius
is (i) 50 mm (ii) 80 mm?

5

When Angela decorates she prefers a roller to a brush. The sketch shows
the container which she partly fills with emulsion paint in order to dip
the roller.
(a) Use the dimensions given on the diagram to find (i) the area of
cross-section of the container in cm² (ii) the capacity of the
container in cm³ (iii) the amount of emulsion paint in the
container when it is filled to half its depth.
(b) Angela has a 9 inch roller. Can she use it with this container?
(1 in ≈ 2.54 cm.)
(c) Each time she has used half the emulsion paint in the container she
refills it to the original level. How much paint does she pour in each
time she tops it up?
(d) She buys a 5 litre tin. (i) How much remains in the tin when she
has filled the container first time to halfway? (ii) How many times
can she top up?

Paper 23

1 Snows Financial Services are ordering chairs for a new office. They are
quoted £1223.25 for 35 identical chairs but decide that they need 45.
How much will 45 cost them?

2 (a) The length of Nicki's pace is 32 inches. How many paces does she
take to walk a mile?
(b) Her boyfriend Ned, is much taller than Nicki. His pace is 39 inches
long. How many paces does he take to walk a mile?
(c) Nicki and Ned spend a week in the Lake District on a walking
holiday. They estimate that they walked 57 miles. How many more
paces did Nicki make than Ned? Give your answer correct to 2 s.f.

3 Over the next 5 years it is predicted that the number of tourists to the UK will increase by 1.5 m. Use the following forecasts to answer the questions that follow.

average length of stay is 14 nights

60% of visitors come in the months of June, July, August and September

50% of the visitors stay in hotels

75% of the visitors staying in hotels require a double room, the remainder require a single room

the planned high season (June to September) occupancy rate is 90%.

(a) How many visitors can be accommodated in a hotel with 20 double rooms and 8 single rooms?

(b) A party of 24 tourists is accommodated in a hotel using the same number of double rooms as single rooms.
    How many rooms do they require?

(c) There were 3 m visitors last year: (i) How many of them stayed in hotels? (ii) How many stayed in single rooms in hotels?

(d) A hotel has 50 double bedrooms and no singles.
    How many tourists do they have for the 18 week high season if every tourist stays for two weeks and they have a 90% occupancy rate?

(e) The ratio of double rooms to single rooms at the Waverley Manor is 3 to 1. They have 44 rooms. How many visitors can they accommodate?

4

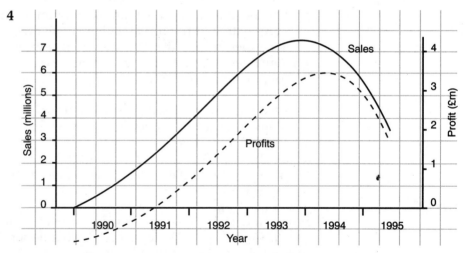

Turner & Newbold introduced a new product in January 1990. The graph shows the number of units sold each month, and the monthly profit generated from these sales, since the product's launch.

(a) Explain why the line representing profits is below the axis during the early life of the product.

(b) When does the product first begin to show signs of making a profit?

(c) During which period did the monthly sales exceed 5 million?

(d) For how long did profits top £3 m?

(e) When was the period   (i) of maximum sales   (ii) of maximum profit?

(f) Would you advise the company to take the product off the market in 1995?
Give your reasons.

5 The Second Severn Crossing is being built by a private consortium at an estimated cost of £300 m. In 1994, the tolls are £3.40 for cars and £10.10 for lorries. 18 m vehicles a year are expected to use the bridge, 50% of whom will pay as they enter Wales. Journeys from Wales into England are free. Until 1996 tolls are allowed to rise annually by 6% plus the rate of inflation, thereafter they can rise by the rate of inflation. It is anticipated that 30% of the vehicles crossing the bridge are lorries, and the remainder cars. Traffic is projected to increase by 5% a year.

(a) How many vehicles a year are expected to pay a toll in
(i) 1996   (ii) 1998?

(b) In each year, how many of these are lorries?

(c) What is the anticipated income in 1994 from
(i) cars   (ii) lorries   (iii) all vehicles?

(d) If the rate of inflation in 1994 is 3% find the maximum permitted tolls in 1995.
(Round each figure down to the nearest 10 p.)

(e) Use your answers to part (d) and assume that the rate of inflation for 1995 is 4.8% to find the maximum tolls for 1996.

(f) Assuming that the rate of inflation for the remaining years of the century is 5% find the maximum possible tolls for each year up to and including the year 2000.

(g) (i) Copy and complete the following table. Some of the answers you have found already.

Item	1994	1995	1996	1997	1998
Inflation					
Inflation + 6%					
% increase in toll					
Toll for cars					
Toll for lorries					
Total traffic paying toll					
Number of cars					
Number of lorries					
Income – cars					
Income – lorries					
Total income					

(ii) As far as you can tell, does it look as though the consortium have made a good investment?

(*Note:* In this question give vehicle numbers and the yearly income in millions, correct to 2 d.p. Give new tolls rounded down to the nearest 10 p.)

Paper 24

1 A badminton club with 200 members has several courts, each of which is available for 100 hours a week. The booking secretary has noted that when a court is used it is always 2 players who use it, and is most interested to find that 20% of the members use the courts for 80% of the time that they are actually used.

   (a) How many members are in the group that use the courts for 80% of the time they are used?

   (b) How many members are in the other group?

   (c) The members belonging to the less active group use the courts for 1 hour a week. For how many hours, in total, do they occupy a court?

   (d) The more active group use the courts 4 times as much as the less active group. How many hours is this?

   (e) How many hours, in total are the courts used in a week?

   (f) If the courts are used for 80% of the available time   (i) how many hours are they used   (ii) how many courts are there?

2 Copy and complete the following order form.

Quantity	Unit (Ea ,Dz box)	Cat. Number	Colour	Description	Unit price	Total value of goods (£)
12	Ream	E 4104	White	Copier Paper	£2.15	
5	Ream	E 4108	Pink	Copier Paper	£2.43	
5	Ream	E 4138	White	Laser Printer Paper	£4.39	
6	Box	E 4183	White	Envelopes	£34.99	
24	each	E 4245	Various	Ring Binders	0.89	
				add £2.90 for delivery		
				please add Vat, 17½ %		
					Total	

What should be the value of the cheque that is sent with this order if full payment must be made with the order?

3 The table shows the position of the clubs in the Sumpter Rugby League before the Christmas matches are played.

Team	P	W	D	L	Tries	Points
Loxhill	13	12	0	1	32	24
Matson	13	10	1	2	40	21
Pennybridge	13	10	0	3	44	20
Waren Hill	13	9	0	4	57	18
Upton	13	9	1	3	28	19
Upper Chute	12	6	1	5	30	13
Bell End	13	5	1	7	19	11
Deal Hall	12	4	0	8	10	8
Ockley	11	3	1	7	16	7
St Days	13	3	1	9	15	7
Quorn	13	2	0	11	15	4
Radley	13	0	0	13	14	0

(a) Two games remain to be played so that all the clubs have played the same number of games. Which games are they?
(b) Which columns should have the same totals? Do they?
(c) How many games should each club play in a season, assuming that each team plays all the other teams twice, once at home and once away?
(d) Starting from the position given in the table, what is the maximum number of points the winner of the league can have by the end of the season?
(e) What fraction of the available points have Waren Hill collected so far?
(f) How do they decide which team comes first in the table when two teams have the same number of points?
(g) What percentage of the available points have Deal Hall lost so far?
(h) Ockley beat Deal Hall 24–8 (Ockley scored 3 tries and Deal Hall scored 1 try) and Ockley lost to Upper Chute 23–6 (Upper Chute scored 3 tries), before any of the other clubs play any further league games. Update the league table.

4 The table shows the purchase price, and the estimated retained value, for seven different makes of car after three years

Car	Mondeo	Xantia	BMW 525	Granada	Mercedes C220	Renault Cabrio	Rover 827
Cost price	£13 600	£17 500	£24 500	£22 000	£24 600	£15 900	£25 000
Value at the end of							
3 years as a % of the purchase price	44%	38%	45%	24%	54%	31%	24%
Cash value after 3 years							
Loss over 3 years							

(a) Copy and complete the table.
(Give your values correct to the nearest £100.)
(b) Tony Hunter has £25 000 which he is prepared to spend, totally or in part, on a new car. He considers buying one of the cars listed in the table. Which car should he buy so that the value of his car after 3 years, together with any unspent money is (i) greatest (ii) least?
(Neglect any interest on unspent money.)
(c) Repeat part (b) on the assumption that he is able to invest any money he does not spend on a car, at 5% per annum tax paid.
(You do not need to do a lot of complicated calculations to answer this!)

(d) How much more, as a percentage, is (i) the Mercedes than the Mondeo (ii) the Granada than the Zantia?

5

Diameter of cable (mm)	Maximum distance between fixing points	
	horizontally (mm)	vertically (mm)
less than 9	600	800
9 or bigger but less than 15	900	1200
15 or bigger but less than 20	1500	2000

The table gives the regulations for the maximum fixing distances between fixing points for mineral insulated cables of various thicknesses, e.g. a 12 mm cable must be fixed at least every 900 mm if laid horizontally and at least every 1200 mm if laid vertically.

(a) What is the maximum distance between the fixing points for cables laid horizontally that have a thickness of
(i) 8 mm (ii) 12 mm (iii) 16 mm?

(b) What is the maximum distance between the fixing points for cables laid vertically that have a thickness of
(i) 5 mm (ii) 10 mm (iii) 12 mm?

(c) Mike wants to lay 24 metres of 15 mm cable horizontally. He has 20 clips.
Will this be sufficient? (Reminder: you need 3 clips to fix 3 m of cable.)

(d) Jane wants to lay 12 metres of 10 mm cable vertically. She has 10 clips.
Is this sufficient?

(e) Sid Golding wants to fix 20 metres of 12 mm cable. Some of it is to be fixed horizontally and the rest vertically. He has 2 packets of clips with a dozen clips in each packet.
Should this be enough?

John Sansom has to lay 120 m of 12 mm insulated cable in a factory unit. 30% of this cable is to be laid vertically and the remainder horizontally.

(f) What length of cable is to be laid (i) vertically (ii) horizontally?

(g) What is the least number of fixing points needed for the cable that is to be laid by John (i) vertically (ii) horizontally?

(h) John can buy the fixing clips in boxes of 25.
How many boxes must he buy?

Paper 25

1 In the budget for next year a local travel operator decides to spend
£18 000 on advertising and promotion. She proposes to divide this
amount in the following way: local TV advertising 45%, local press
advertising 8%, discount vouchers 16%, literature distribution (in
tourist centres and hotels) 8%, bus & aerial advertising 5%, direct mail
8% and the remainder on public relations.
(a) What percentage is to be allocated to public relations?
(b) How much does she propose to spend on   (i) local TV advertising
(ii) direct mailing   (iii) discount vouchers?

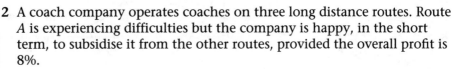

2 A coach company operates coaches on three long distance routes. Route
A is experiencing difficulties but the company is happy, in the short
term, to subsidise it from the other routes, provided the overall profit is
8%.

The price structure and expected number of return fares for next year
are given in the partly completed table.

Route	Number of expected fares	Average price per seat (£)	Total target revenue per route (£)	Target percentage profit at average prices	Target profit (£)
A	10 000	40	400 000	4%	
B	50 000	56			196 000
C	40 000	50			240 000

(a) Copy the table and fill in the blanks.
(b) Does Route *B* provide an acceptable profit?
(c) What is the total target revenue from all three routes?
(d) Find the total target profit.
(e) (i) Express the total target profit as a percentage of the total target
revenue. (ii) Does this figure meet the required overall profit
margin of 8%?

3 Mandy is asked to design a rectangular cardboard box for packing
cylindrical cans of diameter 6 cm and height 12 cm. There are certain
instructions she must observe:
1   The maximum number of layers of cans that can be packed in any
box is 3.
2   The ratio of the length of the box to its width must be 4:3.
3   Each box must hold 96 cans.
4   Assume that the area of cardboard needed is equal to the external
area of the box plus $\frac{1}{5}$.
5   The thickness of the cardboard can be neglected.
(a) Mandy quickly comes to the conclusion that her box must have
two layers of cans. Why?
(b) What are the inside measurements of her box?
(c) How much card does each box require?

4

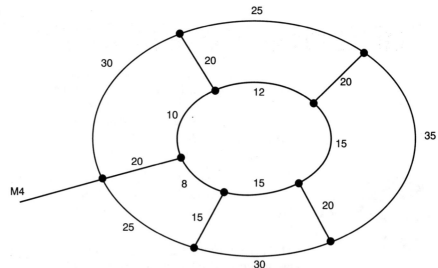

A supplier from the West Country journeys to London twice a week to deliver to the depots marked by dots. The numbers show the time, in minutes, to travel between the depots. Which route should she take to minimise the delivery time?

5 Thomas Buckley manufactures table lamps. They receive an inquiry from the United States for an order of 1000 of a new design. These lamps cost £15 each to produce, to which is added a mark-up of 40% to give the export price. The agreed price is in dollars and at the time of the quotation the exchange rate is £1 = $1.80.

(a) If, apart from the cost of each lamp, there are other expenses that total £1500, find the profit that the company hope to make from the deal.

(b) What is the cost of each lamp to the American importer?

(c) By the time delivery takes place the exchange rate has changed to £1 = $1.86. Find the company's actual profit.

(d) The American importer adds a mark-up of 40% to sell to the retailer.
How much does each lamp cost the retailer?

(e) The retailer adds a mark-up of 60% when he puts the lamps on sale. How much are the American public being asked to pay for the lamps?

(f) Express the original cost price of the lamp as a percentage of the final selling price.
(Use the rate of exchange paid by the importer.

Note: Mark-up = $\dfrac{\text{gross profit}}{\text{cost price}} \times 100$.)

Guidance Notes: Basic Skills

A1 Place value

A figure's place in a number is important. It tells us what that figure is worth. In the number 564, the 4 means 4 'ones' or 'units', the 6 means 6 'tens' and the 5 means 5 'hundreds'. We can write a number by putting each figure under a place heading e.g.

	Thousands	Hundreds	Tens	Units
7261 can be arranged	7	2	6	1
4059 can be arranged	4		5	9

(There are no hundreds so we can leave the hundreds column blank.)

Write down, in figures, the numbers given below.

	Hundreds of thousands	Tens of thousands	Thousands	Hundreds	Tens	Units
(a)			2	9	5	4
(b)			5		7	2
(c)					6	9
(d)					8	
(e)		5	2			
(f)		7		8		6
(g)	6	8		3		5

In the number 3592   the 5 stands for 5 hundreds
            and   the 9 stands for 9 tens.

(h) (i) What does the 7 stand for in the number 5743?
    (ii) What does the 4 stand for?
(i) (i) What does the 6 stand for in the number 63495?
    (ii) What does the 3 stand for?
(j) (i) What does the 4 stand for in the number 458 762?
    (ii) What does the 8 stand for?
(k) (i) What does the 5 stand for in the number 73 522 289?
    (ii) What does the 7 stand for?

A2 The largest and smallest numbers of a set

Look at the 3-figure numbers 352, 325, 253, 235, 532 and 523.
The largest of these numbers must start with the largest possible digit i.e. the largest number must be either 532 or 523. The numbers 532 and 523 have the same first digit. The larger of them is the number with the

larger second digit i.e. 532.
The largest of the six given numbers is therefore 532.

Similarly the smallest of these numbers must start with the smallest possible digit i.e. it must be either 253 or 235.
The smaller of these two numbers is the number with the smaller second digit i.e. 235.
The smallest of the six given numbers is therefore 235.

(a) From the numbers 463, 475, 442, 484 and 462 select
    (i) the smallest number   (ii) the largest number.

Note: Any 4-figure number is larger than every 3-figure number e.g. 1005 is larger than 998. Similarly, any 5-figure number is larger than every 4-figure number, and so on.

(b) From the numbers 848, 1234, 999, 435 and 839 select
    (i) the largest number   (ii) the smallest number.
(c) From the numbers 3301, 867, 352, 1042 and 794 select
    (i) the smallest number   (ii) the largest number.
(d) From the numbers 2904, 973, 1015, 3156 and 538 select
    (i) the smallest number but one   (ii) the largest number but one.

A3 Addition: 1

To add 427, 16 and 1523 put them one beneath the other so that all the unit figures are lined up, all the tens figures are lined up, and so on

```
   427      First step: 3 + 6 + 7 = 16. Put 6 down and carry 1 to
    16      the tens column
 +1523      Second step: 1 + 2 + 1 + 2 = 6
  1966      Third step: 5 + 4 = 9
     1      Fourth step: bring down the 1
```

Find
(a) 456 + 75 + 142   (b) 342 + 2173 + 98
(c) 675 + 8003 + 777   (d) 536 + 253 + 932

A4 Addition: 2

Similarly 2815 + 493 + 745 + 66 is set out

```
  2815      First step: 6 + 5 + 3 + 5 = 19, 9 down, carry 1 to the tens
   493      column
   745      Second step: 1 + 6 + 4 + 9 + 1 = 21, 1 down, carry 2 to the
 +  66      hundreds column
  4119      Third step: 2 + 7 + 4 + 8 = 21, 1 down, carry 2 to the
   221      thousands column
            Fourth step: 2 + 2 = 4, write 4 in the thousands column
```

Find
(a) $643 + 854 + 98 + 3226$
(b) $3354 + 567 + 1723 + 65$
(c) $7674 + 2154 + 863 + 1834$
(d) $352 + 6478 + 12\,234 + 8746$
(e) $33\,445 + 1795 + 8744 + 5009$

A5 Subtraction: 1

To subtract 46 from 278 set 46 beneath 278 with the unit digits lined up

$$\begin{array}{r} 278 \\ -\ \ 46 \\ \hline 232 \end{array}$$
First step: $8 - 6 = 2$
Second step: $7 - 4 = 3$
Third step: $2 - 0 = 2$

(a) Subtract 67 from 285   (b) Subtract 175 from 497
(c) Subtract 215 from 829   (d) Subject 616 from 928

A6 Subtraction: 2

Similarly for $258 - 169$

$$\begin{array}{r} {}^{1\ 14}1 \\ 2\cancel{5}8 \\ -\ \ 169 \\ \hline 89 \end{array}$$
First step: $8 - 9$, cannot. Change the 5 tens to 4 tens and 10 units, $18 - 9 = 9$
Second step: $4 - 6$, cannot. Change the 2 hundreds into 1 hundred and 10 tens then $14 - 6 = 8$
Third step: $1 - 1$ is 0 (which it is unnecessary to write).

If you use a different method from this and usually get the correct answer, stay with your own method.
Find
(a) $345 - 166$ (b) $827 - 339$
(c) $1084 - 738$ (d) $4365 - 2784$

A7 Multiplication by 10, 100, 1000, etc.

When we multiply by 10, the number of units becomes the number of tens, the number of tens becomes the number of hundreds, and so on.

For example $367 \times 10 = 3670$ and $7629 \times 10 = 76\,290$
Similarly $85 \times 100 = 8500$ and $794 \times 100 = 79\,400$

Find
(a) 352×10 (b) 70×100
(c) 123×100 (d) $56\,700 \times 10$
(e) 710×100 (f) 43×1000
(g) 70×1000 (h) $397 \times 10\,000$
(i) $590 \times 100\,000$ (j) 825×1000

A8 Multiplication by other numbers

To multiply two single digit numbers together you should know thoroughly your tables from 2×2 up to 10×10. There is no substitute for this knowledge – you should try very hard to learn them. If this proves too difficult, then you will have to use a calculator.

```
  37
×  4
─────
 148
```

First step: $7 \times 4 = 28$, 8 down, carry 2 tens
Second step: $3 \times 4 = 12$, add 2, to give 14

Find

(a) 82×5 (b) 76×3
(c) 78×7 (d) 83×9

Similarly 285×36 is written

```
   285
×   36
──────
  1710
  8550
──────
 10260
```

First step: $5 \times 6 = 30$, 0 down carry 3 to the tens column
Second step: $8 \times 6 = 48$, $48 + 3 = 51$, 1 down carry 5 hundreds
Third step: $2 \times 6 = 12$, $12 + 5 = 17$
Fourth step: We wish to multiply 285 by 30 which is the same as 2850×3
Fifth step: find the total

(It is of course true that it is much easier to do this multiplication using a calculator, but you will become far more confident with figures if you can do it this way.) Find

(e) 325×34 (f) 653×76
(g) 832×82 (h) 973×51
(i) 742×29 (j) 423×66

A9 Division by 10, 100, 1000, etc.

When we divide by 10, the number of tens becomes the number of units, the number of hundreds becomes the number of tens, and so on.

For example $620 \div 10 = 62$ and $7800 \div 100 = 78$

Find

(a) $8300 \div 10$ (b) $3620 \div 10$
(c) $920\,000 \div 1000$ (d) $44\,000 \div 100$

A10 Division by a single digit

Work out $492 \div 3$

```
   164
3)492
```

First step: 3 into 4 goes once with 1 over
Second step: 3 into 19 goes 6 times with 1 over
Third step: 3 into 12 goes 4 times with no remainder

Find

(a) $536 \div 4$ (b) $795 \div 5$
(c) $1071 \div 7$ (d) $1032 \div 8$
(e) $1470 \div 6$ (f) $5049 \div 9$

A11 Division by a two-figure number

Find $1628 \div 44$

```
      37
44)1628
   132
    308
    308
```

First step: 4 into 16 goes 4 times
Second step: $44 \times 4 = 176$, which is too big. Try 3 times
$\qquad$ $44 \times 3 = 132$, which is less than 162
Third step: Subtract, and bring down the next figure (8)
Fourth step: 4 into 30 goes 7 times. $44 \times 7 = 308$

Find
(a) $1377 \div 17$
(b) $1904 \div 34$
(c) $2496 \div 26$
(d) $3285 \div 45$
(e) $1288 \div 23$
(f) $3654 \div 58$

A12 Division with remainders

What if there are remainders? What is $273 \div 5$?

The answer is 54, remainder 3

```
     54
5)273
  25
  23
  20
   3
```

What is $776 \div 28$?

```
     27
28)776
   56
   216
   196
    20
```

First step: 28 is almost 30, 30 goes into 77 twice, $28 \times 2 = 56$
Second step: Subtract, to give 21; bring down the 6
Third step: Try 7; $28 \times 7 = 196$
Fourth step: subtract

The answer is 27 remainder 20.

Find
(a) $600 \div 23$
(b) $897 \div 34$
(c) $3625 \div 45$
(d) $3026 \div 63$
(e) $6781 \div 51$
(f) $7856 \div 89$

A13 Mixed operations

The order in which you work out mixed operations (which often include brackets and may include the word 'of') is important.

First step: work out the brackets.
Second step: If 'of' is present, replace it by $\times$. Next do the division and multiplication.
$\qquad$ Which of these two you do first does not really matter.
(For example $12 \div 3 \times 4 = 16$ and $12 \times 4 \div 3 = 16$.)
Third step: Complete the addition and subtraction. Once again which of the two comes first does not matter.
(Remember that $1 - 2 + 3$ means 'take away' 2 only, not take away 2 and 3. You may find it better to add together the + numbers first, i.e. $1 - 2 + 3 = 1 + 3 - 2 = 4 - 2 = 2$.)

$$
\begin{aligned}
9 + 5 \times 4 - 3 \quad &= 9 + 20 - 3 && \text{(Multiplication first)} \\
&= 29 - 3 && \text{(Addition next)} \\
&= 26 && \text{(Subtraction last)} \\
46 - 3 \times 7 + 8 \quad &= 46 - 21 + 8 && \text{(Multiplication first)} \\
&= 25 + 8 && \text{(Subtraction next)} \\
&= 33 && \text{(Addition last)}
\end{aligned}
$$

If you wish to keep the order: addition before subtraction

$$
\begin{aligned}
46 - 21 + 8 \quad &= 54 - 21 \\
&= 33
\end{aligned}
$$

$$
\begin{aligned}
18 \div (2 \times 3) \quad &= 18 \div 6 \quad \text{(brackets first)} \\
&= 3 \quad \text{(then division)}
\end{aligned}
$$

The word 'of' is sometimes used with fractions

$$
\begin{aligned}
37 + 15 - \tfrac{1}{2} \text{ of } 62 \quad &= 37 + 15 - 31 && (\tfrac{1}{2} \text{ of } 62 \text{ means } \tfrac{1}{2} \times 62 = 31) \\
&= 52 - 31 && \text{(addition next)} \\
&= 21 && \text{(then division)}
\end{aligned}
$$

Some people like to remember the order in which to do the operations by using the strange looking word BODMAS

i.e.   B – brackets first

O ⎫
D ⎬ 'of', division and multiplication next
M ⎭

A ⎫
S ⎬ addition and subtraction last

Note: Not all calculators use the same logic system. When you have a new calculator you should read the instructions carefully to see that you are using it correctly. Use it to do some simple calculations that can be checked by pencil and paper methods.

Find

(a) $9 \times 8 - 7 \times 4$

(b) $12 \div 3 + 5 \times 6$

(c) $\tfrac{1}{3}$ of $24 + 5 \times 6 - 12$

(d) $(5 + 7) \div (4 \times 5 - 8)$

(e) $5 \times 8 \div 10 - 2$

(f) $(13 - 7 + 8) \div 7 + 4 \times 8$

(g) $(15 \div 3 + 15) + 20 \div 2$

(h) $48 \div 3 \div 4 - 3$

(i) $(7 \times 3 + 12 \div 4) \div 4$

(j) $(24 \div 4 + 6 \times 4) \times 2 \div 5$

(k) $8 - 3 \times 4 + 30 \div 5$

(l) $5 \div 2 \div 3 \div 4 \times 48$

A14 Factors

The factors of 12 are 1, 2, 3, 4, 6 and 12 i.e. they are the numbers that divide into 12 exactly to give a whole number as an answer.
The factors of 27 are 1, 3, 9 and 27.
What are the factors of

(a) 20

(b) 30

(c) 18

(d) 48

(e) 39

(f) 60

(g) 72

(h) 70?

A15 Highest common factor

Two whole numbers always have a common factor i.e. a whole number that goes into both the given whole numbers exactly
e.g. for the numbers 24 (factors 1, 2, 3, 4, 6, 8, 12 and 24) and 30 (factors 1, 2, 3, 5, 6, 10, 15, and 30), 2 is a common factor, as are 1, 3 and 6.
The *highest common factor* (HCF) for these two numbers is 6.
The HCF for 36 and 60 is 12.
Find the HCF of
(a) 18 and 48
(b) 35 and 42
(c) 85 and 68
(d) 18, 54 and 72
(e) 35, 42 and 56
(f) 40, 24 and 16
(g) 98, 56 and 70
(h) 26, 52 and 65

A16 Prime numbers

Any whole number that has no factors other than itself and 1 is called a *prime number*.

　　7 and 17 are examples of prime numbers
　　15 and 32 are not prime numbers.

(a) Which of the following numbers are prime numbers 29, 30, 31, 32, 45, 47, 55, 67?
(b) What are the next two prime numbers after 35?

A17 Lowest common multiple

　　3, 6, 9, 12, 15 and 18 are multiples of 3
and　6, 12, 18, 24, 30 and 36 are multiples of 6
Sometimes a number is a multiple of more than one number.

The multiples of 6 are 6, 12, 18, 24, 30, 36, . . .
and the multiples of 8 are 8, 16, 24, 32, 40, 48, . . .
We see that 24 is the first number to appear in both lists i.e. it is the first number that is a multiple of both 6 and 8. Such a number is called the *lowest common multiple* (LCM).

The LCM of 12 and 20 is 60, the LCM of 4 and 32 is 32, and the LCM of 7 and 12 is 84.

Write down the LCM of
(a) 16 and 12
(b) 10 and 25
(c) 18 and 24
(d) 3, 4, 5
(e) 5, 15, 20
(f) 9, 18, 36

A18 Numbers in index form

The shorthand way of writing $2 \times 2 \times 2$ is 2^3 and the shorthand way of writing $5 \times 5 \times 5 \times 5$ is 5^4. We read these '2 to the power 3' and

'5 to the power 4'. The 3 and the 4 are called index numbers.
In index form $144 = 2 \times 2 \times 2 \times 2 \times 3 \times 3 = 2^4 \times 3^2$.

Express the following numbers in index form
(a) 32   (b) 24
(c) 48   (d) 81
(e) 72   (f) 400

A19 The square of a number in index form

When the index is 2 we call it the square e.g. 5^2 is the square of 5 and 7^2 is the square of 7.
Find
(a) 5^2 (b) 8^2
(c) 12^2 (d) $2^2 \times 5^2$
(e) $3^2 \times 7^2$ (f) $2^4 \times 7^2$

A20 The cube of a number in index form

4^3 is called the cube of 4 e.g. $4^3 = 4 \times 4 \times 4 = 64$.
Find
(a) 2^3 (b) 3^3
(c) 5^3 (d) 6^3

A21 The square root of a number

To find the square root of a number written in index form we halve the index
e.g. $81 = 3^4$, so the square root of 81 is $3^2 = 9$.
(a) Find, in index form, the square root of
     (i) 2^8 (ii) 5^6 (iii) $2^4 \times 3^6$ (iv) $3^4 \times 7^8$.
(b) Express 576 in index form and hence find its square root.

A22 The square root of a number using a calculator

To find the square root of 20 press the following buttons

| AC | 2 | 0 | √ |

The display should read 4.4721 ...
(The symbol we use for square root is $\sqrt{}$.)
Writing down the first 3 figures in the display, the square root of 20 is 4.47.

Find the square root of
(a) 30   (b) 45
(c) 55   (d) 120
(e) 2   (f) 5
In each case write down the first 3 figures in the display.

A23 Correcting to the nearest 10, 100, . . .

The number 2847 is   2850 correct to the nearest 10
2800 correct to the nearest 100
3000 correct to the nearest 1000
Write each of the numbers 1795, 7893 and 35 729 to
(a) the nearest 10   (b) the nearest 100
(c) the nearest 1000

A24 Estimating results

The approximate value of 39×52 is 40×50 i.e. 2000.
The approximate value of 628×173 is 600×200 i.e. 120 000
The approximate value of $8675 \div 523$ is $9000 \div 500$ i.e. 18.

Find the approximate value of
(a) 37×91 (b) 104×78
(c) 493×67 (d) 376×49
(e) $887 \div 48$ (f) $4982 \div 831$

A25 Multiplication of directed numbers

4×2 means $2 + 2 + 2 + 2 = 8$
and $4 \times (-2)$ means $(-2) + (-2) + (-2) + (-2) = -8$:
Since order does not matter when we multiply
$$4 \times (-2) = (-2) \times 4 = -8$$
and $2 \times (-4) = (-4) \times 2 = -8$
Find
(a) $2 \times (-3)$ (b) $4 \times (-5)$
(c) $(-5) \times 4$ (d) $6 \times (-5)$
(e) $(+3) \times (-7)$ (f) $(-2) \times (+6)$
(g) $(-12) \times 1$ (h) $(+4) \times (-6)$

A26 Dividing a negative number by a positive number

Since $3 \times 4 = 12$, $12 \div 4 = 3$
Similarly since $(-3) \times 4 = -12$, $-12 \div 4 = -3$
and $-18 \div 6 = -3$
Find
(a) $(-20) \div 5$ (b) $(-8) \div 2$
(c) $-28 \div 4$ (d) $(-36) \div 6$

B   Fractions

B1 Mixed numbers and improper fractions

We can think of 1 as four quarters so we can write $1\frac{1}{4}$ as $\frac{4}{4} + \frac{1}{4} = \frac{5}{4}$.
When we write $1\frac{1}{4}$ as $\frac{5}{4}$ we are changing a mixed number into an improper fraction.

Similarly $2\frac{3}{4} = \frac{8}{4} + \frac{3}{4} = \frac{11}{4}$

and conversely $\frac{19}{8} = \frac{16}{8} + \frac{3}{8} = 2\frac{3}{8}$.

(a) Express as an improper fraction

  (i) $5\frac{1}{3}$ (ii) $4\frac{3}{4}$ (iii) $7\frac{5}{6}$ (iv) $3\frac{4}{7}$ (v) $8\frac{3}{5}$.

(b) Express as a mixed number (i) $\frac{15}{4}$ (ii) $\frac{12}{5}$ (iii) $\frac{34}{7}$ (iv) $\frac{15}{8}$.

B2 Changing fractions into decimals

Fractions can be changed into decimals by dividing the top of the fraction by the bottom

e.g. $\frac{3}{4} = \frac{75}{100} = 0.75$

$\frac{7}{4} = 1.75$

and $\frac{1}{3} = 0.3333 \ldots$ (the three dots show that the number goes on for ever).

Express the following fractions as decimals

(a) $\frac{1}{2}$ (b) $\frac{5}{8}$

(c) $\frac{2}{3}$ (d) $\frac{7}{20}$

(e) $\frac{5}{12}$ (f) $\frac{4}{7}$

(g) $\frac{15}{2}$ (h) $\frac{19}{3}$

Sometimes it is convenient to use a calculator

e.g. $\frac{69}{115} = 0.6$ and $\frac{96}{352} = 0.272727 \ldots$

Use a calculator to express the following fractions as decimals

(i) $\frac{50}{125}$ (j) $\frac{105}{140}$

(k) $\frac{48}{56}$ (l) $\frac{45}{108}$

(m) $\frac{49}{26}$ (m) $\frac{119}{37}$

B3 Adding fractions

To add fractions they must have the same denominators

e.g. $\frac{2}{9} + \frac{5}{9} = \frac{7}{18}$

and $\frac{4}{5} + \frac{3}{10} = \frac{8}{10} + \frac{3}{10} = \frac{11}{10} = \frac{10}{10} + \frac{1}{10} = 1\frac{1}{10}$

Find

(a) $\frac{2}{7} + \frac{3}{7}$ (b) $\frac{4}{15} + \frac{7}{15}$

(c) $\frac{1}{3} + \frac{1}{12}$ (d) $\frac{2}{3} + \frac{3}{5}$

(e) $\frac{5}{6} + \frac{4}{9}$

To get the same denominator you must look for the Lowest Common Multiple (LCM) of the numbers on the bottom, i.e. the smallest number that the denominators will go into. For example, to express $\frac{2}{3}$, $\frac{3}{4}$ and $\frac{4}{5}$ with the same denominator, the smallest number 3, 4 and 5 will go into is 60.

Then $\dfrac{2}{3} = \dfrac{2 \times 20}{3 \times 20} = \dfrac{40}{60}$, $\dfrac{3}{4} = \dfrac{3 \times 15}{4 \times 15} = \dfrac{45}{60}$

and $\dfrac{4}{5} = \dfrac{4 \times 12}{5 \times 12} = \dfrac{48}{60}$

so that $\quad \dfrac{2}{3} + \dfrac{3}{4} + \dfrac{4}{5} = \dfrac{40}{60} + \dfrac{45}{60} + \dfrac{48}{60} = \dfrac{133}{60} = \dfrac{120}{60} + \dfrac{13}{60} = 2 + \frac{13}{60} = 2\frac{13}{60}$

Similarly for the fractions $\frac{2}{3} + \frac{5}{6} + \frac{7}{12}$ we must express the fractions in twelfths

$$\dfrac{2}{3} + \dfrac{5}{6} + \dfrac{7}{12} = \dfrac{2 \times 4}{3 \times 4} + \dfrac{5 \times 2}{6 \times 2} + \dfrac{7}{12} = \tfrac{8}{12} + \tfrac{10}{12} + \tfrac{7}{12} = \tfrac{25}{12} = \tfrac{24}{12} + \tfrac{1}{12} = 2\tfrac{1}{12}$$

Find

(f) $\frac{11}{12} + \frac{1}{6} + \frac{1}{3}$

(g) $\frac{4}{15} + \frac{3}{5} + \frac{7}{10}$

(h) $\frac{7}{18} + \frac{5}{6} + \frac{2}{3}$

(i) $\frac{7}{18} + \frac{1}{3} + \frac{7}{9}$

B4 Subtracting fractions

Similarly for subtraction

$\frac{2}{3} - \frac{5}{9} = \frac{6}{9} - \frac{5}{9} = \frac{1}{9}$

and

$$\dfrac{11}{12} - \dfrac{1}{4} - \dfrac{2}{3} = \dfrac{11}{12} - \dfrac{1 \times 3}{4 \times 3} - \dfrac{2 \times 4}{3 \times 4}$$

$$= \dfrac{11}{12} - \dfrac{3}{12} - \dfrac{8}{12} = \dfrac{0}{12} = 0 \ (11 - 3 - 8 = 0).$$

Find

(a) $\frac{7}{9} - \frac{4}{9}$

(b) $\frac{1}{3} - \frac{1}{4}$

(c) $\frac{3}{4} - \frac{2}{3}$

(d) $\frac{11}{12} - \frac{5}{6}$

(e) $\frac{3}{5} - \frac{7}{20}$

(f) $\frac{19}{20} - \frac{2}{5} - \frac{1}{4}$

(g) $\frac{3}{4} - \frac{1}{3} - \frac{2}{5}$

(h) $\frac{4}{9} + \frac{2}{3} - \frac{11}{12}$

(i) $\frac{5}{6} - \frac{5}{12} + \frac{1}{2}$

(j) $\frac{3}{25} + \frac{7}{10} - \frac{7}{15}$

B5 Mixed numbers

In dealing with mixed numbers consider the whole numbers first, then the fractional parts.

$4\frac{2}{3} - 3\frac{1}{4} = (4 - 3) + (\frac{2}{3} - \frac{1}{4}) = 1 + (\frac{8}{12} - \frac{3}{12}) = 1 + \frac{5}{12} = 1\frac{5}{12}$

and

$5\frac{1}{2} - 2\frac{2}{3} = (5 - 2) + \frac{1}{2} - \frac{2}{3} = 3 + \frac{3}{6} - \frac{4}{6} = 2 + 1 + \frac{3}{6} - \frac{4}{6} = 2 + \frac{6}{6} + \frac{3}{6} - \frac{4}{6} = 2 + \frac{5}{6} = 2\frac{5}{6}$

Find

(a) $7\frac{1}{2} - 3\frac{1}{3}$

(b) $9\frac{7}{12} - 3\frac{1}{4}$

(c) $6\frac{1}{4} - 1\frac{5}{8}$

(d) $10\frac{3}{4} - 7\frac{7}{8}$

(e) $12\frac{4}{7} - 5\frac{2}{3}$

(f) $6\frac{3}{4} - \frac{7}{12} - 3\frac{9}{16}$

(g) $4\frac{7}{12} - 3\frac{5}{8} + 1\frac{2}{3}$

(h) $5\frac{1}{2} - 2\frac{2}{3} - 1\frac{1}{5}$

B6 Multiplying fractions

To multiply fractions, multiply the top numbers together, and multiply the bottom numbers together

$$\frac{5}{7} \times \frac{2}{3} = \frac{5 \times 2}{7 \times 3} = \frac{10}{21}$$

$$\frac{{}^1\cancel{5}}{\cancel{12}_3} \times \frac{\cancel{4}^1}{\cancel{15}_3} = \frac{1}{9}$$

and $\quad \dfrac{{}^1\cancel{7}}{\cancel{20}_{\,1}} \times \dfrac{\cancel{5}^1}{\cancel{14}_{\,2}} \times \dfrac{\cancel{8}^1}{9} = \dfrac{1}{9}$

Find

(a) $\frac{3}{4} \times \frac{5}{7}$ (b) $\frac{5}{8} \times \frac{3}{10}$

(c) $\frac{3}{5} \times \frac{4}{9}$ (d) $\frac{20}{21} \times \frac{7}{4}$

(e) $\frac{5}{9} \times \frac{3}{20}$ (f) $\frac{7}{12} \times \frac{9}{28} \times \frac{4}{5}$

(g) $\frac{5}{9} \times \frac{12}{25} \times \frac{5}{7}$ (h) $\frac{11}{18} \times \frac{21}{44} \times \frac{9}{14}$

B7 Multiplying fractions that involve improper fractions

To multiply mixed numbers first write them as improper fractions
$$4\tfrac{1}{4} \times 2\tfrac{1}{2} = \tfrac{17}{4} \times \tfrac{5}{2} = \tfrac{85}{8} = \tfrac{80}{8} + \tfrac{5}{8} = 10\tfrac{5}{8}$$

and

$$3\tfrac{3}{7} \times 1\tfrac{5}{12} \times 4\tfrac{2}{3} = \frac{{}^2\cancel{27}}{\cancel{7}_1} \times \frac{17}{\cancel{12}_1} \times \frac{\cancel{14}^2}{3} = \frac{68}{3} = \frac{66}{3} + \frac{2}{3} = 22\tfrac{2}{3}$$

Find

(a) $4\tfrac{1}{2} \times \tfrac{4}{9}$ (b) $1\tfrac{2}{5} \times 2\tfrac{1}{2}$

(c) $5\tfrac{1}{3} \times 1\tfrac{3}{8}$ (d) $3\tfrac{1}{5} \times 1\tfrac{3}{4}$

(e) $\tfrac{4}{7}$ of $4\tfrac{3}{8}$ (f) $2\tfrac{5}{8} \times \tfrac{4}{7} \times 2\tfrac{2}{5}$

(g) $3\tfrac{1}{6} \times 1\tfrac{5}{7} \times 5\tfrac{1}{4}$ (h) $3\tfrac{3}{7} \times 1\tfrac{5}{9} \times 2\tfrac{1}{8}$

B8 Dividing by a fraction

There are eight $\tfrac{1}{2}$ s in 4 i.e. $4 \div \tfrac{1}{2} = 8$.

To divide by a fraction we multiply by that fraction turned upside down
$$5 \div \tfrac{2}{3} = 5 \times \tfrac{3}{2} = \tfrac{15}{2} = 7\tfrac{1}{2}$$

and $\quad 3\tfrac{1}{4} \div 1\tfrac{1}{6} = \tfrac{13}{4} \div \tfrac{7}{6}$

$$= \tfrac{13}{4} \times \tfrac{6}{7} = \tfrac{39}{14} = 2\tfrac{11}{14}$$

Find

(a) $6 \div \tfrac{1}{3}$ (b) $4 \div \tfrac{3}{5}$

(c) $1\tfrac{1}{2} \div 1\tfrac{1}{5}$ (d) $3\tfrac{1}{5} \div \tfrac{4}{7}$

(e) $4\tfrac{2}{5} \div 5\tfrac{1}{2}$ (f) $6\tfrac{2}{5} \div 9\tfrac{3}{5}$

(g) $4\tfrac{1}{3} \div 9\tfrac{3}{4}$ (h) $5\tfrac{1}{3} \div 1\tfrac{1}{7}$

(i) $4\tfrac{1}{7} \div 2\tfrac{5}{12}$ (j) $7\tfrac{2}{3} \div 2\tfrac{7}{8}$

B9 Comparing the size of two fractions

To decide which of two fractions is the larger, express each fraction over the same denominator.

$\frac{2}{3} = \frac{14}{21}$ and $\frac{5}{7} = \frac{15}{21}$
so $\frac{5}{7}$ is bigger than $\frac{2}{3}$

Which fraction is the larger?

(a) $\frac{4}{9}$ or $\frac{7}{12}$ (b) $\frac{2}{3}$ or $\frac{3}{4}$
(c) $\frac{5}{9}$ or $\frac{7}{12}$ (d) $\frac{11}{20}$ or $\frac{5}{8}$
(e) $\frac{8}{9}$ or $\frac{6}{7}$? (f) $\frac{15}{16}$ or $\frac{14}{15}$

B10 Converting a fraction into a percentage

To convert a fraction into a percentage multiply by 100
$\frac{1}{2} = \frac{1}{2} \times 100\%$ i.e. 50%
$\frac{7}{8} = \frac{7}{8} \times 100\%$ i.e. $87\frac{1}{2}\%$

Give each of these fractions as a percentage

(a) $\frac{3}{4}$ (b) $\frac{4}{5}$
(c) $\frac{2}{3}$ (d) $\frac{7}{12}$
(e) $\frac{2}{9}$ (f) $\frac{13}{20}$

C Decimals

C1 Place value

In the number 45.76 the units figure is 5, the tenths figure is 7 and the hundredths figure is 6. In the number 5.927 the tenths figure is 9, the hundredths figure is 2 and the thousandths figure is 7.

For each of the numbers 39.748, 421.947 and 2.763 write down
(a) the number of tenths (b) the number of hundredths
(c) the number of thousandths.

C2 Expressing a fraction as a decimal and a decimal as a fraction

$\frac{3}{10}$ as a decimal is 0.3, $\frac{7}{100}$ is 0.07 and $\frac{29}{100}$ is 0.29
0.6 is six tenths $= \frac{6}{10} = \frac{3}{5}$
and 0.056 is $\frac{5}{100} + \frac{6}{1000} = \frac{50}{1000} + \frac{6}{1000}$
$$= \frac{56}{1000}$$
$$= \frac{7}{125}$$

(a) Give as a decimal (i) $\frac{9}{10}$ (ii) $\frac{17}{100}$ (iii) $\frac{81}{1000}$ (iv) $\frac{26}{100}$

(b) Give as a fraction in its lowest terms
    (i) 0.8 (ii) 0.36 (iii) 0.177 (iv) 0.625

C3 Putting decimals in order of size

To decide which is the larger 5.86 or 5.89

look first at the number of units – they are the same
then look at the number of tenths – they are also the same
finally look at the number of hundredths – 9 is bigger than 6
so 5.89 is larger than 5.86.

(a) Which is the larger   (i) 7.38 or 7.83   (ii) 9.2 or 5.9
   (iii) 3 or 2.98   (iv) 2.587 or 2.584?
(b) Put the numbers 16.7, 15.9, 18.1 and 15.89 in order of size, smallest first.
(c) From the numbers 1.5, 0.57, 12.2 and 1.08 write down
   (i) the smallest number   (ii) the largest number.

C4 Giving numbers in decimal form

Five and four tenths, that is $5 + \frac{4}{10}$, as a decimal is 5.4
Similarly, seventeen and three hundredths, i.e. $17 + \frac{3}{100} = 17.03$
and $15\frac{43}{100}$ $= 15 + \frac{40}{100} + \frac{3}{100}$
$= 15 + \frac{4}{10} + \frac{3}{100}$
$= 15.43$

Write as a decimal
(a) three and seven tenths
(b) four tenths and eight hundredths
(c) twelve and five hundredths
(d) $6\frac{1}{10}$
(e) $12\frac{37}{100}$
(f) $5\frac{7}{100}$
(g) $\frac{3}{10}$
(h) $3\frac{247}{1000}$

C5 Writing a decimal as a fraction in its lowest terms

$0.15 = \frac{\overset{3}{\cancel{15}}}{\underset{20}{\cancel{100}}} = \frac{3}{20}$ and $4.25 = 4 + \frac{\overset{1}{\cancel{25}}}{\underset{4}{\cancel{100}}} = 4 + \frac{1}{4} = 4\frac{1}{4}$.

Write each decimal as a fraction in its lowest terms
(a) 0.75
(b) 0.05
(c) 0.48
(d) 3.35

C6 Expressing a number to a given number of decimal places or significant places

The number 18.478 is

18	correct to the nearest whole number
18.5	correct to 1	decimal place (1 d.p.)
18.48	correct to 2	decimal places (2 d.p.)
18.5	correct to 3	significant figures (3 s.f.)
and 18	correct to 2	significant figures (2 s.f.).

Numbers less than 1 are treated in a similar way

so	0.05784 is	0.1	correct to 1	decimal place

	0.06	correct to 2	decimal places
	0.06	correct to 1	significant figure
	0.058	correct to 2	significant figures
and	0.0578	correct to 3	significant figures.

Give each of the numbers 75.935, 124.963 and 0.7489 correct to
(a) the nearest whole number   (b) 3 significant figures
(c) 2 decimal places.

C7 Addition of decimals

Decimal numbers are added in much the same way as whole numbers. The most important thing to remember is to put the decimal points for the different numbers in a vertical line

We write 1.47 + 0.82 as   1.47 (The decimal points are in a vertical line.)
                          0.82
                          2.29

We find 42.74 + 1.089 + 0.76 in a similar way
  42.740   (Arrange the decimal points in a vertical line.
   1.089   Fill in the spaces with 0s so that each decimal has 3 digits
+ 0.760   after the decimal point.)
  44.589

Find
(a) 5.2 + 3.7   (b) 7.4 + 2.5
(c) 9.7 + 4.62   (d) 5.98 + 3.45
(e) 4.88 + 6.783   (f) 5.837 + 12.64 + 34.883
(g) 7.372 + 0.779 + 3.72   (h) 6.22 + 9.471 + 0.708

C8 Subtraction of decimals

Similar rules hold for subtraction
31.6 − 2.49 is written   31.60 (fill in the space with a 0)
                        − 2.49
                          29.11

Find
(a) 35.4 − 3   (b) 6.7 − 0.66
(c) 25.4 − 9.6   (d) 12.6 − 5.67
(e) 125.8 − 76.45   (f) 7 − 0.83
(g) 18.54 − 1.76   (h) 100 − 38.57
(i) 19.2 − 0.8092   (j) 31.04 − 18.397

C9 Multiplication and division by 10, 100, 1000

To multiply by 10, 100, 1000, we move the figures one, two or three places to the left

e.g. $9.27 \times 10 = 92.7$
$53.94 \times 100 = 5394$
$0.0724 \times 1000 = 72.4$

To divide by 10, 100, 1000, we move the figures one, two or three places to the right
e.g. $5.7 \div 10 = 0.57$
$0.47 \div 100 = 0.0047$
$176.92 \div 1000 = 0.17692$

Find
(a) 4.72×10
(b) $37.4 \div 10$
(c) $54 \div 1000$
(d) 0.083×1000
(e) 0.66×100
(f) $75.8 \div 100$
(g) 1.2×30
(h) $0.48 \div 40$

C10 Multiplication of decimals

The multiplication of decimals is similar to the multiplication of whole numbers.

3.72×4 is written $\begin{array}{r} 3.72 \\ \times \quad 4 \\ \hline 14.88 \end{array}$ (Count the number of places to the right of the decimal point in the first numbers (2) and add to it the number of places to the right of the decimal point in the second number (0). Count this number of places from the right hand side of the final number to give the answer.)

Hence $3.72 \times 4 = 14.88$

5.61×3.4 is written $\begin{array}{r} 5.61 \\ \times \quad 3.4 \\ \hline 2244 \\ 16830 \\ \hline 19.074 \end{array}$ (2 d.p. + 1 d.p. gives 3 d.p.)

(To give the position of the decimal point, count 3 places from the right hand side.)

Find
(a) 6.35×6
(b) 5.87×7
(c) 3.84×8
(d) 8.31×4.5
(e) 25.7×9.2
(f) 9.06×3.14
(g) 2.27×4.78
(h) 0.76×3.86
(i) 0.45×0.83
(j) 0.557×1.46

C11 Division of a decimal by a single digit

Divide 2.08 by 8. To divide by a single figure we shall use short division

$\begin{array}{r} 0.26 \\ 8\overline{)2.08} \end{array}$

i.e. $2.08 \div 8 = 0.26$.

Find

(a) $23.79 \div 3$ (b) $0.55 \div 5$

(c) $1.96 \div 7$ (d) $13.56 \div 6$

(e) $38.43 \div 9$ (f) $7.56 \div 8$

C12 Division that does not give exact answers

Sometimes the answer is not exact

$$\begin{array}{r} 1.8733 \\ 3\overline{)5.6200} \end{array}$$

i.e. $5.62 \div 3 = 1.87$ (correct to 3 s.f.).

Find

(a) $56.6 \div 7$ (b) $33.74 \div 3$

(c) $0.8753 \div 9$ (d) $3.663 \div 17$

(e) $4.963 \div 11$ (f) $7.609 \div 23$

(Give each answer correct to 3 s.f.)

C13 Division of a decimal by a decimal

To divide one decimal by another decimal arrange for the decimal on the bottom to become a whole number

e.g. $56.7 \div 0.7 = \dfrac{56.7}{0.7} = \dfrac{567}{7} = 81$

and $18.46 \div 0.28 = \dfrac{18.46}{0.28} = \dfrac{1846}{28} = 65.928\ldots$

$$\begin{array}{r} 65.928 \\ 28\overline{)1846} \\ \underline{168} \\ 166 \\ \underline{140} \\ 260 \\ \underline{252} \\ 80 \\ \underline{56} \\ 240 \\ \underline{224} \\ 16 \end{array}$$

Find

(a) $19.05 \div 0.3$ (b) $37.6 \div 0.8$

(c) $205.2 \div 0.6$ (d) $7.425 \div 0.9$

(e) $63.88 \div 6.7$ (f) $325 \div 4.2$

(g) $54.3 \div 1.2$ (h) $295.4 \div 0.36$

D   Percentages

D1 Converting a percentage into a fraction

To convert a percentage into a fraction divide by 100 and simplify.

35% as a fraction is $\frac{35}{100} = \frac{7}{20}$

and 75% as a fraction is $\frac{75}{100} = \frac{3}{4}$

Express each percentage as a fraction in its lowest terms
(a) 25%   (b) 55%
(c) 60%   (d) 48%
(e) 35%   (f) 96%
(g) 84%   (h) 87.5%

D2 Converting a fraction into a percentage

To convert a fraction into a percentage multiply by 100
$\frac{1}{2} = \frac{1}{2} \times 100\%$ i.e. 50%
$\frac{3}{8} = \frac{3}{8} \times 100\%$ i.e. 37.5%

Express each fraction as percentage
(a) $\frac{2}{5}$ (b) $\frac{17}{50}$
(c) $\frac{2}{3}$ (d) $\frac{1}{12}$
(e) $\frac{13}{8}$ (f) $\frac{27}{25}$
(g) $\frac{7}{18}$ (h) $\frac{17}{5}$

D3 Converting a percentage into a decimal

To convert a percentage into a decimal divide by 100
$45\% = \frac{45}{100} = 0.45$
and $67\frac{1}{2}\% = 67.5\% = \dfrac{67.5}{100} = 0.675$

Express each percentage as a decimal
(a) 20%   (b) 65%
(c) 82.5%   (d) 42.3%
(e) 2.25%   (f) 12.5%

D4 Finding the percentage of a quantity

40% of 600 is $600 \times \frac{40}{100} = 240$
72% of 450 is $450 \times \frac{72}{100} = 324$

$37\frac{1}{2}\%$ of 192 is $192 \times \dfrac{75}{2} \times \dfrac{1}{100} = 72$

Find
(a) 30% of 8   (b) 10% of 37
(c) $12\frac{1}{2}\%$ of 24   (d) 85% of 750
(e) $67\frac{1}{2}\%$ of 24   (f) 35% of 126

E Geometry

E1 Parts of a revolution

One complete turn or revolution is divided into 360 parts. Each part is called a degree. 360 degrees is written 360°.

The sum of all the angles round a point is 360°.

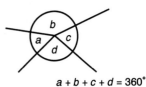

$$a + b + c + d = 360°$$

Half a turn is 180°.
The angles on a straight line total 180°.

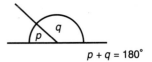

$$p + q = 180°$$

One quarter of a turn is 90°. It is called a right angle and is marked with the symbol

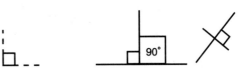

Find the angles marked with letters:
(a)   (b)

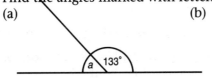

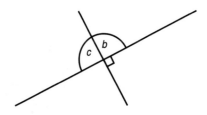

(c)   (d)

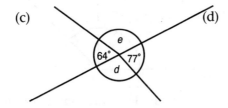

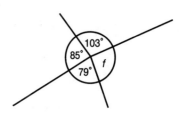

E2 Types of angles

An angle less than 90° is called an *acute* angle.

An angle bigger than 90° but less than 180° is called an *obtuse* angle.

An angle bigger than 180° is called a *reflex* angle.

Look at these three angles:

Angle *a* is acute – i.e. it is less than 90°. It is about 30°.
About 3 angles this size would make a right angle.

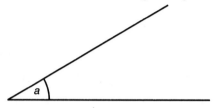

Angle *b* is bigger than 180°, i.e. it is reflex. It is about 180° + 30° i.e. it is about 210°.

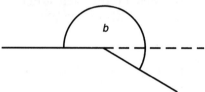

Angle *c* is between 90° and 180°, i.e. it is obtuse.
It is about 90° + 45° i.e. it is about 135°.

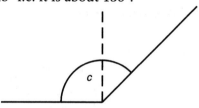

Is each of the following angles acute, obtuse or reflex?
In each case guess the size of the angle.
(a)   (b)

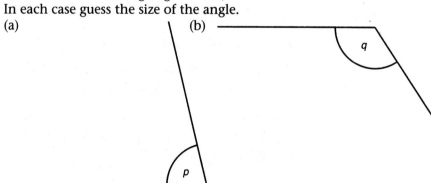

(c)

(d)

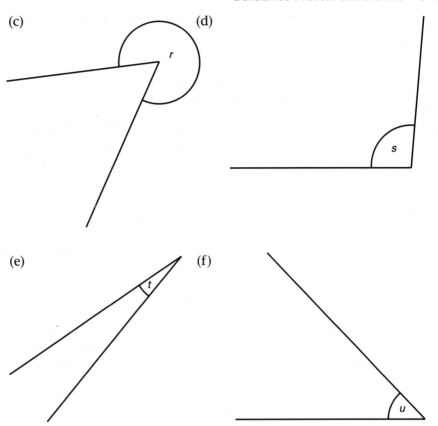

(e)

(f)

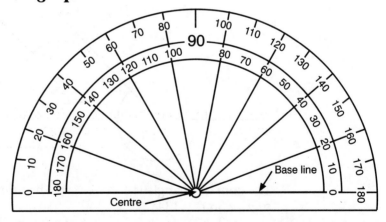

E3 Using a protractor

The sketch shows a protractor, which is what we use to measure angles.
To measure an angle you need to follow five steps:

1 Guess the size of the angle – in particular ask yourself the question:
  Is it less than 90° (i.e. acute), between 90° and 180° (i.e. obtuse) or is
  it bigger than 180° (i.e. reflex)?

2 If necessary extend the lines that form the angle so that they will reach the scale on the protractor.

3 Put the centre of the protractor on the point of the angle and lie the base line along one of the arms that the angle.

4 *Starting from 0* count along the scale until you come to the other arm of the angle.

5 Write down the value you get. Does it make sense when compared with your guess. If not, start again from the beginning.

Now try out these steps on the two angles drawn below.

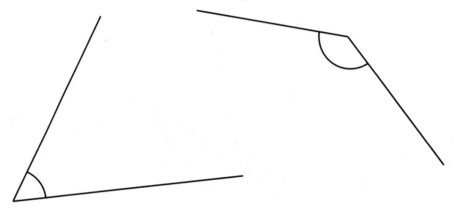

You should find the size of the smaller angle is 58° and the size of the larger angle is 137°

For a reflex angle measure the angle that makes up the full turn and take it away from 360°.

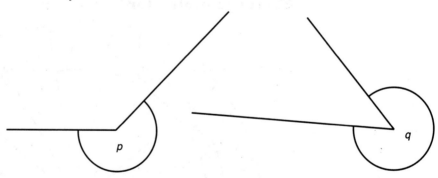

The unmarked angle is 134°
so $p = 360° - 134°$
$= 226°$.

The unmarked angle is 48°
so $q = 360° - 48°$
$= 312°$

Use a protractor to find the angles marked with letters.

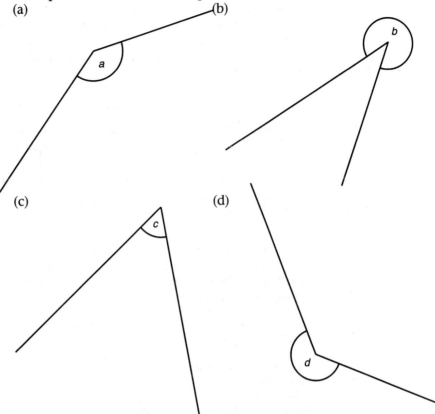

(a)

(b)

a

b

(c)

(d)

c

d

E4 Perpendicular lines and parallel lines

'Perpendicular' means 'at right angles'. If two lines are perpendicular they are at right angles to each other.

Parallel lines go in the same direction. Parallel lines are often marked by arrows.

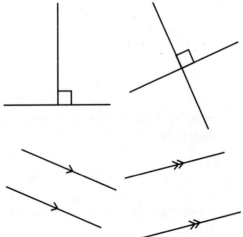

The sketch shows the front of a bungalow. Each point where two lines meet is marked by a capital letter. We can refer to lines using capital letters. For example, the line *CD* is the ridge of the roof.

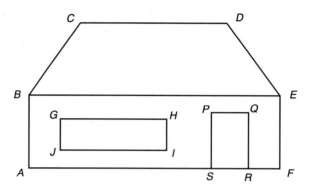

(a) Name three lines that are parallel to *CD*
(b) Name three lines that are perpendicular to *BE*
(c) Name a line that is neither parallel nor perpendicular to any other line on the sketch.

E5 Triangles

A triangle has three sides and three angles.
The sum of its angles is always 180°.

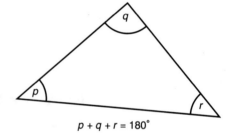

$$p + q + r = 180°$$

Some triangles have special names.

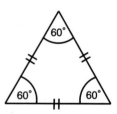

In an equilateral triangle all three sides are the same length and all the angles are 60°.

If a triangle has two equal sides it is called an isosceles triangle.

Find the angles marked with letters.

(a) 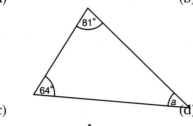 (b)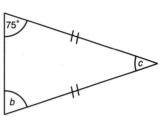

(c) 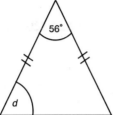 (d)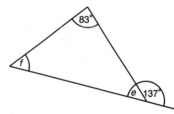

E6 Quadrilaterals

A quadrilateral has four sides and four angles. The sum of its angles is always 360°.

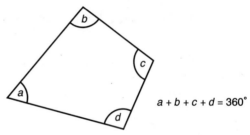

$$a + b + c + d = 360°$$

Some of the quadrilaterals with special names are shown below.

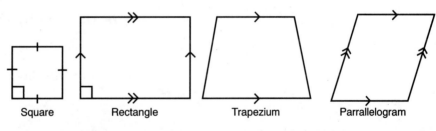

Look at this sketch of the front of a house.
What special name do you give to the shape of
(a) the roof
(b) the front door
(c) one of the downstairs windows
(d) one of the upstairs windows
(e) the front of the house excluding the roof?

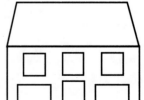

F1 Some equations can be solved by adding the same quantity to each side

If $\qquad a - 4 = 8$

then $\qquad a = 4 + 8$ $\qquad$ (Adding 4 to each side.)

i.e. $\qquad a = 12$

Solve

(a) $b - 6 = 3$ $\qquad\qquad$ (b) $c - 8 = 7$

(c) $p - 10 = 12$ $\qquad\qquad$ (d) $q - 17 = 24$

(e) $y - 4 = 29$ $\qquad\qquad$ (f) $x - 7 = 29$

F2 For others we subtract the same quantity from each side

If $\qquad b + 6 = 14$

then $\qquad b = 14 - 6$ $\quad$ (Subtract 6 from each side.)

i.e. $\qquad b = 8$

Solve

(a) $a + 7 = 21$ $\qquad\qquad$ (b) $c + 11 = 14$

(c) $q + 4 = 13$ $\qquad\qquad$ (d) $9 + r = 36$

(e) $23 + z = 29$ $\qquad\qquad$ (f) $15 + p = 41$

F3 We can divide both sides by the same quantity

If $\qquad 3a = 24$

then $\qquad a = 24 \div 3$ $\quad$ (Dividing both sides by 3.)

i.e. $\qquad a = 8$

Solve

(a) $4b = 16$ $\qquad\qquad$ (b) $5d = 75$

(c) $7e = 42$ $\qquad\qquad$ (d) $8f = 72$

(e) $12p = 96.$ $\qquad\qquad$ (f) $11y = 77$

F4 Or we can multiply both sides by the same quantity

If $\qquad \dfrac{p}{4} = 7$

then $\qquad p = 7 \times 4$ (Multiplying both sides by 4.)

i.e. $\qquad p = 28$

Solve

(a) $\dfrac{a}{3} = 3$ $\qquad\qquad$ (b) $\dfrac{b}{5} = 8$

(c) $\dfrac{y}{6} = 13$ $\qquad\qquad$ (d) $\dfrac{z}{9} = 23$

(e) $\dfrac{w}{12} = 7$ $\qquad\qquad$ (f) $\dfrac{p}{7} = 16$

F5 To solve some equations we may need to use more than one of the above operations

If	$2p + 3 =$	23	
then	$2p =$	20	(Subtracting 3 from each side.)
i.e.	$p =$	10	(Dividing both sides by 2.)

Also

if $\quad\quad\quad \dfrac{q}{5} - 6 \;=\; 3$

then $\quad\quad\quad \dfrac{q}{5} = 9 \quad$ (Adding 6 to each side.)

i.e. $\quad\quad\quad q \; = 45 \quad$ (Multiplying both sides by 5.)

Solve

(a) $3a + 7 = 16$ (b) $5b - 6 = 14$

(c) $6c + 5 = 29$ (d) $8 + 7d = 36$

(e) $6p - 3 = 4$ (f) $\dfrac{y}{2} - 4 = 5$

(g) $5 + \dfrac{z}{3} = 13$ (h) $\dfrac{3x}{5} - 2 = 7$

F6 If the unknown quantity appears in the equation more than once we must collect the terms in the unknown on one side and the number terms on the other side

If	$3b - 5 = b + 7$		
	$3b = b + 7 + 5$	(Adding 5 to each side.)	
	$3b - b = 12$	(Subtracting b from each side.)	
	$2b = 12$		
	$b = 6$	(Dividing both sides by 2.)	

Solve

(a) $3b + 6 = 14 - b$ (b) $3d - 5 = d + 9$

(c) $6c + 7 = c + 27$ (d) $8p - 11 = 5p + 10$

(e) $5y - 4 = 2y - 1$

Although the equation $3p + 14 = 6p - 1$ looks more difficult it is quite simple if we interchange the two sides

i.e. $\quad 6p - 1 = 3p + 14$

$\quad\quad\quad\quad 6p = 3p + 14 + 1 \quad$ (Adding 1 to each side.)

$\quad\quad 6p - 3p = 15 \quad\quad\quad$ (Subtracting $3p$ from each side.)

$\quad\quad\quad\quad 3p = 15$

$\quad\quad\quad\quad\; p = 5 \quad\quad\quad\quad$ (Dividing both sides by 3.)

Solve

(f) $x + 18 = 4x + 3$ (g) $13 - 3z = 1 + z$

(h) $3q + 5 = 7q - 3$ (i) $2y + 7 = 5y + 4$

F7 If there are brackets multiply them out first

$$
\begin{aligned}
5(2p - 1) - 11 &= 14 \\
10p - 5 - 11 &= 14 && \text{(Collect up like terms.)} \\
10p - 16 &= 14 && \text{(Add 16 to each side.)} \\
10p &= 30 && \text{(Divide both sides by 10.)} \\
p &= 3
\end{aligned}
$$

$$
\begin{aligned}
2(q + 4) &= 3(2q + 1) && \text{(Multiply out the brackets.)} \\
2q + 8 &= 6q + 3 && \text{(Take 3 from both sides.)} \\
2q + 8 - 3 &= 6q && \text{(Simplify } 8 - 3 \text{ and take } 2q \text{ from both} \\
& && \text{sides.)} \\
5 &= 6q - 2q && \text{(Simplify } 6q - 2q.) \\
5 &= 4q && \text{(Divide both sides by 4.)} \\
\tfrac{5}{4} &= q && \text{i.e. } q = \tfrac{5}{4}
\end{aligned}
$$

Solve

(a) $2(2a - 7) = 6$ (b) $5(b - 1) + 3 = 8$
(c) $2(3c - 1) - 3 = 13$ (d) $3 + 2(3p + 4) = 41$
(e) $5(x - 1) = 2(x + 8)$ (f) $4(3 - q) = 3(q + 4)$
(g) $3(y - 4) = y + 12$ (h) $7(5 - p) = 2(3p - 2)$
(i) $5(x + 7) = 3(4x + 3)$ (j) $5(p + 2) - 4 = 2(p + 5)$

G   Using a calculator

G1 Which calculator?

There are several different kinds of calculators. If you buy a new one you are advised to buy a *scientific calculator* with *memory* and *brackets* keys. Some keys, such as $\boxed{0}$ $\boxed{1}$ $\boxed{2}$ $\boxed{3}$ $\boxed{4}$ $\boxed{5}$ $\boxed{6}$ $\boxed{7}$ $\boxed{8}$ $\boxed{9}$; the basic function keys $\boxed{+}$ $\boxed{-}$ $\boxed{\times}$ $\boxed{\div}$ and the $\boxed{=}$ and $\boxed{\bullet}$ are the same on all calculators. Other keys can vary from one calculator to another. When you have bought a calculator, it is important that you understand how to use it quickly and easily. Should there be anything you don't understand or feel you are doing incorrectly check with your instruction booklet. The calculator used for calculations in this book is a Casio scientific calculator fx-82C.

G2 Second function keys

On most calculators many keys have more than one function.

For example, on the Casio the key $\boxed{\sqrt{}}$ has two functions. The symbol

($\sqrt{}$) on the key is the first function and the symbol above it x^2 refers to the second function.

To perform the 2nd function you have to press the key marked |inv| in or |shift| or | 2nd F | before pressing the |√| key.

For example, to find the square root of 41 i.e. $\sqrt{41}$ the key sequence is
|AC| |4| |1| |√|

The display shows |6.4031242| . . .

On the other hand, to find the square of 41 i.e. 41^2 the key sequence is

|AC| |4| |1| |inv| |√|

The display shows |1681|

(On *our* calculator we press |inv| |√| to find the square of a number.)

G3 Keys that clear the calculator.

Some calculators have only one *clear* key. To clear the last entry, you press this key once, while to clear the whole calculator you press it a second time. It is more than likely that your calculator has two clear keys.

The |AC| (all cleared) key puts the calculator on or clears it completely while the |C| key clears the last entry but does not clear the memory.

G4 Correcting mistakes

When you use a calculator you must take great care. This includes asking yourself at each stage 'Is my answer reasonable?' If you make a mistake it is probably better to start again.

However, if you do enter a wrong number, it is possible to use the |C| key to remove the error.

To work out 157 − 93 Mike pressed |AC| |1| |5| |7| |−| |9| |7| and realised his mistake straight away.

He pressed |C| followed by |9| |3| |=|.

This cleared his mistake, entered the new number and gave | 64 | in the display, which is the correct answer.

Sometimes you can press the wrong 'operation' key, that is you might press |X| instead of |+| or |÷| instead of |−|. Such a mistake can be corrected easily by pressing the correct key next.

For example to find 84 ÷ 79 Lena pressed |AC| |8| |4| |−|. She stopped here realising that she had pressed |−| instead of |÷|.

The mistake was corrected by pressing |÷| next and then |7| |9| |=|.

The display showed |1.06329| which is the correct answer. Apart from making a mistake when you enter a number, for example keying in 5964 instead of 5694 or 899 instead of 889 or pressing the wrong operation key, take care always to press the $\boxed{=}$ key last. Although you may find that this is sometimes unnecessary, it will never do any harm. It is better to press it when it is not really needed than it is to forget to do so when it is. Finally, take care that you write down the number from the display correctly when you transfer it to your paper.

Check these calculations using your calculator.

(a) $634 + 1219 - 816$

$\boxed{AC}$ $\boxed{6}$ $\boxed{3}$ $\boxed{4}$ $\boxed{+}$ $\boxed{1}$ $\boxed{2}$ $\boxed{1}$ $\boxed{9}$ $\boxed{-}$ $\boxed{8}$ $\boxed{1}$ $\boxed{6}$ $\boxed{=}$

The display shows $\boxed{1037}$

(b) 72×46

$\boxed{AC}$ $\boxed{7}$ $\boxed{2}$ $\boxed{\times}$ $\boxed{4}$ $\boxed{6}$ $\boxed{=}$

The display shows $\boxed{3312}$

(c) $59 \times 23 + 421$

$\boxed{AC}$ $\boxed{5}$ $\boxed{9}$ $\boxed{\times}$ $\boxed{2}$ $\boxed{3}$ $\boxed{+}$ $\boxed{4}$ $\boxed{2}$ $\boxed{1}$

The display shows $\boxed{1778}$ which is correct.

The calculator will multiply 59 by 23 before adding 421. Check that your calculator does this. If it does not, refer to your instruction booklet.

(d) $16^2 - 4.5^2$

$\boxed{AC}$ $\boxed{1}$ $\boxed{6}$ $\boxed{x^2}$ $\boxed{-}$ $\boxed{4}$ $\boxed{.}$ $\boxed{5}$ $\boxed{x^2}$ $\boxed{=}$

The display shows $\boxed{235.75}$

On the Casio fx82C calculator to find the square of a number you have to press $\boxed{shift}$ $\boxed{\sqrt{x}}$ because $\boxed{x^2}$ is written *above* the key.

Always be aware of what you need to do on *your* calculator when you are following a key sequence in a textbook.

(e) $\dfrac{25 \times 39}{42}$

$\boxed{AC}$ $\boxed{2}$ $\boxed{5}$ $\boxed{\times}$ $\boxed{3}$ $\boxed{9}$ $\boxed{\div}$ $\boxed{4}$ $\boxed{2}$ $\boxed{=}$

The display shows $\boxed{23.214285.}$

Most calculators have an 8 or 10 digit display. You will not usually need all the digits. Rounding the answer in the display, which is dealt with in Guidance Notes: Basic Skills, Section C6 (p. 336), is almost always necessary. Every time you round a number, state what you have done. For example, say that you have rounded the number to the nearest 100 or to 3 significant figures.

G5 What about the order of calculation?

Try finding $3 + 4 \times 5$ on your calculator

$\boxed{AC}$ $\boxed{3}$ $\boxed{+}$ $\boxed{4}$ $\boxed{\times}$ $\boxed{5}$ $\boxed{=}$

If your display shows $\boxed{23}$ the answer is correct and your calculator gives priority to multiplication by finding 4×5 before it adds 3.

Maybe your display shows 35. This means that 3 and 4 have been added together and their total multiplied by 5. This is incorrect. On a calculator that does this you must change the order. In this example the order needs to be changed to
| AC | | 4 | | × | | 5 | | + | | 3 | | = |. The display shows | 23 | which is correct.

Now work out $23 + 15 \times 18 - 4 \times 37$
| AC | | 2 | | 3 | | + | | 1 | | 5 | | × | | 1 | | 8 | | − | | 4 | | × | | 3 | | 7 | | = |.
The display should show | 145 |.

Also try
| AC | | 1 | | 5 | | × | | 1 | | 8 | | − | | 4 | | × | | 3 | | 7 | | + | | 2 | | 3 | | = |.

Remember that it does not matter in which order you add and subtract numbers $23 + 270 - 148$ is the same as $270 - 148 + 23$ which is the same as $23 - 148 + 270$.

G6 Working out fractions

Most of the mistakes made in using a calculator are made when working out complex fractions. For example, while $\dfrac{64 \times 79}{82}$ is straightforward (Answer 61.6585 ...) a fraction like $\dfrac{64 \times 79}{82 - 35}$ sometimes causes a problem.

Key in | 6 | | 4 | | × | | 7 | | 9 | | ÷ | | (| | 8 | | 2 | | − | | 3 | | 5 | |) | | = |

The display should show | 107.57447 |
You will not get the correct answer if you leave out the brackets.

Sometimes, it is easier to follow what is going on if you work out the top and bottom separately, making a note of each value and checking that each value is approximately correct.

For example, show that $64 \times 79 = 5056$ (approx. value $60 \times 80 = 4800$), $82 - 35 = 47$ (approx. $80 - 40 = 40$), then find $5056 \div 47$ (approx. $4800 \div 40 = 120$) to give 107.574 ... (This value is not far from the approximate value so is probably correct.)

Find the value of the following fraction

$\dfrac{35^2 - 17 \times 41}{26^2 - 13 \times 19}$ by working out the top and bottom separately

| AC | | 3 | | 5 | | x² | | − | | 1 | | 7 | | × | | 4 | | 1 | | = | The display shows

| AC | | 2 | | 6 | | x² | | − | | 1 | | 3 | | × | | 1 | | 9 | | = | The display shows | 429 |
then | AC | | 5 | | 2 | | 8 | | ÷ | | 4 | | 2 | | 9 | | = | which gives | 1.23076 | ... in the display.

In one sequence the keys to press are

AC (3 5 x^2 − 1 7 × 4 1) ÷ (2 6 x^2 − 1 3 × 1 9) = giving 1.23076.

You should use the method that is *best for you*. The most important thing is to get the correct answer. Do not be afraid to write down values that occur part of the way through a calculation. They will help you if you need to go through it again as a check.

G7 Memory keys

Different calculators can have different kinds of memory keys. The key that puts an entry into the memory is marked
Min (memory in), STO (Store) or M+ (add to memory).

When there is a number in the memory a small m appears in the display. To recall a number from the memory press
MR (memory recall) or RCL (recall) or RM (recall memory).

Sometimes you will want to add the number in the display to the number already in the memory. To do this press
M+ (add to memory) or SUM.

Subtracting the displayed number from the number in the memory requires that you use the M− key or +/− SUM.

The number in the memory can be exchanged with the number in the display by using X↔M (value of display interchanged with the value in the memory) or EXC (exchange).

Some calculators have keys marked
MC (memory cleared) or CM (clear memory),
but you can also clear the memory by pressing
AC Min or on/c STO.

A further method is by pressing
0 Min or 0 STO.
This operation enters 0 into the memory which the same as clearing it.

You will probably not need to use the memory function very often, but one place where it is useful is to test a number for factors.

For example, suppose you wish to find all the factors of 308.
Key in AC 3 0 8 Min (This puts 308 into the memory.)
Then ÷ 2 = gives 154 in the display. Next press ÷ 2 =. This gives 77 in the display. Next press ÷ 2 = which gives 38.5 in the display.

This shows that 2 is a factor twice. The last number displayed is not a whole number so the last time we have divided by 2 it has not divided exactly.

Continue: MR ÷ 3 = gives a display of 102.66 ... so 3 is not a factor

MR ÷ 5 = gives a display of 61.6 so 5 is not a factor

MR ÷ 7 = gives 44 in the display so 7 is a factor and MR ÷ 1 1 = gives 28 in the display so 11 is a factor. Check so far: $2 \times 2 \times 7 \times 11 = 308$. There are therefore no further factors.

G8 Giving a fraction as a percentage

If you have a percentage key % on your calculator you can express a fraction as a percentage by keying in the fraction followed by % for example 4 ÷ 5 % gives 80 in the display that is $\frac{4}{5} = 80\%$.

G9 Negative numbers using a calculator

To get a negative number in the display of a calculator, key in the number followed by the +/− button.

To find $7 + (-12)$
press AC 7 + 1 2 +/− =
The display shows −5 so $7 + (-12) = -5$
Similarly to find $7 - (-12)$
press AC 7 − 1 2 +/− =
This gives $7 - (-12) = 19$

Also to find $-7 + (-12)$
press AC 7 +/− + 1 2 +/− =
which gives $-7 + (-12) = -19$
and to find $-7 - (-12)$
press AC 7 +/− − 1 2 +/− =
which gives $-7 - (-12) = 5$

Now use a calculator to try these
(a) $-7 + (-4)$ (b) $2 - (-5)$
(c) $3 + (-7)$ (d) $-4 - (-7)$
(e) $-8 + 7$ (f) $-5 - (-9)$
(g) $5 + (-7)$ (h) $4 - (-15)$

To multiply $4 \times (-5)$ using a calculator proceed as follows:
AC 4 × 5 +/− = Answer −20

Similarly for $(-4) \times (-5)$ press AC 4 +/− × 5 +/− =
Answer 20

To find $24 \div (-3)$ press $\boxed{AC}$ $\boxed{2}$ $\boxed{4}$ $\boxed{\div}$ $\boxed{3}$ $\boxed{+/-}$ $\boxed{=}$ Answer -8
and to find
$(-12) \div (-6)$ press $\boxed{AC}$ $\boxed{1}$ $\boxed{2}$ $\boxed{+/-}$ $\boxed{\div}$ $\boxed{6}$ $\boxed{+/-}$ $\boxed{=}$ Answer 2

Now try these
(i) $4 \times (-3)$
(j) $(-7) \times (-3)$
(k) $(-9) \div 3$
(l) $6 \div (-3)$
(m) $(-12) \div (-4)$
(n) $-3 + 5 \times (-4)$
(p) $3 - 5 \times (-4)$
(q) $3 + (-5) \times (-4)$
(r) $(-3) \times 5 + 4$
(s) $3 \times (-5) + 4$
(t) $3 (-5) - (-4)$
(u) $(-3) \times (-5) \times 4$

G10 Beware: calculating times and weights

Caution should be used if you use a calculator to add or subtract *time* measured in hours and minutes or *weight* measured in stones and pounds, or pounds and ounces. Suppose you wish to add 5 hr 40 min to 7 hr 47 min. You must not key in $5.40 + 7.47$ since there are not 100 minutes in one hour!

You must add the minutes first ($40 + 47 = 87$), convert this to 1 hr 27 min (since there are 60 minutes in 1 hour), then add the hours ($5 + 7 = 12$) which is finally added to the 1 hr 27 min to give 13 hr 27 min.

Take care in any question involving imperial units, that is yards, feet and inches; stones, pounds and ounces, and so on.

G11 Test your calculator skills

Use a calculator to find:
(a) $739 - 464 + 313$
(b) 82×147
(c) $7521 \div 137$
(d) $13 \times 24 + 63$
(e) $249 - 3.1 \times 62.5$
(f) $49.2 + 293 \div 16.4$

(g) $21.4^2 - 16.9^2$
(h) $\dfrac{5.94 \times 27.6}{32.93 \times 0.94}$

(i) $\dfrac{4.931^2 + 1.826^2}{0.753 \times 21.2}$
(j) $(3.52 + 2.27) \times (21 - 9.37)$

(Give all answers that are not exact correct to 3 s.f.)

Answers

Exercise 1a

1 (a) 44 (b) 527 (c) 27 317 (d) 248 554.
2 (a) £20 000 (b) £16 000 (c) £18 000
   (d) £18 000.
3 £12 000 000.
4 £12 500 000.
5 £956 000 000 000.
6 (a) nineteen ninety five
   (b) one thousand nine hundred and ninety five
   or nineteen hundred and ninety five.

Exercise 1b

1 18.
2 (a) 84 (b) 74.
3 (a) 21st (b) 65th.
4 2885.   5 61 078.
6 85 831.   7 23.
8 208.   9 2318.
10 (a) 1673 (b) 1453.
11 354.   12 270.

Exercise 1c

1 (a) 29 (b) 1044.
2 (a) 48 (b) 288 (c) 16 128.
3 2119.   4 £11 785.
5 560 miles.   6 £840.
7 (a) 675 000 000 (b) 1 116 000 000.
8 (a) 301 000 000 (b) 644 000 000.
9 (a) India (293 m) (b) USA (45 m).
10 (b) (c) (d) (e).
11 (a) 275 (b) 11.
12 22.
13 (a) no (b) no.
14 (a) 3 (b) 5 (c) 6.
15 (a) 5 (b) 7 (c) 8.
16 (a) 10 (b) 7.
17 (a) no (b) 5.
18 (a) (i) Middle East (ii) Europe (b) yes
   (c) 10 000 000 000 i.e. 10 billion
   (d) a thousand billion.
19 (a) 18 (b) Tour A – 1, Tour B – 5,
           Tour C – 44, Tour D – 36
   (c) £14 849 (d) £2447.
20 (a) 25 (b) 47.

Exercise 1d

1 31.   2 35.
3 (a) 14 (b) 17.
4 (a) 72 (b) 5.
5 14.   6 51.
7 (a) 16 (b) 15.
8 405.
9 (a) 14 (b) 1492.
10 (a) one thousand eight hundred and eighty-
    seven or eighteen hundred and eighty-seven
    (b) eighteen eighty-seven.
11 17 mm.   12 800.
13 (a) 1101 (b) 478
    (c) the workforce finishes early.
14 32.
15 2204 i.e. 58 lorries each make 38 journeys.
16 6 bags, 55 CDs.

Exercise 1e

1 (a) (i) thousands (ii) hundreds.
   (b) (i) 27 700 sq ft (ii) 28 000 sq ft.
2 (a) 5840 (b) 5800.
3 (a) 400 (b) 360.
4 (a) 1 576 000 (b) 1 600 000.

Exercise 1f

1 (a) 450 (b) 1550 (c) 1750 (d) 27 550.
2 (a) 849 (b) 1349 (c) 7649 (d) 18 449.
3 (a) 185 (b) 1350 (c) 26 950 (d) 58 500.
4 (a) 749 (b) 1854 (c) 52 049 (d) 38 499.
5 (a) 45 499 (b) 44 500.
6 (a) 23 499 999 (b) 22 500 000.
7 (a) 314 999 sq km (b) 305 000 sq km.
8 (a) greatest 4499, least 3500
   (b) greatest 184, least 175.
9 (a) 9500 hr (b) 10 499 hr.
10 Suppose that 55 499 attended. Correct to the
    nearest 1000 this is 55 000 but correct to the
    nearest 100 000 it is 100 000.

Exercise 1g

1 (a) 90 ft × 50 ft = 4500 sq ft
   (b) 70 ft × 20 ft = 1400 sq ft
   (c) 80 ft × 50 ft = 4000 sq ft
   (d) 980 ft × 90 ft = 88 200 sq ft.
2 (a) 4128 sq ft, 1608 sq ft, 3696 sq ft, 84 999 sq ft
   (b) yes.

357

3 (a) $800 \times 500 \text{ m}^2 = 400\,000 \text{ m}^2$
   (b) $400 \times 300 \text{ m}^2 = 120\,000 \text{ m}^2$
   (c) $1300 \times 600 \text{ m}^2 = 780\,000 \text{ m}^2$
   (d) $9000 \times 600 \text{ m}^2 = 5\,400\,000 \text{ m}^2$.
4 436 506 m², 106 590 m², 831 402 m²,
   5 681 175 m².
5 (a) 1000 (b) 900 (c) 1050 (d) 10 200.
6 (a) 1000 (b) 2000 (c) 4000 (d) 24 000.

Exercise 1h
1 (a) Walk 10 paces down the hill
  (b) Walk 50 paces up the hill
  (c) Walk 100 paces down the hill.
2 I am 1 metre below the surface of the water.
3 I owe my father £30.
4 (a) $-10°C$
  (b) (i) $-5°C$ (ii) $2°C$ (iii) $10°C$ (c) (i) $-16°C$
  (ii) $-23°C$.
5 (a) $-5°C$ by $10°C$ (b) $-18°C$ by $6°C$
  (c) $-6°C$ by $9°C$.
6 (a) (i) $+4$ (ii) -4 (iii) -9 (iv) 6
  (b) (i) $7°C$ (ii) $2°C$ (iii) $4°C$ (iv) $-4°C$.
7 (a) -1 (b) 1   (c) 10.
8 (a) The first, fourth and sixth cars were travelling
      towards London, and the second, third and
      fifth away from it.
  (b) The first is overtaken by the fourth and the
      sixth. The fifth overtakes the third.

Exercise 1i
1 $-6 < 3$.   2 $-7 < -4$.
3 $-4 < -3$.   4 $0 > -8$.
5 $5 > -2$.   6 $-3 > -7$.
7 $-12 < -4$.   8 $2 > -3$.
9 $-3 < 0$.   10 $-4 > -8$.
11 $-5 < 4$.   12 $-3 < -2$.

Exercise 1j
1 -5.   2 -5.
3 -2.   4 -11.
5 -5.   6 -1.
7 -6.   8 -2.
9 0.   10 -9.
11 5.   12 -6.
13 11.   14 21.
15 6.   16 1.
17 -7.   18 1.
19 -15.   20 -7.

Multiple choice questions
1 B.   2 D.
3 D.   4 B.
5 A.   6 A & C are true.
7 C & D are true.   8 B.
9 D.

Self assessment 1
1 (a) £65 000 (b) £5 000 000 000.
2 (a) (i) 405 (ii) 482 (b) 339.
3 136.
4 (a) 72 900 (b) 73 000 (c) 72 850.
5 (a) £16 499 (b) £15 500.
6 741.   7 1800.
8 (a) 23 (b) 1244 (c) 228.
9 (a) about 8200 (b) 8990 (c) 36.
10 (a) (i) £4000 (ii) £10 000
   (b) missing values of sales are: 92, 110, 126 and
   140; the figures for profit (or loss) are: (1), 4, (10),
   (14) and 10 (figures in brackets indicate a loss)
   (c) no (d) no (e) 70 000.
11 (a) £55 overdrawn (b) £300 overdrawn
   (c) £71 overdrawn (d) £90 in credit.

Unit 2

Exercise 2a
1 $\frac{1}{4}$.   2 $\frac{3}{8}$.
3 $\frac{5}{8}$.   4 $\frac{5}{16}$.
5 $\frac{5}{8}$.   6 $\frac{4}{7}$.
7 (a)

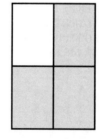

(b)

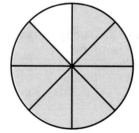

(c)

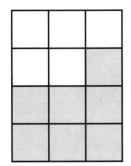

(d)

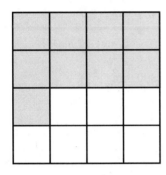

Exercise 2b

1 (a)

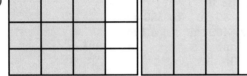

(b) yes (c) $\frac{12}{16}$.

2 (a) $\frac{15}{25}$ (b) $\frac{12}{28}$ (c) $\frac{21}{27}$ (d) $\frac{30}{66}$.

3 (a) $\frac{3}{9}$ (b) $\frac{6}{21}$ (c) $\frac{12}{21}$.

4 (a) $\frac{6}{10} = \frac{9}{15}$ (b) $\frac{15}{20} = \frac{18}{24}$ (c) $\frac{7}{14} = \frac{21}{42}$ (d) $\frac{20}{24} = \frac{25}{30}$.

5 (a) $\frac{2}{10}, \frac{3}{15}, \frac{4}{20}$ (b) $\frac{10}{14}, \frac{15}{21}, \frac{20}{28}$ (c) $\frac{14}{16}, \frac{21}{24}, \frac{28}{32}$

   (d) $\frac{8}{18} = \frac{12}{27} = \frac{20}{45}$.

6 (a) $\frac{8}{16}$ (b) $\frac{15}{20}$

   (c) $\frac{6}{10}$ (d) $\frac{25}{100}$.

7 $\frac{5}{20}, \frac{6}{20}, \frac{10}{20}, \frac{12}{20}, \frac{16}{20}$.

Exercise 2c

1 (a) $\frac{1}{2}$ (b) $\frac{5}{8}$.

2 (a) $\frac{3}{8}$ (b) $\frac{5}{7}$.

3 $\frac{7}{16}$ lb, $\frac{9}{16}$ lb, $\frac{11}{16}$ lb, $\frac{13}{16}$ lb.

4 $\frac{13}{16}$ lb, $\frac{3}{4}$ lb, $\frac{5}{8}$ lb, $\frac{9}{16}$ lb, $\frac{1}{2}$ lb.

5 (a) $\frac{16}{20}, \frac{14}{20}, \frac{17}{20}, \frac{15}{20}$ (b) Mandy (c) Vera.

6 $\frac{5}{14}'', \frac{1}{2}'', \frac{5}{7}'', \frac{3}{4}''$.

7 (a) $\frac{1}{3}$ (b) $\frac{2}{15}$.

8 $26\frac{1}{8}$ lb.

9 (a) $\frac{1}{6}$ (b) $\frac{1}{18}$.

10 15 yd.

Exercise 2d

1 (a) $\frac{1}{2}$ (b) $\frac{1}{4}$ (c) $\frac{3}{5}$ (d) $\frac{17}{20}$.

2 (a) $\frac{2}{3}$ (b) $\frac{1}{6}$ (c) $\frac{3}{4}$ (d) $\frac{1}{10}$.

3 (a) $\frac{2}{5}$ (b) $\frac{3}{5}$.

4 $\frac{5}{8}$. 5 $\frac{1}{8}$.

6 (a) $\frac{1}{35}$ (b) $\frac{1}{5}$.

7 $\frac{2}{3}$.

8 (a) $\frac{2}{5}$ (b) $\frac{1}{10}$.

9 (a) $\frac{2}{5}$ (b) $\frac{3}{5}$.

10 (a) $\frac{3}{10}$ (b) $\frac{13}{20}$.

Exercise 2e

1 (a) £25 (b) £35.

2 (a) 100 g (b) 900 g.

3 (a) 3 litres (b) 5 litres.

4 (a) 30 (b) 4 (c) 6.

5 £50 000.   6 720.

7 (a) (i) $\frac{3}{4}$ (ii) $\frac{1}{4}$ (b) 1200 (c) 400.

8 (a) $\frac{1}{10}$ (b) £2 m.

9 42.   10 40.

11 (a) $4\frac{1}{2}$ sec (b) $26\frac{1}{4}$ min.

12 (a) 30 (b) yes.

13 38 m.

14 (a) £300 (b) £180.

15 (a) yes: receipts £8000, costs £7750

    (b) £4250 (c) £4725, yes £475 more.

Exercise 2f

1 6.7 cm.   2 2.6 cm.

3 13.2 cm.   4 7.3 cm.

Exercise 2g

1 28.5 cm.   2 12.1 m.

3 (a) 4.2 m (b) 4.1 m.

4 (a) 5.6 m (b) 2.6 m.

5 9.7 cm.

6 (a) 74.24 m (b) 9.22 m.

Exercise 2h

1 (a) 3.8 cm (b) 7.3 cm.

2 8.7 m.   3 7.8 cm.

4 (a) 2.6 m (b) 4.4 m (c) 3 m.

Exercise 2i

1 (a) 5.26 cm (b) 5.3 cm.

2 (a) 0.44 cm (b) 0.4 cm.

3 (a) 20.68 cm (b) 20.7 cm.

4 (a) 9.01 cm (b) 9.0 cm.

5 (a) 5.9 g, 5.9 g, 6.0 g, 6.0 g, 6.0 g

   (b) 5.94 g, 5.95 g, 6.01 g, 5.98 g, 6.02 g.

6 (a) 4.7 m, 1.8 m, 1.4 m
   (b) 4.72 m, 1.75 m, 1.42 m.
7 (a) 4 m   (b) 1.7 m   (c) 2.67 m   (d) 1.4 m
   (e) 1.44 m   (f) 0.7 m   (g) 0.02 m   (h) 0.01 m.

Exercise 2j
1 518.4.   2 21.96.
3 34.48.   4 248.6.
5 9. 6 1.9.
7 125.   8 0.05.
9 570 g.   10 9.6 cm.
11 (a) 37.25   (b) £217.54.
12 273 min.
13 (a) 129.6 g   (b) 145.4 g.
14 (a) 1.38 t   (b) 3.92 t.
15 12.6 km per litre.   16 50 m².
17 8.
18 (a) 16   (b) 16 cm.
19 12.   20 £7.42.
21 (a) £16.45   (b) £12.

Exercise 2k
1 34.8.   2 1.8.
3 0.68.   4 16.9.
5 1.1.   6 4.67.
7 648.   8 0.0961.

Exercise 2l
1 £300 000 (600 × £500), £291 152.
2 £72 (9 × £8), £71.10.
3 12 000 g (3000 × 4 g), 11 931 g.
4 (a) 8 m (40 ÷ 5 m)   (b) 6.89 m.
5 £5 (£200 ÷ 40), £5.87.
6 (a) £21 (£7000 ÷ 100 × 0.3)   (b) £19.30.
7 (a) 180 miles (300 × 0.6 miles)   (b) 174 miles.

Exercise 2m
Each measurement could be given to the nearest
1 mm.   2 mm.
3 m.   4 10 km.
5 km.   6 mg.
7 100 cm³.   8 hectares.
9 10 g.
10 (i) nearest 5   (ii) nearest 1000   (iii) nearest 100.
Many other answers are possible, including imperial units.

Multiple choice questions
1 A.   2 D.
3 C.   4 A & D are true, B & C
                              are false.
5 A, C & D are true, B false.   6 B.

Self assessment 2
1 (a) no   (b) (i) $\frac{53}{60}$ (ii) $\frac{7}{60}$.
2 (a) $\frac{1}{8}$ (b) $\frac{7}{8}$.
3 296.   4 $2\frac{3}{4}$ miles.
5 19.
6 (a) 13.782 m   (b) 3.312 m   (c) 3.212 m
   (d) 4.412 m by 3.34 m
   (e) (i) 26.3028 m²   (ii) 26.3 m²   (iii) 26.30 m²
   (f) 3.5 m.
7 (a) 62.5 miles   (b) 181.25 miles.
8 (a) 54 sq metres   (b) 55.4 sq metres.

Unit 3

Exercise 3a
1 (a) 230 cm   (b) 2300 mm.
2 (a) 120 cm   (b) 850 mm.
3 (a) 1430 m   (b) 0.55 km.
4 1.41 km.   5 46 145 yd.
6 3207 yd.
7 (a) 3960 yd   (b) $2\frac{1}{4}$ miles.
8 (a) 71 yd, 12 yd, 7 yd
   (b) 2556 in, 432 in, 252 in.

Exercise 3b
1 (a) 80 cm   (b) 580 mm.
2 (a) 460 cm   (b) 4.1 m.
3 17 m.   4 395 m.
5 66 in.

Exercise 3c
1 Arran 12 sq, Islay 17 sq, I.O.W. 11 sq, Anglesey 22 sq, Jersey 3 sq, I.O.M. 17 sq.
2 Oak 33 sq, Horsechestnut 42 sq, Sycamore 41 sq, Lime 50 sq.
3 (c) 34 sq   (b) 40 sq.

Exercise 3d
1 900 cm².
2 (a) 64
   (b) 12.25 cm²
   (c) (i) square   (ii) square
   (d) (i) 28 cm   (ii) 35 cm
   (e) (i) 784 cm²   (ii) 1225 cm².
3 (a) 16 000 cm²   (b) 2 m by 0.8 m   (c) 1.6 m².
4 (a) 400 yd   (b) 9600 yd².
5 (a) 440 mm   (b) 11 475 mm²
   (c) 13.5 cm by 8.5 cm   (d) 115 cm².
6 (a) (i) 56 in   (ii) $4\frac{2}{3}$ ft
   (b) (i) 192 in²   (ii) $1\frac{1}{3}$ ft².
7 (a) 3 (1 × 12, 2 × 6, 3 × 4)

  (b) (i) 1×12 (perimeter 26 cm)
    (ii) 3×4 (perimeter 14 cm) (c) 12 cm.
8 (a) 4 (2×18, 3×12, 4×9, 6×6)
  (b) 2×18 (c) 6×6 (a square).

Exercise 3e

1 16.   **2** 64.
3 12.   **4** 18.
5 9.
6 (a) 8 (b) 8.
7 1760 cm^3.   **8** 8.
9 (a) 24 (b) 64 (c) 432.
10 (a) 8 (b) 54.
11 16.
12 For box A the yellow cubes (side 2 cm) cannot
  be arranged to give a breadth of 3 cm.
  For box A the white cubes (side 3 cm) cannot be
  arranged to give a length of 4 cm or a height of
  2 cm.
13 (a) 2 cm $\times$ 2 cm $\times$ 2 cm, 8
  (b) (i) yes, $3 \times 2 \times 2$ (ii) no
  (c) 2, 2 cm $\times$ 2 cm $\times$ 6 cm, 2 cm $\times$ 3 cm $\times$ 4 cm.
14 240 in^3.
15 Alf's 3000 mm^3, Ena's 3360 mm^3: Ena.
16 (a) 44.1 cm^3 (b) 45.36 cm^3
  (c) 46.8 cm^3 (d) (i) (c) (ii) (a).
17 $3\frac{1}{3}$ yd.
18 (a) 900 m^3 (b) 900 000 litres.
19 (a) 1728 mm^3 (b) 1.728 cm^3.
20 £3.52 ($0.2 \times 0.08 \times 4 \times £55$).
21 (a) (i) 5062.5 cm^3 (ii) 0.005 062 5 m^3
  (b) 197.
22 (a) (i) 940.5 cm^3 (ii) 7200 cm^2 (b) 10
  (c) 12 (all rows as in (b)) (d) 42, 4
  (e) 288.

Exercise 3f

1 (a) 27 000 cm^3 (b) 27 litres.
2 1000.   **3** 4000.
4 120.
5 (a) 40 cm by 32 cm by 15 cm (b) 19 200 cm^3
  (c) 27 090 cm^3 (d) 7890 cm^3.
6 (a) 3 cm (b) 18 cm by 14 cm (c) 756 cm^3.

Exercise 3g

1 500 g.   **2** 0.005 g.
3 129.6 kg.
2 (a) 7.5 t (b) 12 t.
5 48 litres   **6** 60.
7 40.
8 (a) 90 240 g (b) 90.24 kg.
9 (a) 42 900 cm^3 (b) 343.2 kg.

Multiple choice questions

1 B.   **2** A.
3 A.   **4** D.
5 A & D are true, B & C are false. **6** C.

Self assessment 3

1 (a) 92.5 yd (b) 370 yd^2, 3.08 gal (to 3 s.f.)
  (c) 63 yd^2 (d) (i) 484 yd^2 (ii) $\frac{1}{10}$ acre
  (e) 10 ft by $7\frac{1}{2}$ ft (f) 469 ft^3 (g) 16 in.
2 (a) 196 cm (b) 1.425 m by 0.363 m by 0.245 m
  (c) (i) 3576 mm (ii) 3.576 m
  (d) (i) 0.517 m^2 (ii) 0.089 m^2 (iii) 0.349 m^2
  (each to 3 s.f.), 1.91 m^2 (3 s.f.) (e) 1.01 m^3
  (3 s.f.).
3 (a) 18.5 cm by 11.5 cm, 213 cm^2
  (b) 24 mm, 0.1 mm (c) 5.11 m^2 (3 s.f.)
  (d) (i) 240 g (ii) 1 g (e) 46.9 g (s.f.).

Revision papers for units 1–3

Paper 1

1 14 976.   **2** 1083.   **3** $\frac{8}{80}$.
4 (a) 0.88 km (b) (i) 38 400 m^2 (ii) 3.84 hta.
5 £5.

Paper 2

1 about 27 yrs.   **2** 16.
3 156.   **4** $23\frac{5}{8}''$.
5 (a) 1620 cm^3 (b) 0.00162 m^3.

Paper 3

1 120.   **2** 181 760.
3 (a) $\frac{17}{40}$ (b) 1020.
4 (a) 3240 ft^3 (b) 120 yd^3.
5 (a) *A*   *B*   *C*

  (b) (i) *C* (ii) *A*.

Paper 4

1 280 m.   **2** 79.88 cm.
3 (a) On the first trip out there is no one in Palma
  waiting to fly home and on the last flight
  home no holidaymakers have been flown out.
  (b) 96 (c) 49.
4 (a) (i) 277 000 in^3 (ii) 160 ft^3 (b) 4 ft.
5 30 kg.

Unit 4

Exercise 4a

1 0.85.   2 0.74.
3 0.34.   4 1.35.
5 2.3.   6 $\frac{1}{10}$.
7 $\frac{1}{5}$.   8 $\frac{43}{100}$, $\frac{57}{100}$.
9 $\frac{7}{20}$.   10 25%.
11 65%.   12 68%.
13 28%.   14 32%.
15 41%.
16 (a) 14%   (b) $\frac{29}{50}$.
17 37%.
18 (a) 40%   (b) 60%.
19 (a) $\frac{11}{25}$ (b) no   (c) $\frac{14}{25}$.
20 (a) 140 000 ft^3
    (b) (i) $\frac{23}{50}$ (ii) 64 400 ft^3 (iii) 716 ft^3 (3 s.f.)
    (c) 11$\frac{20}{3}$%.

Exercise 4b

1 $\frac{1}{2}$.   2 $\frac{3}{10}$.
3 $\frac{1}{8}$.   4 $\frac{2}{1}$.
5 $\frac{3}{10}$.   6 $\frac{3}{10}$.
7 $\frac{2}{15}$.   8 $\frac{1}{10}$.
9 $\frac{7}{10}$.   10 $\frac{1}{4}$.
11 $\frac{1}{20}$.   12 $\frac{1}{5}$.
13 (a) $\frac{7}{10}$ (b) $\frac{3}{10}$.   14 80%.
15 48%.   16 40%.
17 20%.   18 40%.
19 25%.   20 65%.
21 55%.   22 (a) 16$\frac{2}{3}$%   (b) 83$\frac{1}{3}$%.
23 101$\frac{1}{4}$%.   24 58%.

Exercise 4c

1 £8.   2 2500.
3 24 cm.   4 68.
5 (a) 1320. (b) 1080.   6 270.
7 £192.   8 1.8 kg.
9 (a) £77.45   (b) £15.
10 (a) 12 kg   (b) 120   (c) 40 kg.

Exercise 4d

1 (a) £35   (b) £288   (c) £50.
2 82.62.   3 £2880.
4 £8.40.   5 87.75 cm.
6 100 kg.   7 £668.50.
8 (a) 55 000   (b) 59 400.
9 (a) £155.10   (b) 90p.
10 (a) 46 412, 56 354
    (b) (i) 10.7%   (ii) 9.7%   (iii) 1.5% (decrease)
      (iv) 11.7%.
    (c) (i) Northern Ireland (an increase)

      (ii) Scotland (a decrease).
    (d) (i) Northern Ireland   (ii) Northern Ireland
    (e) 56 000 000, 47 000 000, 3 000 000,
      5 000 000, 2 000 000
      (i) $\frac{47}{56}$ (ii) $\frac{3}{56}$.

Exercise 4e

1 40%.
2 (a) £210 000   (b) 44.7% (3 s.f.).
3 (a) £5.4m   (b) 63.0% (3 s.f.).
4 (a) £6.75   (b) £7.20   (c) £7.88   (d) £9.
5 (a) 62%   (b) (i) £9.90   (ii) £4.40   (iii) £13.64
    (c) 120%   (d) £20.
6 (a) £7000 loss   (b) 100%
    (c) Share of fixed overheads
    (d) (i) £24 000   (ii) yes, income exceeds fixed
      overheads by £6000   (iii) yes.
7 £80.

Exercise 4f

1 £141.   2 £79.90.
3 £9.99.   4 £98.11.
5 £41.71.
6 (a) £940   (b) Speedstore by £17.63.
7 £34.68, £6.07, £40.75, £2.04
    (a) £38.71   (b) £40.75.
8 £74.55.   9 £52.80.
10 £1.93.   11 £218.75.
12 (a) £9.80   (b) 15%.
13 (a) £10   (b) £2.61   (c) £4.89   (d) 49%.

Exercise 4g

1 (a) £864   (b) £865.28.   2 (b) by £13.88.
3 £55.   4 £166.40.
5 £124.86.   6 £339.08.
7 £1663.08.   8 £2852.92.

Exercise 4h

1 4466.   2 £126.20.
3 £2869.20.   4 9 yrs.
5 (a) about 5030   (b) about 10 100.
6 (a) 1156   (b) 1835.

Exercise 4i

1 (a) (i) £330   (ii) £935   (b) £66 000.
2 (a) £562.50   (b) £6750   (c) £202 500.
3 (a) £72 000   (b) £8000
    (c) (i) £882   (ii) £264 600.
4 (a) £43 520   (b) £110 106.
5 (a) £950   (b) £4430   (c) £630.
6 (a) £243.20   (b) £290.06   (c) £46.86.
7 Bank loan by £33.40.

8 (a) £18.73 (b) £8.90 (c) £355.13.

Exercise 4j

1 £5000.
2 (a) £1200 (b) (i) £3600 (ii) £1200.
3 (a) £19 600 (b) £10 800.
4 (a) (i) £14 400 (ii) £5184
(b) Eastern Woodcrafts by £6560
(£15 200 − £8640) (c) £1870, £2000.
5 (a) £2000 (b) £4000.
6 (a) £5000 (b) £35 000 (c) £11 666$\frac{2}{3}$.
7 (a) £3600 (b) £4800 (c) $\frac{2}{5}$ (d) 40%.

Multiple choice questions

1 C. **2** B.
3 D. **4** A.
5 A & C are true, B & D are false. **6** A.

Self assessment 4

1 (a) $\frac{1}{4}$ (b) 25%. **2** 9%.
3 112%. **4** £2353.40.
5 £13.50. **6** Denhams by 25p.
7 £75. **8** (a) £21.84 (b) £10.37.
9 (a) missing values in order are: £50 000, £25 000, £25 000, £12 500, £12 500, £6250, £6250; £193 750, £6250
(b) 3.1% (3$\frac{1}{8}$%) (c) £38 750.

Unit 5

Exercise 5a

1 (a) £182.40 (b) £190.55.
2 (a) £5.50 (b) £167.20 (c) £211.20.
3 £334.56.
4 (a) 8.00 a.m. (b) 5.00 p.m. (c) 6 hr
(d) 37$\frac{1}{4}$hr (e) £181.04 (f) £36.45
(g) £217.49.
5 (a) (i) one (Thursday) (ii) one (Monday)
(b) 7$\frac{1}{2}$ hr (Thurs 1$\frac{1}{4}$ hr, Fri 1$\frac{3}{4}$ hr, Sat 5 hr, less $\frac{1}{2}$ h, because she finishes early on Monday and starts more than 5 min late on Thurs).
(c) 51$\frac{1}{2}$ hr (d) £256.88.
6 (a) £70 (b) £625 (c) £850.
7 £344. **8** £2585.
9 £149.75. **10** £183.52.
11 (a) £1500 (b) £3820 (c) £1345.
12 (a) £14 880 (b) £44 640 (c) £31 896.
13 Chris by £1836 a year.
14 (a) £1920 (b) £23 040.
15
(a) £152.02 (b) £343 (c) £31.26
(d) £58.12 (e) £13.55.
16 (a) £191.25 (b) £81.60 (c) £272.85
(d) £41.57 (e) £16.37 (f) £195.07.
17

Name	Wages (£)	£20	£10	£5	£1	50p	20p	10p	5p	2p	1p
Brown	197.68	180	10	5	2	50		10	5	2	1
Martin	112.49	100	10		2		40		5	4	
O'Hare	207.37	200		5	2		20	10	5	2	
Hanley	254.76	240	10		4	50	20		5		1

Exercise 5b

1 3980 2024 2426 2642.
2 (a) 1.5 (b) 10 (c) 0.2 (d) 2.5.
3 (a) 10 h (b) 83$\frac{1}{3}$ h (c) $\frac{1}{2}$ h (d) 4 h (e) $\frac{2}{5}$ h
(f) 6$\frac{2}{3}$ h.
4 (a) £5.88 (b) £2.29 (c) 23p (d) £1.19
(e) £1.90 (f) 4 p.
5 (a) (i) 49.92 (ii) 7.5 (iii) 22
(b) 79.42 (c) £6.63 (nearest penny).
6 £445.34. **7** £358.96.
8 £323.84.
9 (a) £579.26.
10 £725.95.
11 (a) £5923.50 for the gas. Total incl. VAT £6959.53.
(b) Cost of gas, excluding standard charge goes up to £6282.86 and total with VAT to £7397.05.
12 (a) £7169.98 (b) £8603.98.

Exercise 5c

1 9 litres. **2** 20 pints.
3 45 m. **4** 15.6 mm.
5 (a) 32p (b) £2.56.
6 (a) 219 miles (b) 6.84 gal.
7 (a) 13.8 gal (b) 1.56 gal (c) 386 miles.
8 10.2 pints. **9** 300 g.
10 12.
11 (a) 62 yd by 22 yd (b) 57 m by 20 m.
12 14' 9", 5' 8", 4' 8".
13 (a) $\frac{1}{8}$", $\frac{3}{16}$", $\frac{1}{4}$", $\frac{5}{16}$", $\frac{3}{8}$", $\frac{7}{16}$", $\frac{1}{2}$", $\frac{9}{16}$", $\frac{5}{8}$", $\frac{11}{16}$", $\frac{3}{4}$", $\frac{13}{16}$", $\frac{7}{8}$", $\frac{15}{16}$", 1"
(b) 15 (c) (i) $\frac{9}{16}$" (ii) $\frac{11}{16}$" (d) (i) $\frac{3}{16}$" (ii) $\frac{11}{16}$"
(e) $\frac{1}{2}$" (f) $\frac{11}{16}$ (g) $\frac{9}{16}$" (h) 23
(i) 15.875 mm, 15 mm (j) 19.05 mm, 20 mm
(k) 10 mm, larger.
14 7 oz brown sugar, 2 eggs, 6 oz self-raising flour, 1 oz cocoa, 2 tablespoons cordial, 4 oz caster sugar.
15 100 g margarine, 100 g caster sugar, 2 eggs, 25 g cocoa, 125 g self-raising flour.

16 6 oz butter, 2 oz caster sugar, 4 oz plain flour (sieved), 1 oz cornflour (sieved), 1 oz cocoa (sieved), few drops of vanilla essence, 6 oz icing sugar, 1 oz cocoa, 3 oz soft margarine, 1 tablespoon warm water.

Exercise 5d
1 (a) 75p (b) £1.14.   **2** £1.07.
3 £2.18.   **4** £1.52.
5 £2.29.   **6** (a) £6.50 (b) £13.50.
7 £9.   **8** (a) £3.25 (b) £4.45.
9 (a) £2.65 (b) £2.05 (c) £1.45.
10 (a) £6.40 (b) no.
11 (a) 55p (£3.80 − £3.25) (b) it's quicker.
12 £6.60.   **13** It is £1440 cheaper.
14 £1271.60.   **15** £110.61.

Exercise 5e
1 (a) 23.622 in (b) 176.37 lb (c) 13.198 gal.
2 (a) 64.374 km (b) 28.328 hectares (c) 76.20 cm.
3 (a) 116.84 cm (b) 145.505 lb
(c) 54.363 acres.
4 (a) 331.855 litres (b) 86.904 km
(c) 28.448 tonnes.
5 (a) 170.877 miles (b) 222.579 hectares
(c) 9091.92 litres.
6 531 miles.

Exercise 5f
1 212°F.   **2** 0°C.
3 115°F.   **4** 38°C.
5 55°C.   **6** 90°C.
7 no, not without extending the scale up to 1000°C.
8 (a) 30.1 inches of mercury (b) 999 millibars.

Exercise 5g
1 (a) £87 (b) 285Ff.
2 £11.50.
3 You will have your own answer here.
4 (a) about 11½ gal (b) about 36 litres.

Multiple choice questions
1 C.   **2** B.
3 B.   **4** D.
5 B & C are true, A & D are false.
6 C.

Self assessment 5
1 (a) 10 (b) 72 (c) 1647, £153.76.
2 (a) Steve £301.80, Nick £287.95
(b) 95.4% (c) Steve by £17.40.

3 (a) 38 h (b) 6½ h (c) £7.14 (d) £180.88
(e) £227.29 (f) £163.95.
4 (a) his new car by 35 cm (b) 62 (nearest whole number)
(c) (i) about 490 miles (ii) about 785 km
(d) 7.9 litres (e) (i) £4441 (ii) £85.41.
5 250 g pasta shells, 60 ml plain yogurt, 10 g butter, 10 g flour, 150 ml beef stock, 350 g plum tomatoes, 1 bay leaf, sprig of thyme, parsley stalks, salt & pepper (weights are given correct to the nearest 5 g).
6 (a) £2.01 (b) £2.89 (c) (i) £3.25 (ii) £4.45.
7 (a) 205.097 acres (b) 113.09 miles
(c) 94.492 tonnes (d) 13.154 kg.

Unit 6

Exercise 6a
1 816 cm²   **2** 500 cm²
3 (a) You have your own diagram here.
(b) (i) 15.65 m (ii) 14.25 m².
4 (a) 1000 m (b) (i) 12 700 m² (ii) 1.27 hectares.
5 (a) 353.4 cm² (b) 150.66 cm² (c) 202.74 cm².
6 (a) 2400 cm² (b) 14 600 cm² (1.46 m²).

Exercise 6b
1 (a) 13.5 cm² (b) 12 cm² (c) 19.74 cm²
(d) 14.82 cm².
2 34 m².
3 *A*: 18 cm². *B*: 16 cm². *C*: 14 cm². *D*: 36 cm².
4 (a) 60 cm by 40 cm (b) 2400 cm²
(c) 1836 cm² (d) 564 cm².
5 870 cm²   **6** 31.8 mm².
7 (a) 1750 m² (b) 1166.
8 1820 cm².
9 (a) *A*: 300 m², *B*: 1400 m², *C*: 600 m²,
D: 800 m², *E*: 200 m², *F*: 450 m², *G*: 1800 m²
(b) (i) 5550 m² (ii) 0.555 hectares.

Exercise 6c
1 1225 cm².
2 95.5 m² (including floor & ceiling).
3 10 640 mm² (106.4 cm²).
4 114 300 mm² (1143 cm²).

Exercise 6d
1 (a) 9 m² (b) 54 m³.
2 (a) 4500 cm² (b) 30 240 cm³.
3 18 816 cm³.
4 (a) 0.75 cm² (b) 23.7 cm³.
5 1.73 m³ (3 s.f.).

6 (a) 37 000 cm³   (b) 0.037 m³.

Exercise 6e
1, 2 You have your own answers and table here.
3 (a) 150 cm   (b) 192 cm.
4 (a) 10 in   (b) 30 in.
5 (a) 225 cm   (b) 225 cm
   (c) (i) 11 250 cm   (ii) 112.5 m.

Exercise 6f
1 (a) 3.14   (b) 3.14   (c) 3.142.
2 283 cm.
3 50.3 cm, 66.0 cm, 84.8 cm.
4 (a) 0.35 cm (0.35 mm)   (b) 1.45 cm.
5 (a) 44.0 cm, 53.4 cm   (b) 97.4 cm
   (c) (i) 100 cm   (ii) 2.6 cm.
6 0.764 m (76.4 cm).
7 (a) 38.2 cm   (b) 33.1 cm   (c) 2.55 cm.
8 (a) 25.1 in   (b) 87.3 yd   (c) 143.
9 (a) 1.88 m   (b) 1.88 m   (c) 531.
10 (a) 4.08 cm, 7.54 cm, 59.7 cm, 66.0 cm,
   99.3 cm, 105.6 cm
   (b) 15.6 cm   (c) 20   (d) 312 cm   (e) 654 cm.

Exercise 6g
1 17.6 m.
2 (a) 34.6 cm   (b) 17.3 cm.
3 47.1 cm.   **4** 30.4 cm.
5 (a) 85 cm   (b) 267 cm   (c) 437 cm.
6 (a) $AB = AD = CD = 140$ cm
   (b) (i) 70 cm   (ii) 220 cm (3 s.f.)
   (c) 640 cm.
7 (a) 32 m   (b) 100.5 m (1 d.p.)
   (c) 401 m (3 s.f.)   (d) 8.02 km.

Exercise 6h
1 50.3 cm².   **2** 1520 m².
3 1130 mm².   **4** 9.05 cm².
5 78.5 yd².   **6** 3180 cm².
7 (a) 4590 cm²   (b) 4090 cm²   (c) 12 800 cm².
8 (a) 661 cm²   (b) 2020 cm².
9 (a) 503 m²   (b) 2268 m²   (c) 1765 m².
10 134 cm².

Exercise 6i
1 (a) (i) 1.32 m²   (ii) 132 m²   (b) 606.
2 3.28 m².   **3** 239 cm².
4 11.0 cm².   **5** 17 700 mm³ (17.7 cm³).
6 50.3 cm³.   **7** 1663 cc.
8 (a) 1.44 cm²   (b) 0.785 cm²   (c) 45%.
9 diameter = height = 18.5 cm.
10 (a) 75 000 cm³   (b) 1364 cm²   (c) 20.8 cm.

11 78.7 mm.
12 (a) 314 cm²   (b) 79.9 cm².
13 55 000 m³.   **14** 0.0415 m³.
15 1290 mm³ (1.29 cm³).

Exercise 6j
1
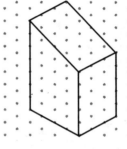

2
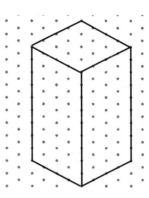

3
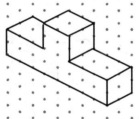

4
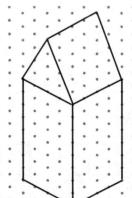

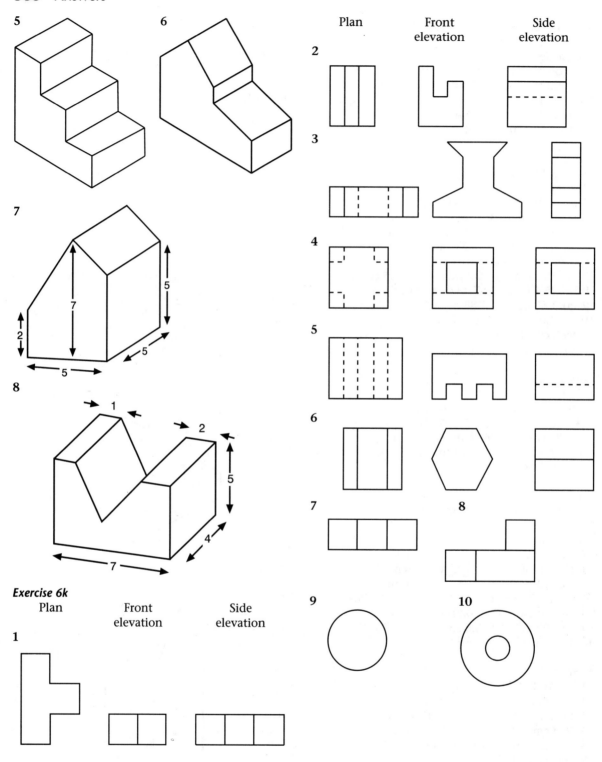

5

6

7

8

Exercise 6k

Plan   Front elevation   Side elevation

1

Plan   Front elevation   Side elevation

2

3

4

5

6

7   8

9   10

11

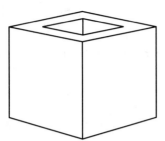

12

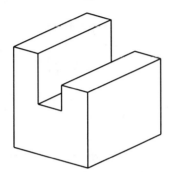

13

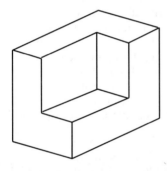

1 (a)

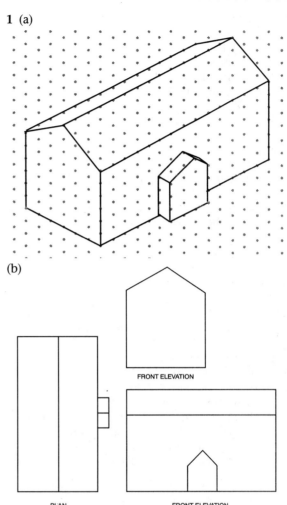

(b)

FRONT ELEVATION

PLAN   FRONT ELEVATION

Multiple choice questions
1 B.   2 B.
3 B.   4 A.
5 B & C are true, A & D are false. 2 D.

Self assessment 6
1 See top of next column.
2 (a) 1: parallelogram, 2: triangle, 3: square,
      4: trapezium, 5: rectangle
  (b) $\frac{1}{3}$ (c) (i) 835 cm² (ii) 461 cm³.
3 (a) $1\frac{7}{25}$ ft² (1.28 ft²)
  (b) $26\frac{14}{25}$ ft²
  (c) (i) 10.2 ft³ (ii) 63.8 gal.
4 (a) 15.7 ft by 20 ft (b) 51.4 ft
  (c) 353 ft² (d) 393 ft³
  (e) 11.7 tons (26 300 lb).

Revision papers for units 4–6

Paper 5
1 172.8 g chromium, 76.8 g nickel.
2 £43.75.
3 (a) £219.38 (b) £58.50.
4 (a) 54 cm² (b) 8.1 litres.
5 (a) 176 cm (b) 176 cm (c) 150 (d) 25.

Paper 6
1 (a) 83.3% (b) 13 100.
2 (a) 36 (b) 3750 g
  (c) 48.95 kg (d) 190 g (nearest 10 g).
3 (a) £31.92 (b) lost £4.32
  (c) (i) £96.40 (ii) £24.60.
4 (a) £24.50 (b) £61.10 (c) £166.10.
5 £348.

Paper 7

1 63 g.
2 (a) £231.13 (b) £287.13.
3 (a) 29.6 m × 9.8 m
  (b) 39.0 ft × 13.0 ft, 81.2 ft × 50.3 ft.
4 (a) (i) 8.5 cm (ii) 2.36 cm
  (b) 22.4 cm.
5 (a) 9.43 cm (b) 276 cm².

Paper 8

1 (a) 116%
  (b) (i) 72 000 (ii) 85 000 (iii) 100 000.
2 (a)

Name	Mileage	Hotel accom.	Hotel meals	Casual meals	Total
B. Ayola					£220.14
C. Love			£52.19		
L. Draigo					
P. Lineen		£89.84			
R. Dence		£242.12		£42.18	
M. Hayes					£400.98
	£619.43		£252.99	£156.81	

  (b) £201.93 (c) 44%.
3 (a) (i) 151 000 (ii) 132 000
  (b) (i) 115 000 (ii) 112 000
  (c) (i) women indoors (ii) men indoors
  (d) (i) 11.2% (ii) yes – it is more than halfway.
4 (a) 63.2 cm × 31.2 cm × 70 cm
  (b) 1.8 m² (c) 0.83 m³.
5 (a) 34 000 sq miles (b) 6000 sq miles smaller.

Unit 7

Exercise 7a

1 (a) 28 (b) 30.
2 no.
3 (a) August (b) May.
4 13.
5 (a) 5 (b) 4.
6 4.
7 (a) Saturday (b) 20 May (c) 7 June.
8 (a) 15 September (b) 7 September
  (c) 18 September.
9 4 September. 10 15.
11 (a) 14 (b) 19 September (c) 10 weeks.
12 (a) 27 (b) 17.

Exercise 7b

1 (a) 14 hr 45 min (b) 2 hr 8 min (c) 32 hr
2 7.20 a.m.

3 (a) 4 hr 4 min (b) 12.18 p.m.
4 (a) (i) 4 hr 10 min (ii) 3 hr 20 min
  (b) (i) 20 min (ii) 30 min
  (c) The January Man by 15 min
  (d) 3½ hr (e) (i) 40 min (ii) 1 hr 5 min.

Exercise 7c

1 (a) 5.35 p.m. (b) 17.35.
2 (a) 712 min (b) 883 min (c) 625 min.
3 14 hr 31 min.
4 (a) 16.10 (b) 09.26 (c) 01.13 (d) 20.50.
5 (a) (i) 09.15 (ii) 12.48 (b) 14 min
  (c) (i) 106 min (ii) 11.51 (iii) 1 hr 53 min
  (d) 09.17.
6 (a) (i) 1 hr 1 min (ii) 1 hr 40 min
  (b) 11 (c) 11.00
  (d) (i) 51 min (ii) 2 hr 32 min (e) 10.00
  (f) (i) 10.26 (ii) 12.58 (iii) 4 hr 32 min.

Exercise 7d

1 (a) 2 (b) 8 (c) 10 (d) 9.
2 (a) 5 (b) 8 (c) 6 (d) 4.
3 (a) 14.00 (b) 20.00 (c) 07.00 (d) 04.00.
4 (a) 3 p.m. (b) 10 p.m. (c) 9 a.m.
5 (a) 2 a.m. (b) 8 p.m. (c) 10 a.m.
6 (a) 7 a.m. (b) 1 a.m. next day.
7 (a) 4 p.m. (b) 4 p.m.
8 (a) 9 hr (b) 0.30 a.m. the following day.
9 (a) 3 p.m. (b) 1 a.m.
10 (a) you gain a day (b) you lose a day.

Exercise 7e

1 (a) 192 miles (b) 186 miles.
2 (a) Leeds and York (b) London and Edinburgh.
3 (a) York (b) Edinburgh.
4 114 miles.
5 (a) 275 miles (b) 186 miles.

Exercise 7f

1 40 m.p.h. 2 15 km/hr.
3 1350 miles. 4 375 m/min.
5 (a) 1.6 miles/min (b) 96 m.p.h.
6 (a) 10 m/s (b) 600 m/min (c) 36 000 m/hr
  (d) 36 km/hr.
7 (a) 1540 miles (b) 4 hr (c) 385 m.p.h.
8 16.8 m.p.h. (16⅘ m.p.h.). 9 60 km/hr.
10 (a) 156 (b) 108 (c) 2376
  (d) 2732 (nearest whole number).

Exercise 7g

1 July and August.
2 (a) about 18°F (b) 7.
3 48.

4 (a) 3 (b) 93.
5 (a) July and August, about 18°F
  (b) April, about 10°F.
6 £566. 7 £1846.
8 (a) 11 May (b) £60 (£30 each).
9 (a) £992, 2 × £347 + £139 + £159
  (b) £1256, 2 × £419 + £199 + £219.
10 Gatwick, Luton, Cardiff, Birmingham,
   East Midlands, Manchester, Newcastle.
11 Gatwick on a Friday, Luton on a Friday,
   Birmingham on a Friday, East Midlands on a
   Friday, Manchester on a Friday.
12 (a) £29 or £19 (depending on flight time)
   (b) £11 (c) 0 (d) £12.
13 £128 (£32 × 4).
14 (a) On a Friday or Sunday between 7–21 July
   (b) £328.
15 (a) £896 i.e. £448 each (b) £16.80
   (c) £54 (d) £1366.80.

Exercise 7h

1 (a) 2175Ff (b) £200.
2 (a) 25 200pta (b) £46.
3 It is cheaper to book when you get there.
4 No. Cost in France is £160.92,
  in Germany £152 and at home £155.
5 £3.25.
6 (a) £1 = $1.55 (b) £1 = 195pta
  (c) £1 = DM2.54.
7 £3.54 (nearest penny).
8 £22 540.
9 gained £12.94.
10 £323.26 (nearest penny).

Exercise 7i

1 £57.38. 2 £80.33.
3 £129.75. 4 £415.20.
5 (a) £87.90 (b) 63p (c) £175.80.

Multiple choice questions

1 B. 2 C.
3 D. 4 A.
5 B & C are true, A & D are false. 6 D.

Self assessment 7

1 (a) 9 hr 35 min (b) 7.55 a.m.
2 (a) 7 July (b) 13 hr 15 min (c) 452 m.p.h.
  (d) 13 hr 37 min (e) 08.17.
3 (a) £1760 (b) (i) £273.30 (ii) £1677.60
  (c) £76.74 (d) (i) £2554.16 (ii) £45.61.
4 (a) 50 min (b) 16 hr 35 min (c) 2 hr 55 min
  (d) 7 hr 25 min (e) (i) 9 hr (ii) 8 hr 10 min

(f) ½ hr. (g) 3 hr 25 min
(h) 4 hr 50 min actual working time.

Unit 8

Exercise 8a

1 Day & date	No of passengers				
	1st trip	2nd trip	3rd trip		
Dolmand					
1st stop					
2nd stop					
3rd stop					
Cripton					
Cripton					
1st stop					
Dolmand					

2					Product					
	A			B			C			
No. produced	Profit / unit	Profit	No. produced	Profit / unit	Profit	No. produced	Profit / unit	Profit	Total Profit

Start with the current figures, then find the total
profits for different possible production numbers of
each product.
3 Although there are many other contributory
factors the point of this survey is to decide how
many of each size of dress to order.

Size	Last year	Year before	Year before that
8			
10			
12			
14			
16			
18			
20			

4

Variety				A	B	C	D
Weight of beans per plant							

5

Traffic census of vehicles entering and leaving Croxton												
	A		B		C		D		E		F	
	in	out	in	out	in	out	in	out	in	out	in	out
6am - 7am												
7am - 8am												

Exercise 8b

1 Satisfactory – clear division of opinion.
2 There is no clear division for an answer.
3 Needs to list the political parties.
4 Good – clear and easy to understand.
5 Good – clear and easy to understand.
6 (b) is all right, the remainder are probably not.
7 (a) Not easy to understand (b) Two questions, not one.
8 (a) (i) 20 (ii) 2
  (b) Not aimed at the right people
  (c) People who had bought a Mondeo should have been contacted.
9 You have your own answers here.

Exercise 8c

1 discrete.   2 continuous.
3 continuous.   4 continuous.
5 discrete.   6 discrete.
7 continuous.   8 continuous.
9 discrete.   10 continuous.
11 discrete.   12 discrete.
13 20–29, 30–39, 40–49.
14 100–149, 150–199, 200–249.
15 $160 \leq h < 165$, $165 \leq h < 170$, $170 \leq h < 175$.
16 $8.95 \leq w < 9.00$, $9.00 \leq w < 9.05$, $9.05 \leq w < 9.10$.
17 (a) $0 \leq h < 10$ (b) $20 \leq h < 30$
  (c) $20 \leq h < 30$ (d) $10 \leq h < 20$.
18 0–100, 101–200, 201–300, 301–400, 401–500.
19 $695 \leq v < 700$, $700 \leq v < 705$,
  $705 \leq v < 710$, $710 \leq v < 715$,
  $715 \leq v < 720$, $720 \leq v < 725$.

Exercise 8d

1 (a)

Person	Man	Woman	Boy	Girl
Tally	ℳ ℳ ℳ	ℳ ℳ ℳ ℳ ℳ ℳ ///	ℳ	ℳ ℳ //
Frequency	15	28	5	12

(b) *Categories of shopper entering a department store*

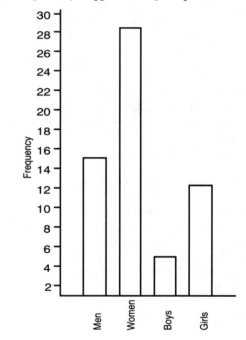

(c) 13 (d) There were 7 more girls than boys
(e) 60.
2 (a) (i) 25 (ii) 2 (b) 33 (c) 16
  (d) 10% (nearest whole number).
3 (a) (i) 65 (ii) 99
  (b)

Age	65 - 69	70 - 74	75 - 79	80 - 84	85 - 89	90 - 94	95 - 99
Tally	ℳ /	ℳ ℳ //	ℳ ℳ ////	ℳ ℳ ℳ ///	ℳ ℳ ℳ //	ℳ ℳ ////	////
Frequency	6	12	14	28	22	14	4

(c) *Ages of 100 people taken into local authority residential care*

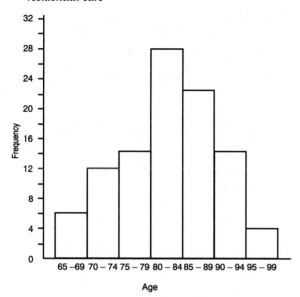

Age

(d) 68   (e) 80–84.

Exercise 8e

1 (a) Pharmaceuticals   (b) (i) £2m (ii) £2¼m
  (c) (i) £½m   (ii) £⅓m
  (d) (i) Pharmaceuticals   (ii) Animal health.
2 (a) (i) £½m   (ii) £1¾m   (iii) £1½m
  (b) yes   (c) (i) *B*   (ii) *B*
  (d) Income from routes *A* & *C* show growth.
      Route *B* appears to be contracting.
3 (a) Health and Social Care   (b) Business
  (c) 51   (d) (i) up   (ii) down
  (e) **A** & **C** true, **B** & **D** false.

Exercise 8f

1 (a) discrete
  (b)

No of flaws	Tally	Frequency
0 - 2	ℍℍ //	7
3 - 5	ℍℍ ℍℍ /	11
6 - 8	ℍℍ ℍℍ ℍℍ ////	19
9 - 11	ℍℍ ℍℍ ///	13
12 - 14	ℍℍ /	6
15 - 17	////	4
18 - 20		0

(c) 10

(d) *Number of plans in a china factory over a 60-day period*

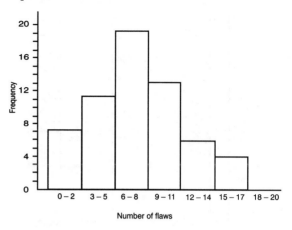

Number of flaws

2 (a) *Time to travel to airport*

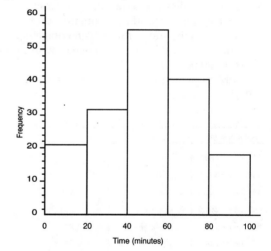

Time (minutes)

(b) 168   (c) 110.

3 (a) (i) *Multiple bar chart: main source of world news for 100 people*

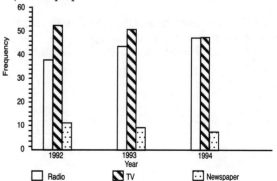

Radio   TV   Newspaper

(ii) *Component bar chart: main source of world news for 100 people*

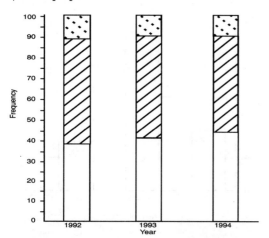

(b) Diagram identical to (a) (ii) apart from 'percentage' instead of 'frequency' on the vertical axis, and a title of 'Percentage bar chart showing the main source of world news for 100 people'.

4 (a) 487 ml (b) If v ml is the amount, then $497.5 \leq v < 498.5$.

(c)

Amount (v ml)	Tally	Frequency
$485.5 \leq v < 489.5$	//	2
$489.5 \leq v < 494.5$	||||| //	7
$494.5 \leq v < 499.5$	||||| ||||| ||||| /	16
$499.5 \leq v < 504.5$	||||| ||||| ||||| ||||| |||||	25
$504.5 \leq v < 509.5$	||||| ||||| ||||| |||||	20
$509.5 \leq v < 514.5$	||||| |||||	10
$514.5 \leq v < 519.5$		0

(d) 55
(e) 500 ml is not a boundary value, so we don't know how many in the group $499.5 \leq v < 504.5$ are above or below 500.

5 (a) (i) *Workforce in employment*

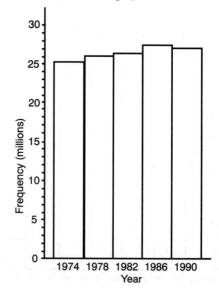

(ii) *Number unemployed*

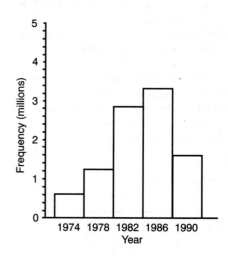

(b) *Percentage of UK workforce employed/unemployed, by year*

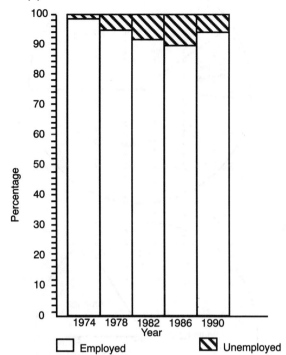

Employed ☐   Unemployed ◩

(ii) *Sales of textbooks*

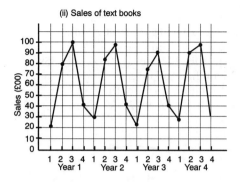

(ii) Sales of text books

(ii) *Axa Travel: holiday bookings*

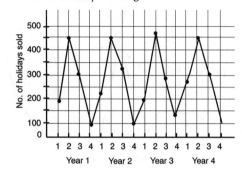

Exercise 8g

1 (a) (i) 10 cm (ii) 25 cm (b) (i) 15 cm
   (ii) 30 cm
   (c) (i) 3rd week (ii) 7th week.
2 (a) (i) £15 000 (ii) £22 000 (b) (i) £21 250
   (ii) £23 750 (c) (i) £10 000 (ii) £10 125
   (d) 1992 and 1993 (£12 500).
   (e) yes, in ascending order second quarter, first
   quarter, third quarter, fourth quarter – the
   overall trend appears upwards.   (f) You have
   your own answer here.
   (g) (i) *Ice cream: sales at Beadle Sands*

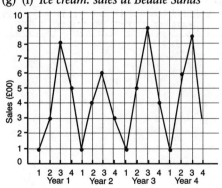

3 (a) 90–100
Line graph: Darren's BAC one weekend
(b)

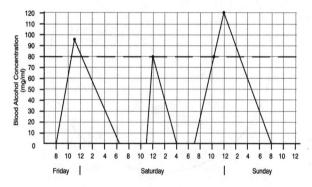

(c) Saturday midnight (d) no – he is over the
   limit
(e) he has probably taken more than 21 units
   (nearer $22\frac{1}{2}$).

Exercise 8h

1 (a) (i) $\frac{1}{12}$ (ii) $\frac{7}{36}$ (iii) $\frac{5}{9}$
  (b) (i) 17 g (ii) 6 g (nearest gram)
  (c) (i) 56 g (ii) 20 g (nearest gram).

2 (a) (i) $\frac{7}{20}$ (ii) $\frac{3}{10}$ (iii) $\frac{13}{20}$
  (b) (i) 27 (ii) 144 (c) (i) 30% (ii) 35%.

3 (a) 62.2 million sq km
  (b) 21.1 million sq km (both to 3 s.f.).

4 (a) (i) $\frac{2}{9}$ (ii) $\frac{47}{72}$ (b) 9:47 (c) £1$\frac{1}{8}$m (d) 43:32.

Exercise 8i

1

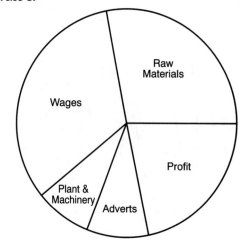

2 (a)

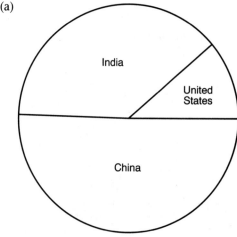

(b)

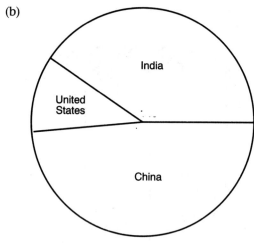

3

America
Former Soviet Union
Middle East
Africa
Asia & Australasia
Europe

4 (a)

Newspaper	Circulation	Readers per copy	Total readership (thousands)	Percentage (%)
Daily Express	1 541 680	2.4	3643	15.7
Daily Mail	1 701 794	2.5	4303	17.3
Daily Mirror	2 918 947	2.8	8035	29.7
The Sun	3 678 897	2.7	9857	37.4

(b)

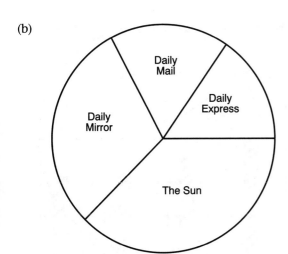

(c) *Tabloid circulation 1991*

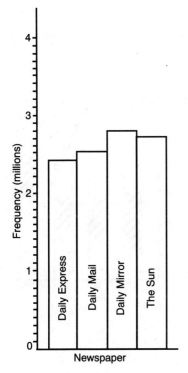

(d) *Circulation and readership of tabloid newspapers, 1991*

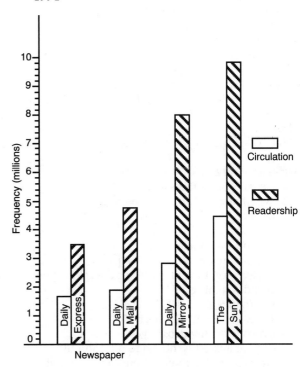

Exercise 8j

1 (a) 20 (b) 38 (c) 1.9 (d) 1 (e) 2 (f) 4.
2 (a) (i) 10 (ii) 94 (b) (i) 9.4 (ii) 0 (iii) 3.5.
3 (a) 13 (b) 80.8 (3 s.f.)
   (c) Two modes, 84 and 88 (d) 53.8% (3 s.f.)
   (e) 82 (f) 31.
4 (a) 7 (b) £3112 (c) £311.20 (d) £256
   (e) the modal weekly basic wage.
5 (a) 1092 kg (b) 546 kg (c) 546 kg (d) 78 kg.
6 74.
7 (a) (i) 288 (ii) 105 (iii) 393 (b) 5.95
   (c) 400 (aaprox).
8 (a) *B* on average has fewer defective
   components than *A* (b) yes.
9 (a) £210 (b) £35.
10 (a) 161 (b) 26.8.
11 (a) 50 (b) 2.

Exercise 8k
1 (a) (i) 18.4 (ii) 16.9 (b) Machine *A*.
2 (a) 6.67 ml (6⅔ ml) (b) 507 ml (3 s.f.).
3 (a) 45 (b) 241 s.
4 (a) 109.5, 129.5, 149.5, 169.5, 189.5
   (b) 147.

Multiple choice questions
1 B.   2 D.
3 B.   4 B.
5 C.
6 B & D are true, A & C are false.

Self assessment 8
1 (a) Possible questions are:
   1 Which age-group do you belong to?
     under 5 □   5–7 □   8–10 □   11–13 □
     14–16 □
   2 Do you watch television? yes □ no □
     (If your answer is 'no' go to question 4)
   3 On average, how many hours a week do you
     spend watching TV?
     less than 5 □   5–10 □   11–15 □
     16–20 □   21–25 □   over 25 □
   4 Do you watch videos? yes □ no □
     (If your answer is 'no' go to question 6)
   5 On average, how many hours a week do you
     spend watching videos?
     less than 5 □   5–10 □   11–15 □   16–20 □
     21–25 □   over 25 □
     and so on with other questions that interest
     you.
(b) The most important questions are:
   1 Do you think every person in the UK over 16
   should carry an identity card? yes □ no □
   2 If your answer to the previous question is
   'yes', do you think that the card should show
   the person's photograph? yes □ no □

2 (a) *Investment of a unit trust company in different
   investment sectors*

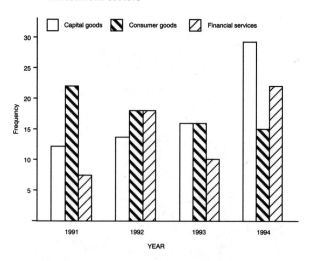

(b) *Investment of a unit trust company in different
   sectors*

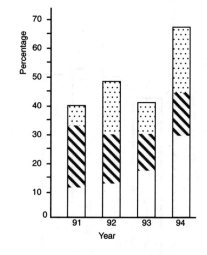

(c) *Investment of a unit trust company in different sectors*

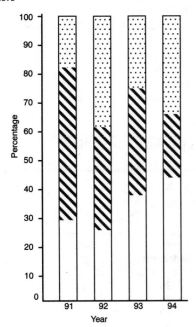

3 (a) (i) $\frac{3}{10}$ (ii) $\frac{3}{20}$ (iii) $\frac{1}{10}$ (b) (i) 680 (ii) 510
(c) (i) 8%
(ii)

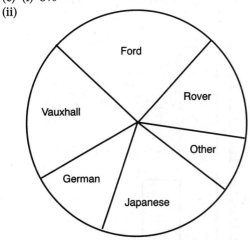

(d) (i) Vauxhall (ii) Rover, Japanese and German (e) Ford.
4 (a) (i) 20 (ii) 0 (b) (i) no (ii) no.
(c) few sit there early, a large number by mid-morning, all of whom leave for lunch, highest number in the afternoon, some leave for tea (perhaps some visitors remain there until tea is over), all leave for supper at 7 p.m., many return to watch TV. All but a few leave soon after 9 p.m. The room is clear soon after 10 p.m.
(d) (i) probably very similar (ii) no.
5 (a) 31 (b) mean 5.00, mode 0, median 3. range 20.
6 (a) 200 (b) $\frac{3}{80}$ (c) 50.8 kg (3 s.f.)
(d) (i) yes (ii) by 169 kg.

Unit 9

Exercise 9a
1 (a) 1997cc (b) 3298cc
2 (a)

Year	1992	1993	1994	1995
Annual sales growth (%)	15.2	13.8	12.6	12.2

(i) decreasing (ii) increasing.
3 (a) 13.1 (b) 11.2.
4 (a) 35.4 tons/passenger (b) 25.8 tons/passenger
(c) 19.2 tons/passenger.
5 9.5 m/min.
6 (a) £26 (b) £2.80 (c) £2930 (d) £84.
7 Mel 100, Wendy 111, Bina 119, Hank 90.
8 (a) 2.52% (b) 2.13%.
9 (a) 3.06% (b) 11.5%.

Exercise 9b
1 (a) 250 (b) 255 (c) 431 (d) 83.
2 (a) No. of components − 512 = 27. No. to start is 539.
(b) No. of components − 387 = 13. No. in basket to start was 400.
(c) No. of bolts = 65 × 4 − 5, i.e. Alan had 255 bolts to start.
(d) No. of washers Sharon had to start = 54 × 7 + 4 i.e. 382.
3 91.　　　　　　　　**4** 1155.
5 1083.　　　　　　　**6** 23, 9.
7 46.

Exercise 9c
1 $p = 26$.　　　　　　**2** $y = 9$.
3 $q = 22$.　　　　　　**4** $a = 52$.
5 $x = 20$.　　　　　　**6** $b = 53$.
7 $b = 17$.　　　　　　**8** $x = 10$.
9 $a = 8$.　　　　　　**10** $b = 8$.
11 $x = 7$.　　　　　　**12** $y = 12$.
13 $a = 45$.　　　　　**14** $b = 48$.
15 $c = 92$.　　　　　**16** $p = 40$.

17 $a = 1.5$.
18 $b = 10.6$.
19 $z = \frac{1}{2}$.
20 $w = 3\frac{1}{4}$.
21 $p = 3$.
22 $q = 8$.
23 $c = 1\frac{1}{2}$.
24 $p = 2\frac{2}{5}$.
25 $p = 5.6$.
26 $q = 9.3$.
27 $x = 71$.
28 $y = 46.9$.
29 $x = 2$.
30 $a = \frac{1}{2}$.
31 $b = 2$.
32 $c = 1\frac{1}{2}$.
33 $a = 10$.
34 $x = 3$.
35 $p = 4$.
36 $q = 1$.
37 $y = 3$.
38 $x = 1\frac{1}{2}$.
39 $x = 3\frac{1}{3}$.
40 $z = \frac{5}{6}$.

Exercise 9d

1 $3a + 6$.
2 $2a + 4c$.
3 $9a$.
4 $12a - 6$.
5 $3p + 5q$.
6 $3p$.
7 $b = 4$.
8 $a = 4$.
9 $p = 6$.
10 $q = 4\frac{1}{2}$.
11 $y = 3\frac{1}{2}$.
12 $x = 1$.
13 $b = 2$.
14 $c = 3$.
15 $p = 1$.
16 $q = 2$.
17 $x = 4$.
18 $a = 6$.
19 (a) 135 cm (b) 150 cm, 165 cm.
20 (a) $3xp$ (b) $8xp$ (c) 25p, 50p.
21 (a) 60p (b) £2.40.
22 (a) 42 acres (b) 210 acres (c) 126 acres.
23 £4, £8.
24 (a) 19 large, 38 medium, 76 small (b) £3135.

Exercise 9e

1 (a) $6x$ (b) $10p$ (c) $24q$ (d) $60y$.
2 (a) $12p - 16$ (b) $30 - 15b$ (c) $7p + 14$
  (d) $6x + 21$.
3 $a = 2$.
4 $x = 16$.
5 $p = 5$.
6 $q = 8$.
7 $a = 9\frac{1}{2}$.
8 $b = 1$.

Exercise 9f

1 4.4 & 4.5.
2 5.4 & 5.5.
3 1.5 & 1.6.
4 5.1 & 5.2.
5 4.7 & 4.8.
6 8.4 & 8.5.
7 7.5 & 7.6.
8 4.4 & 4.5.
9 2.2 & 2.3.
10 2.6 & 2.7.
11 3.4 & 3.5.
12 3.9 & 4.0.

Multiple choice questions

1 C.
2 B.
3 A.
4 C.
5 B & C are true, A & D are false.
6 C.

Self assessment 9

1 537.
2 (a) $a = 29$ (b) $b = 30$ (c) $c = 7$ (d) $d = 16$.
3 (a) Alf 27.1, Ben 25.4, Cliff 22.0, Dave 38.6
  (b) 35.9.
4 (a) $p = 8$ (b) $q = 1.5$ (c) $x = 14$ (d) $y = 3\frac{1}{4}$.
5 (a) $x = 6$ (b) $y = 3$.
6 (a) (i) $10p + 45$ (ii) $21q - 9$ (b) $m = 8$.
7 (a) $3x$ kg (b) $4\frac{1}{2}$ kg and $13\frac{1}{2}$ kg.

Revision papers for units 7–9

Paper 9

1 (a) 54 (b) 9 (c) 5.
2 (a) (i) 96 (ii) 5.
  (b)

Number of bedrooms	Frequency
1–20	39
21–40	19
41–60	6
61–80	2
81–100	4

(c) *Heart of England brochure: Number of hotel bedrooms*

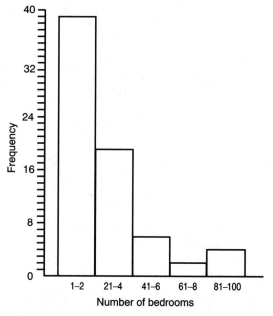

(d) 1–20 (e) 37 (f) 1848 (g) no.
3 (a) (i) 40p (ii) rent, mortgage, holidays

(b) (i) 90° (ii) 45° (iii) 27°
(c) (i) £9 (ii) £45.

4 850°C.

5 (a) 4*p* (b) *p* = 3 (c) 4.4 & 4.5.

Paper 10

1 (a) 11.52 (b) 15.07
(c) 1 hr 47 min (d) 7 hr 7 min.

2 (a) 208
(b) *Silverbridge Argus: Number of columns*

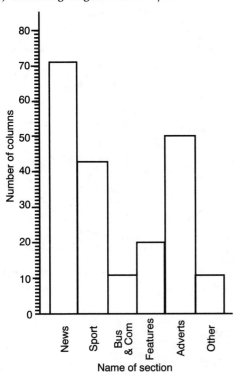

(c) *devoted to various sections*

3 (a) (i) 29 March (ii) 1 April (iii) 6 April
(b) (i) 17 March (ii) 16 March
(c) (i) Wed (ii) Wed.

4 6 st 10 lb.

5 (a) £565.20 (b) £690.80 £188.40.

Paper 11

1 (a) 137 041 francs, discount 7½%
i.e. 10 278 francs if paid within 7 days.
(b) They are £31 worse off excluding any discount.

2 (a) 22 (b) 69 (c) 3.14.

3 (a) *Type of holiday, by agency*

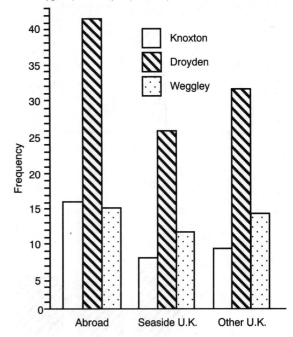

(b) *Type of holiday, by agency*

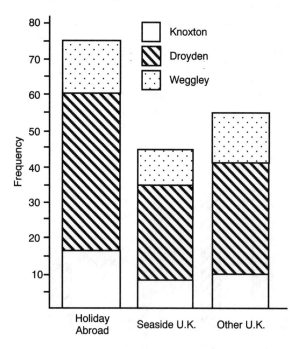

(c) *Type of holiday, by agency*

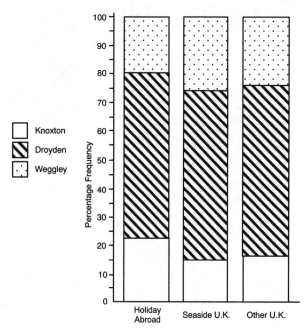

4 (a) $p = 12$ (b) $q = 6$ (c) $a = 6$.
5 (a) 190 (b) 50 (c) 670.

Paper 12
1 (a) 13 (b) 48 (nearest whole number)
   (c) There are two modes: 51 and 55
   (c) 49.
2 (a) 33
   (b) (i) 85 – assumes no female is chosen more
        than once (ii) 80
   (c) 2.58 (3 s.f.) (d) 2.42 (3 s.f.).
3 (a) 7 a.m. (b) 2 p.m. (c) 7 p.m. same day.
4

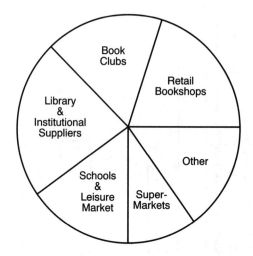

5 (a) (i) 228 g (ii) 253 g (each to nearest gram)
   (b) Majestic.

Unit 10

Exercise 10a
1 2:3.   2 5:3.
3 2:3.   4 7:9.
5 (a) 5:2 (b) 2:5.   6 5:3.
7 3:5.   8 2:7.
9 (a) 2:11 (b) 11:2.   10 (a) 2:5 (b) 5:2.

Exercise 10b
1 (a) 30 lorries: 10 vans = 3:1
   (b) 675 red posters: 540 yellow posters = 5:4
   (c) 3738 seated spectators: 534 standing
        spectators = 7:1.
2 (a) 42 pence compared with 105 pence is the
        same as 2 compared with 5.
   (b) 80 beds empty compared with 440 beds
        occupied is the same as 2 compared with 11.
   (c) 364 shop floor workers compared with 312
        office workers is the same as 7 compared with 6.

3 3:1.   **4** 2:5.
5 1:64.
6 (a) 6:1   (b) 40:3   (c) 8:9   (d) 4:7.
7 7:4.
8 (a) 1:2   (b) 2:1.
9 (a) 3:11   (b) 5:3   (c) 5:2   (d) 8:7.
10 (a) 4:3   (b) 5:2   (c) 3:4   (d) 7:18.
11 (a) 5:8   (b) 5:32   (c) 27:25.
12 (a) $\frac{48}{40}$ (b) 1.225:1.

Exercise 10c
1 (a) 3   (b) 4 lb   (c) 28 oz.
2 (a) 120 kg   (b) 50 kg   (c) 3.
3 (a) 180   (b) 80.
4 (a) 100   (b) 25   (c) £12.50.
5 (a) $\frac{8}{15}$ (b) $\frac{7}{15}$.
6 $\frac{3}{7}$.   **7** 3:7.
8 7:1.

Exercise 10d
1 Dick 16, Ann 20.   **2** Jo £48, Mel £36.
3 £22.   **4** 20 acres.
5 3600.   **6** 7360.

Exercise 10e
1 (a) 70p   (b) £2.10.
2 (a) £1.10   (b) £4.40.
3 £9.75.   **4** 14 oz.
5 611.   **6** 25 litres.
7 £93.96.
8 (a) 360   (b) 15   (c) 20.

Exercise 10f
1 (a) £24 500   (b) 5.
2 (a) 36 days   (b) 45.
3 (a) £64 600   (b) 1700.
4 (a) £26 880   (b) 7   (c) £224 per week.

Multiple choice questions
1 C.   **2** A.
3 B.
4 A & B are true, C & D are false.
5 C.

Self assessment 10
1 (a) 3:2.   (b) 2:3.
2 1:20.
3 18 kg oranges, 36 kg sugar, 9 lemons, 9 litres water.
4 166.

5 (a) missing values are:

Company	Gross profit (£000)	Gross profit as a percentage of sales
Axford Bros	14	$\frac{14}{80}$; 3 100 = 17.5
Besley's	20	16.7
Croxley & Son	330	18.9
Denhams	300	12
Esther & Co	170	17.9

(b) Denhams. Gross profit is much lower than expected.

Unit 11

Exercise 11a
1 (a) (i) 5.4 cm   (ii) 5.6 cm
    (b) (i) 16 km   (ii) 26 km.
2 50 km (approx).
3 yes: Cowes, Ryde, Sandown, Blackwater, Shanklin, Ventnor, Blackgang, Totland, Yarmouth, Newport, Cowes.
4 no.
5 (a) 0.9 km, $\frac{9}{10}$ km   (b) (i) 4.5 cm   (ii) 0.5 cm
    (c) 4.5 km (5 cm on the map).
    (d) north, L Malton Rd, L County Hosp, L Hull Rd, A64, R Fulford, L Nunery Lane, continue around 'ring' road, L Clifton Bootham, R Water End, L Poppleton Rd & Holgate Rd, L Tadcaster Rd.

Exercise 11b
1 (a) (i) 2   (ii) 4   (iii) 4   (b) 6.
2 (a)   (b)   (c)   (d)

2 odd, 3 even   2 odd, 3 even   6 even   4 even

3 (a)   (b)   (c)   (d)   (e)

4

Network	Number of even nodes	Number of odd nodes	Is the network traversable?
(a)	3	2	✓
(b)	3	2	✓
(c)	6	–	✓
(d)	4	–	✓

5

Network	Number of even nodes	Number of odd nodes	Is the network traversable?
(a)	3	2	✓
(b)	5	4	✗
(c)	2	4	✗
(d)	6	2	✓
(e)	–	4	✗
(f)	11	2	✓

6 You have your own answer here.

7 (a) yes (b) yes
   (c) either 0, 1 or 2 (not more than 2)
   (d) none (e) (i) yes (ii) yes.

Exercise 11c
1 (a) 200 (b) 100 (c) 250 (d) 150
   (e) 150 (f) 100.
2 (a) (i) 300 (ii) 450
   (b) (i) 1050 (ii) 950 (iii) 1050 (iv) 900.

Exercise 11d
1 (a) 4 (b) (i) B (ii) A, B & C (c) 19 min.
2 (a) 7 (b) 3 (c) A, C & D (d) no (e) 20 min.

Exercise 11e
1 (a)

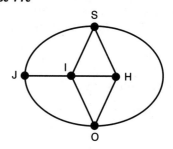

(b) yes.

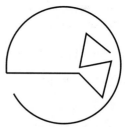

(c) If a bridge is constructed directly between J &
   H.
2 (a) yes – all the nodes are even
   (b) yes.

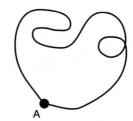

3 (a) 21 miles
   (b) 33 miles (5 + 5 + 6 + 4 + 4 + 2 + 1 + 1 + 1 + 4)
   (c) no, still 33 miles.
4 (a) 53 km (b) 24.6 km.
5 (a) 24 miles (9 + 8 + 2 + 5)
   (b) 50 miles (9 + 7 + 6 + 5 + 5 + 5 + 6 + 3 + 4).
6 (a)

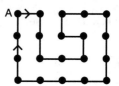

(b) 4 km (20 × 200 m) (c) no.

7 (a) Southampton, Bath, Cardiff, Chester,
Edinburgh, York, Manchester, Birmingham,
Cambridge, London, Oxford, Southampton
(1103 miles)

(b) 28 (nearest gallon), £70.

8 (a)

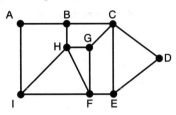

(b) no   (c) yes: *AIHBCGFED.*

Multiple choice questions
1 **B.**   2 **D.**
3 **B.**
4 **A** & **D** are true, **B** & **C** are false.
5 **D.**

Self assessment 11
1 (a) 1.12 km   (b) 1:800 000.
2 (a), (b) and (c)

Network	(a) Number of even nodes	(b) Number of odd nodes	(c) Is the network traversable?
A	10	–	✓
B	12	–	✓
C	1	4	✗
D	2	4	✗

3 (a) 80 min
   (b) (i) 133 min (*ADBCEF*)
       (ii) 178 min (*ABCDEF*)
   (c) *ADEFCBA* (203 min)
   (d) (i) no (ii) no (iii) *ABDACBDECDFCEF*
       (iv) 463 min.
4 (a) 950   (b) 780. (BC cannot be used without
   increasing the distance)
5 (a) yes, from B

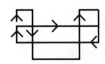

(b) (i) 2200 yd (ii) yes, passes two boxes twice.
   Route as in (a).

Unit 12

Exercise 12a
1 yes.
2 no, Callum was probably a much better player.
3 no, they play in different leagues with very
  different standards.
4 yes.
5 There are an equal number of boys and girls.

Exercise 12b
1 $\frac{1}{6}$.   2 $\frac{1}{2}$.
3 $\frac{1}{4}$.   4 $\frac{1}{6}$.
5 (a) $\frac{1}{6}$ (b) $\frac{1}{6}$ (c) $\frac{1}{6}$.

Exercise 12c
1 (a) $\frac{5}{18}$ (b) $\frac{1}{3}$ (c) $\frac{19}{36}$.
2 (a) yes   (b) (i) $\frac{1}{4}$ (ii) $\frac{1}{26}$ (iii) $\frac{6}{13}$.
3 (a) orange 5, cherries 7, plum 5, lemon 6
   (b) (i) $\frac{1}{10}$ (ii) $\frac{1}{5}$ (iii) $\frac{1}{5}$.
4 (a) $\frac{1}{3}$ (b) $\frac{2}{3}$.
5 $\frac{7}{19}$.

Exercise 12d
1 7.   2 5.
3 (a) $\frac{7}{12}$ (b) $\frac{5}{12}$.
4 (a) $\frac{5}{12}$ (b) $\frac{7}{12}$.
5 (a) 0   (b) 1   (c) 0   (d) 1.

Exercise 12e
1 (a) certain   (b) unlikely
   (c) equally likely as a male
   (d) as likely as getting a tail   (e) certain
   (f) only you know the probability of this!
   (g) unlikely   (h) only you know the probability
   of this!   (i) only you know the probability of
   this!
2 (a) (i) If I spin a coin there is an even chance
          that I will get a head.   (ii) There is a less than
          even chance that it will rain tomorrow.
      (iii) There's no chance that I'll live to be 150.
      (iv) It's certain that we'll all die sometime.
      (v) I'm most unlikely to win a prize if I buy
          1 premium bond.
      (vi) It's very likely that the next plane to land
           at Heathrow will land safely.
   (b) (i) 0 no chance   (ii) 0.01 most unlikely
      (iii) 0 0.45 less than an even chance
      (iv) 0.5 even chance   (v) 0.9 very likely
      (vi) 1 a certainty.

3 (a) 6 (b) 45 (c) 2. Either she's available or she's not.

Exercise 12f
1 $\frac{1}{4}$.   2 0.992.
3 0.32
4 (a) $\frac{1}{22}$ (b) $\frac{21}{22}$.   5 $\frac{44}{45}$.
6 (a) $\frac{1}{3}$ (b) $\frac{10}{153}$ (c) $\frac{26}{51}$.
7 (a) $\frac{15}{22}$ (b) $\frac{7}{22}$ (c) $\frac{1}{22}$ (d) $\frac{3}{11}$.
8 (a) 222 (b) (i) $\frac{3}{14}$ (ii) $\frac{9}{14}$.

Exercise 12g
1 (a) $\frac{1}{6}$ (b) $\frac{1}{10}$ (c) $\frac{2}{9}$ (d) $\frac{2}{7}$.
2 $\frac{1}{21}$.
3 (a) $\frac{3}{5}$ (b) £8.33 (£3.33 + stake, £5).

Exercise 12h
1

		First bag				
		D	D	D	C	C
	D	DD	DD	DD	CD	CD
Second bag	D	DD	DD	DD	CD	CD
	D	DD	DD	DD	CD	CD
	C	DC	DC	DC	CC	CC
	C	DC	DC	DC	CC	CC

2 (a)

		First rail				
		B	B	R	R	Y
	B	BB	BB	RB	RB	YB
Second rail	B	BB	BB	RB	RB	YB
	B	BB	BB	RB	RB	YB
	Y	BY	BY	RY	RY	YY
	Y	BY	BY	RY	RY	YY

(b) 25 (c) 10 (d) 6.

3 (a)

		Lindsay's purse				
		£1	£1	£1	20p	20p
Vicki's	£1	£1,£1	£1,£1	£1,£1	20p,£1	20p,£1
purse	20p	£1,20p	£1,20p	£1,20p	20p,20p	20p,20p

(a) 10 (b) 5 (c) 5.

Exercise 12i
1 (a) $\frac{2}{5}$ (b) $\frac{4}{15}$ (c) $\frac{8}{15}$.
2 (a) $\frac{6}{25}$ (b) $\frac{17}{25}$ (c) $\frac{13}{25}$.
3 (a) 36 (b) (i) 7 (ii) 6
(c) (i) 3 (ii) 30 (d) (i) $\frac{1}{12}$ (ii) $\frac{5}{6}$ (iii) $\frac{13}{18}$.
4 (a) $\frac{3}{25}$ (b) $\frac{22}{25}$ (c) $\frac{17}{25}$.
5 (a) $\frac{6}{25}$ (b) $\frac{13}{25}$.

Exercise 12j
1 (a) 100 (b) 60.
2 (a) $\frac{1}{10}$ (b) 987.
3 1054.
4 24.
5 (a) 52 (b) 80.
6 390.
7 (a) 697 (b) 153.
8 1454.
9 28.
10 (a) 0.16 (b) (i) 624 (ii) 26
(c) 1050.

Multiple choice questions
1 C.   2 D.
3 C.
4 A & B are true, C & D false.
5 A.

Self assessment 12
1 (a) $\frac{1}{10}$ (b) $\frac{1}{5}$ (c) $\frac{3}{10}$.
2 (a) $\frac{7}{12}$ (b) $\frac{5}{12}$.
3 (a) $\frac{9}{10}$ (0.9) (b) 216.
4 (a) $\frac{6}{49}$ (b) $\frac{23}{49}$.
5 (a) 0 (b) 1 (c) 1
(d) $\frac{1}{2}$ (different for different circumstances).
6 695.
7 (a) (i) 25% (ii) 15% (iii) 60%
(b) 0.6 (c) (i) 450 (ii) 1080 (iii) 378.

Revision papers for units 10–12

Paper 13
1 (a) 1:25 000 (b) 7.5 cm.
2 3.
3 1 (i.e. 1.02 corrected to nearest whole number).
4 4:1.
5 (a) (i) 36 km (*ABDECEF*) (ii) 53 km (*ACBDF*)
(b) (i) Not traversable.
(ii) If a new road goes from *C* to *D* it becomes traversable. Start at *B* or *E*.

Paper 14
1 (a) $\frac{2}{5}$ (b) 4.
2

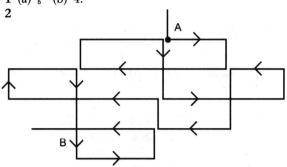

3 (a) no (b) £6.
4 8:9.
5 (a) 7 (b) (i) *B* (ii) *A, B, C & D* (c) 16 min.

Paper 15
1 (a) 703 (b) 733 (nearest whole number) (c) 7.
2 £690 and £90.
3 (a) 275 km (b) 110 litres.
4 (a) 105 gal/min (b) 105 gal/min
(c) 75 gal/min.
5 (a) £12.5m (b) £18m (c) £3m
(d) £15m (e) 1:5.

Paper 16
1 (a) $\frac{10}{21}$ (b) $\frac{3}{7}$ (c) $\frac{11}{21}$.
2 (a) 400 (b) 600 (c) 450.
3 20 days.
4 (a) missing values are 0.54,
0.54/2.13 = 25.4%,
1.13, 1.13/2.81 = 40.2%,
3.22, 0.81/3.22 = 25.2%,
0.59, 0.59/2.59 = 22.8%.
(b) (i) Cranford profit/cost ratio low
(ii) Danely is high, compared with the others.
5 (a) 8, *ABEG, ABDEG, ABDFG,*
ACBEG, ACBDEG, ACBDFG, ACDEG,
ACDFG
(b) (i) *ACDFG* (14 km) (ii) *ACBDEG* (22 km).

General revision papers

Paper 17
1 (a) Norse Direct (£329.80 compared with
£349.50).
(b) W. H. Deakin (£69.90 compared with £73.96).
2 (a) £90 000 (b) £20 400
(c) £7.14 (3 s.f.) (d) £3269 (nearest £)

(e) £10 950 (f) (i) £48 300 (ii) £32 200
(g) (i) £224 650 (ii) £201 175, 89.6%.
3 (a) (i) 169 (ii) 322 (b) 9.01% (2 d.p.)
(c) 29.5% (from 45.9% to 75.4%).
4 (a) 1984cc (b) 95.5 mm.

Paper 18

1

Cash in	Jan	Feb	Mar	Apr	May	Jun	Jul	Aug	Sep	Oct	Nov	Dec
Mike	1220	1220	1220	1260	1260	1260	1260	1260	1260	1260	1260	1260
Sue	850	850	850	850	850	940	940	940	850	850	960	960

(a)

Total	2070	2070	2070	2110	2110	2200	2200	2200	2110	2110	2220	2220
(b) Total cash out	1799	1749	1844	3035	1749	1964	3283	1749	1844	1814	2199	1944

(c)

Monthly balance	271	321	226	(925)	361	236	(1083)	451	266	296	21	276

(A figure in brackets is a debit i.e. is still owed.)

2 (a) £25 690 (b) £24 973 (c) yes.
3 April and July.
4

	Jan	Feb	Mar	Apr	May	Jun	Jul	Aug	Sep	Oct	Nov	Dec
Opening balance	0	271	592	818	(107)	254	490	(593)	(142)	124	420	441
Closing balance	271	592	818	(107)	254	490	(593)	(142)	124	420	441	717

5 yes: April, July and August.
6 (a) £3435: loan £2280, tax £130, Ins. £485,
petrol £540
(b) 13.4%.
7 £1626.
8 £27 100 (nearest £100).
9 yes, just! income c. £27 100, expenses c. £27 000.
10 holidays. 11 180:73.
12 35%.

13 (a)

Cash in	Jan	Feb	Mar	Apr	May	Jun	Jul	Aug	Sep	Oct	Nov	Dec
Mike	1220	1220	1220	1260	1260	1260	1260	1260	1260	1260	1260	1260
Sue	850	850	850	850	850	940	940	940	850	850	960	960
Total	2070	2070	2070	2110	2110	2200	2200	2200	2110	2110	2220	2220
Cash out												
Mortage	750	750	750	750	750	750	750	750	750	750	750	750
Food	300	300	300	300	300	300	300	300	300	300	300	350
Clothes	100	50	50	50	50	50	100	50	50	50	50	100
Gas	38	38	38	38	38	38	38	38	38	38	38	38
Elec	42	42	42	42	42	42	42	42	42	42	42	42
Phone			95			95			95			95
Water				24	24	24	24	24	24	24	24	24
Council tax				38	38	38	38	38	38	38	38	38
Hse Ins								24	24	24	24	24	24
Car loan	190	190	190	190	190	190	190	190	190	190	190	190
TV lic							120					
Car tax				65						65		
Car Ins				41	41	41	41	41	41	41	41	41
Petrol	45	45	45	45	45	45	45	45	45	45	45	45
Life Ins	35	35	35	35	35	35	35	35	35	35	35	35
Credit cds	65	65	65	65	65	65	65	65	65	65	65	65
Bank loan	84	84	84	84	84	84	84	84	84	84	84	84
Hols							1200					
Christmas											450	
Reg saving	100	100	100	100	100	100	100	100	100	100	100	100
Misc	50	50	50	50	50	50	50	50	50	50	50	50
Total cash out	1799	1749	1844	1917	1852	2067	3126	1876	1971	1941	2326	2071

(b) yes. These payments work out at £103 per month from April and increase to £127 per month from July. They now have spare cash at the end of every month. This is shown in the figures given in (a).

14 (a) *Car expenses: bar chart of car expenses*

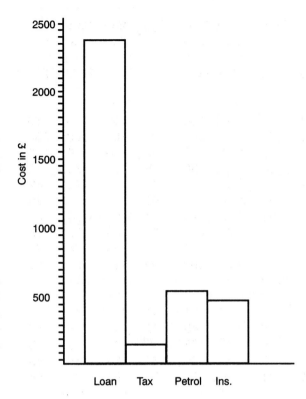

(b)

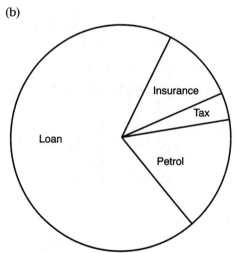

15

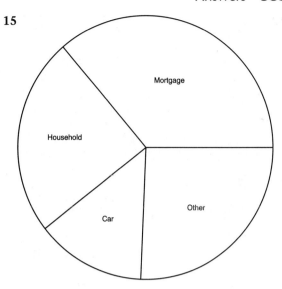

Paper 19

INVOICE

Wally's Food Importers
24 Butler Street
London SE14 0HQ

CUSTOMER
Adams Wholesale
148 Mirror Street
Birmimgham B2 1QR   5/5/95

Invoice No.	Customer Ref.	Invoice Date.

Quantity (Kg)	Description	Unit price (£)	Total (£)
250	Apricots	2.45	612.50
450	Walnuts	3.65	
300	Prunes	1.62	
500	Bran Oats	0.86	
350	Sultanas	1.32	

1 (a) missing values are £1642.50, £486, £430, £462, Grand total £3633
   (b) £3542.18.
2 (a) £4 900 000, £4 864 000, £4 998 000, £5 184 000, £4 982 000, £4 920 000
   (b) £505.
3 (a) about 23 lb, yes, about 15 lb. less b) about 20 lb.
4 (a) $q = 23$ (b) $a = 6$ (c) 5.6 & 5.7.

5 (a) £5455.
 (b) £1399.
 (c) £6745.
 (d) £1290.
 (e) 124% (to 3 s.f.)
6 (a) 1:20 000   (b) about 1140 m   (c) 1200 m.
 (d) Continue along Central Drive, right along
 Albert Rd, left into Regent Rd, straight over
 Church St, continue along Cookson St, left along
 Talbot Rd, left along the Promenade.

Paper 20
1 (a) 8.5 lb   (b) 18% (nearest whole number).
2 (a) (i) $2\frac{1}{2}$ times   (ii) $\frac{7}{5}$ times   (iii) $3\frac{1}{2}$ times.
(b)

	1964–84	1984–94	1964–94
Average house price	8	2.25	18
Family car	5	2	10
TV set	2.5	1.4	3.5
Loaf of bread	3	2.75	8.25
Gallon of petrol	8	1.5625	12.5
(c)Average weekly wage	9.5	1.789	17

(d) (i) 200   (ii) 168   (iii) 212 (all to nearest whole
 number)   (iv) 1984.
(e) (i) 50p   (ii) a. 9.6 min   b. 24 min
(f) (i) a. £5   b. £9.19   (ii) 1984 19 min, 1994
 16 min   (iii) a. yes   b. yes
(g) (i) 250%   (ii) 1600%.
3 £1625.
4 (a) (i) 473 yd^2 (ii) 395 m^2 (each value is
 rounded up to the nearest whole number)
 (b) (i) £11 850   (ii) £12 534.50
 (c) Goodcal by £684.54.
5 (a) 201 600   (b) 10 500 000   (c) 734 000 000.

Paper 21
1 (a) about 9 litres   (b) 12 780 litres.
2 (a) 21   (b) Government wins by 9 votes.
3 (a) 13 km (*ACDF*)   (b) 31 km (*ABDFEDCA*)
 (c) no.
4 (a) less   (b) (i) £223.64 cheaper   (ii) good.
5 length 90 ft 7 in, wingspan 92 ft 10 in, fuel
capacity 3940 gallons, range 2980 miles, maximum
speed 543 m.p.h.

Paper 22
1 (a) 43 doz   (b) 20 doz.
2 (a) *Compound bar chart: showing surface area and
 population for several european countries*

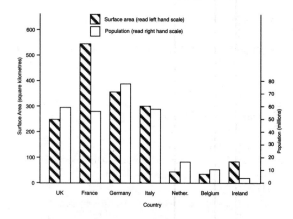

(b) 232, 102, 219, 190, 354, 323, 50 (all to nearest
 whole number)
 (i) The Netherlands   (ii) Ireland
 (c) The Netherlands.
3 (a) *Cost of petrol and amount of tax*

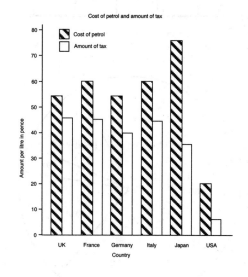

(b) (i)

United Kingdom	France	Germany	Italy	Japan	United States
67%	75%	73%	73%	46%	30%

(ii) France

(c) (i)

United Kingdom	France	Germany	Italy	Japan	United States
18p	15p	15p	16p	41p	14p

(d) France and Germany   (e) UK.
4 (a) (i) 20 mm (ii) 62.5 mm
   (b) (i) 20 mm (ii) 32 mm.
5 (a) (i) 72 cm² (ii) 2016 cm³ (iii) 952 cm³
   (b) yes, 28 cm is more than 9 in
   (c) 476 cm³
   (d) (i) 4048 cm³ (ii) 8 (240 cm³ remains in the tin)

Paper 23
1 £1572.75.
2 (a) 1980 (b) 1625 (nearest whole number)
   (c) 20 000.
3 (a) 48 (b) 16 (8 double, 8 single)
   (c) (i) 1.5 m (ii) 375 000
   (d) 810 (e) 77.
4 (a) Costs are incurred before income is generated.
   (b) mid-1991 (c) mid 1992 to early 1995
   (d) (i) from 4th quarter of 1992 to the 1st quarter of 1995
   (e) mid 1993–mid 1994 (ii) mid-1994
   (f) yes, by late 1995 when it looks as though all profits will stop.
5 (a) (i) 9.923 m (4 s.f.) (ii) 10.94 (4 s.f.)
   (b) (i) 2.977 m (4 s.f.) (ii) 3.282 m (4 s.f.)
   (c) (i) £21 420 000 (ii) £27 270 000
   (iii) £48 690 000
   (d) car £3.70, lorry £11
   (e) car £4, lorry £12.10
(f)

year	1997 £	1998 £	1999 £	2000 £
car	4.40	4.80	5.30	5.80
lorry	13.40	14.80	16.40	18.20

(g)

Item	1994	1995	1996	1997	1998
Inflation	3%	4.8%	5%	5%	5%
Inflation + 6%	9%	10.8%	11%	11%	11%
% increase in toll	9%	10.8%	11%	11%	11%
Toll for cars	£3.40	£3.70	£4	£4.40	£4.80
Toll for lorries	£10.10	£11	£12.10	£13.40	£14.80
Total traffic paying toll	9m	9.45m	9.92m	10.42m	10.94m
Number of cars	6.30m	6.62m	6.94m	7.29m	7.66m
Number of lorries	2.70m	2.84m	2.98m	3.13m	3.28m
Income–cars	£21.42m	£24.49m	£27.76m	£32.08m	£36.77m
Income–lorries	£27.27m	£31.24m	£36.06m	£41.94m	£48.54m
Total income	£48.69m	£55.73m	£63.82m	£74.02m	£85.31m

(ii) yes – the original investment of £300m should be repaid in tolls before the end of 1998. Income, in excess of £90m a year will continue indefinitely.

Paper 24
1 (a) 40 (b) 160 (c) 80 (d) 320
   (e) 400 (f) (i) 80 hr each (ii) 5.
2

Quantity	Unit (Ea.,Dz box)	Cat. Number	Colour	Description	Unit price	Total value of goods (£)
12	Ream	E 4104	White	Copier Paper	£2.15	
5	Ream	E 4108	Pink	Copier Paper	£2.43	
5	Ream	E 4138	White	Laser Printer Paper	£4.39	
6	Box	E 4183	White	Envelopes	£34.99	
24	each	E 4245	Various	Ring Binders	0.89	
				add £2.90 for delivery		
				please add Vat, 17½ %		
				Total		

Missing values in order are: £25.80, £12.15, £21.95, £209.94, £21.36, total £291.20; £294.10, VAT £51.47 (nearest penny); total £345.57.
3 (a) Ockley v. Deal Hall, Ockley v. Upper Chute
   (b) Columns 2 and 4: The number of games won must equal the number of games lost, yes
   (c) 22 (d) 42 (e) $\frac{9}{13}$
   (f) the team with the greater number of tries is placed first   (g) $66\frac{2}{3}$%
   (h)

team	P	W	D	L	Tries	Points
Loxhill	13	12	0	1	32	24
Matson	13	10	1	2	40	21
Pennybridge	13	10	0	3	44	20
Upton	13	9	1	3	28	19
Waren Hill	13	9	0	4	57	18
Upper Chute	13	7	1	5	33	15
Bell End	13	5	1	7	19	11
Ockley	13	4	1	8	19	9
Deal Hall	13	4	0	9	11	8
St Days	13	3	1	9	15	7
Quorn	13	2	0	11	15	4
Radley	13	0	0	13	14	0

4 (a)

Car	Mondeo	Xantia	BMW 525	Granada	Mercedes C220	Renault Cabrio	Rover 827
Cash value after 3 years	£6000	£6700	£11 000	£5300	£13 300	£4900	£6000
Loss over 3 years	£7600	£10 800	£13 500	£16 700	£11 300	£11 000	£19 000

   (b) (i) the Mondeo (ii) the Rover
   (c) (i) still the Mondeo (the largest amount to
       invest)
   (ii) still the Rover (nothing to invest)
   (d) (i) 81% (ii) 26% (nearest whole number).
5 (a) (i) 600 mm (ii) 900 mm (iii) 1500 mm
   (b) (i) 800 mm (ii) 1200 mm (iii) 1200 mm
   (c) yes, he needs a minimum of 17
   (d) no, she needs 11
   (e) yes, he has enough even if all of it is laid
horizontally
   (f) (i) 36 m (ii) 84 m (f) (i) 31 (ii) 95
   (h) he needs 5 boxes + 1 clip i.e. 6 boxes!

Paper 25
1 (a) 10%
   (b) (i) £8100 (ii) £1440 (iii) £2880.
2

Route	Number of expected	Average price per seat fares	Total target percentage revenue (£)	Target profit at average per route (£)	Target (£) prices
A	10 000	40	400 000	4%	
B	50 000	56			196 000
C	40 000	50			240 000

   (a) missing values: Route *A* 16 000;
Route *B* 2 800 000, 7%; Route *C* 2 000 000, 12%
   (b) no, it is below the overall acceptable profit
   (c) £5.2m (d) £452 000 (e) (i) 8.69%
   (ii) yes.
3 (a) To maintain the ratio of length:width as 4:3
the number of cans must be 12 (which gives 8
layers) or 48 (which gives two layers). No other
arrangement is possible. There are therefore 2
layers.
   (b) 36 cm × 48 cm × 24 cm (c) 8990 cm² (3 s.f.).
4 20 + 8 + 15 + 30 + 20 +
15 + 20 + 25 + 20 + 10 + 20.
5 (a) £4500 (b) $37.80 (c) £3823 (nearest £)
   (d) $52.90 (3 s.f.) (e) $84.60 (3 s.f.) (c) 33%.

Guidance notes: basic skills

A1 (a) 2954
(b) 5072
(c) 69
(d) 80
(e) 52 000 (f) 70 806
(g) 680 305
(h) (i) 7 hundreds (ii) 4 tens
(i) (i) 6 ten thousands (ii) 3 thousands
(j) (i) 4 hundreds of thousands (ii) 8 thousand
(k) (i) 5 hundreds of thousands (ii) 70 million.
A2 (a) (i) 442 (ii) 484
(b) (i) 1234 (ii) 435
(c) (i) 352 (ii) 3301
(d) (i) 973 (ii) 2904.
A3 (a) 673
(b) 2613
(c) 9455
(d) 1721.
A4 (a) 4821
(b) 5709
(c) 12 525
(d) 27 810
(e) 48 993.
A5 (a) 218
(b) 322
(c) 614
(d) 312.
A6 (a) 179
(b) 488
(c) 346
(d) 1581.
A7 (a) 3520
(b) 7000
(c) 12 300
(d) 567 000
(e) 71 000
(f) 43 000
(g) 70 000
(h) 3 970 000
(i) 59 000 000
(j) 825 000.
A8 (a) 410
(b) 228
(c) 546
(d) 747
(e) 11 050
(f) 49 628
(g) 68 224
(h) 49 623
(i) 21 518
(j) 27 918.

A9 (a) 830
(b) 362
(c) 920
(d) 440.
A10 (a) 134
(b) 159
(c) 153
(d) 129
(e) 245
(f) 561.
A11 (a) 81
(b) 56
(c) 96
(d) 73
(e) 56
(f) 63.
A12 (a) 26 r. 2
(b) 26 r. 13
(c) 80 r. 25
(d) 48 r. 2
(e) 132 r. 49
(f) 88 r. 24.
A13 (a) 44
(b) 34
(c) 26
(d) 1
(e) 2
(f) 34
(g) 30
(h) 1
(i) 6
(j) 12
(k) 2
(l) 10.
A14 (a) 1,2,4,5,10,20
(b) 1,2,3,5,6,10,15,30
(c) 1,2,3,6,18
(d) 1,2,3,4,6,8,12,16,24,48
(e) 1,3,13,39
(f) 1,2,3,4,5,6,10,12,15,20,30,60
(g) 1,2,3,4,6,8,9,12,18,24,36,72
(h) 1,2,5,7,10,14,35,70.
A15 (a) 6
(b) 7
(c) 17
(d) 18
(e) 7
(f) 8
(g) 14
(h) 13.
A16 (a) 29,31,47,67
(b) 37 and 41.

A17 (a) 48
(b) 50
(c) 72
(d) 60
(e) 60
(f) 36.
A18 (a) 2^5
(b) $2^3 \times 3$
(c) $2^4 \times 3$
(d) 3^4
(e) $2^3 \times 3^2$
(f) $2^4 \times 5^2$.
A19 (a) 25
(b) 64
(c) 144
(d) 100
(e) 441
(f) 784.
A20 (a) 8
(b) 27
(c) 125
(d) 216.
A21 (a) (i) 2^4 (ii) 5^3 (iii) $2^2 \times 3^3$ (iv) $3^2 \times 7^4$
(b) $2^6 \times 3^2$, 24.
A22 (a) 5.47
(b) 6.70
(c) 7.41
(d) 10.9
(e) 1.41
(f) 2.23.
A23 (a) 1800, 7890, 35 730
(b) 1800, 7900, 35 700
(c) 2000, 8000, 36 000.
A24 (a) 3600
(b) 8000
(c) 35 000
(d) 20 000
(e) 18
(f) 6.
A25 (a) -6
(b) -20
(c) -20
(d) -30
(e) -21
(f) -12
(g) -12
(h) -24.
A26 (a) -4
(b) -4
(c) -7
(d) -6.
B1 (a) (i) $\frac{16}{3}$ (ii) $\frac{19}{4}$ (iii) $\frac{47}{6}$ (iv) $\frac{25}{7}$ (v) $\frac{43}{5}$

(b) (i) $3\frac{3}{4}$ (ii) $2\frac{2}{5}$ (iii) $4\frac{6}{7}$ (iv) $1\frac{7}{8}$.

B2(a) 0.5

(b) 0.625

(c) 0.666...

(d) 0.35

(e) 0.416 66...

(f) 0.571 428...

(g) 7.5

(h) 6.333...

(i) 0.4

(j) 0.75

(k) 0.857 142 8...

(l) 0.416 666...

(m) 1.884 615...

(n) 3.2162....

B3 (a) $\frac{5}{7}$

(b) $\frac{11}{15}$

(c) $\frac{5}{12}$

(d) $1\frac{4}{15}$

(e) $1\frac{5}{18}$

(f) $1\frac{5}{12}$

(g) $1\frac{17}{30}$

(h) $1\frac{8}{9}$

(i) $1\frac{1}{2}$.

B4(a) $\frac{1}{3}$

(b) $\frac{1}{12}$

(c) $\frac{1}{12}$

(d) $\frac{1}{12}$

(e) $\frac{1}{4}$

(f) $\frac{3}{10}$

(g) $\frac{1}{60}$

(h) $\frac{7}{36}$

(i) $\frac{11}{12}$

(j) $\frac{53}{150}$.

B5 (a) $4\frac{1}{6}$

(b) $6\frac{1}{3}$

(c) $4\frac{5}{8}$

(d) $3\frac{3}{8}$

(e) $6\frac{19}{21}$

(f) $2\frac{29}{48}$

(g) $2\frac{5}{8}$

(h) $1\frac{19}{30}$.

B6 (a) $\frac{15}{28}$

(b) $\frac{3}{16}$

(c) $\frac{4}{15}$

(d) $1\frac{2}{3}$

(e) $\frac{1}{12}$

(f) $\frac{3}{20}$

(g) $\frac{4}{21}$

(h) $\frac{3}{16}$.

B7 (a) 2

(b) $3\frac{1}{2}$

(c) $7\frac{1}{3}$

(d) $5\frac{3}{5}$

(e) $2\frac{1}{2}$

(f) $2\frac{7}{10}$

(g) $28\frac{1}{2}$

(h) $11\frac{1}{3}$.

B8 (a) 18

(b) $6\frac{2}{3}$

(c) $1\frac{1}{4}$

(d) $5\frac{3}{5}$

(e) $\frac{4}{5}$

(f) $\frac{2}{3}$

(g) $\frac{4}{9}$

(h) $4\frac{2}{3}$

(i) $1\frac{5}{7}$

(j) $2\frac{2}{3}$.

B9 (a) $\frac{7}{12}$

(b) $\frac{3}{4}$

(c) $\frac{7}{12}$

(d) $\frac{5}{8}$

(e) $\frac{8}{9}$

(f) $\frac{15}{16}$

B10 (a) 75%

(b) 80%

(c) $66\frac{2}{3}$%

(d) $58\frac{1}{3}$%

(e) $22\frac{2}{9}$%

(f) 65%.

C1 (a) 7, 9, 7

(b) 4, 4, 6

(c) 8, 7, 3.

C2 (a) (i) 0.9 (ii) 0.17 (iii) 0.081 (iv) 0.26

(b) (i) $\frac{4}{5}$ (ii) $\frac{9}{25}$ (iii) $\frac{177}{1000}$ (iv) $\frac{5}{8}$.

C3 (a) (i) 7.83 (ii) 9.2 (iii) 3 (iv) 2.587

(b) 15.89, 15.9, 16.7, 18.1

(c) (i) 0.57 (ii) 12.2.

C4 (a) 3.7

(b) 0.48

(c) 12.05

(d) 6.1

(e) 12.37

(f) 5.07

(g) 0.3

(h) 3.247.

C5 (a) $\frac{3}{4}$

(b) $\frac{1}{20}$

(c) $\frac{12}{25}$

(d) $3\frac{7}{20}$.

C6 (a) 76, 125, 1

(b) 75.9, 125, 0.749

(c) 75.94, 124.96, 0.75.

C7 (a) 8.9

(b) 9.9
(c) 14.32
(d) 9.43
(e) 11.663
(f) 53.36
(g) 11.871
(h) 16.399.
C8 (a) 32.4
(b) 6.04
(c) 15.8
(d) 6.93
(e) 49.35
(f) 6.17
(g) 16.78
(h) 61.43
(i) 18.3908
(j) 12.643.
C9 (a) 47.2
(b) 3.74
(c) 0.054
(d) 83
(e) 66
(f) 0.758
(g) 36
(h) 0.012.
C10 (a) 38.1
(b) 41.09
(c) 30.72
(d) 37.395
(e) 236.44
(f) 28.4484
(g) 10.8506
(h) 2.9336
(i) 0.3735
(j) 0.81322.
C11 (a) 7.93
(b) 0.11
(c) 0.28
(d) 2.26
(e) 4.27
(f) 0.945.
C12 (a) 8.09
(b) 11.2
(c) 0.0973
(d) 0.215
(e) 0.451
(f) 0.331.
C13 (a) 63.5
(b) 47
(c) 342
(d) 8.25
(e) 9.53 (3 s.f.)

(f) 77.4 (3 s.f.)
(f) 45.25
(h) 821 (3 s.f.).
D1 (a) $\frac{1}{4}$
(b) $\frac{11}{20}$
(c) $\frac{3}{5}$
(d) $\frac{12}{25}$
(e) $\frac{7}{20}$
(f) $\frac{24}{25}$
(g) $\frac{21}{25}$
(h) $\frac{7}{8}$.
D2 (a) 40%
(b) 34%
(c) $66\frac{2}{3}$%
(d) $8\frac{1}{3}$%
(e) $162\frac{1}{2}$%
(f) 108%
(g) $38\frac{8}{9}$%
(h) 340%.
D3 (a) 0.2
(b) 0.65
(c) 0.825
(d) 0.423
(e) 0.0225
(f) 0.125.
D4 (a) 2.4
(b) 3.7
(c) 3
(d) 637.5
(e) 16.2
(f) 44.1.
E1 (a) $a = 47°$
(b) $b = c = 90°$
(c) $d = 103°, e = 116°$
(d) $f = 93°$.
E2 (a) acute, $p = 82°$
(b) obtuse, $q = 125°$
(c) reflex, $r = 300°$
(d) obtuse, $s = 95°$
(e) acute, $t = 17°$
(f) acute, $u = 45°$.
E3 (a) $a = 142°$
(b) $b = 320°$
(c) $c = 57°$
(d) $d = 228°$.
E4 (a) *BE, AF, GH, JI, PQ*
(b) *EF, AB, GJ, HI, PS, QR*
(c) *BC, DE*.
E5 (a) $a = 350$
(b) $b = 75°, c = 30°$
(c) $d = 62°$
(d) $e = 43°, f = 54°$.

E6 (a) trapezium
(b) rectangle
(c) rectangle
(d) square
(e) rectangle.
F1 (a) $b = 9$
(b) $c = 15$
(c) $p = 22$
(d) $q = 41$
(e) $y = 33$
(f) $x = 36$.
F2 (a) $a = 14$
(b) $c = 3$
(c) $q = 9$
(d) $r = 27$
(e) $z = 6$
(f) $p = 26$.
F3 (a) $b = 4$
(b) $d = 15$
(c) $e = 6$
(d) $f = 9$
(e) $p = 8$
(f) $y = 7$.
F4 (a) $a = 9$
(b) $b = 40$
(c) $y = 78$
(d) $z = 207$
(e) $w = 84$
(f) $p = 112$.
F5 (a) $a = 3$
(b) $b = 4$
(c) $c = 4$
(d) $d = 4$
(e) $p = 1\frac{1}{8}$
(f) $y = 18$
(g) $z = 24$
(h) $x = 15$.
F6 (a) $b = 2$
(b) $d = 7$
(c) $c = 4$
(d) $p = 7$
(e) $y = 1$
(f) $x = 5$

(g) $z = 3$
(h) $q = 2$
(i) $y = 1$.
F7 (a) $a = 5$
(b) $b = 2$
(c) $c = 3$
(d) $p = 5$
(e) $x = 7$
(f) $q = 0$
(g) $y = 12$
(h) $p = 3$
(i) $x = 3\frac{5}{7}$
(j) $1\frac{1}{3}$.
G9 (a) -11
(b) 7
(c) -4
(d) $+3$
(e) -1
(f) 4
(g) -2
(h) 19
(i) -12
(j) 21
(k) -3
(l) -2
(m) 3
(n) -23
(p) 23
(q) 23
(r) -11
(s) -11
(t) -11
(u) 60.
G11 (a) 588
(b) $12\,054$
(c) 54.9
(d) 375
(e) 55.3
(f) 67.1
(g) 172
(h) 5.30
(i) 1.73
(j) 67.3.

Index